RELIGIOUS • STUDIES

WALTER H. CAPPS

RELIGIOUS STUDIES

*The
Making
of a
Discipline*

FORTRESS PRESS • MINNEAPOLIS

RELIGIOUS STUDIES
The Making of a Discipline

Cover design: Peggy Lauritsen Design Group

Library of Congress Cataloging-in-Publication Data

Capps, Walter H.
    Religious studies : the making of a discipline / Walter H. Capps.
        p.   cm.
    Includes bibliographical references and index.
    ISBN 0-8006-2535-8 (alk. paper)
    1. Religion—Study and teaching.   2. Religion—Philosophy.
  3. Religion.   I. Title.
  BL41.C36   1995
  200′.7—dc20   95-6956
                                                                          CIP

The paper used in this publication meets the minimum requirements of American National Standard for Information
Sciences—Permanence of Paper for Printed Library Materials, ANSI Z329.4-1984.
                                                                          TM

Manufactured in the U.S.A   AF 1-2535

                                        5   6   7   8   9   10

For
Geo Widengren,
in deepest gratitude for
the example of keen scholarship
and a knowing sense
of how the discipline
is knitted together

C O N T E N T S

P R E F A C E

This book is guided by an assertion that the academic study of religion has been inspired and shaped by a single argument, the development and articulation of which can be approached and traced as a continuous narrative. This assertion has been influenced by recognition that religion is coterminous with human life, while understanding of religion is of rather recent origin. In certain critical respects, what understanding of religion there is is a product of the workings of the distinct methods and traditions of scholarship that came into being during and following the period of the Enlightenment. That is, little objective understanding of religion existed before inquirers learned how to make it intelligible. The means of intelligibility belonged to the methods of description, analysis, and interpretation that were designed for this purpose, and that have been tested, modified, and embellished through the academic study of religion.

Thus the book is directed toward isolating and elucidating the specific argument to which such intelligibility was ascribed, then toward tracing the elaboration and extension of this argument into the several modalities that had been set in motion. The modalities were evoked by virtue of the fact that inquiry into the nature and function of religion could be staged and conducted from a number of vantage points, each of which, however, was methodologically congruent with the force of a fundamental question. The questions themselves are both implicit and explicit in the queries that were advanced, and were (and continue to be) raised by inquirers who identify with a number of fields and disciplines within the humanities and social sciences.

This is to affirm that the existing variety within the academic study of religion derives only in part from the fact that anthropologists, historians, sociologists, philosophers, psychologists, linguists, theologians, and others all understand themselves to have some real, legitimate place and stake in the inquiry, and that they go about their work in varying and distinctive ways. The variety is assured by the fact that the initial single argument was so fertile, resilient, and resistant to resolution that it found itself inciting several modes of potential intelligibility. That is, although significant variety within religious studies results from the fact that scholars representing various fields and disciplines are involved in the inquiry, the more significant variety is due to the fact that the subject itself invites multiple vantage points. The intellectual progression between them can be traced as a continuous narrative.

The approach to the subject being fostered here is one the author has employed while teaching undergraduate and graduate students at the University of California, Santa Barbara. While only an author can take full responsibility for weaknesses and vulnerabilities in the argument, he can also be grateful for the wise counsel of his colleagues as he has been thinking the matter through.

The book is dedicated to its primary catalyst. I had the good fortune to meet Professor Geo Widengren on a trip to Sweden a number of years ago. I profited considerably from the perspective he brought to the study of religion. As the conversations continued I was pleased that he was able to teach for an academic quarter in our department in Santa Barbara. It was then that this book was first conceived. In some respects I wrote the book because Geo Widengren asked for it. The completed project is dedicated to him with affection, esteem, and abiding thankfulness.

J. Michael West was a student at Santa Barbara at the time that Geo Widengren taught there, and may have witnessed the promise that I made. It is particularly gratifying to me that he, now senior editor at Fortress Press, is the publisher of this volume. Special thanks to him, David Lott, Sheryl Strauss, and Thu Pham for expert assistance during the publication process, and to Michael Crandell for dedicated service. Thanks too to Lois, of course (and so much is included in "of course"), for being there at the beginning, at the end, and on the way, and to David August Brostrom for making a grandfather's heart sing.

Santa Barbara, California

INTRODUCTION

The principal objective of this book is to trace some of the ways in which selected responses to fundamental questions about a subject have given content and shape to an intellectual discipline. The subject is religion. The intellectual discipline is most frequently referred to as religious studies.

In the chapters that follow, we shall be probing and inquiring in two areas of intellectual interest. First, we shall isolate a few of the basic questions that have been asked about religion. Second, we shall reconstruct some of the prominent intellectual pathways that belong to religious studies.

The two undertakings would be separate tasks were it not for the compelling fact that the intellectual discipline has been formed and configured by the *questions* that are most frequently asked about the subject. It is within the framework of the intellectual discipline, and by means of its analytical and interpretive capacities, that the questions have been asked over and over again. Disciplines put searching questions before a subject in a rigorous manner, then exercise cultivated memory and practiced intelligence over the inquiries that are formulated as well as the responses that are evoked, elicited, and prove stubborn and troublesome. To call religious studies an intellectual discipline is to recognize that it employs established rules and methods of inquiry to address such issues and to record responses. To make a subject intelligible, disciplines employ methods of inquiry, pursue objects or foci of intellectual interest, and develop reservoirs of information and knowledge upon which to draw. Scholars, teachers, researchers, and students within the field are entrusted with knowing what the methods are and how they function, how the objects and foci are to be approached and addressed, and where the information is to be found and the knowledge utilized resourcefully. The recording and transmission of the products and consequences of such intellectual inquiries assist in shaping the traditions that belong to disciplines. The traditions function to guide continuing intellectual activity. Such ongoing work within the disciplines makes such traditions resilient and dynamic.

Simply put, religious studies provides training and practice (each an essential quality of a discipline) in directing and conducting inquiry regarding the subject of religion. Religious studies (as is the case with all other legitimate subject-fields) utilizes prescribed modes and techniques of inquiry to make the subject of religion intelligible. This is its twofold task: to discover as well as to elicit its subject's intelligibility.

In describing and illustrating the objectives and achievements of religious studies in this volume, we have chosen to proceed by identifying several fundamental questions that have been asked about religion and to illustrate and examine how some theoreticians have responded to them. We have decided to probe these questions, and the modes of inquiry to which they are attached and by means of which they are put forth and elaborated, instead of following the practice of approaching the subject with a proposed definition. We proceed this way for a number of reasons. First, practically speaking, the fundamental questions that have been asked about the subject are relatively few, while possible definitions of the subject are voluminous. Second, it seems imprudent to posit a definition before the inquiry has been undertaken, for the fundamental purpose of the inquiry is to make the subject intelligible. Third, religion is a subject that possesses a variety of referents and can be employed within numerous frames of discourse, and thus can be defined in a multiplicity of ways. One cannot make sense of the word until one knows within which context, frame of reference, or world of discourse the word is intended to register. This is the work of the discipline: namely, to identify such frames of reference so as to understand how questions, frames of reference, modes of inquiry, and subjects cooperate and collaborate in making the subject intelligible.

The variety of ways in which a subject can be made intelligible, together with the implicit complexity of the intellectual frameworks within which such intelligibility is grounded, point to an additional reason for sorting and sifting the kinds of activities that belong to religious studies. When one encounters rather well established academic fields, for example, one is introduced not only to prominent issues and questions, but also to traditions of scholarship, schools of thought, intellectual movements within the field, and, of course, to numerous theorists (some of whom may even qualify as being seminal). To study the field of philosophy, for example, is certainly to learn how to engage in philosophical reflection and to make such reflection one's own. But it is also to find one's way into the reflections of the philosophers that comprise the field—Socrates, Plato, Aristotle, Plotinus, René Descartes, Immanuel Kant, Georg Wilhelm Friedrich Hegel, Bertrand Russell, Ludwig Wittgenstein, Alfred Ayer, Michel Foucault, and Richard Rorty, to name a few of the prominent figures. The same is true of the study of sociology. In studying sociology one is introduced to problems and issues that belong to the field and, in this process, one also becomes acquainted with the history and theory of sociological analysis. At some point in this endeavor the two undertakings coalesce: the student (the scholar) discovers that the problems and issues can (indeed must) be reflected upon in light (and within the framework) of the traditions of scholarship by which the discipline is composed. One also recognizes that one's own intellectual efforts can claim reciprocity with identifiable traditions of learning, the resources of which one can turn to again and again as a kind of permanent, ever-deepening, and enriching resource and legacy.

In principle, the same intellectual expectations pertain to the study of religion. Certainly religious studies has its own schools of inquiry, its patterns of scholarship, and its traditions of inquiry. It exhibits schools, movements, and seminal theorists, just as these can be found in other fields and disciplines. But religious studies is a relatively new subject-field concerning whose intellectual composition there is as yet no consensus. Certainly most of those working within the field agree that the theories of, say, Max Müller, James Frazer, Emile Durkheim, Max Weber, Rudolf Otto, and others of similar eminence have something integrally to do with one another. Each of these scholars and researchers has provided insightful commentary and meaningful exploration of the nature of religion. And yet almost all of these theoreticians—particularly those belonging to the nineteenth and early twentieth centuries—have intellectual roots in other fields and disciplines. Seldom do they enter the terrain of religious studies from the same place or while standing on the same ground. Few of them, if asked, would have identified themselves as being scholars of religious studies. In fact, it is arguable that the principal contributions and prime discoveries within the field of religious studies have been made by scholars and researchers who have understood themselves to be practitioners of the methods and disciplines of other fields: anthropology, sociology, philosophy, history, psychology, theology, and other areas of intellectual interest. This is an indispensable methodological fact about the character and makeup of religious studies.

It is axiomatic that collective intellectual ventures do not qualify to be referred to as fields or as disciplines unless they exhibit a second-order tradition. By second-order tradition we refer to a coordinated account of the primary schools of interpretation, methods of approach, traditions of scholarship, and, most significantly, a shared living memory of the ways in which all of these constitutive factors are related to each other. Religious studies owns such a second-order tradition, and it is dependent on the same for the intellectual directions it has taken as well as for the resources on which it is able to draw. Still, as we have already pointed out, second-order tradition of religious studies is not yet identifiable as a clear, continuous, self-sustaining direct line of communication and transmission. Yet, no matter how difficult to identify, recover, or fashion, a working sense of this second-order tradition is absolutely necessary to the ongoing constructive and creative work of the academic field.

Those working within the field cannot pretend to be instrumentally self-conscious unless they know how to arrange their own seminal texts and to draw upon established patterns and methods of inquiry. An academic field cannot pretend to know its way unless it can relate to its intellectual past in narrative fashion.

All of this clearly demonstrates that what one does within an academic field depends on where one is standing. Where one stands profoundly influences what one discovers. Furthermore, where one stands and what one discovers are implicit in one's scholarly intentions. Taken in its more comprehensive sense, each of these factors also influences the ways in which a subject-field is conceived. It also helps set the operational definitions that are ascribed to the subject.

The complexity and variety of the subject-field are further influenced by the multiplicity of methodological interests and intentions that become appropriate to inquiries of this kind. Some methods of inquiry, for example, are equipped primarily to describe phenomena. Others claim to be able to transcend "mere description," and thus they engage in comparison and contrasting of religions. Other methods function not only to describe, compare, and contrast, but to systematize and synthesize. That is, these are designed to identify or construct integrated systems of thought, or to establish the possibility of stimulating intellectual coherence.

The complexity is further extended when these various methodological intentions are coupled with convictional goals. Scholars can engage in descriptive, comparative, isolative, and synthesizing intellectual activity, sometimes in order to defend the propriety of a subject, sometimes to demonstrate its utility, sometimes to verify it, or, conversely, to explain it away, sometimes to give it sanction, and sometimes to illustrate the attractiveness of a theory of their own. Admittedly, such examples of a scholar's convictional intention are not always manifested in clear or unambiguous form. But convictions do indeed play a formative role in processes of interpretation. Moreover, they are implicit within the distinctive shapes that second-order tradition assumes. This too is a factor that plays a large role in the makeup of religious studies.

Thus we return to an observation that was advanced some paragraphs ago: What gives initial formal structure to religious studies is the fact that only a certain number of basic or fundamental questions can be asked about a subject. Understandably, then, the second-order tradition is constituted by the presence of several modes of inquiry, each of which was prompted and designed to facilitate responses to the fundamental questions. The questions can be asked about virtually any subject; they are certainly not unique to religious studies. The questions include: What is it? How did it come about (or what is its source)? How can it be described? What is its function or purpose? What import does it carry? Our task is to isolate the basic questions that have been asked about religion, and to identify the ways in which these questions—together with the responses they have evoked—have constellated within the field of religious studies. In so doing, we should be able to discern the lines of intellectual inquiry by which the subject-field has been composed, and this will assist us in making the subject intelligible.

In the chapters following, we have identified four basic questions, and three others that have special enduring relationships with religious studies. The four basic questions are: (1) *What is religion?* (2) *How did religion come into being?* (3) *How shall religion be described?* and (4) *What is the function or purpose of religion?* Each of these questions is formative. Each is appropriate. But since each is also distinctive, each looks for a certain kind of answer. Consequently, the answers that are stimulated must be correlated with the questions that are posed. They make no sense in isolation. Furthermore, they cannot be utilized as answers to other questions. And yet religious studies is characterized by the fact that these several basic questions are asked not simply one after another, but all together and, sometimes, all at the same time. This is why it is absolutely crucial that the various questions be distinguished. What is known about a subject is determined in direct correspondence to the question that is being posed and to the responses that the question yields. Questions give expression to interests, and interests reflect the specific ways in which intellectual attention is focused and refined. Interest in religion—so the second-order tradition attests—has always been a multiple interest: intellectual attention has been focused and refined in a variety of ways. And this is compelling evidence of the fact that religion has proven to be an enormously interesting subject. This fact assures that religious studies is a dynamic field of inquiry.

The four basic questions have evoked distinctive responses, and cumulative bodies of information and knowledge. The first ("What is it?") has been utilized to define religion, to identify its nature and substance, and to isolate a fundamental core element. The second question ("How did it come about?") has directed attention to the possible origins of religion as well as to its continuing development from the time of origins into the modern era. The third point of departure ("How shall it be described?") recaptures the intention to be both comprehensive and descriptive. It records some prevalent responses to the question, "How shall religion be portrayed?" And the fourth ("What is its purpose or function?") has been utilized to describe the roles that religion plays in society.

We are proposing that such questions are fundamental and that they reflect common interest in the subject. We have also suggested that the overall approach we are commending will lend access to the composition of religious studies, for it will help identify some of the formative intellectual pathways by which the subject has been addressed. This is to observe that the second-order tradition within religious studies can be characterized by a succession of parallel developments. It is both successive and parallel because religious studies has been composed by a variety of discernible pathways of inquiry. Such pathways are traversed not only once or twice or a few times, but repeatedly, from generation to generation. They are consulted by virtue of the nature of the questions—perennial questions that can hardly be answered once for all, but which provoke accumulations of response and commentary. Those who have inquired have nuanced their questions under the influences of responses that have been generated by questioners who have preceded them. Thus the academic study of religion has never found itself in a fixed or closed position. Because the questions are both fundamental and perennial, the responses can be fresh and new.

Certainly it would be impossible, in either brief or long scope, to reproduce the entire history of the academic study of religion, even restricting that subject to the narratives that can be traced through Western intellectual history. The progression and transitions from one question to the others, however, can be traced, and some of the prominent examples can be cited and explored. This is the format of the chapters and pages that follow.

For example, the past century and a half of religious studies scholarship has been marked by numerous and repeated undertakings to define religion—that is, to identify its fundamental or core element. From Immanuel Kant (yes, even René Descartes) forward, the intellectual tradition is characterized by a series of methodological attempts to isolate a *sine qua non* (or a first principle) for religion, an element that is sometimes referred to as a *religious a priori*. Accordingly, the methods of these researchers and interpreters have been tailored to reduce all qualities, characteristics, and aspects of religion to those core elements that are understood to be absolutely fundamental. The goal is to analyze the ingredients of religion, breaking them down into basic components, so that an unambiguous simple core element might be isolated and identified. Whether that fundamental core element be Kant's moral imperative, Friedrich Schleiermacher's "feeling of absolute dependence," or Rudolf Otto's "the numinous," the isolated first principle in each instance is regarded as *"that without which religion would not be what it truly is."* This controlling intellectual interest has regulated large portions of the inquiry into religion, and forms a major chapter in what we have been referring to as the second-order tradition.

In addition to the question about the nature of religion, the question about the origin of religion has prevailed in the scholarly inquiry. In this situation, the attempt to disclose an underlying core element is merged with the recognition that religion surfaced early in the history of human consciousness and that its substance has probably been significantly affected by the passage of time. Thus what was identified as a quest to isolate religion's *sine qua non* in the first model is transformed, in the second, into an interest in tracing human sensibility back to identify religion's *primordium* (or initial instance, or root-cause). Some have proposed, for instance, that the origins of religion lie in the awareness of the first human beings that they were surrounded by mystery. Others have suggested that religion has come to exist in order to diminish humanity's perpetual underlying fear. Others have seen it as belonging to the desire to lay hold on immortality. And some have contended that religion emerges within the more comprehensive endeavor to construct, create, or design a worldview. It is within this range of intellectual interests—all prompted by more basic human questions—that we must place the work of E. B. Tylor, Andrew Lang, R. R. Marett, Wilhelm Schmidt, and a large group of others. Each was concerned about religion's earliest appearance. All were captivated by questions about the genesis of religion. And all were quickened by efforts to trace religion's evolution and development.

But when serious problems arose in the attempt to isolate the fundamental core element of religion as well as in the desire to trace the subject back to primordial beginnings, much was left to do in discovering ways in which the perceptible ingredients of religion might be understood to relate to each other. That is to say, the work of phenomenology of religion can be understood as having been formed out of a concerted attempt to place the various elements of religion in meaningful order. Instead of trying to identify a single definitive core element, or even to provide an account of religion's origin and development, scholars who have been motivated this way have worked to provide a comprehensive description of the manner and form in which religious phenomena appear in human experience. From here there was an almost natural tendency to link description to function, and to approach religion in terms of purpose and use. Hence, to questions about explanations, causes, and describable characteristics was added the fundamental question about *function:* What is religion for? What needs does it meet? How does it serve society? What does it contribute to culture?

Each of these pathways of inquiry has been responsible for stimulating large bodies of research, discussion, and commentary. All of them have encouraged working definitions of religion, and all have focused on specific items of interest and have been motivated by particular methodological interests. Together they have given constitution to the field of religious studies. And a systematic discernment of their principal lines of inquiry is the first step in the discovery of the contours of religious studies' second-order tradition.

We have selected these four avenues of approach to the subject. Each represents a fundamental point of departure. Each enjoys a formative place within the making of the intellectual discipline called religious studies. They do not represent the only questions that can be asked about the subject, however. Nor are they the only questions that have been utilized to direct scholarly inquiry. We have isolated these four questions for treatment here because they carry a kind of prerequisitional status with respect to all other methods and approaches. In this sense, they are both formative and foundational to the entire discipline of religious studies. In addition, the four approaches we have isolated represent the only methods that have been cultivated for the purpose of coming to terms with the subject comprehensively. All other approaches to the subject aspire only to deal with aspects or dimensions or portions of it or fashion themselves as being equipped to approach the subject from a specific standpoint. Moreover, the four approaches on which we are concentrating are so fundamental and foundational to the making of the intellectual discipline that the progression from one method to the next, and to the next, roughly parallels the historical sequence of intellectual interest in the subject, from the Enlightenment to the present. Thus, in identifying the four approaches and in tracing their successive developments, we shall also uncover many of the basic components of the formative period in the history of religious studies. This will enable us, as we have proposed, to identify the contours of religious studies' second-order tradition.

To the four fundamental questions, we have added three areas of intellectual interest that have also enjoyed large prominence over the years. The first concerns religious language, or the language that is employed when religion is expressed and communicated. This language has been divided into discursive and nondiscursive modes. Thus the fifth chapter of this study, focusing on the subject of the language of religion, is directed by the question, "How is religion expressed?" The second additional area of significant scholarly preoccupation concerns the relationship between the various religious traditions of the world. The chapter that deals with this subject, the sixth in our study, is descriptive of the question, "Are all religions true?" The final chapter in the volume serves as summation and as agenda for the future. The purpose of this chapter is to circumscribe the range of religious studies, to identify what it can and cannot do, and to assess its influence on its subject. Here we will offer a final assessment of the strengths and weaknesses of the initial paradigm, testing it for its ability to make the subject intelligible, acknowledging its capacity too to protect its subject from intelligibility, and exploring the consequences of these strengths and limitations.

It would be inappropriate, therefore, to try to explicate the conclusions of this inquiry in advance. Nevertheless, we are in strong position to advance a principle whose truth is inviolable. The large variety of interests, methods, intentions, convictions, materials, subjects, issues, and skills already referred to should indicate that religious studies is a dynamic subject-field within which selected topics are approached by means of numerous disciplines under the influence of multiple attitudes and methodological sets of interest. This variety is testimony to the fact that no single subject is common to all endeavors. Furthermore, the more specific subjects within the field share no basic likeness, though they always exhibit direct and indirect associations with each other. Such associations need not be organic, however, nor do the likenesses presume some common property.

Moreover, the scholars whose work is cited have been motivated to come to intelligible terms with matters of significant human interest and importance. They have wanted to know where religion comes from, where it fits within the assemblage of human symbolic expression, what human capacities are most significantly and seriously involved and implicated by religion, by what means a test of its potential truth claims can be assessed, and what difference, if any, it makes to the human enterprise. It is important to note this, for the scholars whose work has been cited are not simply interested in the subject for professional reasons. Rather, their professional involvement, in most instances, stems from their desire to bring intellectual light to the questions, interests, puzzles, and other challenges that belong to the subject.

In other words, religious studies is composed of a collection of intellectual interests. It is characterized by a variety of useful endeavors that draw upon a large number of disciplines while involving a multiplicity of subjects. And it is by means of the second-order tradition that subjects, disciplines, and methods can be perceived and understood to cohere.

It is important to recognize, however, that traditions are composed: they are not simply discovered. They are always in process, perennially susceptible to innovation and transformation. They stand as *givens* only after they have been designed and constructed, and their design and construction are always at least partially idiosyncratic and of pragmatic origin. Traditions are used for parameter-setting. They offer working environments within which inquiries can occur and by means of which they are framed. They are not committed to definitional exactness, except the exactness that is internal and contextual. Such traditions are formative but not causal. They are composed; they can hardly be deduced. They are subtle and flexible but not forced. They are like designs that depend on aesthetic nurture rather than like conclusions that can be deduced with precision from logical, discursive, and tightly sequential reasoning process. And traditions involve narratives—stories that can be traced, stories that get retold, stories in whose retelling the traditions find ongoing shape, design, and purposes that may not have been recognized or anticipated by the founders.

But the identification of a tradition is also a matter of discovery. For, as it turns out, the Enlightenment encouraged religious studies' "founding fathers" to ask questions, and to record responses, in a particular way. So prominent were Enlightenment incentives and intellectual sanctions that the tradition of scholarship gives evidence of the utilization of a single methodological paradigm. This paradigm, in its most embryonic form, was devised to isolate and identify the essence of religion, from which basis it was assumed that religion could be defined. And, as we shall see, the same paradigm was modified to support additional intellectual tasks—that is, methodological ventures whose primary intention was not to define religion but, instead, to trace its origins, describe its prominent or permanent features, explain its social and cultural functions, and the like. It is a single paradigm. Its roots lie in a Cartesian temperament, though with significant Kantian refinement and specification. Its influence can be traced in the scholarship that belongs to the field, even up to the present time. Moreover, the presence of the single paradigm is to be found in the questions posed by scholars working from within a wide variety of fields and disciplines. Thus, the primary differentiation within religious studies derives less from the fact that historians, sociologists, anthropologists, psychologists, philosophers, theologians, and others are intensely involved in inquiry, and raise questions from within the frame of interests that belong to their respective vantage points, and much more from the fact that representatives of all of these fields and disciplines are interested in uncovering certain information about the subject and pursue it via raising fundamental questions.

The chapters that follow have been organized according to these large, controlling questions. The chapters, taken cumulatively, illustrate that the study of religion is a significant ingredient in Western intellectual history. They also confirm that the continuing attempt to make the subject of religion intelligible is a serious enterprise, requiring the best analysis and interpretations of which scholars are capable. But to make vivid sense of this contention, we will turn directly to the first question in the analysis: namely, to the Enlightenment attempt to identify and isolate "that without which religion would not be what it is." This is the first question that was asked. Thus, this is the question that is most responsible for the construction of the paradigm that carries influence over the subject-field to the present day. Once the paradigm was constructed, everything followed, almost as if in clockwork fashion, as if once the stage was set the plot was directed by some intrinsic script that explained to all involved how intelligibility was to be understood. Our intention is to illustrate the unfolding of the plot by tracing the actions of many of the principal players. Toward this end we have been more concerned about expressing sequential development accurately than in abiding by some strict chronological order. That is to say, the chapters have been organized according to constellations of positions and methodological orientations. We have sought to identify the theorists who have made contributions to the articulation of these respective positions before progressing to a consideration of other positions and orientations.

What makes the plot intriguing is that those most responsible for its construction, in numerous instances, were subsequently disqualified from reaping what they assumed would be its benefits. Perhaps this is what they intended—namely, to disclose the rudiments of a subject and, at the same time, to protect this subject from full or otherwise compromising disclosure.

A crucial factor in the organization of this volume deserves an explanation. In selecting the theorists whose scholarship is reflective of the work of religious studies, we have tried to identify both formative influence and prominence. That is, the sequence of discussion within each chapter is directed by an intended conversation between individuals who have expressed themselves in noted exemplary fashion on the subjects under discussion and elucidation. Without question, many of religious studies' most formative theorists have been given proper (though never full or adequate) place within this volume. Unfortunately, however, not everyone could be included; and, it goes without saying, some of those who should have been included may not yet have been properly recognized by the author. Moreover, since it is the discussion between theorists that forms the content of this book, greater consideration was given to a developmental tracing of arguments than to strict chronological order. We intend to prepare a sequel volume that will concentrate on some of the most engaging and current theoretical trends and developments. The intention, this time, is to identify the prominent pathways by which the discipline achieved formation. It is to the first of these that we now turn.

THE ESSENCE OF RELIGION

If religion is going to be defined, the inquirer must work through surface or peripheral characteristics to penetrate to core or root elements. Such is required of a definition. To engage in this task, one must adopt a kind of reductive analytical technique, probing one's way, as the tradition puts it, to "that without which the subject would not be what it is." At the same time, the inquirer must make some crucial decisions about what shall count as being important, and on what basis definitional priorities will be established. Intellectual effort must be directed, too, toward the construction of an effective frame of reference. Religion can be defined only if it is explained and interpreted in certain specific senses, and not in every sense. Thus, the inquirer must protect the fact that the quest for "that without which the subject would not be what it is" is not the same as an attempt to list the multiplicity of ways in which the word *religion* might be used. This implies that when religion is defined, it is always with respect to some specific sense of the subject that the definition is determined. The inquirer cannot presume to be able to define religion in every conceivable sense, for such an intention runs contrary to the nature of a definition. It is only after the subject has been captured within a specific frame of reference that the inquirer can proceed to formulate a definition.

A Cartesian Temper, a Kantian Method

When we look within the history of the discipline for examples of the framing of this interest, we find ourselves, again and again, encountering the influence of the philosopher René Descartes (1596–1650). It was not that Descartes gave either accepted or standard definition to religion, nor even that he formulated the crucial questions adequately. And we are not deferring to him simply on grounds that he is generally acknowledged as the first truly modern philosopher.

The philosophy of René Descartes forms the starting point for the making of the discipline of religious studies by virtue of the way in which it established the terms, conditions, and basis of intellectual inquiry. Descartes contributed enormously to the shape and content of religious studies because of the disposition he established for the workings of critical intelligence in general. It is significant, in this respect, that he trained that intelligence to foster the methods by which definitions are formulated and essences are identified.

Descartes' fundamental contribution lay in formalizing the human disposition to doubt. He made doubt a means of access to truth. He thought that everything ought first to be doubted to discover whether anything can withstand the ravages of doubt. He wished to reckon with the power of doubt before offering any serious claims about truth. He reasoned that by eliminating and discounting everything possible, one might discover some principle that would resist this relentless force. And by proceeding in this manner, the analyst should eventually come upon certain bedrock factors—that is, if such elemental bedrock factors are to be found. And these would serve as the absolutely reliable basis on which a sure and defensible philosophical position would be established.

Previous thinkers and schools of thought—Plato, Aristotle, the medieval system-builders (such as Albertus Magnus, Bonaventura, Thomas Aquinas, to name some of the prominent ones)—approached intellectual work out of contrasting motivation. Instead of doubting everything initially, they attempted to affirm, to posit, to validate. Their interest, in contrast to the motivations of the Enlightenment thinkers, was to construct a system by which these necessary elements could be understood to relate to each other. Their disposition was to make the depiction they offered as inclusive as the content they intended to comprehend. Plato, for example, provided a system of thought that had an appropriate place for the several diverse kinds of knowledge of which human beings are capable. Aristotle, for another, created an organic philosophy in which all of the branches of the sciences were accorded proper and integrated status. Thomas Aquinas, the supreme medieval philosophical system-builder, offered a scheme of thought in which natural truths about the world could be harmonized with the convictions of religious faith, the teachings of the Bible, and the cardinal doctrines of the Christian religion. The intention of such constructivist thinkers was to put the elements in order and relationship, to create a comprehensive picture of the world, to identify the design by which the order of the world might be reflected in thought, idea, and concept. They were motivated by the aspirations of a constructive intelligence. Their shared goal was certainly not to work resolutely to eliminate everything from one's grasp of reality to determine whether there might be something that would not fall victim to such epistemological budget-cutting.

Descartes' driving compulsion was just the opposite. Instead of trying to gather the elements together, collecting and organizing, in order to create systematic coherence, he worked diligently to discount whatever he could. He believed that previous systems of philosophy had functioned excessively and extravagantly to coordinate more than can be properly contained and controlled. He deemed it necessary systematically to remove all that had been assembled superficially and peripherally so that philosophy could be grounded on those absolutely primary elements of reality that could not be discounted even under the most rigorous critical scrutiny. His assumption was that whatever resisted the most determined challenges of doubt could hardly be false. His program became vastly different in tone and temper from the majority of philosophers who had preceded him. He wanted intelligence to culminate in something distinctive. He offered philosophical reflection a compelling alternative to conceptual system-building.

This is not to suggest, however, that Descartes made a clean or complete break with the philosophical traditions preceding him. On the contrary, he shared with previous thinkers a confidence that the world is indeed intelligible, and that philosophy can elucidate such intelligibility. He was also aware, with his predecessors, that the mind is capable of a variety of mental operations, and that these exhibit distinctive functions and intentions. For instance, he provided a kind of lexicon as to how intelligence passes from intuitions to logical deductions to an enumeration of component parts. He recognized that these mental processes are interdependent in highly complex ways. Accordingly, his investigation of mental processes was directed toward identifying substances of an indubitable philosophical status. Hence, the uniqueness of his orientation, as contrasted with those of his predecessors, was his desire to root philosophical certainty on a rigorous analysis and examination of distinctive mental activities. He was as concerned about how knowledge is possible as he was about identifying and classifying reality's components.

Being resolutely committed to certainty, his attention was riveted on elemental factors. He wanted to isolate the unambiguous simples—those elements that stand as being foundational to everything else. Only in this way, he surmised, could philosophy establish an unimpeachable basis of certitude. Thus, complex entities had to be broken down into simple ones. This meant that intellectual analysis would follow *decompositional* pathways. In no surer way could inquiry identify reality's underlying and fundamental *first principles*, which Descartes understood to be the conditions on which everything else depends. He assumed that once the elemental base was discovered, it would serve as the foundation on which a more elaborate structure might be constructed. Hence, systematic doubt was not intended to be an end in itself. Rather intelligence moved from an identification of first principles *(reductio)* to an enumeration of necessary and constituent components *(enumeratio)*. But, from start to finish, for Descartes, the indispensable basis of indisputable certitude was made the condition of all truth.

It was this Cartesian temperament—this most distinguishing fundamental tendency in his philosophical reflection—that came to influence inquiry, in subsequent generations, into the nature of religion. Indeed, the Cartesian temperament is prominent in theoretical approaches to the subject of religion even up to the present time. Honoring the time-tested Cartesian proclivities, philosophers of religion have approached their subject by trying to identify religion's *sine qua non*, its irreducible and fundamental core element. Through the centuries, they have sometimes named this element the *religious a priori*—that is, the principle that stands as the condition for the possibility of religion. And when they have identified this fundamental core element, they have named it "that without which religion would not be what it is." In proceeding in this fashion, they have emulated the sequence of analysis that Descartes established, utilizing it as the model effectively to come to terms with the nature of religion.

In working the method through, Descartes discovered that almost everything can be doubted, at least initially, or provisionally. One can doubt the existence of things like buildings, rocks, trees, and fence posts. One can doubt the existence of persons other than oneself. One can even doubt the real existence of one's moods and temperaments; or, at least, one can explain such feelings as having an origin or source in something else. When encountering experiences of this kind, it becomes easy to "explain things away." The mind can become adept in such exercises in systematic doubt. One can proceed, one discovers, by submitting more and more candidates to the discounting and falsifying intellectual shredder.

But, Descartes attested, the process of systematic doubt is brought to a halt when it seeks to abolish the reality of the self that is doubting. Ultimately, that is to say, Descartes found it impossible to doubt the existence of the mind that is engaged in doubting. The doubter, the knower, must exist in order to be engaged in the act of doubting.

This discovery gave Descartes his first certitude, which he described in the phrase *cogito ergo sum*, meaning, "I think, therefore I am." The attempt to reduce complex entities to unambiguous simples, an intellectual process that functions to eliminate and discount everything that is possibly falsifiable, reaches a stopping point. One cannot deny the reality of the doubter while the doubter is engaged in doubting. And this recognition carries profound epistemological consequences.

This is as far as the reductive process need go. There is no need to probe deeper or to explain the matter more fully. For, at this point, Descartes has established an indubitable starting point, a first principle from which the remainder of philosophical reflection can be understood to follow. Once one has vouchsafed the existence of the self, one can proceed to describe why it is appropriate that other things should exist as well. The outline of the argument can be stated as follows: If there is a self, an indubitable self, there must be other indubitable realities as well. In formal terms, the isolation of first principles makes the enumeration of other ingredients possible and certifiable.

Thus the affirmation *cogito ergo sum* became Descartes' basis for postulating realities in addition to that of the self. Eventually, this became the basis and occasion for affirming (1) the reality of an external world, and (2) the reality of that being who is conceived as being independent of all other realities, namely God. Descartes was consistent throughout. The postulation of both world and God was based on *a priori* identifications necessary to positing the reality of the self. In this fashion, Descartes secured an incontestable place for the three fundamental components of a carefully constructed worldview: self, world, and God. He also provided compelling epistemological evidence for the propriety of thinking about the subject of religion.

When assessing Descartes' contribution to our understanding of religion, therefore, it is important to distinguish his philosophical method from the conclusions he reached by means of it, including his portrayal of the dynamics of religion. It was not his conception of religion that became basic to religious studies' second-order tradition. It was not even Cartesian philosophy as such that assumed such a fundamental status. Rather, it was the approach that was calculated to secure first principles. Simply put, Descartes' intention to uncover and isolate a *sine qua non* was incorporated into the inquiry about the nature of religion. The same procedures he used to place philosophy on a firm foundation were adapted to identify the essence, or fundamental core element, of religion.

It took some time, of course, for the application to occur. The primary instigator and practitioner of the method and the new movement was Immanuel Kant (1724–1804). The context was the philosophy of the Enlightenment, and the specific driving ambition was to differentiate natural from revealed religion.

In jumping this quickly from Descartes to Kant, however, we do not want to leave the reader with the impression that there was no interest in this subject during the intervening century. On the contrary, the period between Descartes' and Kant's times was filled with both theological and religious controversy, and produced a number of thinkers of considerable substance and influence. Jean Bodin (1530–1596), for example, author of the *Colloquium of the Seven about Secrets of the Sublime* (written in 1593, published in 1857), was able to penetrate beyond Catholic-Protestant disputes to raise searching questions about the truth of religion. In comparing Christian and Jewish claims, and in giving serious considerations to the possible legitimacy of claims other religions could make, Bodin questioned whether any tradition qualified as being exclusively true. Moreover, the period between Descartes and Kant is marked by the critical philosophy of one of the most highly respected authors of all time, Baruch Spinoza (1632–1677), a Jew of Amsterdam. Spinoza's pioneering work in biblical criticism and fascination with mystical religion, the summation of which is included in his famous *Tractatus Theologico-Politicus* (published posthumously in 1670), remains a pinnacle in the understanding of religion. The same period brought the highly influential writings of David Hume (1711–1776), the Scottish empiricist who sought to locate religion in erroneous conceptions of causality, and thus stands as one of religion's most famous alleged detractors. In his *Dialogues Concerning Natural Religion* (published posthumously in 1779) Hume traced the development of religion from polytheism to monotheism, linking the entire history to the human misconception that causality is embedded in things instead of being explained subjectively as a factor that makes knowledge possible. Since nothing beyond the range of sense perceptions can be demonstrated, there is no conceivable way, Hume attested, to prove the reality of the deity or of deities. The primitives can hardly be faulted for their superstitions, Hume explained, but moderns are worse in that the same fallacious inferences are fueled by dogmatism, intolerance, and zealotry. Hosts of others were involved in such conversations about matters central to an understanding of the makeup of religion and its role within society. Yet it remains accurate to suggest that the makeup of religious studies is the product of a blending of Cartesian and Kantian instincts and talents.

For our purposes, the link between Descartes and Kant is provided by the methodological legacies each transmitted to the study of religion. In basing their reflections on the quest for first principles, both thinkers developed methods that could be employed to identify religion's core element. Their contributions were thus utilized by subsequent thinkers in the search to isolate the essence of religion. Yet even though the legacies of Descartes and Kant flowed together, they retained their distinctiveness. Descartes unleashed the intellectual energies; Kant organized the relevant materials. Later thinkers forged a combination of resources by placing the Cartesian temper with a Kantian conceptual framework. The product was a series of attempts to name "that without which religion would not be what it is." It goes without saying that this intellectual interest has continued up to the present time.

The Kantian Paradigm

Immanuel Kant's work on the subject grew out of the distinction between natural and revealed religion. Natural religion, for him, referred to the common religious sensibilities to which any person, simply by being human (that is, irrespective of any specific religious influence), could lay claim. Revealed religion was the religion of the church, the religion of the institution, the religion of specific authority, with its doctrines, dogmas, creeds, liturgies, theologies, prescribed rituals, traditions, and perennial suspicions of others. By contrast to revealed—or "received"—religion, natural religion was understood to be accessible and available to all. It was inviting and tolerant, though not always very specific. Natural religion, for instance, carried no special membership requirements, other than one's humanity. Its convictions and affirmations were publicly accessible. It could be verified empirically, and required no approvals or sanctions from ecclesiastical authorities. Furthermore, it was the religion toward which many individuals found themselves moving after experiencing emancipation from what Kant referred to as "dogmatic tyranny," that is, bondage to the religion of an unresponsive Christian orthodoxy. Natural religion sought to secure individual autonomy so that one could arrive at a religious viewpoint independently of ecclesiastical or creedal pressures.

The distinction Kant worked with was not a new one. He simply started where others had left off, and went further, with more elaborate and sophisticated philosophical analysis. For example, Bernard le Bovier de Fontenelle (1657–1757) had already spoken for other thinkers when he attested that God manifests Godself in the law-governed system of nature. The same deity, according to de Fontenelle, was not the god of any historical religion. And another, Claude Adrien Helvetius (1715–1771), extending the distinctions between natural and revealed religion, criticized the obvious restrictiveness of "the mystery religion of Christianity" because it placed obstacles in the path of the fulfillment of humankind's most edifying social interests. Opposed to all forms of ecclesiastical monopoly over the subjects of religion and morality, Helvetius offered this alternative in his famous *Treatise on Man:* "The will of God, just and good, is that the children of the earth should be happy, and enjoy every pleasure compatible with the public welfare. Such is the true worship, which philosophy should reveal to the world."

Given these assumptions, the need for a specially contrived set of theological dogmas disappeared. Such dogmas were regarded as being poor and uninspiring substitutes for a living, authentic religion. Indeed, for Helvetius—as for many—revealed religion seemed to function as the principal instrument of human tyranny. Where it prevailed, minds were held in subjection. Revealed religion, in short, stood as a suspiciously powerful tool to perpetuate intellectual enslavement.

Credit the Enlightenment temper for Helvetius' insights. This temper required that everything—and religious beliefs and attitudes in particular—should be grounded not in some divine will, special providence, creedal formulation, or ecclesiastical authority, but in natural, public, human factual experience. Thus, if any previous religious orientation was to be sustained, it had to undergo a thorough humanizing transformation. This meant transformation via a process of naturalization, or, more precisely, a renaturalization. If so-called "revealed religion" was to be sustained, it had to be stripped of its excesses. Its claims had become extravagant. The process of limiting its influence to manageable size involved a specific application of the now familiar methods by which a subject is reduced to its primary core elements.

The first step in the process—we are associating it with the work of Immanuel Kant, though others employed the same intellectual methods—was a matter of principle. The intention was to approach meaningful religion by certifying its individual human accessibility. It was time to get down to basics. To paraphrase the Cartesian terminology, religious claims of a peripheral or secondary nature had to be discounted. The objective of the inquiry is to reach *certifiable* (and not simply abstract, theoretical) *first principles.*

The second step involved identifying the specific environment within which the inquiry, and thus the search for first principles, was to be conducted. Here the Enlightenment thinkers simply posited the view that religion should be approached as being something eminently *human*. Then, within the context of what is involved in being human, the inquirers worked to identify that human habit, human capacity, human temperament, or human quality to which religion is directly attributable or with which it is fundamentally associated. This involved the inquirers in a kind of taxonomy of human habits, capacities, and qualities so that one of these might be identified as religion's intrinsic point of reference.

It is important to recognize that the Enlightenment attempt to define religion was undertaken within a more comprehensive effort to describe and define the essential characteristics of human nature. Kant and numerous thinkers from his time recognized that the human is a complex organism, and to say this is to affirm that human nature involves the effective interaction of a multiplicity of temperaments, habits, capacities, functions, and qualities. Thus, it is grossly misleading to define *human* as "rational animal," as Aristotle had, as if the human being could be defined in terms of a single quality or capacity that is most distinguished from all other entities within the range of animate life. Certainly the human being is rational, or, at least, possesses the capacity to be so. Humans are also sensitive; that is, they experience emotion and feeling, as in knowing happiness, grief, sadness, elation, and the like. In addition, human beings possess a capacity for moral judgment. One makes willful decisions about actions that ought to be taken, and, faced with moral and ethical dilemmas, one makes choices as to which of several alternatives is most responsible. But the distinctiveness of the human being is that these several fields of interest and attention are impinging upon the psyche at the same time. The human being is referred to as being an organism by virtue of the fact that human nature consists of the interaction of all of these at once. In the end, the Enlightenment thinkers attested that thoughts, actions, and feelings constitute the three fundamental functions or capacities of human nature. Thus, their redefinition of what it is to be a human being occurred with reference to these fundamental capacities. And, when they engaged in this inquiry, they understood that they were pursuing a pathway of analysis that was rigorously reductionistic in its intent.

Understandably, the definition of religion was approached in the same manner, and within the same taxonomic framework. Once the turn toward "the natural" was taken—that is, once the decision was made to approach religion in human terms, as a subject that belonged to human experience, regardless of how analysis might eventually account for it—it became appropriate to ask: *To what range or capacity of human experience does religion most fundamentally and directly belong?* The question was designed to help fix a locale, or specify a quality, or identify a fundamental habit or temperament. It was an effort in contextual identification and refinement, all of it being undertaken with an interest, as Descartes had encouraged, in establishing *first principles.* The goal of the inquiry was to make religion intelligible by discovering where precisely it is situated within the wide range of interactive human powers and faculties.

Therefore, under the inspiration of the dynamics of *reductio,* the large question about the nature of religion broke down into smaller, more penetrating questions. These questions were made appropriate by the basic schematic framework of Enlightenment inquiry:

1. Does religion belong to the human capacity to think, cogitate, and reason from premises to conclusions? Is religion, therefore, to be associated first of all with *the world of thought or idea?* Is what happens to human beings when they engage in religion a matter of thought and reflection, first of all? Is mental activity religion's intrinsic human locus?
2. Or does religion pertain first to *moral or ethical considerations?* Is the human capacity for moral judgment the intrinsic locus of religion? That is, does religion belong to the personal recognition of obligation or sense of duty? Does the human capacity for meaningful practical action constitute religion's fundamental human basis?
3. Or does religion pertain to the human capacity to sense and appreciate order, harmony, balance, and proportion? Is religion fundamentally *aesthetic?* Is its essence to be associated with human feeling? Does it emanate from beauty more directly than from truth or from goodness?

These, within the Enlightenment approach, were the three prevalent possibilities. The assumption was that one of the frames of reference could be identified as helping to account for religion as a human reality. In other words, the inquirers assumed that one could talk about religion by exploring and examining the worlds of philosophy, ethics, and aesthetics. These constituted the appropriate frame of reference. The expectation was that religion would be very much like one of these, or maybe all of them, or, at least, some combination of them. But this is the way to conduct meaningful inquiry if the objective is to define religion by identifying "that without which it would not be what it is."

Notice from the progression of the argument that two significant steps have been taken. The controlling assumption is that religion is rooted not in divine revelation or some form of ecclesiastical authority, but in something eminently natural and human. The next task is to identify that particular human power, faculty, or capacity to which religion belongs intrinsically. Here the analyst can choose from a menu of three possibilities, identified on the basis of distinctions between the true, the good, and the beautiful. Immanuel Kant selected the second category, the ethical, as the basis of religion, since, in his judgment, religion pertains most directly to moral and ethical sensitivity. Friedrich Schleiermacher, as we shall consider later, selected the third of the three options, aesthetics, and identified religion as being "a matter of *feeling*." Other analysts looked to the first category as providing the appropriate locale. Some others responded to the conceptual scheme by working to expand or extend its range so as to include other categorial possibilities. But, however the selection is made, religion is approached as belonging to the range of natural human abilities and interests. Religion is explained on the basis of human nature. In this sense, it is natural to be religious—just as natural as being reflective, being ethical, or being sensitive to the compulsions of beauty.

At this point, the analysts insert a proposal of their own. They contend that the human capacity or faculty in question lacks completion unless the religious factor is functionally present. In other words, the religious factor is treated as a complement to the faculty or habit with which it is associated. It is understood that the religious element adds something to the human activity with which it is associated and in reference to which it is explained. It augments, or complements, or fulfills, and even transforms. It gives an "overplus of meaning," in Rudolf Otto's words, to the faculty or power in question. This implies that this designated faculty or power could not function properly, or develop fully, except in dependence on the religious factor. Ethical virtue is not true virtue, the argument ran, unless ethics is grounded in religion. The human moral sense is only partially developed (according to the same argument) until it is influenced and pervaded by religion. Similarly, appreciation for order and harmony becomes constricted unless it includes the sensitivities of the religious factor. Human knowledge falls short of its potential unless the religious factor is acknowledged. In summary, it is an inviolable rule that the designated natural capacity or power cannot function completely or fully until it is provided with religious reference, orientation, and nurture. As a general rule, whenever the religious element is omitted or short-changed, the human faculty or power with which it is associated must be regarded as being impoverished, undernourished, or fundamentally misaligned. And all of this is involved in "Part One" of the methodological inquiry. All of it is required if religion is to be established on natural (that is, non- or extrarevelational) grounds. This is the work of *reductio*.

After the reductive technique has been applied successfully, attention is directed next toward recuperating whatever might have been lost in shifting religion from revelation to natural grounds. That is, the second phase of the inquiry involves a kind of turning back, a veritable return to the beginning of the inquiry, and a revisitation of the distinction between natural and revealed religion.

This is *enumeratio*. *Enumeratio* is employed to help describe and defend the reasonableness of the details of revealed religion. That is, *enumeratio* certifies the contents of revealed religion but without certifying revelation. For it attests that once the conditions of religion have been established as being something eminently human, the contents of the Christian religion can be reasserted on these same natural grounds. Perhaps the portrayal of the contents of the religious tradition comes out the way it would have before the inquiry was set in motion. But the basis is different, for this time the support comes from an identification of the fundamental conditions of what it is to be a human being, as distinct from some conception of transcendent messages that have been dispensed from the sky.

This two-part approach—*reductio* followed by *enumeratio*—enabled Enlightenment philosophers of religion to claim (or provide assurances) that nothing of substantive or spiritual importance had been lost in the reconceptualization of religion on a natural base. The truly important ingredients were neither discounted nor explained away, but were merely placed on a more resilient and confident foundation. As a result of this transformation, the very heart of religious aspiration was conceived to have a firmer rootage than ever before.

Some Enlightenment thinkers went further. They viewed the transposition from revelation to natural grounds as involving something more than resourceful ways of placing, rooting, and certifying the validity of religious experience. For them, this transaction was a way of breathing new life into the Christian religion. They were bold and optimistic. They claimed that everything meaningful in Christianity could be evinced simply by unpacking the ingredients of the human capacity with which natural religion had become associated. An in-depth scrutiny of human nature, the thinking went, would confirm the fundamental insights and teachings of the Christian religion. Had these fundamental elements not been transmitted by tradition, they would inevitably have surfaced through a careful inventory of what is required in being a human being. But this was merely the basis for a much grander claim: The Christian religion is superior to all other religions because of its unique capacity to articulate the aspirations of the human spirit. Christianity enjoys this status, so the theorists asserted, because, under its influence, the articulations of such aspirations reach their highest human limits.

Immanuel Kant's own literary work illustrates the movement from *reductio* to *enumeratio* that we have been describing. It is significant, in this respect, that he wrote three fundamental critiques: (1) *The Critique of Pure Reason*, which addresses the question "How is knowledge possible?"; (2) *The Critique of Practical Reason*, which focuses on the question "What ought one to do?"; and (3) *The Critique of Judgment*, dealing with aesthetics, which responds to the question "For what shall one hope?" Having decided that religion is approached most resourcefully within the second framework—that is, in the analysis of ethical duties and moral compulsions—Kant closes the sequence with the book *Religion within the Limits of Reason Alone*. This latter book is a portrayal of the teachings and tenets of the Christian religion. It is also a reasonable defense of the plausibility of some of the central doctrines of Christianity, but it takes nature, as distinct from revelation, as the starting point. It is as if had the articles of Christian faith not been taught, one could discover them nevertheless simply by becoming responsibly self-conscious regarding one's own moral sensibilities. To state it more carefully, the Christian religion is both philosophically compelling and morally self-consistent.

Having analyzed religion in these terms, Kant left his successors three procedural possibilities. (1) They could develop his own position further, strengthening its base, extending its range, and bringing methodological and conceptual fortification to its primary assertions. (2) They could seek out other possibilities available to them within his tripartite schematic patterns. That is, instead of concentrating on morality as the locus of and occasion for religion, the analysts could look to ratiocination, to aesthetic judgments, or some additional interpretive category as providing a more appropriate setting. (3) Or they could work to fashion another paradigm altogether, one that worked in some other way, had some other intention, or was motivated by another set of intellectual expectations.

This latter alternative, the cultivation of an alternative or an additional paradigm, required a rather monumental conceptual effort and a genius for being able to see beyond the interpretive possibilities Kant identified. Hence, it was not an option that was taken by many thinkers and philosophers of religion very early. In keeping with an implicit law by which the development of patterns of thought (as well as styles of art) seems to be regulated, the alternative approaches did not surface mightily until the creative energy of the initial *reductio-enumeratio* sequence had been spent. Thus, the first responses were not designed to revise the paradigmatic outline but, instead, to probe whatever conceptual flexibility lay within it. In fact, the Kantian framework, with its Cartesian inheritance, reigned supreme for nearly a century.

Schleiermacher's Shift to the Aesthetic Mode

Friedrich Schleiermacher (1768–1834) was not compelled to criticize the framework itself. On the contrary, he found Kant's threefold categorization of the fundamental human faculties thoroughly convincing. He even agreed that it was appropriate and necessary to separate religion from rationality. Kant had said, "I have denied knowledge in order to make room for faith," and Schleiermacher agreed with the emphasis within this assertion. He, too, wanted to identify religion with something non- or extrarational. But he was not pleased with Kant's identification of religion with the category of morality. He recognized that Kant had argued his case forcefully, but he understood aesthetic sensitivity—what is being referred to here as the third category—to be religion's most appropriate and fundamental locus.

Thus, Schleiermacher's response to Kant's proposals found him selecting the third of the three categorial options. (Significantly, Kant himself left various hints and suggestions that he had given serious consideration to this possibility himself; and yet, when the crucial choice had to be made, he came back to his initial postulation of ethics.) It was Schleiermacher's intention to keep the comprehensive paradigmatic framework intact, while seeking to reorder its internal emphasis.

Having selected the third category, the author of *On Religion: Speeches to Its Cultured Despisers* proceeded to define religion as a kind or quality of feeling. He understood feeling to be an expansive and inclusive reality, something akin to deep sensitivity. Feeling connotes a manner of inwardness, an interior self-consciousness, an awareness of the kind we speak of when we say that something "moves" us deeply. More specifically, it means self-consciousness of our "creatureliness" (the sense of having been created and, thus, of being finite and fragile). Eventually Schleiermacher came to define this wellspring of religion (within personal self-consciousness) as "the feeling of absolute dependence."

Of course, Schleiermacher did not arrive at his contention in this calculated, almost mechanical way. It was no mere matter of making an orientational selection from a list of conceptual possibilities set forth by Immanuel Kant. Rather Schleiermacher's formulations grew out of personal conviction; his ambition was to defend authentic religion against the criticisms and cynicisms of determined detractors.

Religion, he was aware, had come upon hard times. It was encountering significant opposition and indifference within the culture, and particularly among the more educated people. In defense and in response, Schleiermacher proposed that personal self-consciousness be probed, and that this become the avenue through which the conversation about religion take place. He accused his adversaries of presuming to know more than they actually did; thus he referred to them as "the all-too-knowing ones." Presuming that they had thought their way past religion, they had only become victims of their own cultural deprivation. In their professed cultural sophistication they had become shallow. Indeed, they had lost touch with their own feelings; that is, with the foundations of their own sensibilities. It was a strong countercharge to make, but the diagnosis followed from Schleiermacher's fundamental conviction that the ground of religion lies in human sensitivity or feeling. As a restorative, he offered a refined portrayal of religion as belonging to the aesthetic mode.

Thus, it was to the "sophisticated ones" that he addressed his remarks in his book *On Religion*. He began his address with a plea for a hearing. Schleiermacher assumed that he could appeal successfully to the professed openness of the educated people. They claimed to be willing to listen to a presentation on any worthwhile subject by anyone who had devoted a lifetime to study. Schleiermacher, who certainly met this qualification, asked that he be granted an attentive hearing.

He based his defense of religion on observations and judgments regarding human nature. The first of these focused on the dynamics of the self—the essence of personhood—and he described an interior rhythm of which every self-conscious person can be made aware. He said:

> The human soul, as is shown both by its passing actions and its inward characteristics, has its existence chiefly in two opposing impulses. Following the one impulse, it strives to establish itself as an individual. . . . The other impulse, again, is the dread fear to stand alone over against the Whole, the longing to surrender oneself and be absorbed in a greater, to be taken hold of and determined.

Schleiermacher observed that "every soul shares in the two original tendencies of the spiritual nature." The first tendency of the soul is described as a "passing beyond the self." The second tendency—"the longing to be absorbed in the greater"—is described as an "abiding in the self." Every person exhibits both tendencies. The human soul (the seat of consciousness) is marked by the two dispositions.

For some individuals the tendencies are so diminished that they often go unrecognized. In others they are blended and harmonized. Schleiermacher reserves high praise for those rare souls who, possessed of both tendencies, unite the two in a personally fulfilling manner. Such persons "seek order and connection, right and fitness, and they find these qualities just because they do not lose themselves." These unusual, incomparable individuals strive to "awaken the slumbering germ of a better humanity, to kindle love for higher things, to change the common life into a nobler one, to reconcile the children of earth with the heaven that hears them, and to counterbalance the deep attachment of the age to the baser side." It is this personal equipoise, this harmonizing of dispositions, that "adorns humanity." This sort of adornment even registers in a cultural sense.

Schleiermacher explained that he was not trying to defend religion directly. Rather, he was involved in an effort to probe human nature and, more specifically, to come to terms with the dynamics of the human spirit. His intention was to take his readers into places within the human spirit where feelings and conceptions receive form. Once there, his intention was to identify the instinctual impulses from which religious feeling proceeds. Then he wished to specify (in typical Kantian style) how religion can function as a complement or amplification of that mode or form of human consciousness which is highest, dearest, and best.

He recognized the necessity to correct all impressions that religion should be identified first with doctrines, theology, and articles of belief. It was not this kind of religion that he was referring to when probing the dynamics of the human spirit. In other words, the basis of natural religion (not revealed religion) is what Schleiermacher wished to confirm first. Having conceded that the "cultured despisers" have good reason to keep their distance from doctrine, formal theology, and creeds, he praised his adversaries for their caution and condoned their disengagement. Certainly his intention was not to defend revealed religion, at least not in the form in which it had been presented to them. Yes, he wanted to make all appropriate concessions so that he could approach the subject from a vantage point that demonstrates his complete sincerity. As much as possible, without giving ground he would eventually need to recapture, he intended to sympathize with those who found themselves critical of traditional (or received) religion.

It was from this vantage point that he asked his hearers to think first not of the claims of formal religion but, instead, of their own natures. Specifically, he requested that they examine their own consciousnesses. "I ask . . . that you turn from everything usually reckoned religion, and fix your regard on the inward emotions and dispositions, as all utterances and acts of inspired men direct." Then he stated his own case:

> I maintain that in all better souls piety [religion] springs necessarily by itself, that a province of its own in the mind belongs to it, in which it has unlimited sway; that it is worthy to animate most profoundly the noblest and best and to be fully accepted and known by them.

He added:

> The sum total of religion is to feel that, in its highest unity, all that moves us in feeling is one; to feel that whatever is single and particular is only possible by means of this unity; to feel, that is to say, that our being and living is a being and living in and through God.

Thus Schleiermacher proposed feeling as the *sine qua non* of religion. He called this feeling "the consciousness of being absolutely dependent, or, which is the thing, of being in relationship with God." This is the abiding in the self, the longing to be absorbed by something (or someone) greater: "Seers of the Infinite have ever been quiet souls. They abide alone with themselves and the Infinite, or if they do look around them, grudge to no one who understands the mighty Word his own peculiar way."

Religion is located there where "the world fashions itself as feeling." The strong and unmistakable implication is that those who have not detected its presence and come under its influence, despite their protestations to the contrary, are exhibiting an impoverished state of human consciousness. They may understand themselves to be cultured, but the most distinguishing characteristic of their beings has gone relatively uncultivated and undernourished.

By this point in the argument, Schleiermacher has established a basis for religion within the subject, namely as a mode of consciousness: the basis of self-identity. "The religion [which he is commending] is neither a knowing nor a doing, but a modification of feeling, or of immediate self-consciousness." And in approaching religion in this manner, Schleiermacher gave full credence to the distinction between natural and revealed religion. His case for religion was made on natural, public, even empirical grounds, not on the basis of anything circumstantial or to which human beings have special access on the basis of privilege or special qualifications. Then, having isolated the natural basis and locus of religion, Schleiermacher also contended (following the dictates of the fundamental paradigm) that the natural aesthetic impulse is complemented and strengthened by the active presence of the religious factor. In coming to this conclusion, Schleiermacher was merely allowing the force of paradigmatic processes to lead the way. The corollary followed: namely, that until one recognizes that the isolated distinguishing human characteristic carries explicit religious overtones, the life of feeling (or individual self-consciousness) has not yet been directed toward its proper destination; it has not yet found or reached fulfillment. As a consequence, the person within whom this activity is transpiring is not yet whole or complete.

This, as the Kantian precedent illustrates, is just the first of the three important steps. At this stage of the argument, Schleiermacher has only accomplished the first of three related tasks. He has made the case for religion on natural grounds. He has identified the formal categorization. But the content of religion, so far, has only been hinted at.

The next steps require other books as the program reaches beyond what could be covered and elucidated in *On Religion*. In the sequel, called *The Christian Faith*, the author builds upon the case he has made for the validity of religion by exploring the content of religion in light of the cardinal teachings of the Christian religion. Traversing ground he has already covered, Schleiermacher opened *The Christian Faith* with a summarized portrayal of the dynamics of feeling. As might have been expected, he explained feeling in light of the three categorial possibilities (knowing, doing, and feeling) that the Enlightenment paradigm had isolated. Here he opted for the third category (aesthetics), explaining that there is no fourth possibility.

The familiar territory is covered anew when Schleiermacher approaches the Christian faith by describing human life as being constituted by the alternation between "abiding-in-self" and "passing-beyond-self." The next task is to clarify how the mode of feeling (religion's basis) can be conceived as "abiding-in-self." The first step is to differentiate the various kinds of dependency that register within this attitude of "abiding-in-self." He recognizes that the human self is characterized by degrees of dependency, running from minor or moderate to complete and absolute forms. The absolute form of dependence intrigued him most, for this is the basis of religion. This unqualified state of dependence is reserved especially for one's relationship with God. Thus, it is within this context that religion is defined as "the feeling of absolute dependence." "If the feeling of absolute dependence, expressing itself as consciousness of God, is the highest grade of immediate self-consciousness, it is also an essential element of human nature." Note the correspondence. First, the feeling of absolute dependence denotes the fullest expression of religious sensibility. Second, that same feeling leads sensibility to its most appropriate heights. Finally, within the same process, human nature recognizes that it needs to be brought to such an awareness. All of this can be said about religion—following Kant—on purely natural grounds. And all of it has already been said in the predecessor volume, *On Religion.*

Before exploring the contents of the Christian religion, Schleiermacher gives some consideration to the religious traditions themselves, to the religions that exist throughout the world. But, with the exception of Christianity, he has nothing very specific to say about any of them. It is the category of religious tradition that he needs; that is, his exposition requires the "religions" as formal, categorial entities. But his exposition and argumentation require little in the way of detailed description or elucidation. That is, it was not troubling to Schleiermacher to recognize that there is more than one major religion of the world, and he felt no obligation to compare and contrast their competing claims. He expected a natural religious base to lend expression to numerous religious systems, and he simply assumed that one of these (he knew which one) would facilitate the fullest and most exact recognition of the workings and yearnings of the human spirit.

Christianity is the exalted expression of all that is best within the life of piety, in Schleiermacher's view. Would one expect anything other than this from a dedicated Christian theologian? He put it succinctly:

> It appears that, just as in the realm of nature the species are less definite on the lower
> levels of life, so in this realm of religion also the uniform consummation of the out-
> ward and the inward unity is reserved for the higher development; and thus in the
> most perfect form (*which we say in advance is Christianity* [emphases editor's]) the in-
> ward peculiarity must be most intimately bound up with that, which forms the his-
> torical basis of our outward unity.

Christianity is identified as embodying "the higher development" of the religious history of humankind. It is "the most perfect form" of religion because it consists of a precise and satisfying meshing of outward historical expression and inward religious requirements. In other words, the cardinal tenets of the Christian faith are in closest keeping with the religious dictates of the life of inwardness. Thus, before he finished, Schleiermacher understood himself to have made an impressive case for the contention that the journey to religious self-consciousness is all but synonymous with the gradual unfolding of fundamentally Christian religious convictions.

This, we recall, was Immanuel Kant's position too. Both expositions of religion enjoyed the strong support of the controlling paradigm. And if Friedrich Schleiermacher's writing seems to reflect more personal warmth, greater sensitivity, increased humaneness, and less dispassion than Kant's, this may be a consequence of the language he selected for his exposition. Schleiermacher couched his portrayal of religion by probing and examining the world of aesthetics. He was taken by the dictates of beauty, by the emotions that hold one captive when experiencing or encountering a great work of art or an incomparable piece of music. This gives his portrayal of religion an obvious expansiveness, even into sentimental and romantic realms. Kant's product, by contrast, is an examination of moral imperatives. It is therefore marked by ethical seriousness. But despite variations in language and tone, both Kant's and Schleiermacher's renditions follow the prescribed steps of the paradigmatic outline.

That is, Schleiermacher was also obedient to the sequence from *reductio* to *enumeratio*. Indeed, there is a close correlation between these two conceptual movements and the respective subjects of Schleiermacher's two major works. The first, *On Religion*, was an attempt to certify religion on grounds to which rational, natural, empirical, experiential, and public appeal could be made. Then, once these conditions were established beyond reproach, Schleiermacher could write the sequel, enumerating the characteristics of religion in Christian terms. As he proceeded with the second book, *The Christian Faith*, he remained true to both the convictions and the program unveiled in the first book. The argumentation was the expected one, sanctioned throughout by a formal conceptual paradigm that encouraged inquirers and analysts to move from *reductio* to *enumeratio*. The final step—stage three in the process—involved crowning the Christian religion as the cultural entity that must successfully gave expression to the compulsions and yearnings of the human spirit.

Albrecht Ritschl: Revival and Updating of Kant's Position

The nineteenth century was a time of significant reflection on religion. As we shall see in subsequent chapters, not all of this attention was focused on definitions of religion. There was also great interest in accounting for the origin of religion. Moreover, attempts to commit religion to comprehensive description were undertaken in the nineteenth century. Increased exposure to anthropological data gave scholars a much larger body of materials to work with.

Kant's reflections on religion, for example, occurred in relative isolation from religions other than his own. Indeed, this was characteristic of the Enlightenment more generally: the accounts of religion offered did not pretend to be empirical accounts; nor were they presented as comprehensive summaries of concrete data concerning actual living religious traditions. When the Enlightenment thinkers offered their interpretations of religion as universal accounts, they assumed that human mental and sensitive capacities were uniform the world over. They believed that all rational persons came to clarity in the same way, and that human beings everywhere had the same mental makeup. Thus, Kant had confidence that his account of human rationality could be applied generally and universally. An extension of the same presupposition gave Enlightenment thinkers confidence that their accounts of the nature of religion were also generally applicable. Not until almost the mid-nineteenth century did anyone try to assemble hard empirical data to uncover concrete facts concerning, for example, the religions of so-called archaic peoples. Not until then was extensive disciplined investigation undertaken of other religions and cultural possibilities. When this occurred, religious studies became something of an empirical science. Yet, even after this development, the *sine qua non* interest continued to find adherents.

One of these adherents, Albrecht Ritschl (1822–1889), was opposed to what he considered Schleiermacher's romanticizing of religion. In contending against Schleiermacher's formulations, he sought to revive and update Kant's association of religion with a practical, ethical, or moral ideal. This led him to view Christianity in practical, ethical terms—as a religion that disclosed both a perfect moral ideal and the exemplification of that ideal in the person of Jesus Christ. Ritschl regarded Christ as the perfect historical embodiment of the human moral ideal. In his view, the ideal had to be historically manifested to remain ideal. Thus he understood the Christian religion to attest that the Kingdom of God is brought into being through the cultivation of the spiritual personality. This established the conditions of the possibility of "a spiritual dominion over the world." The yearning for the realization of this possibility, Ritschl believed, is present in all persons of religious sensitivity. The distinctiveness of Christianity is that it provides the conditions of the possibility of fulfillment. It certifies that the ideal must be rooted in concrete historical form.

Ritschl knew this fundamental religious quest to be characteristic of all religions. The desire for "spiritual dominion" is a universal religious phenomenon. This is true because religion derives from (and belongs to) moral sensitivity, and moral sensitivity is a characteristic of human nature.

In true paradigmatic fashion, Christianity is elevated to be regarded as a superior religion because, in Ritschl's view, it effectively responds to the universal religious yearning by disclosing the interconnectedness of the ideal and the practical, the eternal, and the historical. Christianity also effectively blends the eternal and the historical. That is to say, the Christian religion illustrates that the ideal can be realized on earth, within the plane of human existence. Thus the Christian religion assists and sustains moral obligation toward effective practical realization. All of it follows from Ritschl's version of the attempt to identify religion's *sine qua non*, and the way in which he proceeded illustrates the movement from *reductio* to *enumeratio*.

Rudolf Otto: The *Sine Qua Non* as "The Holy"

The interest in discovering the *sine qua non* of religion has been pursued with great force and intensity from Kant's and Schleiermacher's times forward, through the nineteenth and twentieth centuries, even to the present. The contribution of Rudolf Otto (1869–1937), German theologian and philosopher of religion, constitutes a central chapter in this ongoing story. Otto's classic text, *Das Heilige* (published in 1917 in German and in 1923 in English translation, *The Idea of the Holy*) has come to be regarded as the most compelling portrayal of this interest. Here, once again, the familiar sequence of *reductio* to *enumeratio* is present in clearly discernible outline.

From the outset, the inquiry reflected in *Das Heilige* shows its affinity with Kantian traditions of scholarship. In typical Kantian form, Otto initiated his study by acknowledging the severe limitations placed on our understanding of deity when this subject is restricted to ratiocinative approaches. Otto understood how the human mental framework persuades itself to approach deity in such terms, but he believed that such an approach promises more than it can reliably deliver. Agreeing with Schleiermacher in the latter's response to Kant, Otto contended that those things to which we refer through use of our rational capacities cannot be completely understood through use of those capacities alone. In other words, he argued that there is a truer religion than the one made accessible by the methods of ratiocinative reasoning.

In beginning his book this way, Otto set the stage for his proposal that irrational elements belong to the essence of religion. This implies that an overemphasis on the rational components of religion produces an unbalanced, impoverished, and inaccurate portrayal. Otto believed that orthodox Christianity, with its stress on right belief, true dogma, and correct teachings, was one of the chief violators of this rule. As such, it became a victim of its own excess. Overstresses and overemphases led Christian orthodoxy to conceive of God in a way that Otto found "one-sidedly intellectualistic and rationalistic." From its opening paragraphs, *The Idea of the Holy* is presented as a necessary corrective to such one-sidedness.

The opening sentence of the second chapter of the book makes reference to the Kantian paradigm and indicates the uniqueness of Otto's use of it. Otto wrote that "the holy" is "a category of interpretation and valuation peculiar to the sphere of religion." In this view, holiness is unique to religion. It should be distinguished first of all from rationality. When this is done, one sees that holiness is most closely associated with goodness, and religion is most closely associated with the ethical. But even "the good" does not fully convey the core element of religion. Otto found even stronger ties to "the category of the beautiful," that is, to the aesthetic. Philosophy was closed out; ethics was understood to fit more appropriately. But, finally, religion was perceived to have most in common with aesthetics. The possibility remained, however, that Kant's three options did not exhaust the variety of human capability.

Otto's treatment of the paradigm's threefoldness was intelligent and distinctive. His intention was to test the possibility that the word *holy* refers to "a clear overplus of meaning"—what remains of religion when the ethical and rational components have been excluded. This means that religion is both like and unlike aesthetics. It is more closely associated with aesthetics than with the other categories. At the same time, Otto insisted that the category of *heilige* be regarded as a distinct category of interpretation. In brief, the range of categorial possibilities must be expanded from three to four: the true, the good, the beautiful, and also the holy.

The word Otto selected to designate the addition, or "overplus" of meaning, is *numinous* (from the Latin *numen*, meaning "dynamic, spirit-filled transhuman energy or force"). In Otto's portrayal, the term refers to an intangible, unseen, but compelling reality that inspires both fascination and dread. It designates the irrational, nonrational element most characteristic of vital religion.

Otto had in mind Schleiermacher's formulations of the essence of religion. Indeed, it was impossible for him to identify the religious *a priori* without referring to Schleiermacher's attempt to provide an alternative to Kant's formulations by ascribing religion to an extrarational faculty. But Otto also disagreed with Schleiermacher. He found Schleiermacher's viewpoint objectionable because it does not penetrate deeply enough. He conceded that religion ought to be associated with feeling, but feeling alone provides nothing more than a close analogy to religion's true root. More precisely, "feeling"—even in "the feeling of absolute dependence"—is a response to the religious condition; it is not that condition itself. Likewise, feeling is not the occasion for religion, but what is prompted by the occasion.

Otto further objected to Schleiermacher's treatment of "feeling" because it is restricted to the perspective of subjectivity. To view the matter as Schleiermacher does limits aesthetics to the category of self-consciousness. Otto insisted that the subjective self-consciousness attending "feeling" is a concomitant to an objective divine reality. And so he constructed an alternative concept—the *numinous*—to point more effectively to a reality outside the self. "Feeling" retains a close relationship with "numinous experience," but it is neither the source, condition, or root of religion.

When Otto undertook to describe the *numinous* in detail, he faced certain problems. Since the term had been defined as an "overplus" of meaning, it can be approached only through metaphors, analogies, and other symbolic expressions called "ideograms." Recognizing these difficulties, Otto still believed that it makes sense to talk about the *numinous*. He selected the term *mysterium tremendum* for this purpose: the term describes the "deepest and most fundamental element in all strong and sincerely felt religious emotion." He described the experience as follows:

> The feeling of it may at times come sweeping like a gentle tide, pervading the mind with a tranquil mood of deepest worship. It may pass over into a more set and lasting attitude of the soul, continuing, as it were, thrillingly vibrant and resonant, until at last it dies away and the soul resumes its "profane," non-religious mood of everyday experience. It may burst in sudden eruption, up from the depths of the soul with spasms and convulsions, or lead to the strangest excitements, to intoxicated frenzy, to transport, and to ecstasy. It has its wild and demonic forms and can sink to an almost grisly horror and shuddering. It has its crude barbaric antecedents and early manifestations, and again, it may be developed into something beautiful and pure and glorious. It may become the hushed, trembling and speechless humility of the creature in the presence of—whom or what? In the presence of that, which is a mystery inexpressible and above all creatures.

The overall portrayal involves two distinct steps. First, Otto placed religion within the proper category, utilizing the threefold scheme that Kant had proposed. Here he has explained that the essence of religious experience should be identified neither with the rational, ethical, nor the beautiful, but, instead, with the numinous element. Second, he tried to attribute content to (or discover content within) the category. It was at this point that he selected and fashioned one concept, the *mysterium tremendum*, as a description of the numinous.

In the process, Otto discovered that he could be much more precise about the characteristics of the numinous. For example, the adjective *tremendum* breaks down into the elements of awe, majesty (translated as "overpoweringness"), and urgency (unusual energy). The noun *mysterium* resolves into various terms signifying "wholly otherness"—that which is distinct from everything else. Yet Otto insisted that while it remains distant, uncommon, and unique, the *mysterium* also attracts and fascinates. It is both transcendent and compelling, both distant and attracting, at once:

> These two qualities, the daunting and the fascinating, now combine in a strange harmony of contrasts, and the resultant dual character of the numinous consciousness,

to which the entire religious development bears witness . . . is at once the strangest and most noteworthy phenomenon in the whole history of religion.

Otto found precedent for this formulation in the distinctions Martin Luther made between God's wrath and God's love, while asserting, nevertheless, that both characteristics belong simultaneously to God's nature. Otto also found parallels in Friedrich Nietzsche's distinction between the Dionysian and Apollonian temperaments. But he went even further. In surveying the entire history of human religious awareness, he argued that this fundamental contrast inherent in the *mysterium tremendum et fascinans* was always present. The two aspects of the numinous come bound up together. Further, they parallel the interpenetration of rational and nonrational factors in religious sensitivity.

Otto speculated that the first human beings, experiencing the first stage of religious awareness, were captivated solely by the daunting aspect of the numinous. Such persons lived under the threat of divine wrath. They had not yet become acquainted with the other side of the numinous experience. When this latter awareness dawned, their religious activity grew into something more than a series of attempts to appease a powerful, threatening, even menacing deity. The second stage created the occasion for a "positive self-surrender to the *numen*." Otto went on to read the same contrast as that between magic and religion. Magic, he contended, develops the daunting aspect of the numinous. Religion, contrariwise, implies a discovery and cultivation of the corresponding positive side.

At the peak of his evolutionary speculations, Otto applied his understanding of the dialectical character of the numinous to the history of religious experience. This led him to draw theological conclusions about the superiority of Christianity similar to those drawn by previous users of the Enlightenment paradigm. He argued that the alternation between the repelling and the alluring aspects of the numinous, when expressed in the rational and nonrational idioms of religion, constituted the pulsebeat of human religious history. (He referred to this ongoing chronicle as the "history of salvation.") The balance between the *tremendum* and *fascinans*, and between their rational and nonrational expressions, provided for Otto a yardstick for the evaluation of all religions:

> By the continual living activity of its nonrational elements a religion is guarded from passing into "rationalism." By being steeped in and saturated with rational elements it is guarded from sinking into fanaticism or mere mysticality, or at least from persisting in these, and is qualified to become religion for all civilized humanity.

It is within this context that Otto talked about the preeminence of the Christian religion in contrast with the other major religious traditions of the world: "The degree in which both rational and nonrational elements are jointly presented, united in healthy and lovely harmony, affords a criterion to measure the relative rank of religions—and one, too, that is specifically religious." Now, for the key line: "Applying this criterion [i.e., the extent to which rational and nonrational elements are balanced], we find that Christianity, in this as in other respects, stands out in complete superiority over all its sister religions." Further, Otto believed that the history of achieving this balance—the "salvation history" to which he made reference—describes the self-unfolding of God. Hence, these contrasting religious currents are not mere products of the understanding. Nor are they human conceptions of divinity. Rather, they describe the "ever-growing self-revelation of the divine."

This is to follow the tendency of the prevailing paradigm to its logical conclusion. To recapitulate, Otto's intention was to portray the holy, in Kantian terms, as being a "purely *a priori* category." His argument for this was that whatever attributes of independence and necessity Kant ascribed to the human capacities to perceive the true, the good, and the beautiful also apply to the human capacity to perceive the holy. Moreover, all four of these categories must be regarded as conditions of the possibility of human experience.

> The facts of the numinous consciousness point therefore—as likewise do also the "pure concepts of the understanding" of Kant and the ideas and value-judgments of ethics or aesthetics—to a hidden substantive source, from which the religious ideas and feelings are formed, which lies in the mind independently of sense experience.

Hidden in this large claim are two smaller, related contentions. First, the holy, like the true, the good, and the beautiful, stands as an *a priori* condition (or "hidden substantive source") of the experiences that are drawn from it. Second, the holy carries the status of being self-standing: it has the quality of being *a priori*. This gives it an independence equal to that of the true, the good, and the beautiful. Consequently, it cannot be derived from any of these or even from the sum of them together. In short, the holy stands by itself, and without it there would be no religion. Thus, having stated his case for its *a priori* status, Otto can refer to the holy as "a hidden predisposition of the human spirit." This predisposition is a "religious impulse that only finds peace when it has become clear to itself and attained its goal." The holy, as an *a priori* "category of mind," also manifests itself in outward appearance. It can be perceived in religious experience. It motivates mystical sensitivity. And, as we have seen, it even provides access to the nature of God. Furthermore, because of its ability to give large place and appropriate recognition to the holy, Christianity can be judged to be a valid religion—indeed, the most exemplary of all of the great religions.

In moving from a consideration of the *sine qua non* of religion with direct reference to natural human capacities to according Christianity the highest place among the religions of the world, Otto's portrayal illustrates each step in the paradigmatic progression. Indeed, he followed the paradigmatic route precisely, from *reductio* to *enumeratio*.

Anders Nygren and the Quest for a Religious *A Priori*

After Otto, the search for the essence of religion, in Western scholarship, is not easily traceable. The paths of recent and contemporary intellectual inquiry pay allegiance to a wide range of interests, in various combinations, so that such inquiry rarely remains single-minded. Before this pronounced modification and proliferation of interest took full control, however, the search for religion's *sine qua non* received at least one more classic systematic treatment. It came in 1921, shortly after Otto wrote his best-known work, in a book by the Swedish theologian and bishop Anders Nygren (1890–1979) called *Religiöst Apriori* (English translation, *The Religious A Priori*). This important book illustrates the workings of the fundamental paradigm in almost architectonic fashion.

Nygren's work encompasses the two movements with which we have become familiar, *reductio* and *enumeratio*. The first movement is orchestrated in his early books, the chief one of which (besides *Religiöst Apriori*) is *Filosofi och Motivsforskning* (English translation, *Philosophy and Motif-Research*). Both of these books show large dependence on Kant and Schleiermacher, to whose writings Nygren often refers. Both are used to place religion on firm natural grounds. In both, Nygren remains true to the Kantian point of departure by first examining philosophy, ethics, and aesthetics as possible loci for religion. After doing this, Nygren—like Otto—proposed that religion be understood as a *sui generis* reality. To call it *sui generis* is to indicate that it stands on its own—unique and irreducible. It is related to philosophy, ethics, and aesthetics, while also being independent of them.

Nygren worked out a distinctive place for religion by assigning it to a fourth category: not to the true, the good, or the beautiful, but, in Nygren's words, to the eternal, to that which abides when all else passes away. Formally speaking, the eternal is a category on which the other categories depend. For example, if something is true temporarily or even occasionally, it is not true in the fullest sense. If something is good, either temporarily or even occasionally, it is not good in the fullest sense. The quality of permanence is accorded the true, the good, and the beautiful by the religious factor—namely, the category of eternality. Religion, in Nygren's view, is centered in the category of the eternal.

Enumeratio, as we would expect, follows *reductio* in Nygren's work. Thus, his next step involves describing the content that belongs to the category of the eternal. To find and identify this, he turns to the religious traditions themselves. Nygren justifies this move on the basis of his conviction that the religions were formed in response to the question about the eternal. That is, when Nygren speaks of "the eternal" he also intends to say that religions can be understood as giving expression to permanence. Religions are responses to the question, "What is eternal?" The Christian religion responds to the question by means of the affirmation, "God is love." Thus, the religious traditions name the permanent elements of reality and provide appropriate orientation to them. The differentiae of the various religions lie in the particular expressions they give to the category of the eternal. In functioning thus, religions bear a certain resemblance to philosophies. Philosophies are formed by the category of truth. Ethics derives from the category of goodness. But the specific manifestations, the concrete examples of any given philosophy or ethical system, construe the content of the category in distinctive ways.

These were Nygren's fundamental intentions, but his work was only partial and preliminary. After working out the schematic framework, Nygren concerned himself with only one religious tradition, namely Christianity, and, by contrast, with those traditions (Judaism and Platonism) that interact with it within Western civilization. In proceeding in this fashion Nygren honored the paradigmatic tendency to treat Christianity as being superior to the other traditions with which it is associated: it is superior, as we have come to expect, because it offers the religious category the fullest opportunities for self-expression.

The comparative analysis of the three traditions is the subject of Nygren's book *Agape and Eros*. As can be anticipated, the three traditions are presented as having formulated distinctive attitudes toward permanence (or toward the category of the eternal). Nygren contended that these distinctive attitudes are implicit in the fundamental motifs of the three traditions (for Christianity, *agape*; for Platonism, *eros*; for Judaism, *nomos*). In appropriate paradigmatic fashion, a fundamental motif is defined as "that without which the respective tradition would not be what it is." In short, *agape* is the Christian enunciation of the category of the eternal. *Agape* is "that without which Christianity would not be what it is," and the category of the eternal is "that without which religion would not be what it is." *Reductio* has put the elemental realities in place. The remaining intellectual work can be assigned to *enumeratio*—that is, the *agape*-motif needs to be described in fuller measure.

It was at this stage that Nygren utilized the assistance of one of his colleagues, Gustaf Aulén (1879–1978), also a theologian and bishop, to complete the paradigmatic cycle. We refer principally to Aulén's work *The Faith of the Christian Church*, which stands to Nygren's *Religiöst Apriori* and *Agape and Eros* the way Schleiermacher's *The Christian Faith* stands to Schleiermacher's *On Religion*. The first stage of scholarship establishes sure conditions for the possibility of religion. The second puts flesh on the skeleton, filling in structure with content. In other words, phase one makes the case for the validity of religion as a distinctive form of human experience. Phase two fills out the account by elaborating religion's significant characteristics. Thus Aulén's *The Faith of the Christian Church*

was constructed upon the methodological and philosophical base e.
Nygren's critical works. The typical paradigmatic sequence was fol.
different from the examples we have cited before, two scholars rather
were involved in completing the cycle. Yet the prevailing tendency was
followed by *enumeratio*, with the conclusions being that religion is indeed
form of human experience whose most effective and integrated form of e.
sion is the Christian tradition.

An Example of Otto's Influence: Erwin R. Goodenough

As noted, from this point forward, the strands and trajectories of *sine qua non* scholarship go here, there, and virtually everywhere. In identifying some of the more prominent intellectual pathways among them, we return to Rudolf Otto's formulations and to a position that was inspired by them. We refer to the orientation of Erwin R. Goodenough (1893–1965), well-known historian of religions, who specialized in early Christianity, the religions of the Hellenistic period, and Jewish symbols in the Greco-Roman world. Our intention in reviewing Goodenough's proposals is to illustrate still another variation on *sine qua non* themes, and to trace Otto's influence into the history-of-religions territory.

Both Rudolf Otto and the Kantian framework are apparent in Goodenough's statement that "religion of one sort or another is one of the two or three universal and basic aspects of human life." Religion, understood in this larger sense as something basically human, must be distinguished from religion understood as "organized or traditional faith." (We note that Goodenough's starting point, thinly veiled, is the familiar distinction between natural and revealed religion.) Approaching religion as a universal human phenomenon, he wanted to identify the "common religious element." He believed that this element could be disclosed in the cumulative religious history of humankind as "the universal quest for security." He explained the situation this way:

> The common element is that of a devotion to something on which the people committed seem to themselves to depend, in which they hope for security, or in which they actually find it. Whether it is by the security given by a fetish, by a ritual, by a creed, by the church, by the loving Jesus, by one's social status, by a substantial bank account, by a title (whether the title be "president of the bank," "professor," or "marquis"), or by creativity in art or science, when one or more of these becomes the focus of our lives, we have accepted the security as our religion.

The quotation illustrates that the roots of religion lie in the human desire for security. In describing how the need has become discernible, Goodenough offers a genetic account. All persons, he says, seek release from anxiety and from threats to their existence. Security is sought as the mode of release. It is just this simple. And it can be stated in clear psychological terms.

But the same analysis can be used to illustrate the propriety of Rudolf Otto's definition of religion. Goodenough believes that threats to human existence are expressed as an awareness of what Otto called the *tremendum*. According to Goodenough, Otto himself made the connection in *The Idea of the Holy*. He explains:

> I call these threats or sense of threats collectively the "tremendum," a Latin word which Rudolf Otto used in a somewhat different sense and which has, as I use it, its simple original meaning of "that which must be feared" or "the source of terror." I use it precisely because its strange vagueness best conveys the most terrifying part of our predicament, the very inchoateness of the terror without and within us.

Continuing with assistance from the field of psychology, Goodenough argues that there are compelling ways of explaining why persons have found it difficult to face the *tremendum*. First, people find it impossible to live with ignorance. They always want to know more about the world in which they live. They desire to attribute no more than is absolutely necessary to mystery. And, second, people find it impossible to tolerate their own feelings of helplessness in the face of this situation.

Thus, in Goodenough's view, human beings are motivated to know more about the world so that they may more readily approach the possibility of bringing it under their own means and methods of control. This "drive for control" is the chartering cause of civilization, culture, and institutions. Religion, too, is created this way, which helps explain the utility of its function:

> Man's rituals make the individual participate in the *tremendum* to a slight extent, at least, and give him a feeling that by these acts he appeases the *tremendum* or makes it more apt to befriend him. By the rituals, he also keeps himself from consciously facing the *tremendum*'s unfathomable depth and power, the actual abyss of the uncontrollable.

What religion provides is a mode of adjustment. Goodenough defines religion as "man's adjustment to the *tremendum*." For Rudolf Otto, we recall, religion was not simply a matter of adjustment. Rather it involved discovering the secret of the rhythms by which demonic and benevolent aspects of the holy interact and alternate with each other. Goodenough understands his own view to be a variation on Otto's proposals. In his view, the daunting quality of the *tremendum* helps explain the repeated attempts to appease the uncontrollable and incomprehensible deity that appear in the history of humankind.

We recall that Otto's formulation of the *tremendum* includes a second side too—the side of the *tremendum* which compels and fascinates. Here a substantial difference exists between Goodenough and Otto. For Otto, *fascinans* is a positive disposition that is able to attract human beings and assist in making them whole. Goodenough neglects this aspect of Otto's formulation. He limits his portrayal of the *tremendum* to the adjustments it evokes on the part of those who are subject to its daunting power. Religion, in his view, supplies the most obvious ritualistic and mythological means of adjustment.

> Man throws curtains between himself and the *tremendum* and on them he projects the accounts of how the world came into existence, pictures of divine or superhuman forces or beings that control the universe and us, as well as codes of ethics, behavior, and ritual which bring him favor instead of catastrophe.

He summarizes the same point with a telling concluding line: "So has man everywhere protected himself by religion."

In spite of what might appear to be the case, Goodenough insists that he has no interest in explaining religion away. He understands his attitude toward religion to be positive. He acknowledges that religion serves a useful function. Indeed, he even goes so far as to recommend that religious aspiration continue, and that persons try to bring the *tremendum* under firm control—if not by magic and distinctly ritual practices, perhaps by scientific invention. He wants human desires, fancies, and visions to be directed toward improving personal and collective environments. He reasons that if persons have constructed hedges against the *tremendum*, it is because the *tremendum* must be hedged.

Furthermore, in Goodenough's view, more basis for optimism exists today regarding the religious quest (or, in his words, the religious "search") than ever before. Scientific advances have removed many of the illusory curtains that have been thrown up to protect humankind against the powers of the *tremendum*. In the modern era, through scientific discoveries, people are enabled to live by continually revised hypotheses (since good hypotheses lead to better and better hypotheses) instead of mythological contentions that often masquerade as absolute truths.

> The truly modern men are steeplejacks climbing to dangerous heights; indeed, they are mountaineers scrambling far beyond the peaks of Everest or descending into inconceivable depths. The ones who become dizzy are those who watch them from what they suppose is the real ground. To the modern mind, there is no ground any more, no fixed level or point of meaningful reference. Such a world is not for cowards, but such is the world in which modern man lives.

Thus, what began as an attempt to lend definition to religion culminates in a challenge to cease approaching the unknown with obsolete categories of interpretation. Goodenough contends that the practice of raising curtains in the face of the *tremendum* sometimes constitutes a deception. Some human effort qualifies as true adjustment; much of it, however, must be seen as the perpetuation of meaningless and illusory compensation.

Goodenough is committed to "the quest for reality" even while recognizing that the quest can only be undertaken provisionally. He understood his goals for religion to be analogous to the patriotic imperative of Abraham Lincoln's "Call to Prayer":

> The dogmas of the quiet past are inadequate to the stormy present. The occasion is piled high with difficulty, and we must rise to the occasion. As our case is new, so we must think anew and act anew. We must disenthrall ourselves, and then we shall save our country.

From Otto to Barth and Tillich

We have cited an example of the employment of a *sine qua non* approach from the writings of Erwin R. Goodenough, a historian of religion. We turn now to two Christian theologians, Paul Tillich (1886–1965) and Karl Barth (1886–1968), both of whose approaches were inspired and fashioned by the fundamental distinction between natural and revealed religion. The two are regarded as being among the most significant Protestant theologians of the twentieth century.

Tillich was much taken by Otto's portrayal of "the idea of the holy," but he believed it appropriate and necessary to extend its range. This underlying element, what Tillich came to refer to as "the depth dimension of religion," is to be found, he proposed, in all meaningful cultural activity. All of it—in art, in music, in literature, indeed, in all modes of cultural expression—gives evidence of being nurtured by this depth dimension, or a dimension of depth.

Barth was impressed by Otto's portrayal too, but he preferred to construe it within narrower, restricted, and refined boundaries. The champion of the movement called Neo-Orthodoxy in Protestant theology, Barth took the alternate view that God is "the wholly other," and God is therefore deemed so inaccessible that only relevation provides trustworthy religious knowledge. The difference between the two positions is fundamental and decisive. Tillich placed the *sine qua non* within the framework of natural human experience, so as to define the essence of religion in broad and comprehensive cultural terms. Barth judged that Tillich's proposals violated the sanctity of authentic religion's authoritative *sine qua non* by entangling it within the world of natural phenomena. Barth stood opposed to this point of view because he reckoned that the only authoritative basis for authentic religion lies in revelation. Thus, one can view Barth and Tillich as having taken Otto's inspiration and applied its principles within the two contrasting frames of reference implicit in the Enlightenment distinction between natural and revealed religion.

For Barth, revelation is religion's authoritative context. In speaking of the substance of revelation—both its source and its content—Barth emphasized "the Word of God." With specific reference to Otto's proposals, Barth offered this comment in the first volume of his *Church Dogmatics:*

> Rudolf Otto's "Idea of the Holy," whatever it may be, is at all events not to be regarded as the Word of God, for the simple and patent reason that it is the numinous, and that the numinous is the irrational, and the irrational something no longer distinguishable from an absolutised power of nature. Upon the very distinction everything depends, if we are to understand the concept of the Word of God.

This makes it clear that it is invalid to accord meaningful religion a public, accessible, natural *sine qua non.* Neither can there be something called "religious experience." Rather, Barth makes a concerted attempt to separate such pretentious "natural" religion from the authoritative and specific revealed—or, in Enlightenment terms, "received"—religious truth, which is the religion of revelation, which alone carries the capacity to lead to salvation.

For Barth, the fundamental paradigm remains intact. But at the initial selection point, he gives unqualified preference to revelation and excludes natural religion. From this point on, all subsequent paradigmatic choices follow the same preference. Eventually something like a Cartesian indubitable element emerges— Barth calls it "the Word of God." But, in this case, it is understood to be the fundamental core element of revealed rather than natural religion. For Barth, revealed religion and so-called natural religion are qualitatively and categorically dissimilar.

Tillich, on the other hand, was also sensitive to the differences between religion "in the narrow sense" (the religion of revelation) and religion "in the larger sense" (or religion as "an aspect of the human spirit"). Like Kant, Schleiermacher, and those thinkers who were impressed with the apparent power and influence of religion within culture, Tillich's intention was to keep the two forms of religion in appropriate relationship with each other, so that each would be accorded appropriate respect. His method lay in specifying the workings of the sequence of *reductio* and *enumeratio.*

He began by defining religion not as "a special function of man's spiritual life, but [as noted] the dimension of depth in all of its functions." This meant that instead of trying to isolate a specifically religious human impulse or temperament—say, the life of feeling, or moral awareness, or sense of order, and so on— Tillich talked about a dimension of human life that possesses the ability to transform all of life. He was fond of Otto's phrase, "clear overplus of meaning," but instead of wanting to identify, locate, or name this force more specifically, he sought to demonstrate that it is implicit in all aspects of human life. In his view, everything the human being thinks, feels, does, or otherwise experiences is simply that much greater, deeper, and more multivalued because of the active presence of the religious (or depth) dimension. The underlying religious dimension enables one to tap a subterranean range of significance and emotion. As he put it: "Religion is the aspect of depth in the totality of the human spirit."

Furthermore, Tillich contended, there is no occurrence in human affairs that is removed from potential religious interpretation if such occurrences are probed and comprehended in terms of the presence of this depth dimension. Social relationships have religious significance. Political events carry religious meanings. And cultural expressions exhibit religious influence.

Consequently, Tillich detected the presence of the dimension of depth in specific works of art, in painting and sculpture, in novels, films, plays, and musical compositions—although, of course, in various forms and degrees. Art, music, drama, literature, philosophy, and other forms and modes of human expression are not simply self-contained subjects and objects of cultural interest and attention; rather, they are the vehicles that bear life's meaning. They are symbolic carriers through which religious meaning is conveyed. All of them betray a dependence on some deeper, more fundamental aspect of reality from which they glean significance in the world. For example, the meaning of a novel or a play is not exhausted by whatever it is able to make apparent; rather, both novel and play reflect more basic human issues that affect everyone, whether or not they are explicitly aware of this fact. Music cannot be reduced to the interrelation of melodies, rhythms, harmonies, and tones. Rather, music taps that subterranean world in which deep and rich universal issues are being played out. After referring to each of these three basic ranges of human experience, as identified within the original Kantian paradigm, Tillich says in summary (and with a tone that reflects the passion of Schleiermacher's "speeches to religion's cultured detractors"): "You cannot reject religion with ultimate seriousness, because ultimate seriousness, or the state of being ultimately concerned, is itself religion." Then comes the summary statement: "Religion is the substance, the ground, and the depth of man's spiritual life." This, Tillich adds, is "the religious aspect of the human spirit."

Throughout his analysis, Tillich follows the several initial steps of the Kantian scheme. He makes it clear from the outset that he is not thinking of religion in the narrow sense. ("Narrow," in this case, means the religion of Christian revelation conceived of as special.) Instead, he is speaking more comprehensively of all justifiable religion; that is, the natural religious capacity of the human person. So, instead of linking religion to one of the human subcapacities—thinking, acting, and feeling—he construes religion as a pervasive dimension that lends depth to all human capacities and functions. Religion, he attests, belongs to the workings and aspirations of the human spirit. Having approached the religious factor this way, he is in position to talk about how the human spirit is impoverished, truncated, and imbalanced when the same dimensional factor is not appropriately acknowledged. In positive terms, human life is enriched, or, indeed, rightly oriented when the religious dimension is accorded proper place. This conclusion allows Tillich to contend that without conscious recognition and dependence on the religious dimension, human life cannot become what it is meant to be.

At this point in the outline, Tillich returns to the beginning of the sequence to recover whatever might have been lost when he applied the original distinction. That is, having spoken of religion in the broad sense, he needs to give some description to religion in the narrow sense. For the viability of his formula depends on his keeping these two differentiated contexts in specific relationship with each other.

"But now the question arises," he acknowledges, "what about religion in the narrower and customary sense of the word, be it institutional religion or the religion of personal piety?" He paraphrases his own question: "If religion is present in all functions of the spiritual life, why has mankind developed religion as a special sphere?" In short, what does the treatment of religion in the larger, more expansive human sense imply regarding "religion in the narrower and customary sense of the word"?

Tillich's answer is twofold. In the first place, he confesses that he regards religious traditions—particularly if they have been formed in a mutually exclusive manner—to be the product of human self-estrangement from the ground of being. The institutionalization of religion occurs, in his judgment, when religion becomes just another social, political, and cultural artifact. This occurs when persons fail critically to apply a perspective of depth to their own religious experience. Such a perspective rescues persons from treating the specifics of their own religious situations in an idolatrous manner.

But Tillich goes further to make positive affirmations too. In his view, the specific religions—the religious traditions of the world—find their true sustenance in the underlying, primary substratum of reality. Only when they point beyond themselves to the realm of being which they make accessible—but which they can never pretend to comprehend or contain—do they fulfill their role of facilitating the human quest for meaning.

Thus, all persons (Christians, Jews, Muslims, and all others alike) should be taught to place their confidence neither in this nor in that specific creed or deity, but in what Tillich calls "the God beyond the gods." Christians, for example, should be taught not to assert that Jesus of Nazareth *is* the Christ. To draw such a literal equation is to destroy the symbolic interconnections between the visible world and reality's underlying substratum. Instead, Christians should talk of Jesus *as* the Christ. Or, again, a flower is not simply a flower, but a reality that points to a more fundamental set of conditions from whose resilience it receives its own reality. Because everything thus refers beyond itself, the entire world takes on symbolic significance. The components of the sociocultural world, whatever they are, symbolize something more fundamental: they point to the active presence of the dimension of depth. And all find their life-meaning in the nurture that flows from this deeper dimension.

In Tillich's view, religion pertains to this underlying, subterranean grounding of all things. Instead of having reference to a separate preserve, religion pertains simply to everything that it records in its dimension of depth. Tillich explains in his *Theology of Culture:*

> What does the metaphor *depth* mean? It means that the religious aspect points to that which is ultimate, infinite, unconditional in man's spiritual life. Religion, in the largest and most basic sense of the word, is ultimate concern. And ultimate concern is manifest in all creative functions of the human spirit.

Then, with explicit reference to the fundamental paradigm we have been identifying and delineating in this chapter, Tillich adds:

> It [religion] is manifest in the moral sphere as the unconditional seriousness of the moral demand. . . . Ultimate concern is manifest in the realm of knowledge as the passionate longing for ultimate reality. . . . Ultimate concern is manifest in the aesthetic function of the human spirit as the infinite desire to express ultimate meaning.

For Tillich, one of the most compelling warrants for this proposal is the understanding of deity that belongs to the Hebrew Bible. When asked who he was, the God of Israel, YHWH, conveyed to Moses that he should be identified simply "I am who am." Tillich takes this declaration to mean that the true God, the God of revelation in a sustainable sense, and the God of religion in the larger sense, is the Ground of all Being. The name of God in Hebrew, YHWH, also implies this etymologically. The gods who inspire worship and adoration have their bases in the God who is identified most specifically as the Ground of Being.

Thus, specific religious traditions must be partial to their own circumstances and destinies, for natural human religious aspirations find expression within the traditions and are stimulated by them. Those traditions that acknowledge the necessary human affirmation of the Ground of Being embody the truest and surest natural religious currents. But these natural religious impulses never run pure and free within any one religion. Hence, every religion, in Tillich's view, is marked and governed by mixed motivations. A perennial tension exists within the traditions between their specific destinies and their capacity to allow these natural religious compulsions to break free. Religious traditions tend to function both as affirmation and negation of the natural religious impulse. Religion, viewed as ultimate concern, provides an overplus of meaning that none of the religious traditions by itself can adequately comprehend or express. Nor is this overplus of meaning rightly placed unless the religious traditions conceive of themselves as carrying out prescribed and necessary symbolic functions. Natural and revealed religions are interconnected. Properly conceived, revealed religion is a refinement of natural religion, through which resources it is also sustained. This thesis, we have discovered by now, lends expression to one of the cardinal tenets of the Kantian proposal. In keeping with the spirit of that proposal, Tillich believes he has demonstrated that the treatment of religion with reference to natural human capacities does not rob its subject of its vitality, but, on the contrary, infuses it with sufficient resilience and durability to support religion in its narrower senses.

The *Sine Qua Non* as Prereflective

While all of this was happening, another response to the original set of Kantian proposals offered a significant revision. Recall that the fundamental paradigm had identified three chief spheres of human capacity—in correspondence with the true, the good, and the beautiful—to which religion might be related when religion was understood to reflect the experience that characterizes human beings *qua* human beings. Recall, too, that each of the three spheres has been tested repeatedly concerning the ability to give religion a fitting location. Recall, finally, that the history of the making of the discipline also provides graphic evidence of disciplined attempts to expand the range of logical possibilities. Rudolf Otto wanted to add the holy to the list of the true, the good, and the beautiful. Anders Nygren, under the influence of the same compulsion, believed the eternal to be religion's appropriate category, and Paul Tillich described ways in which the three given categories find appropriate balance with each other through the workings of an identifiable dimension of depth, or fullness, which is most distinctively to be identified with religion.

There are additional logical possibilities. One of these keeps the original tripartite categorial formula intact but proposes modifications that give one of those orientational points considerable additional flexibility. This approach affirms that religion and truth go together, an equation that is fundamental to all additional interrelationships between religion and ethics as well as religion and aesthetics. In other words, Kant's first category is the normative one for religion. Religion, in its most fundamental and primary aspect, pertains to cognition. Its more comprehensive subject is *knowledge*. In certain respects, this perspective affirms that Kant's initial insight was the correct one.

But, then, how does it handle Kant's statement, "I have denied knowledge in order to make room for faith?" And what will it do with the seemingly countless problems associated with inconsistencies between the insights of faith and the truths of reason, the claims of religion and the certainties of science? If religion belongs to knowledge, how is one to protect it from philosophy's menacing criticisms?

The answer is to be found in distinctions between various modes of cognition, specifically in the distinction between *reflection* and *prereflection*. The proposals that are offered come from a group of thinkers, sometimes referred to as Neo-Thomists, who found it useful to talk about the role of insight, intuition, and personal knowledge. Among the first to make such proposals was Joseph Marechal (1878–1944), a Belgian Jesuit, and they are also represented in the works of two well-known twentieth-century Catholic philosopher-theologians, a German, Karl Rahner (1904–1984), and a Canadian, Bernard J. F. Lonergan (1904–1984).

The starting point is the belief that distinctive kinds of knowledge exist, only one of which qualifies as the matrix for religion. The thesis is that prereflective knowledge is different from discursive knowledge, and that prereflective knowledge is the normative context for religious belief. Prereflective knowledge is marked by a desire to gain an immediate and total grasp of a subject. After having been grasped in its totality, the subject may be deciphered, analyzed, investigated, and otherwise interpreted, but the two mental operations are not of the same kind. It is important to discern how they affect the essence of religion.

The Marechal proposal has it that prereflective knowledge is able to grasp a reality in its totality and unity. Conceptual knowledge, by contrast, involves the application of the methods and techniques of analysis, division, distinction, separation, judgment, and so on, to that intuited whole. Religion has its roots in intuitive knowledge—that is, in the immediate, spontaneous, total grasp of a subject that stands as preface to the process of conceptualization.

The implication is that the Enlightenment-inspired paradigm did not carry sufficient sensitivity to the force of such prereflective knowledge. Thus, when Immanuel Kant offered his description of knowledge, whether he recognized it or not, he was writing exclusively of ratiocinative cognition, or discursive knowledge, and this is merely one aspect in the reflective process. Furthermore, Kant was correct to separate the roots of religion from a ratiocinative context. But in making the correction, it was not necessary for him to separate religion from knowledge. It would have sufficed to identify the precise form of knowledge, or moment in the cognitive process, from which authoritative religion emanates. Failing to find the appropriate locus for religion within the ratiocinative process, Kant looked to extrareflective contexts. The Thomist revisionists understand the reasons for Kant's search, but they propose that the adequate context is not to be found in something *extra*reflective, but in the *pre*reflective. Their revisionist proposals enable them to retain the sense that religion is an intellectual endeavor.

Once the prereflective category becomes an option, virtually endless suggestions arise regarding religion's locus. With reference to the process of intellection, the prereflective may refer to intuition, as distinct from analysis, or as comprehensive as differentiated from discursive reasoning. But with reference to the catalog of cultural expressions, prereflective can stand for prelogical, which can be translated as mythical or mythological in contrast to conceptual. Once this line of response to the Kantian formula is advanced, inquirers can look for religion in mythological literature, assisted, for example, by the work of Ernst Cassirer's proposals regarding "a philosophy of symbolic forms." But Cassirer is not alone in offering materials for religious studies' scrutiny. We cite his work to illustrate that a judgment against Kant for construing knowledge in terms that were too narrow to be inclusive of religion can easily express itself in a proposal that the roots and locus of religion lie in prelogical mythic, intuitive, or imaginative consciousness. This proposal provides amendments and revisions, without calling for an alternative paradigm.

Sine Qua Non Inversions: Ludwig Feuerbach

We have referred to a number of examples of *sine qua non* approaches to religion that are based on a conceptual paradigm whose roots lie in the philosophical stances of René Descartes and Immanuel Kant. Instead of citing additional examples, we find it instructive to look at some alternatives and reversals that belong to an intriguing variant on the original design. The variant belongs to a branch of continental philosophy of religion that is indebted to the thought of Ludwig Feuerbach (1804–1872) as well as being particularly aware of the insights of Sigmund Freud (1856–1939). This "school" keeps the Kantian approach intact but, like surrealism in art, allows the ingredients of the design's extension to produce results that the original paradigm would find incongruous. At the same time, the variation on the original pattern has proved to be of widespread intellectual interest and can claim a number of significant thinkers in support.

According to the paradigm as originally conceived, there was an assumption that if one could identify the *sine qua non* of religion, one could also assert religion's reality or validity. This assumption was included in the operational intentions of *reductio*. All methodological techniques were formulated in light of the interest in isolating the one thing that cannot be doubted. When applied to the subject under our scrutiny, this was translated as religion's indubitable, underlying, unambiguous core element. As we have seen, the approach was fashioned to isolate one thing, and then to establish everything else by virtue of that one thing's formative centrality. To lay hold of religion's essence was to have its reality, in full and utter Cartesian simplicity. The same assumption is also a variation on the classical ontological argument that holds, respecting the deity, that the very thought of the reality of God implies the existence of that reality.

The new wave of Feuerbachian-inspired thinkers turned the paradigm in another direction. They considered the proposal that religion owns a *sine qua non*, but they were unwilling to assume by this that religion possesses an indubitable quality. In their view it is quite conceivable that religion has an essence, but it is possible, too, that the essence is unreal. What if religion is a mere projection? This is what Feuerbach called it, and Karl Marx as well, following his influence. What if it turns out to be mere illusion (as Sigmund Freud proposed)? What if it is produced out of the resources of the imagination? Or, instead of being a product of rationality, ethical awareness, or aesthetic sensitivity, what if it is elicited simply out of whatever mental apparatuses are responsible for creating fictions and figments?

This, it seems, is the thrust of Ludwig Feuerbach's contention that the essence of religion is something unreal, something unsubstantial, and thus something fundamentally deceptive. Religion may indeed exhibit reality, but it need not be the reality that was alleged or expected. That is, the same categorial apparatus that is invoked to support affirmation can be retrofitted to defend disclaimer.

In arguing this way, Feuerbach was merely extending the insights of such thinkers as David Friedrich Strauss (1808–1874), who, in his book *Leben Jesu, kritisch bearbeitet,* proposed that the content of Christian faith is the product of the wish-making aspirations of the earliest Christian community. Strauss could indeed speak meaningfully of religion's essence, but the essence was of the nature of an idea: It was ideal, as opposed to being factual. The essence possesses reality in the way that a thought possesses reality; but these ideal realities must be differentiated from objective realities, or, for that matter, from factual histories. Furthermore, Strauss wanted to insist that the analysis he rendered regarding Christian origins would be applicable, *mutatis mutandis,* to any and all religions. In every instance, the essence of religion is something that registers only mythologically. Whatever else myth, or religion, might be, its essence is neither objectively nor empirically real. Religious belief, according to this view, functions creatively: it advances imaginary ideals; it projects transcendental possibilities and gives wing to hopes and aspirations. Thus, to lay hold of religion's essence is not to gain access to anything essential. In the Cartesian sense, the reality Strauss talked about could still be doubted.

The record ought to show, too, that Strauss's convictions were Hegelian through and through. Even the notion that reality is idea (or ideal) bespeaks G. W. F. Hegel's (1770–1831) contention that the self-unfolding of the Absolute occurs in three steps, from being to essence to idea. In idea, the Absolute is, if anything, more rather than less real, for it is here that its participation is both full and final. For Hegel, ultimate reality is spiritual, and the word *spiritual* connotes subjective consciousness. Thus, in speaking of religion as the highest manifestation of Absolute Spirit short of absolute knowledge, and in seeing Christianity as the religion which best captures the sense of that highest manifestation, Hegel gave Strauss the idealist tendencies that the latter's writings so vividly display. He was also following the dominant paradigmatic tendency. Hence, to require the content of religion to be something objectively (that is, factually, historically, or empirically) real, from this vantage point, is to lapse back into one of the previous phases of dawning religious self-consciousness. In Hegel's terms, Strauss had to say what he did to prevent religion's essence from becoming obsolescent.

Bruno Bauer (1809–1882), who was also influenced by Hegel, found it difficult to hold the view that the content of religion derived from the myth-creating imagination of its adherents and devotees. Rather, in Bauer's view, the source of religion should be identified as the minds of the writers of scriptures. This keeps the paradigm intact. It even sustains the turn toward an ideal essence. The disagreement is simply over the appropriate identification of that which stands as religion's *sine qua non*.

As we have already noted, however, Feuerbach is the key figure in this phase of the post-Enlightenment attempt to identify and isolate religion's *sine qua non*. Feuerbach challenged Hegel's assumption that the most real is mental or spiritual, and he had difficulty attributing the reality of all things to spiritual or mental consciousness, even when the latter was understood in an absolute sense. To make amends for Hegel's deficiencies in this respect, Feuerbach argued that consciousness should be understood as a product of nature, and not the reverse. Hence, whatever sense can be made of religion must start with the concrete (instead of with some abstract) reality of man. For Feuerbach, the dilemmas placed before philosophy were the opposite of what Hegel thought. The problem was not that of linking up the ideal with the concrete, as though the reality of the former could be assumed and the reality of the latter was very much in question. Instead, one had to work from the other direction. The starting point is always the concrete, for the concrete is the only reality to which appropriate and confirming reference can be made. The ideal, not the concrete, is in jeopardy.

Thus, in Feuerbach's view, religion (a major component within the idealist project) is both delusional and fallacious. And not only that: its deceptions frustrate all human attempts to promote and take responsibility for a better society. By according highest status to a supernatural deity, humankind forfeits the opportunity to improve its own lot. Poor people remain poor; the hungry stay hungry; society remains in a state of disrepair; and God is given all honor and glory, especially by poor people, hungry people, and those who suffer most from the pervasive state of disrepair and economic inequality. The false promises of religion delude humans into thinking that they need not, or cannot, improve their own social and economic conditions. This only demonstrates to Feuerbach that religion is the product of misplaced enthusiasm. The real religious energy ought not to be expended where it can only be wasted, but ought to be directed toward improving the human condition.

Under the idealist transposition, religion is a fabrication, and the instrument of fabrication is simple projection. Human beings project their needs and aspirations skyward. Religion is created and sustained by speculative mental exercises in transcendental extrapolation. Religion may have an essence, all right, but it is not the essence believers intend, covet, or profess. Moreover, a *sine qua non* may indeed be isolated, but much more is required if religion is to exhibit a certifiable first principle that compels and sustains human virtue.

Marx: Idealist Analysis and Revolutionary Program

Although Karl Marx (1818–1883) is known primarily as the German social and economic theorist who laid the philosophical basis for the revolutionary principles that inspired communist ideology, it is important to recognize that he was also a careful student of the philosophy of religion as this subject was presented to him in the writings of Hegel, Strauss, Bauer, and Feuerbach. Indeed, as with Feuerbach, Marx took Strauss's and Bauer's arguments regarding the mythologies of early Christianity and applied them as critique of religion itself. As has been noted, both Bauer and Feuerbach had regarded mythologized religion as an obstacle to political and cultural progress. Marx simply supplied the specifics to the social, cultural, and political situation Europe (particularly Germany) faced in the mid-nineteenth century, and proposed a programmatic remedy that was far-reaching in intention and influence.

By Marx's time, the Hegelian school was asserting that religion is the instrumentation by means of which alienated human beings project needs, wants, and aspirations into some transcendental, supernatural realm, to which human beings also attach expectations of satisfying remedies. Feuerbach was critical of this ploy, as has been noted, because it tends to separate human beings from those abdicated rights and goods to which they possess proper title. Marx wanted to push the analysis further. For him religion represents a protest against whatever dehumanizing conditions keep human beings in social and political bondage. Were the dehumanizing conditions not present, religion would not be necessary. In other words, the fact that religion exists is testimony to the need to eliminate all forms and occasions of dehumanization, to correct the social, cultural, and political situation from which religious aspirations spring.

Thus, when describing the essence of religion, Marx employed the well-known phrase, "the opiate of the people." Rather than whatever delusionary happiness religion was called upon to provide, Marx wanted real and lasting happiness. Rather than being content to decipher alienation and explain the relationships between its actual and transposed content, Marx wanted alienation overcome by an understanding and a politically consequent program that was socially and politically effective. For him, the practice of religion is the sign that emancipation has not yet been achieved. Thus, if human beings are fully to enjoy a real and lasting happiness, they must be emancipated from the ineffective treatment of fundamental alienation that religion stands for. That is, to realize true happiness, human beings must be emancipated from religion. Religion, in short, has been created out of the alienation that is the fact of life for human beings. To the extent that it confronts alienation, religion can be viewed as protest against alienation. To the extent that it provides concessions and appeasements, religion remains under the control of the alienating forces with which it pretends or purports to deal effectively. For Marx, religion is an obtrusion that perpetuates the misguided expectation that alienation will eventually be overcome through the instrumentation of thought, imagination, or theological and philosophical reasoning. The pervasive human unhappiness that calls religion into operation can only be effectively overcome, in Marx's view, through basic changes in socioeconomic relationships, changes that require revolutionary political action.

Marx's views on religion belong intrinsically to the discussion of the subject that occurred within the Hegelian school. Thus, like his predecessors, Marx was intent on identifying the core of religion by isolating that without which it would not be what it is. He exhibited a slight shift from the paradigmatic model, however, in that he worked from an analysis of Christianity to a description of the nature of religion, and not the other way around. Nevertheless, what he discovered concerning the nature of Christianity stands as disclosive example of the nature of religion. With the necessary correlations in place, Marx could work in the other direction: that is, what is characteristic of the nature of religion is also characteristic of the intentions of the religions themselves. Indeed, when the state entertains religious aspirations, what is characteristic of a religion is also characteristic of the state: the state too can find intrinsic ways to perpetuate alienation by frustrating the drive toward emancipation that is human nature's most powerful motivational force. When the state functions this way, it behaves symptomatically. The only remedy, in Marx's view, is a successful effort at pervasive humanization through which the inhuman conditions that frustrate the desire to reach full potential are finally eliminated. It is utopian thinking, of course, requiring the elimination of economic class conflict, followed by the instituting of a socialist agenda.

Freud and Bloch: Religion as Illusion

Sigmund Freud's attitude also resonates with Feuerbach's, though Freud employed the word *illusion* rather than *projection* when identifying religion's deception. The outcome of the investigation, however, is virtually the same. Human beings fabricate religion, Freud agrees. Religion is produced out of a desire to fulfill a wish. The wishes are products of human weakness and a recognition of helplessness. Hence, religion is reflective of nothing more than the dynamics of aspirational life, dynamics that produce apparitions. The entire religious enterprise is filled with deception, for it is nothing more than the objectification of the content of wishes. Thus, Freud's chief book on the nature of religion is entitled *The Future of an Illusion*, and the book in which he describes the way in which religion functions in culture is called *Civilization and Its Discontents*. It is apparent, from both treatises, that the deceptions Freud identifies are no mere aberrations of otherwise meaningful religion, as if they ought to be performing more effectively than they are. On the contrary, when Freud speaks of illusion and deception, he is referring specifically to the intrinsic functions of both Christianity and Judaism. They become party to the need to raise up protections against overpowering external forces. The concept of "Chosen People," the desire to call God "Father" and to think of oneself as being God's "child," and the hope that a "benevolent Providence is watching over us" are all indications of the way in which "the religious system" works to exorcise the threatening powers of nature and to assist the human being to confront human weakness and helplessness. But the doctrines that are produced in this way are not representative of any confirmable and substantial truths. Instead, "they are illusions, fulfillments of the oldest, strongest and most urgent wishes of mankind." In summary:

> [T]he terrifying impression of helplessness in childhood aroused the need for protection—for protection through love—which was provided by the father; and the recognition that this helplessness lasts throughout life made it necessary to cling to the existence of a father, but this time a more powerful one. Thus the benevolent rule of a divine Providence allays our fear of the dangers of life; the establishment of a moral world-order ensures the fulfillment of the demands of justice, which have so often remained unfulfilled in human civilization; and the prolongation of earthly existence in a future life provides the local and temporal framework in which these wish-fulfillments shall take place.

Furthermore:

> Answers to the riddles that tempt the curiosity of man, such as how the universe began or what the relation is between body and mind, are developed in conformity with the underlying assumptions of this system.

Freud calls them "illusions" because "they are derived from human wishes." A belief is an illusion, he attests, "when a wish-fulfillment is a prominent factor in its motivation." Freud thinks he is on firm ground in approaching religious beliefs in this way because he has noticed that whatever claims to truth they make are "unsusceptible of proof."

The Feuerbachian-Freudian counterproposal gains an added new twist in the mid-twentieth century when it is declared, first, that religion has a *sine qua non* element; second, that this core element is illusionary; and, third, that the status of illusions as illusions must be given credibility. This proposal, which extends the Feuerbachian contention, had been in process for years. It is not necessarily a proposal with which either Feuerbach or Freud would disagree. But its expression gained force in the contentions of a group of scholars whom some refer to as philosophers of hope.

The philosophy of religion of the German revisionist–Marxist philosopher Ernst Bloch (1885–1983), for example, author of *Das Prinzip Hoffnung*, can be placed in this context and interpreted this way. It is significant too that Bloch can work his variations on the fundamental paradigm without disturbing it greatly. But what makes Bloch's alternative most interesting is his claim that true, vital sustainable religion is atheistic. In his view, the initial genius of Christianity was that it was atheistic too. Original Christianity was atheistic, according to Bloch, until the early Christians gave in to debilitating loss of nerve.

For Bloch atheism is not just negation of something previously maintained. It is not a deficiency, a lack, or the absence of a good. Rather it is the condition for creative, constructive work, for it provides a workable occasion for the postulation of human hopes and dreams. Human hopes and dreams do not get far unless they can be sustained within an open field. Nor can they long endure within a context of things that are already fixed. Dreams and hopes become malnourished and uncourageous if their sphere of operation is already cluttered with presumed-to-be objectivizable deities—that is, with a god, or God, who monopolizes the entire territory. For Bloch, illusions and projections must be taken seriously, for they supply the vital stuff of reality. And by virtue of their energetic formative influences, they can be depicted as being more real than anything else.

In Bloch's perspective, religion is tied directly to that which is envisioned. Thus, to be captivated by illusion is (perhaps) to fall under the influence of religion's driving force. For Bloch the choice is not between illusion and reality but between illusions that disappoint and those that sustain the hopes of the human spirit. To call religion illusion is not to explain it away, or rob it of its essence. It is rather to provide status, location, function, and to confirm its reality. For Bloch, something can be ascribed to the world of the not-yet (indeed, even to the world of the still-not-yet) and enjoy a reality as strong and as undeniable as the reality of the future. The future of an illusion, in Ernst Bloch's view, is a future the religiously sensitive can learn to trust.

William James: Varieties of Religious Experience

The sequence of intellectual development that has been traced so far in this chapter is rooted primarily (indeed, in places, rather exclusively) in European discussion and debate. Certainly students and scholars in other parts of the world have been affected by it and, in numerous respects, have contributed significantly to its nuances and continuous progression. Yet none of it qualifies as being distinctively American, or even cooperatively American. It is European discussion, conceived and transmitted by Europeans, even if it has been adopted in other parts of the world.

Something distinctively American is born, however, with the work of William James (1842–1910), whom many regard as being one of the greatest philosophical minds America has ever produced. His book *The Varieties of Religious Experience*, published in 1902, qualifies as a classic statement on the subject of the essence of religion. As distinct from theorists who search for definitions that require an establishment of specific distinctions between human faculties, capacities, and sensibilities, James looks to experience itself. He was aware of some of the other attempts to define religion that are reviewed in this chapter, but he suspected that the resulting formulae were contrived and therefore could easily degenerate into dogmatisms. Having examined the attempts the others made to identify the particular faculty or capacity to which religion is most fundamentally attached, he had this to say: "One man allies it [religion] to the feeling of dependence; one makes it a derivative from fear; others connect it with the sexual life; still others identify it with the feeling of the infinite." The examples cited, and the manner in which they are cited, support the impression that the list is almost random and, as such, could be extended much further. James was not tempted to engage in any such isolating analyses or to posit some locus for religion of his own. He was convinced that religion cannot be reduced to any one entity or quality. His conclusion is that there is "no one elementary religious emotion, but only a common storehouse of emotions. So too is there no single religious object and no single essential kind of religious act."

James's most astute observations on this subject were provided in *The Varieties*, which stands as the prestigious Gifford Lectures of 1901–1902. The title is well chosen, for it was James's contention that useful scholarly inquiry into this matter is obliged to focus on pluralities—that is, on varieties of religious experience—instead of on potential single explanatory elements. His emphasis lay on both "varieties" and "experience," and the data with which he worked were provided by a wide assortment of writers and spokespersons who had been intent on coming to terms with religious experience. These included writers such as George Fox who concerned themselves with mystical experience. James simply assumed that whatever these writers had identified was qualified to be examined as religious experience. That is, at least initially, he did not dispute the reports that Fox and the others had filed. Furthermore, he sensed that religion is something that is experienced before it is thought about, dogmatized, or otherwise institutionally adopted and organized.

This conviction encouraged James to make rather sharp distinctions between personal and institutional religion. While he tried not to ignore institutional religion, the focus of his analysis was personal religion, from which he developed the following working definition of religion: "Religion . . . shall mean for us the feelings, acts, and experiences of individual men in their solitude, so far as they apprehend themselves to stand in relation to whatever they may consider the divine." To put the matter in briefer form but broader scope: "Religion, whatever it is, is a man's total reaction upon life."

From this point, James's analysis focused on the functions religion performs within the lives of sensitive human beings. He understood that religion is formed within that set of responses and reactions to what human beings regard as a (or perhaps *the*) primal reality. He recognized that varieties of responses are in order, depending in significant part on the attitudinal orientation of the individual. At this point, the fundamental working distinction is between "the religion of healthy-mindedness and the religion that is formed out of a maximization of the fact and presence of evil." The latter is described as the disposition of "the sick soul." The former orientation, which derives from the temperamental ability some humans have to encourage optimism to carry formative influences, is characterized by a willingness not to tussle with reality but to commit oneself and one's fundamental interests, with no discordance, to the fundamental powers of the universe. James described it as an act of "espousal." The latter disposition is the contrast, an orientation to life that does not regard the events and components of life to be good, but regards the recognition of the world's evils as the surest path to reliable meaning. James knew that the distinctions between these two modalities lay largely in temperament, and he was concerned to distinguish the voluntary and involuntary aspects of such temperamental inclinations.

> The personal attitude which the individual finds himself impelled to take up toward what he apprehends to be the divine . . . will prove to be both a helpless and a sacrificial attitude. That is, we shall have to confess to at least some amount of dependence on sheer mercy, and to practice some amount of renunciation, great or small, to save our souls alive.

From this vantage point, James offered this insight concerning the nature and function of religion: "Religion thus makes easy and felicitous what in any case is necessary." Further, religion "becomes an essential organ of our life, performing a function which no other portion of our nature can so successfully fulfill." But none of this can be taken for granted; none of it is automatic. Rather, religion is a kind of experiment established by the believer who wishes successfully to relate to that over against which he or she is most definitively identified. James recognized that there are a variety of conceivable and actual responses to this practice. But none of them is easily formulated philosophically except as an extension of a dispositional response from within which the content of religion is born, shaped, and tested.

John Dewey: From Varieties to a Common Faith

John Dewey (1859–1952), eminent American philosopher, psychologist, and educator, took James's point of departure, namely experience, and transformed the concomitant conception of the functions of religion into an intentional program. James had attributed to ideas and concepts some practical utility; indeed, these belonged to the strategies implicit in making a harmonious response to what the human being understands to be the primal reality. Dewey, by contrast, was far less interested in distinguishing temperaments or in correlating distinctive temperaments with identifiable responses. For Dewey such an appraisal of James's insights was much too passive and continued to leave the human being under debilitating dependencies, as if action is assigned by the place and position one inhabits in some comprehensive cosmic scene. Dewey asserted that the human being is an agent of change; that is, if the human being realizes his or her true being and function. The response to the primal reality is a moral response, asserted by the human being, in support of a disciplined sense of prescribed moral ends that will enable humankind to realize deep-seated human aspiration.

James had stated that healthy-mindedness represents an attitudinal disposition that wishes to live beyond tension, in some trusted equilibrium, in harmony with all of that in relationship and response to which one's destiny is cast. Again, Dewey's transformation of James's insight derives from employing instrumentalist terminology to insure that such harmony is sought via an active, dedicated project. Throughout his writings, from those that deal primarily with psychology or education to his treatises on religion and philosophy, he frequently employs terms like *activity, process,* and *growth* and gives each of these central position. Virtually everything in which the human being is involved is directed toward resolving tension and easing strain. In education, for instance, the student is understood to be subject, and the eventual goal is the effective mastery of the subject's environment. The same principles are made applicable to the spheres of morality and religion. Morality derives from compulsions that are recognized to be necessary to the realization of ends required by the achievement of the good society. And the good society is one within which the citizens are given access to the instrumentations through which they will find self-fulfillment in mutually supportive ways. The same is true for religion: here Dewey pleaded for attention to effects that are produced rather than on speculation about God or about religion's origin. Reality is the active relationship between a living organism and the environment, and the large questions concern the ways in which this active relationship is to be carried out. In short, Dewey raises the relationship of stimulus and response to a kind of transcendent dimension, attesting that this describes the career of the human being within and in relationship to its primary environment. He was not interested in speculative matters, or in approaching religion as a distinct *sui generis* sphere of activity.

Such matters were spelled out systematically when Dewey was invited to deliver the Terry Lectures at Yale University in 1934, lectures that produced the book *A Common Faith*. Here he distinguished between traditional theistic belief, which he could not support, and the eminently supportable religious attitude. He rejected creeds, institutions, and institutional practices while affirming the value of religion as a mode or quality of experience. So far Dewey's position is Jamesian through and through, particularly in the way in which he draws implications from the critical distinction between institutional and personal religion. But he goes beyond James in showing little or no interest in the viability of the kind of religious experience to which the mystics give attestation. Rather, faith, for him, belongs to the quality of "being religious," a quality that refers to the active practice of unifying the self via allegiance to prescribed ideal ends. Therefore, when Dewey employs the word *God*, he has defined it in such a way that signifies the unity of ideal possibilities which are actualized through human intelligence and action. As he put it:

> We are in the presence neither of ideals completely embodied in existence nor yet of ideals that are mere rootless ideals, fantasies, utopias. For there are forces in nature and society that generate and support the ideals. They are further unified by the action that gives them coherence and solidity. It is this *active* relation between ideal and actual to which I would give the name "God."

In other words, as Dewey stated it, "the self is always directed toward something beyond it," as all religions attest, but Dewey was insistent that such transcendent references be construed in active and natural rather than passive and metaphysical senses. In his formulations, William James's treatment of religion as experience is accorded a thoroughly pragmatic translation. For each, the *sine qua non* of religion is identified with the human's *will to believe*, which in James is approached descriptively and in Dewey is understood instrumentally.

By this time, it should not surprise us that the reconstitution of religion on natural, experiential grounds, which was introduced by an operational distinction between personal and institutional religion, is accompanied by an effort to reconceive the religious tradition in such reconstituted definitional terms. In *The Varieties of Religious Experience*, James provides repeated evidence of wanting to think through the role of the churches in contributing toward or detracting from a prescribed religious healthy-mindedness. In his assessment, Lutherans and Catholics, for example, are given mixed reviews, while thinkers like Leo Tolstoy and Baruch Spinoza are understood to be positive contributors. In like fashion, he considers established religious practices—conversion, repentance, saintliness, and mystical awareness, for example—in light of the specific interpretation of religion's manifest functions. Throughout his portrayal, there are aspects of institutional religion against which the human being should be protected, while, rightly understood, there are behaviors, occurrences, and practices that are accorded institutional sponsorship which are most strongly to be reaffirmed and supported. Although always considered so provocative that he could not escape being controversial, William James delivered lectures in churches, and was listened to by persons who sat in church pews and sang hymns following his addresses.

From institutional vantage points, John Dewey was perceived to be far more radical. The fact that he had no tolerance of a supernatural deity and was really at great pains to discount any potential argument on such behalf on the basis of mystical experience does not mean that he wished thoroughly to throw out traditional religion. The problem with the latter, for Dewey, is that it draws legitimate religious interest away from legitimate religious obligations toward a debilitating otherworldliness as well as to esoteric doctrines associated with theistic belief. God, for Dewey, is no supernatural being, but can be properly identified as the unity of ideal possibilities that human beings carry responsibility to actualize. Similarly, he was intent upon distinguishing theistic from naturalistic views of moral law and the moral purposes of society. Within this context, the word *God* can still properly be employed, but with reference to the realization of the best interests of society and not to salutary acts originating from outside the human sphere.

Dewey would have a difficult time trying to demonstrate that his religious views reflect the viewpoint and attitude of any of the great religious traditions, but this would not stop him from offering himself as a reformer. If his views were adopted, the religions themselves might be transformed and refreshed. In this sense, at least, he has gone full circle. That is, he has separated institutional from personal (real) religion, has described and analyzed the latter, and then has contended that a reinterpretation of tradition in light of his portrayal of defensible religion would bring new vitality to the institutions, and would assist in ushering in an era within which a "common faith" would most certainly be instrumental in improving the conditions of society. The institutions are there to create perspective and establish moral priorities in the recognition that human beings are called upon to deal with forces beyond their control. Religions teach that human beings cannot expect to realize the ideal simply by resolute striving, but via the securing of harmony with nature, which critical purpose the religions serve. Dewey was worried, of course, that these legitimate purposes would be jettisoned in favor of various institutional self-interests and presumptions. As we have noted, he worked diligently to emancipate legitimate religious interest from religion, affirming that religious values and ideals are too important to the resilience of individual and collective life to be restricted to professed creeds and cults. But when any religion behaves the way Dewey wishes it to, it can command favor. Dewey, like James before him, is committed to the standard *reductio-enumeratio* method of analytical investigation.

A Summation

We have traced a sequence of intellectual development, from Descartes, via Kant, to Marx, Freud, James, Dewey, and Bloch, from an insistence on basing religion on what cannot be doubted to a discovery of religion in illusion, projection, and value construction. Throughout the entire sequence, the fundamental methodological paradigm has remained intact and has been utilized to inspire a wide variety of resourceful formulations regarding the nature or essence of religion.

From this vantage point, virtually three centuries of individual and collective intellectual work have been devoted to reducing religion to its most essential and fundamental characteristic. This has required analysts to discern religion's core element by distinguishing it from everything tentative, occasional, circumstantial, or otherwise peripheral or marginal. At the outset, this methodological disposition seemed to encourage a programmatic distinction between natural and revealed religion (revealed religion being regarded as being of circumstantial origins). And yet, throughout the long sequence of intellectual development that we have been tracing, there is an inviolable assumption that what can be learned about natural religion (whether employed to defend or discredit religion) is also applicable to revealed religion. The hypothesis is that whatever is responsible for religion fundamentally—that is, whatever is identified as religion's core element—is also the basis and foundation of the religions. The *sine qua non* of religion, in its generic sense, is coextensive with the *sine qua non* of religion in its narrower or more specific senses.

From Descartes through Kant, to the present, *reductio* is followed by *enumeratio*. The first principle is established, and then its content is unpacked and identified. The condition for the possibility of religion is established; then that condition is probed for purposes of eliciting formal content that might be transposed into the expression of that possibility. In the Western world—note that we are surveying chapters in Enlightenment and post-Enlightenment Western intellectual history—the possibility is elucidated most frequently in Christian terms.

But we come to the end of the sequence without a firm decision as to whether the basis of religion is discovered or created, or even as to which of these two possibilities is preferable religiously. Clearly, the controversy is not going to be resolved easily or quickly, for, as Descartes recognized, it is impossible to give additional credibility to what is posited as being most fundamental.

It is important to recognize, however, that what is being said about religion belongs to the language of the schema by which the entire inquiry has been formed. The scheme is conceived to expose a fundamental core element. It exposes this element so that the essence of religion can be named. But all of this is achieved within the specific context of the paradigm. Apart from the workings of the paradigm there is no identification or isolation of religion's core element. Moreover, so far, at least, the intellectual tradition offers no more effective way to lend definition (that is, rigorous definition) to religion. The truth of the matter is that what stands as religion's *sine qua non* is a name assigned to the paradigm's central regulative principle. The condition of the possibility of a core element is created by the dynamic and integral workings of the paradigm. Religion can be shown to have an essence within an intraschematic sense. Its core element is identified within an intelligible orientation to a subject that is designed to disclose a *sine qua non*. And, as Immanuel Kant repeatedly emphasized, the effective functioning of a regulative principle cannot be utilized to demonstrate the objective reality of some subject that may correspond to that principle. As others have noted, an essence may possess the status of logical validity without such qualities entailing that it also enjoys some objective reality.

Perhaps, then, to name the core element "illusion" is to recognize that the search for a *sine qua non* for religion is fundamentally a logical exercise. And to lend content to a category of logic is not to answer the obvious questions regarding objective and substantive status. Or, put in other words, the means of establishing the conditions of the possibility of something cannot be used to decide, in complete confidence, whether that possibility is subjective instead of objective, or real rather than illusionary. Such arguments serve only to give such distinctions conceptual and contextual reference. In short, there is no inviolable basis on which to attest that whatever does function logically as a first principle also enjoys translogical reality, status, or function. The methodological movement within *enumeratio*, since its capacities for extension are effective only within the boundaries of the schema, can make no additional disclosures beyond's *reductio*'s logical validations. In religious studies terms, there is no easy way to transpose René Descartes' *cogito, ergo sum* into a constitutive function, for the simple reason that it is impossible to translate a definition into a truth claim.

It is also abundantly clear that the intellectual temper that drives these definitions is reflective of a predominantly Christian theological mindset. In fact, in many instances, the quest for the *sine qua non* of religion is closely related to the desire to know who God is, if there is such a supreme reality. The identification of the essence of religion that is frequently offered is one that would apply equally appropriately to a description of the nature and function of the deity. To identify the essence of religion as "the ineffable" (as Rudolf Otto does, in one of the strongest of his portrayals) is to attest that God too, in God's nature, is unknowable. To identify religion as "illusion" is to propose that there can be no certitude that references to God actually point to some transcendent reality. But the most telling evidence of the presence of a theological cast of mind is that the search for the *sine qua non* of religion is doubtless of more interest to theologians than it is to scholars of religious studies. From this vantage point, it is virtually impossible to distinguish the two endeavors; that is, religious studies, as a distinguishable subject-field, has not yet emerged or broken free. Although the writers we have surveyed claim that their essays consist of analyses of the nature of religion, the products of their inquiries belong first to the history of theological reflection in the Western world and, to lesser extents, to philosophy of religion. Within such frameworks, religion, as an identifiable entity, is hardly configured at all. Yes, there are nascent attempts at comparative religion in Rudolf Otto, and to an extent in Anders Nygren, but such endeavors are always made subservient to convictions about the essence of Christianity. In other words, the other religions, when they register at all, are identified primarily in qualitative contrast to the norms that are employed to insure the superiority of the Christian religion. The *sine qua non* approach is not activated from an objective, neutral, or unprivileged vantage point in spite of all of the claims made that the evaluative criteria employed are reflective of critical judgment itself. When *sine qua non* is the driving intellectual force, the findings belong as much to theology as they do to embryonic or prolegomenal religious studies. The identification of the nature of religion invokes descriptions of the fundamental attributes of God. When no such ascription is being intended, the definition of the subject takes refuge in terms like *illusion, deception*, and *projection*, terms that denote an absent or inverted essence and stand as a defensible theoretical foundation for atheism as opposed to religious belief.

If the *sine qua non* approach is more closely associated with theology than with religious studies, and if religion as an identifiable entity hardly emerges from within this methodological sponsorship, why is this chapter included in our survey? The answer is twofold. First, it was the Enlightenment form of argumentation that prompted intellectual inquiry into the nature and function of religion, and the academic study of religion did indeed occur within this inquiry. It was under *sine qua non* auspices that the rules and sequence of argumentation were first devised. Thus, this chapter describes the methodological formulations and theoretical presuppositions by which all subsequent inquiries were set in motion. Apart from acknowledgment of this initial formative chapter, each of the consequent chapters would make considerably diminished sense. Second, the initial paradigm, conceived within Enlightenment philosophy, carried a pair of fundamental inclinations regarding the accessibility of the essence of religion (now regarded as a form or mode of human experience). From the one side the theoreticians were intent on coming to intelligible terms with the subject, just as they wished to understand the dynamics of the other forms or modes of human experience. But, from the other side, their respect for this subject prompted them to insist that important ingredients or qualities of the subject were inaccessible to objective, impartial inquiry. Such inaccessibility was confirmed, for example, in Kant's vocational confession that he had "denied knowledge in order to make room for faith." It became explicit too in Rudolf Otto's description of *das Heilige* as being attracting and repelling at one and the same time. Espousing such convictions regarding the *sine qua non* of religion, the Enlightenment theoreticians devised approaches that made religion accessible to human knowledge while also protecting it from epistemological accessibility. This is what is at stake in transferring its locus from philosophy (namely, Kant's world of pure reason) to other modes that are identified and circumscribed primarily in distinction to the philosophical mode of address. The one conviction all *sine qua non* theorists shared is that the essence of religion is only partially accessible to human knowledge. What the knower learns is that the *sine qua non* is beyond comprehension and understanding.

We will find in subsequent chapters in this survey that when religious studies became sharply distinguished from theology, and was encouraged to emerge entirely on its own terms, most if not all *sine qua non* motivation was jettisoned too. The consequence was that religion became difficult to define as a predominating entity. Such proposals were advanced but, increasingly, were replaced by descriptive or functionalist alternatives. That is, when emancipation from theological sponsorship is effected, some significant loss of essentialist terminology occurs too. Are we suggesting that the formative theorists enforced protections of religion in such fashion that inquirers who did not accept the methodological terms they had established were prevented from talking meaningfully about the essence of religion? That is, since their formulae sanctioned accessibility and inaccessibility to the subject simultaneously, did they intend that rejection of their terms of accessibility would simply strengthen the protections they had established? Well, it begins to look this way from the evidence we have assembled so far. A preliminary conclusion seems to be that whatever theological residue is present in the beginnings of the making of the intellectual discipline is hardly anachronistic, but rather is solidly ingredient in the intellectual motivation through which the analytical and interpretive processes were placed in motion.

C H A P T E R • T W O

THE ORIGIN *OF* *RELIGION*

One way to identify the core element of religion, as we have illustrated in the previous chapter, is to search for an essence. Another way, as we shall illustrate in this chapter, is to try to isolate the origin; that is, the source, primary causal factor, root, or that from which everything flows or stems and to which all meaningful explanation must eventually be referred. The quest to identify the essence of religion can easily disregard the influences of time, history, change, and process on the subject, but the attempt to uncover religion's origins must account for the presence of these very factors.

The fundamental insight incorporated within this approach is that human beings have always been involved in worship or in imagining the ways of deity and their relationships thereto. Indeed, from this vantage point, the origins of religion seem synchronous with the beginnings of humanity. Thus, in seeking to come to terms with its subject, this approach needs to be equipped to reach back through time and history—even into a realm of "prehistory"—to reestablish the situation and conditions of religion's origins. As the attempt to recover this origin unfolds, an interesting combination of methodological cogwheels is set in motion. First comes the resolution to identify the beginning point, the *primordium*. This interest can only be exercised via the positing of a chronicle; namely, a narrative account of the distinct stages of development that have pertained from the time of origins to the present era. In some renditions the chronicle is understood to encompass all of human history, from the beginning through the present, even into the future. In other versions the scope is more specific and less expansive; only a particular segment of history is included. But, regardless of how its range and scope are determined, the chronicle is marked by successive periods, stages, and moments. Such periods function to measure and distinguish identifiable temporal units. Such units are reckoned to be like each other in that all belong to and are ingredient in the process. But they are also understood to be unlike each other in that each one represents a distinctive or unique time or stage within the process. Furthermore, the characteristic units of the chronicle—the elements of "the time line"—are not only distinguished and described. They are also given value, indeed comparative and contrasting value. That is, they can be approached not only with respect to their characteristic place within an ongoing temporal sequence, but also with respect to the degree to which they come to approximate a norm. The norm may be understood to reside outside the time line, within the time line, prior to the initiation of sequential development, or even at the culmination of the entire process. Whatever formulation is proposed requires a decision regarding the period or stage in the process that comes closest to the norm. This is the period or stage by and from which the other segments in the chronicle are measured and judged.

It is customary, in some renditions of this approach, to accord highest place to the first point or stage in the chronicle. Within this scheme, whatever lies closest to the beginning is judged to be qualitatively superior to everything that follows thereafter. Thus, the movement of time that is measured by the chronicle exhibits a regressive rather than a progressive tendency. Of course, the movement of time can be given positive evaluation too, an assessment that pertains when the chronicle is judged to exhibit a progressive tendency. In these versions, time is regulated by a kind of forward tending, as in the conviction that "the best is yet to be." Between regressive and progressive models stands a version which holds that chronicles *per se* are qualitatively neutral: they imply neither regressive nor progressive movement necessarily; the motion they encompass does not always signal advance, but neither need it imply loss or deterioration. In this neutral version, the stages of the chronicle are just that—a succession of distinctive forms of knowledge or consciousness, all of which rightly belong to the more comprehensive pattern. Thus attention can be focused on any period, stage, or time quotient within the chronicle, and descriptive ways can be found to distinguish the period being focused on from all of the others. The periods themselves can be compared and contrasted, but they need not be approached as being either greater or lesser approximations to some identifiable norm.

It is customary in all of these portrayals to emphasize that reality is indeed dynamic, and its dynamism can only be captured in linear or horizontal diagrams. The dynamic portrayal, expressed linearly or horizontally, is designed to take account of the force of the passage of time. Thus it happens that the interest in identifying the origins of religion always involves some detailed description of the evolution or development of religion. The one cannot be undertaken without the other. The two foci are conceptually interdependent: origin refers to the initiation of sequential motion; development has reference to the stage-by-stage unfolding or expression of the sequence.

The chronicle itself serves a variety of conceptual functions. It can be used to provide access to the beginning, that is, to facilitate the methodological passageway backwards. Or it can be seen as that by which the essence (as *primordium*) is enunciated and expressed. It can even be employed as a basis of projecting what may lie ahead, as the periods and epochs that belong to it are understood to reach into the future.

So far, in this chapter, we have approached our subject formally and schematically. We have said little, if anything, about how usage of the approach affects an understanding of the nature of religion. Instead, we have concentrated on formal factors to illustrate that, in this approach too, identification of the content of religion follows the workings of the conceptual framework. What is learned and said about religion is what the schema makes possible. If origins are being sought, origins will be found, for it is precisely for this purpose that the schema is designed. Knowledge of the workings of the formal schematic pattern will help us anticipate content and results.

For example, some scholars in religious studies, employing this approach, have assumed that religion carries many direct associations with the primal origins of human consciousness. Thus they have employed the chronicle to help find a way back to the beginnings—to the beginnings, say, of human consciousness, or to the first stages of recorded human awareness. At times they have tried to correlate the beginnings of religion with the beginning of the chronicle of consciousness. And at times they have placed religion back there prior to the beginnings of the designated process. When they have followed this latter alternative, they have frequently judged the chronicle to signal a detraction from religion's purer original nature. When religion is situated prior to the chronicle that is measured by time, it becomes appropriate to explore religion's genetic ties, for example, with mythological awareness—awareness that can then be understood to possess a quality of timelessness. It is also appropriate to consider the nature of so-called primitive societies and how such peoples come to terms with life, the world, or reality. Primitive societies become the object of interest because they are understood to represent a way of life that is correlative with stages of awareness situated early in the chronicle.

But we have gone about as far as we should, for the moment, in formal methodological terms. Ways in which these basic methodological tendencies have been worked out can be portrayed in narrative fashion as well. And while the story is not as easy to recover as the one concerning the quest for the essence of religion, there is indeed a story to be told as well as threads of development that can be isolated and traced. It is a story that carries us all the way through to the present era of scholarship about the nature of religion.

Background: From Descartes and Kant to a Dynamic View

In contrast to the orientation we are about to portray in this chapter, the viewpoints of both René Descartes and Immanuel Kant seem to have envisioned a static world. Neither's rendition allowed for much movement, flexibility, or change. In neither interpretation was time, history, or sequential development considered seriously. Both seem almost oblivious to spontaneous occurrences. Both, it seems, sought a basis for permanence and, thus, conceived reality in terms of unchanging categories.

Descartes' intention, for example, was to set forth a system of universal knowledge. To achieve this, he thought it necessary to isolate the clear indubitable premises from which all other propositions could be deduced. He wanted to develop an orientation to reality that would be valid for all time, without regard to special circumstances and situations. For him, the ideal was a rational system of both permanent and universal validity. This norm he found symbolized in mathematics. Mathematics was the normative model of reflection because it made timeless truths accessible. As Descartes implied, timeless truths also include timeless truth:

> [O]f all the disciplines known by others, only arithmetic and geometry are pure from every taint of falsity and incertitude.... We must observe further that ... deductions, or a pure inference from one thing to another ... can never be erroneously executed by an intellect even minimally rational.

Using clear, incontestable mathematical truth as his model, Descartes added:

> [F]rom all this one must conclude, not, indeed, that one must learn nothing but arithmetic and geometry, but only that those who seek the right of truth ought not to occupy themselves with any object concerning which they cannot possess a certainty equal to that of the demonstrations of arithmetic and geometry.

The goal of philosophical reflection, in Descartes' view, is to cultivate "some general science explaining all that can be investigated concerning order and measure, without application to a particular material." This Descartes is quite willing to identify as "universal mathematics."

Given these aspirations and criteria, it is understandable that Descartes' method would not be very sensitive to the dynamics of time and change. Nor was his approach equipped to embrace chronological development, or even to consider that the dynamics of evolution or progress might function as important bearers of important truths.

The same can be said, generally, about the perspective of Immanuel Kant. Kant adhered to the Cartesian ideal for precision and certitude, which, after significant revisions, he also carried forward. His goal, as we have observed, was to identify the fundamental principles that are implicit in all valid knowledge. It goes without saying that the truths he sought are those that are invariable and unalterable. They cannot be affected by time and change. They are not to be modified by changing or shifting circumstances. They are fixed, uniform, permanent, absolute, universal, and changeless—qualities that make them absolutely dependable. Although Kant tended to root such principles in the knower's capacity to know rather than in objects to be known, he was convinced that mathematical or geometrical certainty is the ideal. It is true that the relation between knower and the knowable is understood to be a dynamic relationship, from the Kantian perspective. But this does not imply that the world is in flux or, in more technical terms, that reality is in process. Kant's grammar of reflection could deal only with formal constants. The very titles of his works illustrate his thoroughgoing desire for deductive purity.

Developmental Alternatives

The outlook of Georg Wilhelm Friedrich Hegel (1770–1831) represented another point of departure. Hegel affirmed with both Descartes and Kant that the universe is intelligible. He also believed the search for fundamental principles to be worthy of philosophical attention. But he shifted the mode and context of the search significantly. Descartes had sought to root knowledge in "a self that cannot doubt itself." Kant tried to expand the range of reflective self-consciousness by tracing the process by which the knower comes to know. Hegel judged Kant's capacity-to-know as being too narrowly contained. He offered, as substitute, an inclusive consciousness that was both individual and collective. In making this shift, Hegel pledged appreciation for the reality of time, change, and development.

He criticized Kant's method because it produced nothing more, as Hegel saw it, than "a skeleton with tickets stuck all over it, or a row of boxes kept shut and labelled in a grocer's stall." In Hegel's view, Kant's method was out of touch with the living and dynamic reality of the concrete fact. He accused it of being able to gain access to nothing more than "dry bones with flesh and blood all gone."

Hegel offered an alternative to Kant's formalism—indeed, nothing less than an elaborate plan for portraying the progressive unfolding of consciousness within human history. Developmental stages were given place. Process and change were taken seriously. Truth was understood to be correlative with time. The product was a comprehensive history of consciousness, which Hegel referred to as "the dialectic process which consciousness executes on itself." His was an attitude that implied the reality of "things emerging and being revised."

But, while it may have been the grandest, Hegel's was certainly not the only formulation that included motion, change, and progressive development in its portrayal of reality. Nor was Hegel alone in making the history of consciousness the fundamental stuff of the primary developmental process. The concepts of time, process, and development were already part of the general philosophical heritage. They had helped form an important chapter in Western philosophy from the time when Heraclitus, in the fourth century B.C.E., described reality using the metaphor of a stream or river "into which one cannot step twice in the same place." Hegel's thought gave modern philosophical respectability to this disposition. It also reinforced it, augmented it, and brought it up to date. Furthermore, Hegel found a way to develop a progressive perspective that remained in conversation—even while stating a difference of opinion—with Kantian thought. Not everyone agreed with the Hegelian orientation, of course, not even all of those who had come to acknowledge the propriety of sequential development. But Hegel accorded credibility to the point of view by developing a language and conceptual framework within which the orientation could be expressed systematically and comprehensively. The product was a comprehensive philosophy of history.

Hegel had many precursors. Jacques Bénigne Bossuet (1627–1704), a French bishop who lived during the reign of Louis XIV, developed a "providential" view of human history as early as the seventeenth century. Bossuet also cultivated a way of speaking about the "development of Christian doctrine." In Bossuet's view, both providence and development require that the world be understood as a reality not already permanently fixed.

Antoine-Nicholas de Condorcet (1743–1794) was a French mathematician, philosopher, and revolutionary thinker whose book *Esquisse d'un tableau historique des progrès de l'esprit humain* was referred to again and again by subsequent thinkers who viewed the world in progressive, developmental terms. For Condorcet, history is "the story of man's progress from superstition and barbarism to an age of reason and enlightenment." Condorcet understood the story to consist of ten chapters. It began with the dawning awareness of the primitive or savage tribes, and eventually reached beyond Condorcet's own time into a future he could only dimly envision. Significantly, the movement from stage to stage is regulated by successive increments of intelligence, cognitive sensitivity, and conceptual precision.

Condorcet's first stage finds savage humankind being formed into tribes. The second stage is marked by a transition to agriculture as the tribe's primary *modus vivendi*. Stage three traces the progress of agricultural peoples up to the invention of the alphabet. Then, turning more specifically to the Greco-Roman culture, Cordorcet focused on the division of the sciences. The sixth stage chronicles the decline of knowledge during the Crusades. The next stage includes the rebirth of scientific knowledge to the time of the invention of the printing press. Stage eight is regulated by the liberation of philosophy from scholastic theology, religious intolerance, and outmoded ecclesiastical authority.

> The human mind was not yet free but it knew that it was formed to be so. Those who dared to insist that it should be kept in its old chains, or to try and impose new ones upon it, were forced to show why it should submit to them; and from that day onwards it was certain that they would soon be broken.

The ninth stage reflects the full flowering of French Enlightenment thought. A tenth stage was projected that was to bring a progressive eradication of social problems and a diminution of the inequalities of wealth, status, and education.

Condorcet did not claim that the pathway of development went forward regularly and consistently without opposition. Rather, the path is marked by periods of progress followed by retrogression, clear journeys into enlightenment followed by retreats to ignorance. But, in the main, Condorcet was sure that the general tendency of things is progressive, liberating, and inexorable. He was confident too that, despite the obstacles, ways could always be found "so that genius can continue undisturbed on its path."

> The strengths and the limits of man's intelligence may remain unaltered; and yet the instruments that he uses will increase and improve, the language that fixes and determines his ideas will acquire greater breadth and precision and, unlike mechanics where an increase of force means a decrease of speed, the methods that lead genius to the discovery of truth increase at once the force and the speed of its operations.

Significantly, Condorcet identified religion, throughout the cycles, with superstition and intellectual bondage. It followed, he affirmed, that human progress requires the abolition of such false beliefs and release from such intellectual fetters. Religious influences must be overcome or circumvented. This point of view—prevalent among Enlightenment thinkers—was in complete accord with Kant's statement that "enlightenment is man's release from self-incurred tutelage. Tutelage is man's inability to make use of his understanding without direction from another." Religion, for Condorcet, is that from which the "geniuses" ("the eternal benefactors of mankind") save humans. Early in human history, humans needed to be saved from the superstition of tribal savagery. Humans needed to be saved, once again, during the Middle Ages when intelligence regressed, being subverted by religious authority. And the same task is necessary in the modern period. Viewed comprehensively, the evolution of the human mind is understood to be a story of human progress from superstition and barbarism to an age of reason and enlightenment. Thus Condorcet's optimism regarding the outcome derived from his conviction that humans were becoming increasingly and unavoidably irreligious.

As noted, Condorcet argued that the human race had progressed stage by stage, from an elemental barbarism through enlightenment toward the possibility of achieving perfection. He argued further that the stages of progress were not just theoretical or speculative constructs. Rather, they could be correlated with precise periods and epochs of history. For example, the age of the Enlightenment stood as the ninth stage of human history. And a tenth was to follow. The tenth stage would find nations equal to each other, and all inequities and inequalities between classes and persons would be abolished. The scheme even proposed that humans eventually would become perfected. But, always, the movement toward that aspiration was marked by distinct moments and epochs. None of this could be expected to happen in a moment or a flash. Rather, the formative current was the ongoing underlying progressive chronicle, and the chronicle supplied a clear means of reckoning progress.

A similar "progressivist scheme" was enunciated in the writings of Louis Gabriel Bonald (1754–1840), a French politician and philosopher, who is known for his book *Essai analytique sur les lois naturelles de l'ordre social*, published in 1800. Unlike Condorcet, whose pro-Enlightenment and pro–French Revolution sympathies made him a democrat, Bonald employed his formulae to defend the natural propriety of the monarchy in both ecclesiastical and temporal realms.

Prior to both Condorcet and Bonald, the Italian thinker Giambattista Vico (1668–1744), a legal philosopher and cultural historian, used his comprehensive *Scienza Nuova* (1725) to chronicle both a theogony (the birth and generation of the gods) and "the course of nations." Vico's goal was to develop a multiperspectival, comprehensive history of humanity. As a student of Roman law and of Greek philosophy, and a teacher of rhetoric in Naples, Vico drew upon the combined resources of law, poetry, myth, and language in composing *Scienza Nuova*. The organization of ingredients is complicated, primarily because Vico understood the course of human history to be more complex than either simple linear progression or cyclical repetition would capture. In Vico's view progress occurs, certainly, as human awareness becomes more expansive and discerning, but it is progress without fixed destination and with no guarantee of success. Rather than leading to an inevitable perfecting of the human race, the movement often produces decadence and a recurrence of the fall of humans from their desired state. When this occurs, the age of barbarism is reenacted. But the movement toward barbarism can easily be followed by movement toward order and a consequent rebirth of civilization. Once achieved—or reachieved—civilization flourishes for a time, only to produce a legacy of renewed barbarism.

Vico's complex view of things is multidisciplinary and multiperspectival. He recognized that various organic entities—nations, the world, history, world history, as well as human creative ventures—pass through their own respective stages of development. Each of these develops in complicated interdependence with the others. Vico admitted that the cycles of progress are not enacted at the same pace within all contexts, nor is there a single comprehensive chronicle that sweeps all of them along together. Thus, a variety of approaches becomes necessary to analyze fully the nature and importance of history.

Saint-Simon and Auguste Comte

Other significant figures help form the background of our story. For instance, the founder of socialism, Claude-Henri de Rouvroy, Count de Saint-Simon (1760–1825), is known both for his visions of social reform and for his interpretations of the history of civilization. With regard to social reform, Saint-Simon opposed the militarism of Napoleon by offering the alternative that those who know science should take control of society. His model of "takeover" was influenced by his conception of the role played by ecclesiastical officials during the Middle Ages. With regard to his interpretations of the history of civilization, Saint-Simon suggested many of the ideas about the complexion of evolutionary development that were subsequently elaborated by Auguste Comte. Both in social reform and in historical theory, Saint-Simon's objective was to identify the ingredients necessary for the construction of an international community. He reasoned that medieval society functioned well because there was true harmony between the ideas and the institutions of the time.

Historical chronology was implicit in Saint-Simon's point of departure. Social and ideological harmony were present, he believed, at the time of the Middle Ages, but this harmony had been broken by the Reformation. It was injured further by the growth of scientific knowledge, and suffered even more under the religious skepticism of the eighteenth-century rationalists.

Saint-Simon conceded that the possibility of returning to the earlier medieval synthesis was gone forever; too much damage had been done. But the compulsion to rebuild the interface between social realities and intellectual pronouncements, and thus to create a new harmony, remained ever present. Furthermore, the logic of historical progress tended to assure that such reforming and harmonizing measures would be successful.

In Saint-Simon's view, human awareness had already passed through the stages of polytheism, monotheism, and metaphysics. The stage of positive science—next in the sequence—was just beginning to occur. Having come to this new stage, it was essential that humans identify the general ideas necessary to the construction of a new rapprochement between intellectuals and a society as a whole. Saint-Simon's goal was to develop an encyclopedia of such general ideas. The ideas were to carry social reformative capacity, he contended, and be consistent with the confirmable scientific knowledge of the time. Saint-Simon used Thomas Aquinas's *Summa Theologica* as a model. For its time, the *Summa* provided the basis for a synthesis of philosophy and social order in a manner that was both socially and intellectually compelling. Saint-Simon wanted to construct a new "Summa" to correlate the current scientific knowledge with the social needs of the late eighteenth and early nineteenth centuries.

Thus, even prior to Comte, one can find reference to "positive science" in a context in which history is viewed as chronological sequence composed of stages or epochs. Saint-Simon wrote: "We have advanced by stages so far that there remains only a step further to arrive at a universal conception." In another place, he wrote:

> The progress of the human mind, the revolutions which occur in the development of knowledge, give each century its special character.
> The sixteenth century was rich in theologians; or rather the predominant interest in this century was such that nearly all writers dealt with theological questions.

He noticed a significant change: "In the seventeenth century the arts flourished, and the masterpieces of modern literature were born." Bringing the chronicle closer to his own time, he observes:

> The writers of the last century were philosophers. They opened men's eyes to the fact that the most important social institutions were founded in prejudice and superstitions and in the powers which were built on them. This was the century of revolutions and of criticism.

There were lessons to be drawn from such analyses of the shifts of interest and attention that have come to characterize the various time periods. Saint-Simon observed that "the philosophy of the last century was revolution." By contrast, the philosophy of the nineteenth century must be "constructive." Put in sweeping fashion, "the social order has been overturned because it no longer corresponded to the level of enlightenment; it is for you to create a better order."

In his essay "New Christianity," Saint-Simon made similar proclamations:

> The more society progresses morally and physically, the more subdivision of intellectual and manual labor takes place; in the course of their daily work, men's minds are occupied with things of more and more specialized interest; as the arts, science, and industry progress, the more necessary it is that the form of worship remind me . . . of the interests common to all members of society, of the common interests of the human race.

And, again, in another place: "In order to rejuvenate Christianity it is not enough to enable it to triumph over former religious philosophies. I must also establish its scientific superiority to all the philosophic doctrines which have discarded religion." When one listens long enough, one recognizes that all of the necessary components are there: a view of history that organizes time according to periods and stages; an affirmation of the pervasiveness of human progress; and unqualified enthusiasm for the capacities of positive science.

The stages of history were elaborated more precisely and dramatically by Auguste Comte (1798–1857), a French mathematician who, while being influenced by Saint-Simon, also carried on lengthy correspondence with the English writer John Stuart Mill (1806–1873). Comte's goal, like Saint-Simon's (though without the latter's revolutionary-organizational fervor), was to employ a progressive view of human history so that humankind's social and political condition might be improved.

According to the famous "law of three stages," Comte perceived human thought—in the sense of human consciousness in general—to pass from theological to metaphysical to more current scientific interests. In the third stage, both the controlling substantive interest and the methodological scope had shifted dramatically. Instead of being concerned with absolute truth and ultimate explanations, positive science is being directed toward disclosing "the actual laws of phenomena." Such laws are made accessible through the powers of reason and empirical observation. Comte attested that positive science functions in the following way:

> [It] endeavors to discover, by a well-combined use of reasoning and observation, the actual laws of phenomena, that is to say, their invariable relations of succession and likeness. The explanation of facts, thus reduced to its real terms, consists henceforth only in the connection established between different particular phenomena and some general facts, the number of which the progress of science tends more and more to diminish.

The inference is that religion is to be associated with theological thinking—the beginning stage in the development of human intelligence. Comte accorded lasting value to theology; that is, without the theological outlook, the process of knowledge could not have been set in motion. This means that theology did indeed identify some proper issues, and formulated provisional responses that subsequent modes of thought could examine, react against, improve upon, and eventually transcend. His candid feelings about theology can be expressed as follows: The purpose of theology is to so arrange the ingredients of the universe that humans are compelled to find a way beyond the theological construction of reality. In Comte's view, earliest intelligence needed something large, comprehensive, intriguing, and captivating—all of which features are provided by theological speculation—to sustain that same intelligence.

Thus the theological mode of intelligence stands as a provisional stage in the pathway toward surer knowledge. Metaphysics, by contrast, is not provisional but transitional. The metaphysical mode serves chiefly as a means of transference and exchange between theology and positive science. Comte explained the relationship this way:

> Theology and physics are so profoundly incompatible and their conceptions are so radically opposed in character, that, before giving up the one in order to employ the other exclusively, the human intelligence had to make use of intermediate conceptions, which, being of a hybrid character, were eminently fitted to bring about a gradual transition.

After the shift from theology to positive science has been facilitated by metaphysics, the interests of the theological frame of mind are left behind. From within the scientific mode, for example, Comte observed that any "search after what are called causes, whether first or final, is absolutely inaccessible and unmeaning."

For Comte, the entire sequence followed with inevitability. It was no simple matter of preferring the scientific mode to its predecessor theological and metaphysical orientations. Nor was the transition from the first to the second and the third stages explicable simply in terms of shifting styles or fashions. Rather, an underlying rationale—a law of sequential progression—makes it impossible (or, at least, manifestly anachronistic) to take up the concerns of the theological state of mind after human intelligence has come to recognize the propriety of positive science. Such progress is sequential; it is also deliberate. "There exists in this regard an invariable and necessary order which our various classes of conceptions have followed, and were bound to follow, in their progressive course."

The primary implications regarding the status and significance of religion are clear. Religion has its roots in the first stage of human mental development when apperception was most daring, and, simultaneously, most fragile, untutored, inexact, and precarious. This first stage has been superseded by a second stage, which, in the course of its unfolding, makes the first stage obsolete. The second transitional stage gave way to a third, a surer mode of knowledge in which all remaining abstractions were replaced by empirical knowledge of fact. The achievement of this third stage not only makes the first stage obsolete, but it also transforms it into a vestige from a time gone by. Furthermore, the entire sequential development is regulated by a law which demands that the movement take place just as Comte has been able to describe it. This law says that once a stage in the pathway of human intelligence has been superseded by a subsequent stage it is no longer appropriate or viable.

However one looks at it, this interpretation refers religion to the mental childhood of the human race. Religion may have performed a useful function in its time, but that function retains no utility once that time has been passed. Taken comprehensively, the historical chronicle witnesses that religious sensitivity helped set humankind on the pathway toward a more useful comprehension of human surroundings. But once those surroundings were comprehended in more effective, accurate, and trustworthy terms, all previous stages or forms of understanding became obsolete. Chronologically, the theological mode of awareness represents humankind's first way of making sense of the world. Retrospectively, the theological orientation represents an archaic mode of awareness. Theology, in other words, is both first-stage and superannuated. And the judgments against theology apply with equal force to religion. Comte understood religion and theology to be of the same cloth.

Lévy-Bruhl and Primitive Mentality

Comte's views were consulted again and again, particularly within French thought, and specifically by Lucien Lévy-Bruhl (1857–1939), anthropologist, philosopher, and historian of philosophy. Lévy-Bruhl shared the widespread enthusiasm for the law of three stages—the Comtean way of lending categorization to the evolution of human intelligence. He was also quite familiar with the evolutionist theories of such scholars and writers as E. B. Tylor, Andrew Lang, and Sir James Frazer, three British thinkers to whom we shall be turning our attention later in this chapter. As a consequence, Lévy-Bruhl brought intellectual rigor, fresh empirical data, and impressive scholarly versatility to the evolutionist approach. For, in addition to philosophy and anthropology—his major fields—he worked in psychology, sociology, moral philosophy, and (though he may not have recognized the description) the scholarly study of religion.

Influenced by Emile Durkheim, Lévy-Bruhl was trained to explain the discrepancies between the reasoning processes of archaic and civilized humans. He did so by focusing on their distinctive mental habits. He approached the same by trying to identify the mode of human intelligence which was most unlike that of civilized human beings. This contrast could be established, he conjectured, were he to concentrate his attention on the thought process of primitive (or rudimentary) peoples. Two large and important works—*How Natives Think* (1910) and *Primitive Mentality* (1922), which he described as "one and the same work in two volumes"—are the products of this analytical and descriptive task.

Lévy-Bruhl's contention was that human intelligence in primitive peoples can be described as being mystical, prelogical, and pervaded by a sense of "affectional participation." To say that primitive mentality is mystical is to recognize that it is "at all times oriented to occult forces." To call it prelogical is to acknowledge that it is "indifferent as a rule to the laws of contradiction." This means that primitive mentality is diametrically opposed to the pathways and procedures that post-Enlightenment peoples have followed in recognizing, measuring, and practicing rationality. And by "affectational participation" Lévy-Bruhl wanted to signify the sense of connectedness that primitive peoples felt with other persons and objects. That is, in primitive comprehension, the data of experience tend to flow together and associate with each other in many complex ways rather than being regulated by strictly cause-and-effect relationships.

For example, Lévy-Bruhl contended that a tendency toward immediacy and attachment influences the way primitive peoples formed mental associations:

> Now there is one element which is never lacking in such relations. In varying degrees they all involve a "participation" between persons or objects which form part of a collective representation. For this reason I shall, in default of a better term, call the principle which is peculiar to "primitive mentality"—which governs the connections and the preconnections of such representations—*the law of participation.*

Admitting that it is difficult to formulate this law in abstract terms, and that it is more effective to illustrate it by means of examples from the life of primitive peoples, he offered the following tentative and approximate definition: "I should be inclined to say that in the collective representations of primitive mentality, objects, beings and phenomena can be (though in a way incomprehensible to us) both themselves and something other than themselves." Being "both themselves and something other than themselves," Lévy-Bruhl elucidates, "they give forth and receive mystic powers, virtues, qualities, influences, which make themselves felt outside, without ceasing to remain what they are." He recognized that these capacities may be difficult for the modern mind to fathom. Yet, this is just the point: primitive mentality is under no obligation to follow the rules of understanding that characterize human intelligence in the modern period. "In other words, the opposition between the one and the many, the same and another, and so forth, does not impose upon this mentality the necessity of affirming one of the terms if the other is denied, or vice versa."

Lévy-Bruhl provided illustration of his contentions. He was taken by the fact that some tribes tend to think of themselves as animals or birds. He believed that, when this occurs, such tribes are not simply thinking metaphorically or symbolically. Nor do they mean to suggest that after they die they will become animals or birds. Instead, the equation implies actual participatory identity. Again, this may be difficult for the modern mind to fathom—for the modern mind no longer orders intelligence in this way—but Lévy-Bruhl was convinced that his observation was sure and his description accurate. "That they can be both the human beings they are and the birds of scarlet plumage at the same time appears to be inconceivable, but to the mentality that is governed by the law of participation there is no difficulty in the matter."

Thus, the attempt to describe the primitive, prelogical mentality led Lévy-Bruhl to take up the comprehensive task of giving an account of primitive language. This involves a treatment of the ways in which primitive peoples measure and classify; and this, in turn, involves a description of the numbering systems they utilize. All of this, in turn, involves analyses of correlations between language forms and ritual practices. The product of all of this, when completed, would be a rigorous and complete account of the rudiments of primitive collective representations.

His contribution to knowledge of the earliest human beings was considerable, and his way of approaching this subject intrigued others. But both what he uncovered and how he approached it reflect some strong assumptions about the dynamics of mental coordination. Lévy-Bruhl believed that he could isolate some fundamental differences between primitive and modern human beings by comparing and contrasting the mental habits that give form to knowledge in the two instances. Thus we have included his contribution to the study of religion within a chapter that concentrates on origin-and-development inquiry. Lévy-Bruhl's work belongs here by virtue of its strong intention to identify the rudimentary components of the worldview of the earliest peoples.

It is clear, however, that the same strategy can be employed for additional or alternative purposes. Rather than simply focusing on the coordinated mental habits of so-called primitive peoples for purposes of outlining a possible primitive world of thought, the scholar can attempt to decipher coordinated mental habits wherever they occur. That is, if one can effect this accomplishment by concentrating on primitive cultures, one should also be able to achieve the same goals with respect to other and, perhaps, all cultures. Indeed, we should note that a half-century after Lévy-Bruhl's death, Stanley Tambiah, an American anthropologist, made an impressive case that participation should stand as a universal category, representing one of two coexisting mentalities in humankind everywhere, the other being the rational-logical mentality.

This broadening of focus was an expected outcome of Lévy-Bruhl's technique, a method he learned from Emile Durkheim (1858–1917). But when Durkheim employed it, the interest in origin and development became somewhat ancillary to another intention: he wanted to comprehend the workings of mental coordination. Hence, in the work of Durkheim, an initial interest in identifying origin and development carries the scholarly study of religion to another paradigm. For this reason, we have chosen to treat Durkheim's position more fully in chapter 4, which concentrates specifically on "organic coordination." Suffice it to observe here that "organic coordination" was originally conceived as a methodological focus for isolating the most significant and formative social, mental, and religious characteristics of the earliest peoples.

Before tracing developments within France further—a task that would take us from Durkheim through the work of Henri Hubert and Marcel Mauss, indeed, all the way on to an analysis of the intentions of modern-day structuralism—we must turn to Great Britain, where related origin-and-development inquiry was occurring. In crossing the English Channel, we have chosen to focus our chronicle on the work of the two giants, Max Müller and Sir James Frazer first, and then turn to a sequence of inquiry that was sponsored within anthropological circles more strictly defined. Following our descriptions of the positions of Müller and Frazer, we shall take up the contentions of Herbert Spencer, E. B. Tylor, their successors, critics, and commentators.

Max Müller: The Creation
of a Science of Religion

Max Müller (1832–1930), German born but a resident of England throughout most of his scholarly life, is one of the most prominent of those figures to whom the history of the study of religion refers when giving an account of its genesis and history. A Sanskritist by both training and profession, Müller was also well schooled in philosophy from his work at the universities of Leipzig and Berlin. He was trained first as a Hegelian, and also became well acquainted with neo-Kantian thought. But the greatest philosophical influence in his education came from Friedrich Schelling (1775–1854) in Berlin. Through Schelling, Müller also became acquainted with a metaphysical system that had been elaborated on the basis of a philosophy of nature. Thus, many features within Müller's more mature attitude toward religion were formed by Schelling's natur-philosophie. For example, Müller's contention that the infinite is present in all things finite was first phrased in Schelling's terms and with the assistance of Schelling's point of view. But Schelling gave Müller much more than attitude and terminology. In addition, the constellation of interests characteristic of Schelling's philosophy became part of Müller's preconception of the nature of religion and mythology. Schelling helped train his attention. And what Müller perceived continued to belong to Schelling's perspective.

Müller had left Germany in 1846 to travel to England to edit a translation of the Rig Veda. Following the completion of the project, he stayed on in England, taking a post at Oxford. There he taught comparative philology until 1875, when he was appointed curator of the Bodleien Library. In the same year he became the editor of a fifty-volume collection of scriptures of Eastern religious traditions, called *The Sacred Books of the East.* Thus, Müller came to the study of religion via the study of language and mythology.

He is important to our chronicle for two large reasons. First, he must be regarded as one of the chief founders—as well as one of the most prominent sustaining patrons—of the new science of the study of religion. Even in his earliest writings, he displayed an interest in establishing and nurturing this new discipline. Because he was conversant with the writings of theologians, philosophers, philologists, anthropologists, and cultural historians, Müller wished to speak to no single group of persons or scholars, but to a variety of persons within an interdisciplinary context. This is significant not only because it goes against the conventionally atomizing scholarly thrust, but also because it shows that Müller understood that researchers and theorists within a wide variety of fields were addressing the same subjects.

Müller's remarks indicate that he did not assume that the history of religions was to be classified as a separate field or discipline. History of religions—he called it "science of religion"—had no developed conscious sense of its range, capacities, and ongoing tradition. In fact, a tradition had not as yet been formed. The makeup of the subject-field was still fluid, and its capacities were embryonic and, thus, untested. Müller employed his essay, *Introduction to the Science of Religion*, to unify interdisciplinary interests. As a consequence, the essay can be referred to as one of the original documents that lent self-consciousness and gave impetus to the emerging subject-field.

The second major reason for Müller's importance lies in the attention he gave to mythology. Manuals on the subject credit him with popularizing the study of mythology and sometimes cite his book *Essays in Comparative Mythology* (1856) as the first serious, disciplined study of the subject. Müller brought the two elements together. They coalesced, inasmuch as the study of mythology became the primary means of access to the religion of the earliest peoples. That is, a probing of mythology held the promise of disclosing the origins of religious awareness.

He developed his approach in several stages, all of which build upon a definition of religion that roots it in natural human awareness and then, more specifically, within the dynamics of perception. Consequently, much of Müller's effort was directed toward trying to illustrate how the distinction between finite and infinite is perceived. Within this context, he defined religion as "a mental faculty which, independent of, nay, in spite of, senses and reason, enables man to apprehend the infinite under different names and under varying disguises." He elaborated, as follows:

> Without this faculty, no religion, not even the lowest worship of idols and fetishes, would be possible; and if we will but listen attentively, we can hear in all religions the groaning of the spirit, a struggle to conceive the inconceivable, to utter the unutterable, a longing after the infinite, a love of God.

These are rich phrases: "the infinite in the perception of our senses," "the groaning of the spirit to conceive the inconceivable and utter the unutterable," and "the longing after the infinite." Given this richness of expression, Müller was quick to acknowledge, however, that one should not expect to find either a perfect or fully developed idea of the infinite in the earliest instances of individual or collective religious experience. Rather, this was an idea that developed gradually. As he put it: "Religion begins as little with the perfect idea of the infinite as astronomy begins with the law of gravity: nay, in its purest form, that idea is the last rather than the first step in the march of the human intellect." Yet, while he acknowledged the fact of evolution in religious awareness, he also took deliberate steps to assure his readers that he could not subscribe to Comte's reading of human history. He was particularly opposed to the suggestion that the roots of religion lie, purely and simply, in a primordial fetishism—that is, in the belief that certain objects have magical power.

The perception of the infinite is always tied to something tangible, Müller argued. It was so when religious awareness first dawned; it is no different in modern times. The idea of the infinite always includes a sensuous or perceptual quality. Müller explained:

> [B]eyond, behind, beneath, and within the finite, the infinite is always present to our senses. It presses upon us, it grows upon us from every side. What we call the finite in space and time, in form and word, is nothing but a veil or net which we ourselves have thrown over the infinite. The finite by itself, without the infinite, is simply inconceivable, as inconceivable as the infinite without the finite.

But, in the development of religion, the perception of the infinite becomes extended and transformed into a concept. What originated as a datum of sense is subsequently subjected to reason and reflection. And when subjected to reason, religion is judged by selected canons of truth. Hence, religion evolves. The stages in its development are distinguished on the basis of the different forms and modes of apprehension by means of which it is comprehended.

For example, Müller held that the earliest conceptions of deity were actually personifications of natural phenomena. Again, with Schelling's lead, Müller's philosophy of nature held that the sun, moon, wind, thunder clouds, stars, sky, rivers, the dawn rain, and other primary astral or solar phenomena gave the earliest humans an intuition of deity and the invisible reality beyond. In the course of the development of language, these touchstones of reality were deified, and the infinite was described in a personified manner. Thus Müller held "disease of language" accountable not only for personified conceptions of deity, but also for the origins of mythology. Recognizing that language supplies tools to thought, Müller believed that mythology arises at a particular stage within the growth of a language when some key words lose their original metaphorical or symbolic meaning and their referents are transformed into supposed objective realities. Müller wished to "depersonify" and then "re-naturalize" all references to gods and divinities. Yet he took the tendency to deify natural phenomena as indication that peoples everywhere, and in all times, have had an intuition of the divine.

He favored "pure religion," the simple apprehension of the infinite. He displayed a negative attitude toward what happens to religion in the course of its subsequent development—when the content of such intuitive insights are objectified so as to be transposed into a foreign, and thus deceptive, frame of reference. Müller advocated a return to the simplicity of the original vision, knowing that this would occur only through some cultivated sensitivity to the power of language in overlaying the content of perceptions with extraneous materials. For only then can the extraneous be discarded. That the "extraneous" exists is further evidence that the infinite has always resided beyond the veil of nature and within the human spirit.

Although many of the details of Müller's position were corrected and amended in subsequent scholarship, his work belongs permanently to the composition of religious studies. He shaped an origins-and-development approach into a respected science of religion.

Sir James Frazer: Magic, Religion, and Science

One of the clearest and most comprehensive portrayals of the view that magic, religion, and science belong to an evolutionary sequence was provided by Sir James George Frazer (1854–1941), perhaps known best for his book *The Golden Bough*, a twelve-volume collection of materials on "the savage mind," which was issued from 1907 to 1915. Frazer's interpreters are quick to point out that *The Golden Bough* constituted both a testing ground for a large hypothesis regarding the relation of magic to religion and a rich source of data from primitive cultures. The same interpreters often take the position that Frazer's evolutionist theory is now thoroughly suspect, but his repository of ethnological and anthropological information remains useful. All evaluators, however, should be clear about Frazer's intentions. By means of the data he gathered and the system of classification he devised, he intended to provide description of "the chemistry of the mind." It was not enough simply to uncover graphic examples of artifacts from primitive cultures. His original program was larger, grander, and more precise.

According to Frazer, human intelligence formed progressively. The formative process of development, he thought, could be measured. This developmental process—Frazer is prepared to call it a "chain"—stretches from the beginning of time to the present, and it remains unbroken. Hence, the thought of the earliest humans contained the germs out of which more complex ideas developed.

Within this broad sweep of things, Frazer focused his attention on two large issues. He wanted to know how magic came into being, and he wished to identify the fundamental differences between magic and religion. Under the first heading, Frazer contended that magic pertained to the attempt to manipulate or control natural forces through ritual, ceremony, and incantation. Such practices are common among primitive peoples. Frazer based his contentions on E. B. Tylor's thesis that magic developed from forms of association—associations of ideas because they are similar to each other, and associations of ideas because they are continuous in either time or space. Frazer explained his contention this way:

> If we analyze the principles of thought on which magic is based, they will probably be found to resolve themselves into two: first, that like produces like (or that an effect resembles its cause); and, second, that things that have once been in contact with each other continue to act on each other after the physical contact has been severed.

Frazer had names for these rules. He called the first the Law of Similarity and the second the Law of Contact or Contagion. It is by means of these categories that Frazer can illumine the fact that the magician "can produce any effect he desires merely by imitating it." This, in other words, is enunciation of the law of similarity. But the magician can also infer that "whatever he does to a material object will affect equally the person with whom the object was once in contact." This is exemplification of Frazer's second law. Both activities of the magician assume that nature is orderly and its laws are regular.

Examples are useful in this regard, and Frazer offers a host of them. The most familiar of the first set of activities, he suggests, is the attempt that is frequently made to hurt or destroy an enemy by hurting or destroying an image of the foe. The assumption is that whatever is represented by the image will be affected by the way the image is treated. The principle, again, is that like produces like—expressing the law of similarity. For the other set of activities, Frazer cites the instance of the maidservant who objected to the throwing away of a child's baby teeth. She warned that if the teeth were found and gnawed by an animal, "the child's new tooth would be, for all the world, like the teeth of the animal that had bitten the old one." The principle operating in this situation can be expressed as follows: "Things which have once been conjoined must remain associated ever afterwards, even when quite dissevered from each other, in such a sympathetic relation that whatever is done to the one must similarly affect the other."

In Frazer's view, magic relies on an interpretation of mental associations that is logically suspect. The mistake lies in conceiving the natural order of things as an extension of the order in which ideas present themselves to the mind. Magic gives way to religion when it is discovered that "the succession of natural events is not determined by immutable laws." When this assumption holds, the appropriate response lies in the realm of magic—to believe that one can employ regular natural order for one's own ends and manipulate it accordingly. After the assumption has been discredited, however, the belief in natural order is replaced by the religious view, which sees natural events occurring in the world because of the invisible presence and intervention of supernatural beings. Because of their recognition that magic rituals do not work, the earliest humans cultivated a reliance on supernatural beings. In Frazer's portrayal, the transition occurred this way: "[I]n the acuter minds magic is gradually superseded by religion, which explains the succession of natural phenomena as regulated by the will, the passion, or the caprice of spiritual beings like man in kind, though vastly superior to him in power." This led Frazer to the following definition of religion:

> By religion, then, I understand a propitiation or conciliation of powers superior to man which are believed to direct and control the course of nature and of human life. Thus defined, religion consists of two elements, a theoretical and a practical element, namely, a belief in powers higher than man and an attempt to propitiate or please them.

The next transition in sequence—from religion to science—occurs because of dissatisfaction with the view that events are to be explained by reference to the activities of spiritual realities or divine beings. The scientific mode shares the attitude with its predecessors that nature follows regular patterns of order. But the scientific response to this fact attempts to transcend the naiveté of the magical outlook. In the case of science, the natural order is fixed only on the basis of careful empirical observation and exact analysis. This is a more rigorous apprehension of the world than can be achieved by any of the sensitivities given credence in magic. And the same holds true in the relationship between religion and science. Science supplants recourse to explanation on the basis of the power of deities by employing empirical observation and rational analysis. But this is not to suggest that science is indeed the final stage in the series. Frazer suggests that

> as science has supplanted its predecessors, so it may hereafter be itself superseded by some more perfect hypothesis, perhaps by some totally different way of looking at the phenomena—of registering the shadows on the screen—of which we in this generation can form no ideal.

The entire sequence—from magic to religion to science and beyond, perhaps, to science's successor—stands as an eloquent expression of the insatiable human quest for reliable knowledge of humanity's surroundings. Yet each distinct stage contains the products of the former stage. And the final accomplishment meets aspirations that have been present from the beginning:

> The advance of knowledge is an infinite progression toward a goal that forever recedes. We need not murmur at the endless pursuit. . . . Great things will come of that pursuit, though we may not enjoy them. Brighter stars will rise on some voyager of the future—some great Ulysses of the realm of thought—than shine on us.

In short, "the dreams of magic may one day be the waking realities of science."

Frazer's overall intention, it is evident, was to find access to the mentality of primitive peoples. He assumed that by identifying some of the primary components of "the chemistry of the mind," he might make a significant contribution toward propelling human beings forward and expediting the path of human progress. Theodor Gaster, the editor of one abridged version of *The Golden Bough*, judged Frazer's ultimate contribution to human learning to be analogous to Sigmund Freud's:

> [W]hat Freud did for the individual, Frazer did for civilization as a whole. For as Freud deepened men's insight into the behavior of individuals by uncovering the ruder world of the subconscious, from which so much of it springs, so Frazer enlarged man's understanding of the behavior of societies by laying bare the primitive concepts and modes of thought which underlie and inform so many of their institutions and which persist, as a subliminal element of their culture, in their traditional folk customs.

And yet, because of its emphasis on disclosing an underlying grammar of thought, Frazer's was also a Kantian project, but in both psychological and cultural terms.

In addition to those scholars and inquirers who worked self-consciously to create comprehensive descriptions of the mental capacities of the earliest human beings, others in Great Britain, chiefly some pioneer figures in the field of anthropology, developed evolutionist models that included definite conceptions of the place and function of religion. To some of these—Herbert Spencer and Edward Burnett Tylor, first—we now turn.

Herbert Spencer: Religion and Evolution

Herbert Spencer (1820–1903) was a railway engineer, later turned evolutionary philosopher, whom the scientist Charles Darwin called "the greatest living philosopher in England." It has been claimed often that Spencer is the founder of the theory of evolution. This honor belongs either to Spencer or E. B. Tylor (whose point of view we shall be examining in the next section of this portrayal)—though Darwin himself perceived the presence of evolution in the thought of the German romantic poet-philosopher Johann Wolfgang von Goethe (1749–1832) sometime before either Tylor or Spencer made strong use of it. Spencer and Tylor carried on an extended and sometimes bitter public conversation over just who was the first to conceive of evolutionary theory. As can be expected, commentators more sympathetic to Spencer contend on his behalf; but his opponent in the controversy also has impressive supporters. The quarrel need not detain us here.

In 1852, Spencer published his influential and now famous article, "The Development Hypothesis," in which he rejected the doctrine of special creation as a means of explaining differences between species in animals. He also argued on behalf of a theory of "a process of organic evolution through successive modifications."

Then, in a companion article called "Progress: Its Law and Cause," published in 1857, two years before Darwin's *The Origin of the Species* appeared, Spencer expanded his views on evolution to include the application of his new theory to society and to the universe itself. Eventually the theory of evolution came to apply simultaneously to the universe, Earth, the development of biological forms, the human mind, and, as we have indicated, even to society. All of these were understood to have assumed their present forms through a process of progressive development.

The full elaboration of Spencer's theory was left for his comprehensive work, *Synthetic Philosophy*, which consisted of: *First Principles* (1862), two volumes of *The Principles of Biology* (1864–1867), two volumes of *The Principles of Psychology* (1855–1872), three volumes of *The Principles of Sociology* (1876–1896), and two volumes of *The Principles of Ethics* (1892–1893). For each of these studies, the same principles applied. Defining evolution as "a change from a state of relatively indefinite, incoherent, homogeneity to a state of relatively definite, coherent, heterogeneity," Spencer sought to trace the process by which homogeneity constantly breaks up into increasing variety. For example, just as animals evolve from simple to complex species, so too does society evolve into a perpetual proliferation of functions, grades, and offices—priests, kings, prophets, scholars, workers, and so on. The same process occurs in the growth of knowledge, wherein disciplines, fields, individual sciences, and distinctive subfields are produced as homogeneity becomes displaced by increasing differentiation. In all of these instances, splittings-off, borrowings, shadings, modifications, and mutations occur. Eventually the same disciplines, fields, and sciences give rise to new subdisciplines, subfields, and subsciences, which in turn give rise to additional forms of integration and coherence.

Throughout the process, increasing specialization and variegation arise. Yet each moment in the process sustains its interdependence on and interrelationship with the sum total of other moments. Consequently, any entity—be it an animal, a species of animal, animal as genera, the human body, society, even the universe as a whole—can be viewed as a distinct organism that is undergoing the process of increasing differentiation and heterogenization. At the same time, those same parts or ingredients of heterogenization continue to stand in a relationship of reciprocal interdependence with each other. Consequently the process of increased differentiation is also regulated by a tendency toward ultimate integration. Spencer had confidence that in time—literally, *in time*—every possible variety of being would find the possibility of actualization:

> This process from general to special in priesthoods, has, in the highest nations, led to such marked distinctions that the original kinships are forgotten. The priest-astrologers of ancient races were initiators of the scientific class, now variously specialized; from the priest-doctors of old have come the medical class with its chief divisions and minor divisions; while within the clerical class proper have arisen not only various ranks from pope down to acolyte, but various kinds of

functionaries—dean, priest, deacon, chorister, as well as other classes such as curate and chaplains.

Similarly, if we trace the genesis of any industrial structure, as that which from primitive blacksmiths who smelt their own iron as well as make implements from it, brings us to our iron-manufacturing districts, where preparation of the metal is separated into smelting, refining, puddling, rolling, and where turning this metal into implements is divided into various businesses.

The transformation here illustrated is an aspect of that transformation of the homogeneous into the heterogeneous which everywhere characterizes evolution. But the truth to be noted is that it characterizes the evolution of individual organisms in especially high degrees.

When one probes Spencer's theories for the attitudes to religion that are implicit there, one can draw something of the following sketch: Religion belongs to the constitution of social organisms, that is, to societies. It has been present from the beginnings of civilization. It regulated the earliest forms of social organization, and it performs the same function today. Whenever it appears in culture, it functions as a means of social control. For example, in primitive tribes, religion often served to marshal and support military success and control: the war gods, for example, are propitiated by bloody rites to insure the success of the tribe in battle. This helps explain the frequency with which the earliest mythologies represented their deities as conquerors in battle. It also illustrates the striking interdependence of political and theological forms of government, as well as the remarkable similarities between military and ecclesiastical organization. In Spencer's view, there are undeniable linkages and close correspondences between religious and military interests and functions. The close relationships are manifested, for example, in the functions of rituals and ceremonies. Everyone recognizes that rituals have religious significance, but Spencer attested that the same rituals also serve a military function. That is, they provide a means of social control. They regulate "interhuman conduct before the appearance of institutions of control." The same associations are apparent in the close ties between religion, ancestor worship, and the prevalence of monarchical forms of government within primitive tribes.

The ultimate explanation for the persistence of religious ideas, for Spencer, lay in what might be called the dynamics of symbolic projection. These are not Spencer's own words. He did not employ such terminology exactly, but it represents an apt description of his reading of the genesis of religious ideas.

He came at it as follows, by asking his readers to reflect upon their own experience and upon the ways in which concepts are related to empirical referents. Notice, Spencer continues, that for a large number of working concepts, no precise empirical referents exist at all, but simply an "insensible transition"—a series of infinitesimal steps to higher and more comprehensive abstract concepts. Spencer made much of the example of starting with small pebbles and then building up to a notion or concept of earth. From an empirical thing, the mind generalizes, thus moving to a concept of higher generality.

Great magnitudes, great durations, great numbers, are none of them actually conceived, but are all of them conceived more or less symbolically; and so, too, are all those classes of objects of which we predicate some common fact.

Those concepts of larger magnitudes and more extensive classes which we cannot make adequate, we still find can be verified by some indirect process of measurement or enumeration. And even in the case of such an utterly inconceivable object as the Solar System, we yet, through the fulfillment of predictions founded on our symbolic conceptions of it, gain the conviction that this symbolic conception stands for an actual existence.

The process by which the mind moves from specific things to generalizations about specific things is capable of producing additional impressions. For example, it is this same process that may give the impression that a symbolic conception is identical with an actual existence. This, in Spencer's mind, is how religion is created. Religion comes about when conceptions (of high generalization) are understood to refer to actual realities. Religion is a product of these conceptions "of highest magnitude," or by the tendency to engage in "general thinking." Spencer wrote:

> To the primitive man sometimes happen things which are out of the ordinary course—diseases, storms, earthquakes, echoes, eclipses. From dreams arises the idea of a wandering double; when follows the belief that the double, departing permanently at death, is then a ghost.
>
> Ghosts thus become assignable causes for strange occurrences. The greater ghosts are presented supposed to have extended spheres of action. As men grow intelligent and conceptions of these minor invisible agencies merge into the conception of a universal invisible agency, there result hypotheses concerning the origin, not of special incidents only, but of things in general.

In Spencer's view, the origin of religion is to be traced to the mental tendency to engage in transempirical generalizations; that is, to explain particular actions in terms of an overarching agency.

Another side to Spencer's contentions is worthy of our attention. Having explained religion by identifying the procedures by which the mind generalizes upon empirical data, he felt confident offering an acknowledged personal view on valid, legitimate religion. Here he referred to religion as mystery, within the context of which Spencer called attention to "the omnipresence of something that passes comprehension." In his words:

> For every religion, setting out though it does with the tacit assertion of a mystery, forthwith proceeds to give some solution to this mystery; and so asserts that it is not a mystery passing human comprehension. But an examination of the solutions they severally propound shows them to be uniformly invalid. The analysis of every possible hypothesis proves, not simply that no hypothesis is sufficient, but that no hypothesis is thinkable. And thus the mystery which all religions recognize turns out to be a far more transcendent mystery than any of them suspect—not a relative, but an absolute mystery.

In other words, after all is said and done, there is a permanent occasion for religion, which lies in mystery, the mystery to which no powers of reasoning or rational explanation have satisfying access.

This led Spencer to say something about scientific pretensions. He believed that religious explanations constitute attempted translations of mystery into something explainable. In claiming to be able to know, understand, and explain the mystery—if only by giving it a name—religion transgresses into the field of science. Science, in turn, frequently forces religion to abandon its dogma. But then science makes a similar mistake, in Spencer's view, when it tries to replace religion with metaphysical terminology. When scientists do this, they transgress their own limitations. Sometimes science, after learning that it has overstepped its bounds, has functioned to restore the mystery; and the mystery is returned to its original place.

In approaching his subject in this manner, Spencer registered two large claims. First, he associated religion (that is, truly sustainable and certifiable religion) with reality's fundamental mysterious nature. Second, he provided an explanation for the "ongoing warfare between science and religion"—a conflict that will continue, so he estimated, "as long as the process of differentiation is incomplete." With respect to the latter point, he offered some predictions: "Gradually, as the limits of possible cognition are established, the causes of conflict will diminish. And a permanent peace will be reached when science becomes fully convinced that the mystery it contemplates is ultimate and absolute." Where will it end, and when? When will differentiation yield to integration? This is Spencer's answer:

> By continually seeking to know and being continually thrown back with a deepened conviction of the impossibility of knowing, we may keep alive the consciousness that it is both our highest wisdom and our highest duty to regard that through which all things exist as *The Unknowable*.

In summary, Herbert Spencer approached religion as being the mode of intelligence that is able to recognize and encounter mystery. By approaching the unknown, religion set in motion a process of progressive cognitive discernment. This process will continue as long as it remains necessary to differentiate one thing from another. But the permanent source of religion is mystery. Thus, over the course of its long career, religion has been called upon again and again to affirm the presence and power of the mysterious.

E. B. Tylor: The Emergence of a Science of Culture

Spencer carried on a lifelong conversation—sometimes rather caustically—with Sir Edward Burnett Tylor (1832–1917), who is also credited with fashioning evolutionist categories to trace the ongoing pathway of culture. Tylor is cited in the textbooks for his view that religion issues from animism (which, too summarily, is described as belief in souls or spirits). But his contribution to religious studies is much larger and more sophisticated than this. Our description of his views is based primarily on an analysis of his book, *Primitive Culture: Researches into the Development of Mythology, Philosophy, Religion, Language, Art and Custom*, which many regard as his most important work.

One of the cardinal assumptions with which Tylor began is that "mankind is homogeneous in nature, though placed in different grades of civilization." In Tylor's view, diverse cultures can be counted on to produce identical classes of artifacts, though certainly not at the same time and not always in the same way. Furthermore, in Tylor's view, the same cultural artifacts appear in particular contexts and locales according to a predictable sequence:

> The quality of mankind which tends to most make the systematic study of civilization possible is that remarkable tacit consensus of agreement which so far induces those populations to unite in the use of the same language, to follow the same religion and customary law, to settle down to the same general level of art and knowledge.

On this basis Tylor generalized:

> Progress, degradation, survival, revival, modification, are all modes of the connection that binds together the complex network of civilization. It needs but a glance into the trivial details of our own daily life to set us thinking how far we are really its originators, and how far but the transmitters and modifiers of the results of long past ages.

The case for development has been made. Tylor found confirmation of his views in the fact that the conditions of the earliest human beings mirror exactly the situation of modern savage [his word, not ours] tribes. That is, the earliest stage of human development (namely, the first stage in the long march toward civilization) is present in both instances. The main tendency of culture is described as the movement from savagery toward civilization. This occurs in stages, of course. In some locales, advances have hardly occurred at all. In other places, most forms of primitivism have been left behind almost totally. But while the movement between the primitive and civilized human states is correspondingly accelerated and decelerated, the stages themselves are cultural variants. Tylor thought there was ample empirical, anthropological evidence to support his view.

Having established this base, Tylor was free to move in any one of several directions. His overall intention was clear: to illustrate and support the thesis that "the savage state in some measure represents an early condition of mankind, out of which the higher culture has gradually been developed or evolved, by processes still in regular operation." Having affirmed this, he was free to chart the process of evolution, dividing its contents into distinguishable stages of periodization. Or, should he choose to, he could focus on any one or more of the periods of developments that had been thus demarcated.

Clearly, Tylor's interest focused more particularly on the first stage of human development, primitive culture, than it did on providing a full-scale history of culture. So that his endeavors in this regard would bear fruit, he decided first that he should identify those cultural forms, artifacts, and expressions that highly civilized people share with savage peoples. These include language, mythology, custom, and religion. Thus, second, he stated that his means of access to the primitive state, in addition to what he could learn by observing savage tribes (and interpreting others' reports about them) is a more calculated form of analogical inference. The basis for this second move is his assumption that "the civilized mind still bears vestiges, neither few nor slight, of a past condition from which savages represent the least, and civilized men the greatest advance." In other words, by delineating how something came to be, Tylor believed he could understand what that something is or what it was originally. To put the matter in a slightly different manner, Tylor supposed that on the basis of its surviving vestiges, one can reconstruct the society and culture of earlier times. Given these assumptions, the means of access to the earliest state of man is analogical. Tylor's analysis is therefore expanded into a version of the history of human culture conceived on the basis of an identification, description, and chronological tracing of selected ideal types. The vestiges of earlier days function as ideal types that are repeated over and over again, though in various degrees of fullness, as civilization marches on. The history of culture, in Tylor's rendition, becomes the history of the survival, reformulation, and redefinition of these preselected types.

Tylor's attempt to understand the mind of primitive peoples focused, as we have suggested, on language, mythology, custom, and religion. Each of these headings includes a variety of component entities. For example, the discussion of language includes careful treatment of gestures. The discussion of myth includes analyses of the means by which thought is composed and ideas are arranged and interrelated. The study of mythology tends to focus on recurrent imaginative processes, and points to a discussion of mental laws and "consistent structures of the mind." Thus, when Tylor refers to gestures, words, pictures, and writing, he has in fact distinguished some of the prominent ways in which thought gains expression. Gestures, words, pictures, and writing are categories of expression of thought.

It is in this context that much of what Tylor says regarding the close association between religion and animism is placed. A prime reason for proposing that religion be defined in terms of animism (in his words, "religion is belief in spiritual beings") is to enable missionaries, ethnographers, and others to have a more realistic sense of the levels and types of religious apprehension they will encounter on native soil. Tylor believed that the missionaries and others who deal with native tribes have probably failed to perceive the true religious character of tribal behavior because they have sought to approach the same through their understanding of religious beliefs, attitudes, and practices that belong to advanced stages of religious development. In other words, when religion is understood to consist of refined beliefs in God and sophisticated doctrines about life and death, and is associated with elaborate rituals and conceptualized mythological systems, much of what belongs to true tribal religion, Tylor fears, is "excluded from the religious category." When this happens, obviously, the religious significance of tribal behavior goes unrecognized.

As was his custom in working from products of cultural development back to their genetic sources, Tylor was concerned that interests in tribal behavior be reconstructed so that "the deeper motive that underlies" religion be properly discerned. Interpreting religion in its most elementary and fundamental sense, he wrote: "Here, so far as I can judge from the immense mass of accessible evidence, we have to admit that the belief in spiritual beings appears among all low races with whom we have attained to thoroughly intimate acquaintance." With all exceptions to the rule being accounted for in other ways, Tylor stated that whenever information has been accumulated regarding earliest peoples, "belief in spiritual beings" emerges as a necessary motive force. By "belief in spiritual beings," Tylor has reference to the "belief that man has a soul capable of existing apart from a body it belongs to, and continuing to live, for a time at least, after the body is dead and buried." "Soul" or "spirit" is defined as follows:

> It is a thin unsubstantial human image, in its nature a sort of vapor, film, or shadow; the cause of life and thought in the individual it animates; independently possessing the personal consciousness and volition of its corporeal owner, past or present; capable of leaving the body far behind, to flash swiftly from place to place: mostly impalpable and invisible, yet also manifesting physical power, and especially appearing to men waking or asleep as a phantasm separate from the body of which it bears the likeness: continuing to exist and appear to men after the death of that body: able to enter into, possess, and act in the bodies of other men, of animals, and even in things.

Tylor cited dreams as being one source of the belief in souls, for human shapes and forms appear in different modes in dreams and visions. He also listed waking and sleeping, undergoing a trance, recognizing disease, and questions about death as related sources of beliefs in souls:

> It seems as though thinking men, as yet at a low level of culture, were deeply impressed by two groups of biological problems. In the first place, what is it that makes the difference between a living body and a dead one; what causes waking, sleep, trance, disease, death? In the second place, what are those human shapes which appear in dreams and vision? Looking at these two groups of phenomena, the ancient savage philosophers probably made their first step by the obvious inference that every man has two things belonging to him, namely, a life and a phantom.

Then, having recognized the reality of both of these factors, the earliest human beings tended to conceive of the phantom as a kind of "second self." Tylor conjectured that "both are also perceived to be things separable from the body, the life as able to go away and leave it insensible or dead, the phantom as appearing to people at a distance from it." Then, when this conception was extended, it became appropriate to conceive of life and the phantom as being one:

> A second step would seem easy for savages to make, seeing how extremely difficult civilized men have found it to unmake. It is merely to combine the life and the phantom. As both belong to the body, why should they not also belong to one another, and be manifestations of one and the same soul? Let them be considered as united, and the result is that well-known conception which may be described as an apparition-soul, or a ghost-soul.

Thus, the animistic theory of vitality was interpreted by Tylor as the generative source of religion. Indications of the plausibility of this conclusion are implicit in our own language. Tylor called attention to the frequency with which such words as life, mind, soul, spirit, ghost, and so on are interchangeable. The same animistic theory of vitality finds expression in the belief that in dreams the sleeper's soul goes on journeys, that human souls sometimes come to visit the sleeper in dreams, and, of course, in perceptions of the close correlations between dreams and waking thoughts.

Tylor proposed that such apprehensions are possible because primitive human beings did not make rigorous distinctions between subject and object. Nor were they adept at differentiating imagination and reality. This implied that animism is not a valid philosophy once scientific knowledge has been introduced as norm. Once scientific knowledge comes to prominence, the content of a previous religious apprehension gets called by other names. For example, under the influence of scientific investigation, human beings recognize dreams to be dreams and the journeys that souls appear to make to involve the employment of figurative, metaphorical language.

Tylor recognized that within time, the primitive imagination (characterized by the animistic theory of vitality) must be abandoned in favor of a perspective that claims a clearer and more refined scientific accuracy. And yet, while refinements occur along the way—refinements that are both progressive and successive—there is an "unbroken line of mental connection" pertaining to souls and spirits, which stretches from the "savage fetish-worshipper" to "the civilized Christian."

In Tylor's view, animism is the generative source of religion. In asserting this, he did not mean that animism is religion's *sine qua non*, but only its generative source. He was altogether willing to leave the connections between primitive animistic belief and more highly developed theological doctrines to others. He claimed no special expertise in this area. His primary concern throughout was to depict the religious apprehension of primitive peoples.

Lang and Marett: Variations on Evolutionist Themes

From Tylor, the trajectories of thought about religion's origin and evolution move in several significant directions. One of the boldest, because it runs directly counter to Tylor's contentions, was that supplied by one of his students, the Scottish literary figure Andrew Lang (1844–1912). Because of the large range of subjects on which he published essays, Lang was frequently accused of being a dilettante. To be sure, his interests were extensive. Along with tutored research work in folklore and anthropology, he engaged in journalistic enterprises. He also collected fairy tales, rewrote fairy tales, composed new fairy tales, and wrote poetry. He was also taken by Homer's writings and became something of a specialist in giving them interpretation. He wrote a lengthy *History of English Literature* (1912), which was published just two days after his death.

Lang was suspicious and sharply critical of Tylor's hypotheses about the origin of religion and its roots in belief in souls. But there was much in Tylor with which Lang could agree. For example, he accepted evolutionism as the prevailing underlying pattern for religious development. He agreed with Tylor regarding the genesis of the belief in souls. He too suspected that such beliefs derive from psychic occurrences. He even found much cogency in the prominence Tylor gave to animism. But, sharing all of this, Lang found himself unable to accept many of the implications Tylor drew. For example, Lang challenged Tylor regarding the chronological primacy of the animistic stage. He contended that earlier stages of human awareness had preceded the animistic stage. The animistic stage was neither the first stage of human development nor the first chapter in the story of man's religious awareness.

Similarly, Lang questioned the accuracy of the chronology regarding the origin of belief in God. Against Tylor, Lang argued that the idea of God did not develop late in the development of self-consciousness. In fact, he disputed Tylor's contention that belief in God had its genesis in belief in souls. This is a significant alternative to Tylor's account. For in denying that belief in souls is the genetic source of belief in God, Lang really wanted, first, to reverse the chronological order, and, second, to abolish the causal relationship that regulated the two in Tylor's account. Giving expression to a viewpoint that was later to gain prominence in the writings of Wilhelm Schmidt, Lang argued that belief in God is found among the most primitive and simplest peoples. This fact would not seem to corroborate the conviction that belief in souls, when more fully developed and extended, produces belief (or faith) in identifiable deities. But it does imply that what primitive peoples did or did not believe in is a complicated matter, not easily reducible to a presumed animistic core:

> Now in addition to the objections already noted in passing, how can we tell that the Supreme Being of low savages was, in original conception, animistic at all? How can we know that he was envisioned originally as Spirit? We shall know that he probably was not, that the Maker and Father in Heaven, prior to Death, was merely regarded as a deathless Being, no question of "spirit" being raised. If so, animism was not needed for the earliest idea of a moral Eternal.

Having criticized Tylor in this way, Lang proceeded to make his own suggestion, drawing upon the functions of making and creating. Earliest human beings, he proposed, recognized that some of the items they encountered had been made or created by someone (or something) else. As Lang told of it:

> [A]s soon as man had the idea of "making" things, he might conjecture as to the maker of things which he himself had not made, and could not make. He would regard this unknown Maker as a "magnified non-natural man." . . . This conception of a magnified non-natural man, who is Maker, being given, his power would be recognized and fancy would clothe one who had made such useful things with certain other moral attributes, as of Fatherhood, goodness, and regard for the ethics of his children—these ethics having been developed naturally in the evolution of social life. In all this there is nothing "mystical," nor anything, as far as I can see, beyond the limited mental powers of any beings that deserve to be called human.

How Lang accounted for it is probably not as important as is his basic proposal that, logically and chronologically, the "indeterminate idea of a Supreme Being" may have occurred prior to the evolution of the idea of ghost or spirit. To say it with force: "The ghost theory . . . by the evidence of anthropology itself, is not needed for the evolution of ghost propitiation and genuine dead-ancestor worship. Therefore the high gods described were not necessarily once ghost—were not idealised mortal ancestors."

In sum, then, Andrew Lang criticized Tylor on grounds that animism is neither the necessary logical antecedent to theism nor a necessary chronological antecedent. Furthermore, he found animism to be an ineffective explanation for belief in God, which, he affirmed, seems present in tribes that exhibit little if any interest in ghosts and spirits. Not until Wilhelm Schmidt made similar proposals were Lang's views taken seriously. It was too easy for some of his hearers to attribute such views to Lang's dilettantish temper.

R. R. Marett's (1866–1943) position with regard to the origin and development of religion is subtle. He has frequently been described as having espoused a theory of "pre-animism" or even "anti-animism" when attempts are made to distinguish his viewpoint from that of Tylor. But a more responsible interpreta-tion finds Marett to have wanted to reconcile ideas and viewpoints he had uncov-ered in various theories and sourcebooks. Clearly he suffered from the fact that the presentation of his viewpoint by others was often simplistic and sloganized. Hence he felt obliged, again and again, to explain himself and to distinguish his own position from the prevailing misrepresentations.

From his own vantage point, his "chief concern," in his words, was "to urge that primitive or rudimentary religion, as we actually find it amongst savage peo-ples, is at once a wider, and in certain respects a vaguer, thing than 'the belief in spiritual beings' or Tylor's famous 'minimum definition' allows." This statement indicates that Marett did not reject animism out of hand. Rather, by broadening the base of application, he sought to clarify what should have been meant when the term was employed.

Marett's objection to Tylor's formulation focused chiefly on the ease with which animism could be employed as a *sine qua non*. Marett objected to identifying primitive religion with any one, pervasive common denominator. As an expanding and broadening alternative, he suggested first that, if there is animism, there is also a pre-animism and an extra-animism. But this simply meant that there are large ad-ditional non-animistic phenomena and data that belong in the picture and that tend to go unrecognized when the scholar's attention focuses too narrowly on animism.

Marett was not trying to trace religion's origin and evolution. Concerning origins, for example, he remained agnostic. "For me, the first chapter in the his-tory of religion remains in large part indecipherable," he asserted. This statement expressed his attitude regarding the suppleness and vagueness of "primitive" reli-gion. He was unwilling to reduce religion to a formula or even to isolate a funda-mental common denominator. To do either would give an inaccurate rendering of the situation with which scholars were intent on coming to terms. He argued that additional steps needed to be taken before such conclusions were even approach-able: "Before our science ventures to dogmatize about genesis, it must, I think, push on with the preliminary work of classifying its data under synoptic headings." The reason is that the first examples of religion are both broader and more complex than any narrow category of "animism" can acknowledge.

In addition to calling for a broadening of perspective and additional interpre-tive categories, Marett had some definitional proposals of his own. These carried him from the origin-and-development paradigm to a consideration of religion as a multifaceted organism. In fact, Marett referred to religion as an "organic complex of thought, emotion, and behavior," prefiguring the schools of thought that went to work after evolutionism was more thoroughly discredited. Marett understood religion (chiefly in "its psychological aspect") to be a "mode of social behavior." Then he argued that religion is furnished more by emotions than by ideas, since the emotions are more fundamentally the source of social behavior. "Thus awe, in the case of religion, will, in this view, have to be treated as a far more constant factor in religion than any particular conception of the awful." This insight enabled him to approach animistic theory from a psychological perspective. On balance, he understood animism to denote an idea (an intellectual construct) that, he surmised, must have had numerous psychological and emotional antecedents in the experiences of the first human beings. In short, before there were animistic conceptions there were experiential encounters with inexplicable vital forces.

In summary, then, Marett was neither anti-animist, pre-animist, non-animist, nor animist solely, but one who refused to portray animism in any of the ways that would make such typological references exact:

> In regard to religion thus understood I say not that its evolution proceeds from abstract to concrete—which would be meaningless—but that it proceeds from indistinct to distinct, from undifferentiated to differentiated, from incoherent to coherent. And that, I claim, as a hypothesis which has the best part of evolutionary science at its back.

In his view, the term *animism* (in all of its modalities) is an intellectual construct. Before yielding to any such constructs, religion ought to denote primary, first-order, almost raw human experience, and particularly in its emotional or psychological aspects.

Thus, by working against Tylor and by treating the origin of religion by broadening and expanding the operational framework, Marett moved effectively toward another intellectual orientation. In referring to the ways in which religious emotion, behavior, and thought stand in reciprocal relationships, he previewed some treatments of religion as "cultural system" (for example) that were worked out by subsequent thinkers, by Clifford Geertz in particular.

Marett knew what he was doing. He recognized that Durkheim's theories could become instrumental in giving the study of religion a new focus. Without deliberate reference to Durkheim, he also acknowledged that social psychology constituted the prime methodological means of access to religious phenomena, since religion consists of emotional, behavioral, and rational components. Moving away from an emphasis on origin-and-development, Marett came to approach religion as a sociological datum or, as it was to be said later on, as a sociocultural system.

It is significant that Marett's alternative to origin-and-development theory is a position that has been influenced by Durkheim, for we recall that the same culmination can be associated with the distinctively French line of progression through evolution theory—from the dominant precursors through Saint-Simon, August Comte, to Lévy-Bruhl. Eventually, with both English and French contexts, the interest in isolating religion's *primordium* came to focus on *primordia*. Within both contexts, the expectation that scholarly inquiry would uncover a single causal factor yielded to a recognition that scholarly inquiry needed to focus on a number of factors all at once. Thus, instead of attempting to identify the unambiguous simple core element, intellectual inquiry worked to make sense of pluralized organic coordinates. This simply describes the process by which an original schema was revised as it was used and tested. That is, before the paradigm was criticized in total, it was criticized for this and that detail. Without the initial workings of the paradigm, the inquirers would not have known how to criticize the paradigm. Such is the process by which scholarship progresses.

Wilhelm Schmidt: Antievolutionist Monotheism

For example, Wilhelm Schmidt (1868–1954) was sharply critical of evolutionist theory because of what it seemed to say about the traditional monotheistic grounding of religious belief. A German anthropologist, linguist, ethnologist, and, by vocation, Catholic priest, Schmidt found support from Lang in challenging the views of Tylor, Spencer, and other developmentalists. In Schmidt's view, the earliest human beings, regardless of where they are found, believed in a supreme being. Thus, monotheism is not a late arrival within the history of religious consciousness. Rather, it represents the earliest perception of deity. In Schmidt's view, there was monotheism before there was polytheism: polytheism, that is to say, represents monotheism in a degenerated state.

Schmidt did not deny the fact and force of evolution. Nor was he unaware of the variety, variability, and flexibility in belief and attitude that was characteristic of the first human beings. He recognized that societies and cultures develop into more complex states, and that evolution is a social and cultural fact. He found it easy to refer to "stages of development." After all, tribes, peoples, and societies did not and do not remain the same. Yet in granting that evolutionary processes are present in human development, Schmidt could not agree that they are uniform: not all tribes and peoples evolve or progress at the same rate of speed, through the same motions, by means of the same influences. And, most important of all, the fact of progress and evolution cannot be employed to question or undermine the fact— Schmidt believed it to be an empirical fact—that the first human beings had a conception of the Supreme Being. In his view, the first dawning of religion was inherently and unquestionably monotheistic.

Schmidt devoted his two-volume work *Der Ursprung der Gottesidee* to this subject. It was written between 1912 and his death in 1954 (the twelfth volume being published in 1955). Whether his attention was trained on the Pygmy tribes, the Tierra del Fueguans, the Bushmen, the Kurhai, Kulin, Yuin, or the native North Americans, Schmidt argued that self-consistent attitudes and viewpoints toward deity were indeed expressed therein, viewpoints that were unmistakably monotheistic. He explained this occurrence as follows:

Man needs to find a rational cause; this is satisfied by the concept of a Supreme Being who created the world and those that dwell therein. Man had social needs; these find their support in belief in a Supreme Being who is also the Father of mankind, who founded the family and to whom, therefore, man and wife, parents and children, brothers and sisters and kinsfolk owe allegiance. Man has moral needs; and these too find their stay and support in a Supreme Being who is lawgiver, overseer, and judge of the good and the bad, and is himself free from all moral taint. Man's emotional wants, trust, love, thankfulness, are satisfied by such a being, a Father from whom comes all good and nothing but good.

But this is just the beginning. Schmidt continues:

Man needs a protector to whom he can resign himself; this need is supplied by this Being, who is supreme and great above all others. Thus in all these attributes this exalted figure furnished primitive man with the ability and the power to live and love, to trust and to work, the prospect of becoming the master of the world and not its slave, and the aspirations of yet higher, supermundane goals beyond.

Having amassed this evidence, Schmidt concludes:

Only through this conception of deity can we explain the power of our earliest ancestors to struggle onwards; and the most precious of human energies—labor, responsibility, aspirations, upward feeling for the unity of all mankind—still trace their origin to these primeval days. We thus find, among a whole series of primitive races, a notable religion, many-branched and thoroughly effective.

Schmidt, following accepted practice, referred to the idea as *Urmonotheismus* (primordial monotheism), but he was not interested only in having the basis to posit this concept. He was also interested in being able to enumerate some of the characteristics of this monotheistic God, or Ur-deity.

As it turned out, these characteristics bear striking resemblance to the sanctioned theological attributes of the God many Christians worship. For instance, Schmidt referred to the eternity of God, noting that God was understood to have existed before all other beings were brought into existence. God is also regarded as being omniscient, all-knowing. He is both beneficent and moral. Likewise God is omnipotent, all-powerful. God, as the Supreme Being, is understood to have the authority to punish evil and reward good behavior. In thus meting out rewards and punishments, God also insures that the universal moral code is safeguarded. But this is not all. The Supreme Being is also creator, though Schmidt admitted that the name "creator" does not occur as frequently among primitive peoples as do references to the deity's "power to create."

Thus, when one reads through Schmidt's account, one cannot help but notice that the catalog of divine attributes which, he claims, is an accurate rendering of the religious beliefs of the earliest human beings is strikingly similar to the list of divine attributes set forth in Catholic catechetical manuals. Schmidt wanted to affirm that the God the earliest human beings acknowledged is the God Christians worship. There is but one true God. Monotheism, that is to say, is universal. The one true God who was revealed more fully in the Christian narrative, the God whom Christians worship, has also been recognized, no matter how dimly, by a host of persons in a host of tribes reaching back to the beginnings of recorded history, and even before.

> Comparing the primitive cultures with the later ones, we may lay down the general principle that in none of the latter is the Supreme Being to be found in so clear, so definite, vivid, and direct a form as among peoples belonging to the former. We may now proceed to supplement this by another principle of no less importance. This Supreme Being is to be found among all the peoples of the primitive culture, not indeed everywhere in the same form . . . but still everywhere prominent enough to make his dominant position indubitable.

In Schmidt's view, monotheism functions as the genetic source of religion. It is consonant with religion's *primordium*. In some respects, monotheism is the religious *primordium*; and it is *primordium* and not *primordia*. Thus the human witness to the power of deity is uniform. What was still is. What is has always been. The God the first human beings worshiped, in Schmidt's view, is also the God of modern societies. Called by various names, it is one and the same God, nevertheless.

Raffaele Pettazzoni: Religious Belief among Primitive Peoples

The Italian scholar Raffaele Pettazzoni (1883–1959), well known in scholarly circles for his large study of divine omniscience (entitled *L'omniscienza di Dio*) argued, like Schmidt, for a belief in a supreme being among earliest societies. Unlike Schmidt, however, Pettazzoni did not want to argue on behalf of an original monotheism. He knew what Schmidt had wanted to do: to reconcile the "theological speculations concerning deity" with "the data of anthropology." He knew, too, that Schmidt coveted scientific support for the Christian doctrine of revelation. But he judged the entire enterprise to be suspect, no matter how much he may have been sympathetic to it on personal religious grounds. In Pettazzoni's view:

> The theory of primitive monotheism is founded on an equivocation and on an error. The equivocation consists in calling by the name of monotheism what is nothing of the kind, in mistaking for true monotheism the savage peoples' idea of Supreme Beings. The error consists in supposing that to be primitive, which is not so, in transferring to the most archaic religious culture the idea of God which properly belongs

to our western civilization, that which found its way from the Old Testament into the New and then was elaborated by Christianity.

In other words, Pettazzoni acknowledged with Schmidt that singular deities were acknowledged among earliest peoples, but he could not agree that this sufficiently makes the case for a primitive monotheism. Pettazzoni charged Schmidt with working with a highly developed, Westernized, Christianized conception of deity, transferring this conception back to earliest historical times, then claiming that the two forms of deity were indeed identical. According to Pettazzoni, this equation is produced by confused projection or misguided transferring of qualities. While acknowledging that the earliest human beings may have worshiped a supreme being, Pettazzoni was unwilling to identify this being with whatever theological elaboration of the concept of deity is found in Christian dogmatics:

> What we find in them [primitive religions] is the notion of a Supreme Being. Is it allowable to identify such an idea with monotheism? If we do, are we not running the risk of importing among the uncivilized [peoples] an idea peculiar to the sphere of the great modern monotheistic faiths?

In other words, when one wants to learn about monotheism, one should not consult the beliefs and attitudes of the first human beings, but instead "the great monotheistic religions, those whose monotheism is past all doubt, which have declared themselves monotheistic from their very birth, and have always represented themselves as that and nothing else. . . ."

Part of what Pettazzoni achieved was cogent criticism of Schmidt. But after doing so, he offered proposals of his own. That is, after disengaging the religious sensibilities of the earliest human beings from the belief system of demonstrable monotheistic religions, he pushed intellectual inquiry in several directions. He was concerned with tracing the true genesis of monotheism in those instances where it is actually present: in Judaism, Christianity, and Islam. In each of these religions, Pettazzoni noted that monotheism was the product of antagonisms resolved within a previous polytheistic religious framework. "Every one of them [the monotheistic religions] arises as a new religion out of a previously existing polytheistic environment." Pettazzoni could be more specific. In every instance, monotheism results from the resolution of a controversy and is the product of the success of an identifiable reform movement. To take the case of Judaism: "We can verify this for the case of Israel, the monotheism of Moses and the prophets, as opposed to the polytheistic cults of the Ancient East." The same principle holds for Christianity and Islam. In the latter instance, the prophet Mohammed pitted his monotheistic reforms against "the polytheism of the Iranian peoples' traditional religion," and was successful in doing so. The pattern is the same in each instance, in Pettazzoni's view. Monotheism develops out of resolution of stresses and strains within polytheistic frameworks. This observation leads Pettazzoni to conclude:

> Monotheism therefore is later than polytheism. Only, it does not evolve from it, as the evolutionist theory supposed. Far from developing out of it by an evolutionary process, monotheism takes shape by means of a revolution. Every coming of a monotheistic religion is conditioned by a religious revolution. Far from arising out of speculative thought, the formation of monotheism springs from religious life, from a fulness of religious life, such as has but seldom come to pass in the course of human history, and only by an unusual coincidence of favorable circumstances.

This observation provided the basis on which Pettazzoni could offer an assessment of the origins of the idea of a single supreme being:

> The idea of the Supreme Being is not the reflexion of an abstract monotheistic idea of God made up of all the highest attributes theoretically inherent therein, one of which is omniscience. It is a concrete historical formation which takes different shapes, including at times diverse attributes, according to the cultural environment in which it appears.

Then, to make certain that his views will not be confused with those of Tylor, Schmidt, or any of the others who have offered opinions on the matter, Pettazzoni offered this summary judgment:

> This is not to say that monotheism is derived from polytheism by a gradual and inevitable development, as the evolutionist theory would have it. It derives from it, if at all, by revolution, by a radical religious upheaval, the work of some great religious personality, the herald of a new world.

The conclusion follows: Despite their worship of a singular supreme being, the earliest human beings could not have been monotheistic in this prescribed sense of the term.

Yet, once the distinction had been made, Pettazzoni still had the large task of explaining how it happened that the earliest human beings were preoccupied with a singular supreme being. There was no short answer to this question. Indeed, Pettazzoni found the question so rich that his response, *L'omniscienza di Dio*, came to six hundred pages. Pettazzoni employed the category of omniscience to fix and illustrate the differences between actual historical primitive religious structure and a properly articulated monotheism. His chief contention was that omniscience is a divine (and, on occasion, a human) attribute attached to no "particular religious environment, monotheistic, polytheistic, or other." Characteristically, omniscience is attributed to deity, but this does not necessarily imply "supreme being." In other words, contrary to Schmidt's view, Pettazzoni found that omniscience need not be attached to monotheism: "The attribute of omniscience is therefore not inherent in the monotheistic idea of God, nor is that of a Supreme Being, nor again is that of deity in general." Rather, the power to be all-knowing is closely associated with the power to be all-seeing, and both, it seems, are typical of sky-gods and astral deities.

> The plain fact is that according to the evidence it is mostly sky-gods and astral gods, or gods connected with the heavenly realms of light, to whom omniscience is ascribed. This is not to be wondered at, if we remember that . . . divine omniscience is a visual omniscience, which naturally depends upon light. . . . The attribute of omniscience is not generally implicit in the idea of deity generally, but organically connected with the peculiar nature of all-knowing gods, who are all-knowing because all-seeing and all-seeing because they are luminous, as being in the first place sky- and astral gods . . . .

Therefore, in Pettazzoni's view, omniscience is an attribute of a specific type or class of deity. It is not common to all deities, or even inherent in the concept of deity itself. Consequently, omniscience cannot be conceived in comprehensive but only in specific terms. In the case of primitive religions, omniscience always implies something manifestly specific. It is not that the deity knows all things, for example, but, instead, that what human beings say and do is known and understood, and is recognized as such. Words, actions, inmost thoughts, and secret desires, because they are understood to be seen and known by God, are the sources of the notions of divine omniscience. Pettazzoni explained:

> The manner in which divine omniscience comes about is quite definite, for it is founded upon a power of universal vision, completed on occasion by similar powers of hearing, by omnipresence and the like. This divine omniscience is not merely passive and contemplative, but gives rise to a sanction, generally punitive, which in its turn is not of any and every kind, for usually its instrument is the weather.

More specifically:

> The elements that make up the complex of divine omniscience, subject and object, purpose and method, conditions and effects, have an organic connection with one another. An internal logic joins the luminous nature of the omniscient beings with the powers of sight on which their universal knowledge depends, the visibility (from above) of human actions (also the audibility of human speech and so on), and the meteorological nature of the sanction which is attached. By virtue of this internal correlation and interdependence of its component parts, the complex of ideas concerning divine omniscience is really a complex, that is to say, an organic whole, well-defined.

This self-sustaining complex, this well-defined organic whole, is very much different from a monotheistic structure. Similarly, the deportment of omniscience within this organic complex is different from the role played by omniscience in monotheism. The former complex of ideas belongs to an anthropomorphic and mythic framework. The second structure is the product of additional and subsequent intellectual activity. And yet, omniscience appears in both contexts. Pettazzoni's point was that the two examples of omniscience are not rooted in the same way, since the contexts in which they are placed are incomparable linguistically and dissimilar ideologically.

Contrary both to the methods and contentions of the evolutionists, Pettazzoni insisted that all postulations about omniscience be rooted within carefully defined cultural contexts. It is not surprising, then, that he also defined religion in such cultural-contextual terms. He understood each culture to be an organic complex within which there are nexuses between the elements that comprise the organism. "Religion," Pettazzoni affirmed, "is one of these elements, and the Supreme Being is part of religion." In this way Pettazzoni acknowledged the pervasiveness of the belief in a supreme being in primitive cultures, and contended, against Wilhelm Schmidt, that this belief is something quite different from any sort of *Urmonotheismus*. His judgment in this respect is based on a comparative treatment of omniscience. Subsequently he was to conduct a comparative study of confession of sins for the same purpose. On this latter issue he concluded:

> The differences that divide the savage rite from the Christian sacrament are many and deep. The two have nothing in common, neither the form of the ceremony nor the accompanying circumstances nor the motives which bring them nor the kinds of sin which they deal with.

Once again, the alternative to the origin-and-development instinct is an approach to the subject matter that insists that all elements of religion be placed and treated in cultural contexts. What may appear on the surface to be the same or similar frequently turns out to be decidedly different when the distinctiveness of the context is acknowledged.

Evolutionism, as an interpretive tool, raised numerous problems. Pettazzoni was aware of most of them, but he chose not to attack or defend the schema itself. Wilhelm Schmidt was less cordial, as we have seen. And yet Schmidt's criticism of origin-and-development theory can be regarded as a side skirmish for him. His more basic intention was to secure a place for Christian theological interpretation in the history of religious consciousness. Under those auspices, Schmidt worked to identify a religious *primordium* in both history-of-religion and theological terms.

The more forceful and sustained critique of the evolutionist approach came from those scholars who shifted from a single to a plural focus, and who abandoned the quest for origins in favor of descriptions of organisms. This led to a shifting of allegiances from one mode of inquiry to another. As we shall observe, the transfer was facilitated by some major criticisms of the original orientation.

The Development of
Antievolutionist Views

It happened here, there, and everywhere. Evolutionism, with its attendant progressivist understanding of the workings of history, seemed to be reflected with such impressive validation that most attention had been focused on attaining an accurate understanding of distinctions between stages. Indeed, scholarly interest had virtually been concentrated on equating the onset of distinct stages with the cultivation of distinct mental capacities, all of which tended to argue that the occurrence of religion came very early in the history of humankind. But perhaps facts about religion were much less known than facts about distinctive mental habits and practices. Thus, it was not always clearly demonstrated that the hypotheses that developed had verification capabilities in the religious beliefs, practices, and attitudes that were being referenced. What seemed better known was the way in which the development of human consciousness could be segmentally chronicled.

Questions were bound to arise. Geo Widengren (b.1907), Uppsala historian of religions, wrote a book entitled *Religionens Ursprung*, in which he challenged and attempted to discredit the evolutionary viewpoint. Indeed, Widengren challenged the fundamental hypothesis directly: he rejected the idea that religions always develop from simple to more complex. When this hypothesis was being honored, the scholar of religion could work back from complexity to singularity, and thus to an eventual identification of a primordial *sine qua non*. In challenging this assumption Widengren also raised serious questions concerning the equating of "chronologically first" with "phenomenologically primitive." Said clearly, the religions of earliest peoples were not necessarily the most simple or the most primitive. Nor are the religions of subsequent peoples necessarily more complex or sophisticated than the religions of the first peoples. In Widengren's mind, there is no necessary correlation between being "precivilized" in a cultural sense and holding to simple religious views. Under this sort of analytical questioning, the assumptions under which the search for the origin of religion was undertaken encountered some tough resistance.

Widengren found support for his views in the writings of the American anthropologist Franz Boas (1858–1942), who argued consistently and persistently throughout his long career that "there is no fundamental difference in the ways of thinking of primitives and civilized." This statement puts the matter in negative terms. Put positively, Boas contended that physical endowment and cultural experience work together to form human character, wherever one finds it. Further, he found this to be true regardless of the time or the place to which peoples are oriented. Boas was familiar with the best of the claims on behalf of evolutionism. Thus his reaction against that theory is based on something more than rejections of the familiar equations between child life and primitive life, or unsound mental life and normal primitive life. Such equations appeared to Boas as "fancies in which neither the aspect of primitive nor that of civilized life is sustained by tangible evidence."

The more solid bases for evolutionary theory can also be challenged, though they must be taken with more seriousness. Boas perceived that the concept of evolutionism presumes the fact of unilinear cultural development. A theory of unilinear cultural development holds that

> different groups of mankind started at a very early time from a general condition of lack of culture; and, owing to the unity of the human mind and the consequent similar response to outer and inner stimuli, developed everywhere approximately along the same lines, making similar inventions and developing similar customs and beliefs.

Boas found the theory intriguing, and yet his archaeological findings led him to challenge it. Support for the theory would require the recurrence of step-by-step cultural progression among the peoples of humankind, and this the archaeologist simply cannot verify:

> While it is certainly true that analogues can be found between the types of culture represented by primitive peoples and those conditions which prevailed among the ancestors of the present civilized peoples at the dawn of history, and that these analogues are supported by the evidence furnished by survivals, the evidence of archaeology does not support the complete generalization. The theory of parallel development, if it is to have any significance, would require that among all branches of mankind the steps of invention should have followed, at least approximately, in the same order, and that no important gaps should be found. The facts, so far as known at the present time, are entirely contrary to this view.

In other words, because growth depends on the contrapuntal play of a number of variables—principally, physical endowment and cultural experience—it does not necessarily occur uniformly or unilinearly except where the variables have been influenced in identical or similar ways. Therefore, the unilinear pattern of development would apply only in those situations "in which the same group of people are involved and in which the same kind of activity persists." Furthermore, Boas did not believe that one can certify that "every people in an advanced stage of civilization must have passed through all the stages of development which we may gather by an investigation of all the types of culture which occur all over the world."

Boas' contentions were put with force and zeal by two of his students, Robert H. Lowie (1883–1957) and Paul Radin (1883–1959). For Lowie and Radin, it was not primarily a matter of discrediting the methodological use of evolutionism in the studies of early cultures, but a demand to fashion a viable methodological alternative. Both, under Boas' influence, developed positions that concentrated on the intrinsic patterns of sociocultural organization of specific tribes. Both, significantly, turned their attention to Native American tribes: Lowie engaged in detailed research of the Crow Indians, for example, while Radin analyzed the culture of the Winnebago tribe. Radin also pioneered in the use of autobiographical documents to gain access to the internal, intrinsic makeup of the tribe. In expressing his strategy in concerning himself with *The Autobiography of a Winnebago Indian*, Radin wrote:

> One of the greatest drawbacks in the study of primitive peoples is the difficulty, one might almost say the impossibility, of obtaining an inside view of their culture from their own lips and by their own initiative . . . .
>
> For a long time most ethnologists have realized that the lack of "atmosphere" in their descriptions is a very serious and fundamental defect, and that this defect could only be properly remedied by having a native himself give an account of his particular culture. Unfortunately, however, natives never spend much time trying to get a general idea of their culture and are consequently unable to describe it when pressed . . . . Unprepared as a primitive man is to give a well-rounded and complete account of his culture, he has always been willing to narrate snatches of autobiography . . . .

Thus, Radin turned to autobiography as a way of filling in the details of "atmosphere": "Atmosphere" has reference to "presenting the facts in an emotional setting."

The same sort of multidimensional, coordinated sociocultural, "atmospheric" approach is recommended by Lowie, who, after surveying the history of ethnological theory for more than a century, recommended the following as the goal of anthropological research:

> [W]hatever preference the individual worker may gratify, our science as a whole can neglect no aspect of social life as intrinsically inferior to the rest. Specifically, material objects must be studied as embodiments of their makers' craftsmanship, aesthetic taste or spiritual aspirations. Subjective attitudes and personality must also be investigated as social symbols . . . . This topical breadth will be matched by the massiveness of the regional approach.

It is understandable that Lowie, given these interests, also turned his attention to kinship theory. The study of kinship makes the intrinsic organization and coordination of a tribe perceptible. It happened this way also, as we shall see, in the development of contextualist approaches.

Origin-and-Development Revised: Radcliffe-Brown and Malinowski

This development can be perceived in the writings of British theorist A. R. Radcliffe-Brown (1881–1955), whom some refer to as the father of modern anthropology. Radcliffe-Brown was committed to a process orientation (if not to evolutionism, *per se*), and his works are dotted with references to the contentions of Herbert Spencer. It is clear that he regarded Spencer's insights as a stimulating point of departure. But, when thinking about process, he was more microscopic than macroscopic. His concern was not to reconstruct the grand sweep of anthropological history in process-dominated terms. Instead, he was content to treat this or that particular social system as a process rather than as an entity. This follows from his conviction that social systems must be examined in dynamic rather than in static terms. For Radcliffe-Brown, the fundamental frame of reference is contextualist rather than evolutionist, but within the context process rules:

> My own view is that the concrete reality with which the social anthropologist is concerned in observation, description, comparison and classification, is not any sort of entity but a process, the process of social life. The unit of investigation is the social life of some particular region of the earth during a certain period of time. The process itself consists of an immense multitude of actions and interactions of human beings, acting as individuals or in combinations or groups. Amidst the diversity of the particular events there are discoverable regularities, so that it is possible to give statements or descriptions of certain *general features* of the social life of a selected region. A statement of such significant general features of the process of social life constitutes a description of what may be called a *form of social life*. My conception of social anthropology is as the comparative theoretical study of forms of life amongst primitive peoples.

Thus, there is need to view social reality as process and organic coordination simultaneously.

Process terminology is retained, but it is fitted to its own context. Radcliffe-Brown uses the word *dynamics* frequently, but it too is treated in contextualist terms. He talks of the need to study "social dynamics" so as to establish "generalisations about how social systems change." This implies, in turn, that analyses of social systems will take cognizance of the dynamic element to the fullest extent methodologically possible. But the focus is on the system, a system regulated by a process. The system is the comprehensive term, and process is significant as a regulator of the dynamics of the system.

Radcliffe-Brown's departure from evolutionist conceptualization is particularly apparent when he treats religion. A typical evolutionist attitude would relate religion to magic and science. Radcliffe-Brown, however, treated religion alongside morality and law, understanding all of these to be essential elements or components of "the social machinery." In his view, religion is necessary to the makeup or constitution of a society. It functions to articulate the society's sense of dependence. The articulation of the sense of dependence is made coherent with the society's sense of obligation and its sanctioning of the rules of behavior. Always, religion is viewed as being party to the general makeup of a society. The process temperament is retained, but outside the evolutionist schema.

A similar transition is perceptible in the writings of Bronislaw Malinowski (1884–1942), a contemporary of Radcliffe-Brown's, whose initial point of departure was made explicit in the title of his most influential essay, *Magic, Science and Religion.* Malinowski knew the history of evolutionist inquiry into religion very well. He was also well acquainted with the classic *sine qua non* approaches. Thus, his essay reads like a comprehensive assessment of the methodological stances that had been tested before his time. Tylor, Frazer, Lang, Marett, Schmidt, Lévy-Bruhl—all of these "origin-and-development" figures are given place. But in his description of the attitude of Lévy-Bruhl, Malinowski makes a significant transition. From this point on, he is deep into the insights of Robertson Smith and Emile Durkheim. Robertson Smith captures his attention for his contention that primitive religion "was essentially an affair of the community rather than of individuals." Malinowski refers to this principle as "a Leitmotiv of modern research." Durkheim he finds convincing because of his correlation of "the religious" with "the social."

Malinowski's alternative to "origin-and-development" is a view of the *composite.* Instead of viewing magic, religion, and science as successive modes that are regulated by an ongoing, developmental continuum, he understands them to be interrelated components of the social matrix. Each has a unique function. These functions do not belong to any era, epoch, stage, or state of mental, emotional, or conceptual development. Therefore, instead of employing the language of developmental stages, Malinowski refers to the "three-cornered constellation of magic, religion, and science." It is "three-cornered" because it belongs to a "constellation" of components. The word "constellation" signals that the conceptual framework has been revised. The components of the original sequence have been retained: the prime elements are indeed magic, religion, and science. But the interrelationships between them are much more complicated than the original formulas indicated. The prevailing interpretive scheme can no longer be held together by the resources of the evolutionist model. In Malinowski's work, an obvious turn has been taken toward the imagery of organic coordination.

Summary Criticism: E. E. Evans-Pritchard

The classic summary-critique of evolutionist theory, as applied to "theories of primitive religion," was presented under the same title by E. E. Evans-Pritchard (1902–1973), a student of Radcliffe-Brown's. Acknowledging that his evaluation may appear to some as being "severe and negative," Evans-Pritchard traced the history of evolutionistic theory from its origins to its mid-twentieth-century representations. Along the way he examined the dominant sociological, psychological, and anthropological approaches to religion within both British and French schools of thought. Particularly interested in examining the logic of the approaches—that is, the assumptions on which methodological strategies as well as the prominent reasoning processes are based— Evans-Pritchard found numerous examples of questionable procedure. Even though the theories invited discrediting, Evans-Pritchard thought there was value in their having been posited.

> If we are now able to see the errors in these theories purporting to account for primitive religions, it is partly because they were set forth, thereby inviting logical analysis of their contents and the testing of them against recorded ethnological fact and in field research.

Yet his ability to perceive something positive in the enterprise did not persuade him to qualify his conclusion that the theories of religion's origin and development are of questionable explanatory value: "Indeed, I have to conclude that I do not feel that on the whole the different theories we have reviewed, either singly or taken together, give us much more than common-sense guesses, which for the most part miss the mark." The prime reason that their utility is suspect is that they have been produced by a question that is wrongly put: the origin of religion cannot be uncovered because "origin" itself is inaccessible. "About all these broadly speaking intellectualist theories we must say that, if they cannot be refuted, they also cannot be sustained, and for the simple reason that there is no evidence about how religious beliefs originated." Thus, believing that the theories cannot be argued persuasively one way or the other, Evans-Pritchard suggested that the theorists of primitive religions should shift their focus from origins and development to intrinsic relationships: "the writers were seeking for explanations in terms of origins and essences instead of relations." Had they been searching out relationships, they would have phrased questions that were equipped to elicit compelling responses. But to do this, they needed to shift their attention from an anticipated single explanatory source to the complex interaction between a multiplicity of ingredients.

And this seems to be the story. The search for origins always focuses attention, eventually, on the nature of the originative context, and the originative context can hardly be interpreted or described in terms of one isolatable, distinguishable feature. Rather, intellectual attention is always evoked by the diverse kinds of components that belong to the originative context. The intention, from here, is to understand and illustrate how all of these elements come or belong together. Thus, instead of discovering a *primordium* for religion, the story of the search for that *primordium* stimulates a wealth of materials which demonstrate clearly that the religious factor is but one of the fundamental components of the collective life. The quest for a single *primordium* uncovers and sometimes unlocks a plurality of *primordia*. Within the context of plurality, it is appropriate to identify religion as either the basis or means of coordination. The phrase "religion as cultural system" denotes this function. Or religion can be included as one of the units that are being coordinated. But when this happens, clearly, another paradigm has been invoked.

Before we turn to an analysis of another orientation, however, we must ask if this outcome was not implicit at the starting point. At least as early as Durkheim—for in Durkheim the matter is made explicit—it is understood that there is no *primordium* but only *primordia*. Those who persist in searching for a *primordium* (witness E. B. Tylor) are forced rigorously to deal with the criticism that the selected (yes, preselected) *primordium* cannot be expanded far, widely, or deeply enough (witness R. R. Marett or E. B. Tylor) to account for the incidence and formation of the large assortment of ingredients that the search for origins uncovers. Soon, it seems, the focus shifts from origins to process of formation, or, if both are retained, to the rudiments of the original formation. The attempt to work back through a series of developmental stages to the beginning is replaced by a descriptive account of organic formation. In the original Durkheimian version, this account tends to apply primarily to the earliest example: to primitive religious consciousness. But, as the next chapter will illustrate, the same focus can be trained upon any of the other almost countless instances of sociocultural religious coordination that have marked the ongoing history of humankind. There need be no compulsion any longer that the normative element be placed chronologically first.

We cannot leave a survey of attempts to identify religion's origin or to trace its development without making reference to an intriguing attempt to revive evolutionist theory within the scholarly study of religion. We have already observed that when origin-and-development interest is abandoned, it is frequently replaced by the recognition that religion is a complex but organically coordinated cultural system. Thus, the shift from one interest to the other invokes a change in mode of inquiry. Religion's organic system is depicted differently from religion as *primordium*. The focus differs, as does the methodological interest through which the subject is approached. But what about an origin-and-development focus that is cognizant of these differentiating factors?

The Evolutionist Model Revived: Robert Bellah's Proposals

When we call attention to this modal shift, we should also be prepared for the possibility of a fusion. When the models are combined, religion is approached as an organic system that can be treated in developmental—yes, even in evolutionary—terms. Such is the prospect held out in some of Robert Bellah's (b.1927) essays, within which an argument is set forth concerning the development of religion as symbol system from lesser to more complex forms. Bellah's viewpoint is instructive.

In reviving evolutionist thinking, Bellah is specific about its point of application. It is not that earliest human beings were either less or more fully religious than subsequent human beings. Neither is Bellah proposing that the deity has evolved. It is rather that the symbolization of religion has become more complex. Such symbolization is more complex by virtue of the fact that the societies to which it relates have also become increasingly complex. That is, the symbolization itself has undergone a process of development.

Giving religion the working definition of "a set of symbolic forms and acts that relate man to the ultimate conditions of his existence," Bellah has noted that monotheistic religions "involve a much more differentiated symbolization of, and produce a much more complex reaction to the ultimate conditions of human existence than do primitive religions." It is not purely and simply a matter of religion's advancement from simple to complex forms. Rather, societies evolve into advanced stages of complexity. When they do, their religious components and qualities are encouraged to keep pace, for religious expression and religious understanding are always coordinant with social organization.

In other words, the characteristics of a religion of a given society are influenced by established relationships within that society. Consequently, as sociocultural organization becomes more detailed, intricate, and complicated, so also does symbolic religious interaction become more highly sophisticated. Sociocultural development is mirrored in the conception and depiction of the human's relationship to the ultimate conditions of existence. Increased differentiation and complexity at one level produces increased differentiation and complexity at all levels of sociocultural organization. Or, in slightly different words, increased organizational differentiation and complication is interlaced with increased symbolizational differentiation and complication.

Illustrating his proposal, Bellah distinguished a series of stages—from (1) primitive, (2) archaic, (3) historic, (4) early modern, to (5) modern—in the evolution of religious consciousness. In each case, he sought to depict the relationships that pertain between the form of social organization and the conception of the ultimate conditions of human existence. His expressed intention was to

> examine at each stage the kind of symbol-system involved, the kind of religious action which occurs, the kind of social organization in which the action occurs, and the implications for social action in general that the religious action contains.

For example, one large difference between primitive and archaic religion is that the latter depicts mythical beings in a much more definite, less tentative and fluid manner. Coupled with this is an increased specificity and definiteness regarding the principles of social organization. At the stage of development of archaic religion, things are given both specific and proper place. So also is symbolic structure made definite. Priests assume specific and concrete roles. The cosmos is populated in a specific way. Patterns of worship and sacrifice are regulated by particular prescriptions. The systematic character of both religion and sociocultural organization develops in a way that is only foreshadowed in primitive societies. As this process of increased differentiation and greater complexity moves forward, it encourages subsequent stages in human cultural and religious development.

Bellah does not want to say that modern humans are any more or less religious than their earlier counterparts. It is not in such terms that the evolutionary process is worked out. Nor is he willing to call one of the early or later stages a "religious era" as distinct from a stage that is either "pre-" or "postreligious." The age in which humans currently live is depicted, significantly, not as being "postreligious," but as being "posttraditional." The religious dimension can be perceived at each stage in the evolutionary process, but, of course, in terms that are appropriate to the larger social and cultural conditions and circumstances that pertain. In short, Bellah's view can be classified as a revised version of evolutionism that is nurtured by the dynamics of organic coordination. In his work, evolutionism has been revived and updated by being placed on a thoroughly revised methodological base. In fact, Bellah's updating is undergirded by a significant methodological fusion. The same fusion forms a transition to the subject of our next chapter.

Concluding Observations

Before we trace the methodological pathways from the evolutionist approach to one that views religion as being a matter of integrated and coordinated organization, however, we must draw one or two important conclusions.

First, the evidence shows that the interest in human origins is always associated or combined with an interest in human development. The interest in how things came to be involves one in analyses of both genesis and ongoing development. Inquiries that intend to identify the one are always obliged to decipher the other. It is impossible to engage in the first object of analysis without engaging in the other.

Second, the authors we have cited—from Tylor to Bellah—tend to approach the matter of origin-and-development by means of analyses of the processes of mental reasoning. That is, the tracing of religious development is coordinate with the tracing of development of human intelligence. Implicit in this is the assumption that there are distinctive ways of making meaning, and making meaning is dependent on the attitudes and perspectives the knower can take with respect to the object of knowledge. From some vantage points, knowledge is immediate, and the mode of apprehension is virtually a kind of engagement. From other vantage points, knowledge is arrived at through the mechanisms of an elaborate analytical process. And, from still other vantage points, what becomes known is knowable because the knower is conscious of how knowledge is possible and practices such self-consciousness even while the act of knowledge is being exercised. From the time that the paradigm was first conceived, it was recognized that distinct forms and modes of knowledge can be correlated with distinctive mental acts; and distinctive mental acts give rise to distinctive genres. The writing of narrative portrayals, for example, involves different mental sensitivities from those required to elucidate primary philosophical principles. The one may find expression in mythological accounts. The other will involve discursive forms of reasoning, as would be appropriate, say, to philosophical essays.

The commanding insight of the origin-and-development orientation is that these distinctive mental habits tend to prevail during certain periods—called "stages" when the sequence is viewed as a whole—in the evolution of human awareness and intelligence. Hence, the views of the world that can be associated with these distinctive periods or stages are formed by the respective prevailing mentalities. Put more simply, processes of mental reasoning involve the cultivation of distinctive perspectives on the world. These same perspectives seem to have developed in both a discernible and a sequential fashion.

Thus, an account of the origins and development of religion is tied to descriptions of the development of specific perspectives on the world. The scholars whose work we have summarized have all felt obliged to identify these several perspectives and to provide a convincing account of their relationships to each other. Appropriately, such accounts are rendered in sequential—and, sometimes, even chronological—order. The perspectives themselves come to stand as stages or periods in the development of a more comprehensive pattern or design. The pattern is regulated, in turn, by a succession of distinctive styles of mental reasoning. Indeed, all of the approaches we have identified—from the time of Tylor's probing to the revival of evolutionist terminology in Bellah's essay—seem to approach the matter this way. All treat religion in terms of a progressive unfolding of an ongoing coordinated process of distinctive mental acts. The task and challenge, of course, is to explain why and how rationality is capable of such diversity of forms of sensibility. And to know this, one needs to distinguish those diverse forms while accounting for the fact that the human species has been capable of devising worldviews via the instrumentation of all of them.

Should this approach to the subject be taken with less seriousness because more recent developments in religion have not occurred according to expectation or prediction? We refer specifically to two powerfully challenging, seemingly interrelated global events in the 1980s: the rise of religious fundamentalism, and the sudden, dramatic demise of Marxist philosophy. Neither was predicted, and neither should have happened had the progressivist model been in force. The power of Marxist philosophy was based on the assumption that government throughout the world was moving more and more in the direction of the socialist model, and the increasing elimination of religious fundamentalism had its roots in the expectation that Enlightenment philosophy would simply extend its rightful range of influence. Under such compulsions, the dogmatisms of religion would be placed in interpretive frameworks through which most zealotry could be defused. And the Marxist influence would insure progressive development toward classless societies, within which all persons would share all available resources equally. But throughout Eastern Europe and the Soviet empire, Marxism collapsed. And throughout the world—whether in Christian, Muslim, Jewish, Hindu, or even Buddhist circles—fundamentalism had regained strength, in spite of the fact that self-proclaimed enlightened human beings had long ago known it to be obsolescent.

Such developments indicate that progressive lines forward are always more complex and certainly more conflicted than might be apparent. Ernest Gellner, the British philosopher who has devoted a lifetime of scholarly service toward understanding such phenomena, contends that whatever obstacles progressivism encounters simply manifest the orientation's fundamental "moral unacceptability." Such orientations are morally unacceptable, in Gellner's view, because they encourage human beings to suppose themselves sitting outside the world, sitting in judgment upon it. Gellner contends:

> [W]orld-growth stories will not do: not only the Hegelian, but equally the other versions, more closely connected with some science and less metaphysical, such as the Marxian or Darwinian ones . . . . They will not do because . . . trends do not dictate norms, even if trends were clearly discernible.

The debate, of course, will continue, and the consequences for an understanding of religion are extensive and profound. Even though Gellner raises strong objections to the hypotheses, he believes the progressivist orientation to be worthy of "a sympathetic understanding," since, as he wrote, it "provided a stirring answer to a real question." This has been religious studies' experience with it too.

THE DESCRIPTION OF RELIGION

The preceding two chapters examined a number of prominent attempts to make religion intelligible by concentrating the focus of analysis on unambiguous simple elements. Approaches surveyed in the first chapter took the unambiguous simple element to be the essence (or *sine qua non*) of religion. In the second chapter, the simple unambiguous element was approached as the root or genetic source of religion. We referred to this source of origination as the *primordium* of religion.

Both chapters gave us opportunity to trace the workings of a reductive methodological technique. In the first instance, the contents of religion were reduced to an essential core element, that is, an irreducible basis identified as "that without which religion would not be what it is." In the second set of approaches, the methodological tendency was to work back through specific developmental sequences to recover religion's first datum. Both approaches illustrate what happens when inquiry is designed to identify, isolate, or disclose a single and primary core element. Temperamentally, each approach is characterized by a deliberate radical singleness of mind and intent. Each illustrates how coherence, explanation, and interpretation can be effected and established via the instrumentation and workings of a single schematic organizing principle.

Another clear set of intellectual interests takes over, however, when religion is approached as not being divisible into any simple reality. The alternative is to approach it as consisting of a multiplicity of elements, but a multiplicity that exhibits some definite arrangement. In this situation, analysis is directed not toward a *sine qua non* or a *primordium*, but to an assemblage of elements, a constellation of ingredients—even, possibly, a pattern of interrelatedness. In this approach, religion is considered to be a composite reality, a composition, perhaps, and its composite features can be identified and described in their intrinsic interconnectedness and interdependencies.

The effects of this change of interest and perspective will be felt immediately and forcefully. In the first place, the shift from single core element to pattern of relatedness gives recognition to the power of plurality. Instead of being approached as being of a simple and single essence, religion will be viewed as consisting of a number of components. Similarly, the shift from singles to plurals is accompanied by diminishing interest in trying to penetrate through empirical or surface factors to some underlying root or core. Instead, there is a larger willingness to approach the characteristics of religion in terms of whatever intrinsic patterns of interrelatedness seem to be exhibited. Thus, the methodological task is to discern the form of the composite, the pattern of interrelatedness, and the way in which coherence has been established. In short, the shift from a single to a plural focus is accompanied by a dramatic change in intellectual interest. Deduction-and-enumeration expectations, a la the Cartesian precedent, are increasingly abandoned in favor of less isolative and more inclusive systematic and comprehensive description.

Varieties of Focus and Description

One can trace this transition simply in formal conceptual terms. The shift from singles to plurals, from an isolative interest of reason to a desire to provide systematic classification, is tantamount to fashioning a distinctive methodological paradigm—a specific way of making religion intelligible. One must recognize, at the same time, that there are strong empirical encouragements for the conceptual shift we are describing. For it is evident, after all, that religion has something integrally to do with the ways in which religion appears in culture and society. That is, religion must have something fundamentally to do with religions—for example, with religious traditions, and with the other ways in which religion can be characterized in terms of organized patterns of multiplicity.

Thus to focus on patterns of intrinsic interrelatedness in the study of religion is to pay attention to crucial matters. It is to employ a method whose fitness is more than secondhand. It is to fix attention on natural groupings, on patterns of arrangement that are intrinsic, fundamental, and actual. Furthermore, these patterns can be approached objectively, empirically, and descriptively. Their natural composition tends to invite scholarly objectivity and impartiality. In addition, their evident "facticity" diminishes the possibility that religion will be approached through techniques of interpretation that are alien, stereotyped, or contrived. Furthermore, because an approach of this kind can be conducted crossculturally, it is equipped to give equal attention to all of the major religious traditions of the world and to take religion seriously wherever it is found. The approach carries built-in supports for being impartial, objective, and tolerant of the views of others. If and when it becomes more selective in its intellectual interest, it can specify the basis on which such selectivity has been exercised. In other words, it carries an impressive claim to be intellectually fair-minded.

It is evident, therefore, that this approach can be exercised by focusing on the religious traditions themselves. For religious traditions are primary examples of integrated patterns of multiplicity; they are composites; they are examples of organic coordination. Supporting analogies can be found in other academic fields. The study of philosophy, for instance, can be approached through a study of philosophical schools, philosophical systems, and philosophical movements. Sociology can be undertaken via a study of distinctive societies. Political science can be effected through portrayals and analyses of political systems and interest groups. The study of art can be approached through treatments of selected artistic styles and schools. For all of these reasons, it makes eminent sense that the study of religion should be carried on through a study of the religious traditions of the world.

Certainly, however, religion-as-religions is not the only form this methodological interest takes. The shift from unambiguous simples to organically interrelated plurals also represents a historical and theoretical turn taken by scholars of other approaches, many of whom choose to refer to themselves as "phenomenologists of religion." The word *phenomenology* is important and appropriate, for it denotes an intention to concentrate on phenomena—that is, on the perceptible, manifest, empirical, and sometimes visible features or characteristics of religion. Again, instead of trying to identify the single and definitive core element, or providing an account of religion's origin and development, phenomenologists have worked to describe the manner and form in which religious phenomena appear in human experience. Rather than searching for underlying causes, essences, or comprehensive and exhaustive explanations, they have focused on those components that can be perceived and portrayed. Their eventual goal is to provide as complete an account of religion's form, structure, and visible contours as is possible. Terms like *structure, description, morphology, characterization,* and *phenomenology* have become prominent in their vocabulary.

Such phenomenologists contend that the subject can be approached by a method which combines empirical exactness with a kind of intuitive grasp. When this approach is carefully employed, the investigator is able to identify, or decipher, the subject's rudimentary ingredients. Proper employment of the method encourages the manifest features of the subject to stand out, as it were, for the investigator to identify. Thus phenomenology of religion concentrates on perceptible characteristics within the context of their own manner of interrelatedness.

There is still another prominent way—a third way—in which "intrinsic interrelatedness" is approached in the academic study of religion. This third way combines characteristics of the two orientations to which we have already made reference. Like the others, this orientation also concentrates on coordinated plurals and on manifest features. But it is different from the others in that it makes something other than "religion" the direct object of inquiry and attention. For example, the specific focus might be society, or culture, or even language or symbology, each of which organism is described in terms of its own constituent components. Characteristically, religion is approached as being one of the significant ingredients within the more comprehensive composite. It becomes appropriate for the scholar to refer to religion *in* society or culture, or to speak of religious aspects. It is possible, too, that religion will even emerge as the cohesive principle by means of which society or culture (or whatever the comprehensive term) is formed. In all such interpretations, something other than religion is identified as the primary and dominant organism, and religion is accounted for when the organism is described. Thus, it also happens that the descriptive account can easily become a functional account too: religion becomes known in terms of the function it performs within the workings of the more comprehensive primary system or organism.

We shall devote this chapter, first, to an overview of the development of the phenomenological approach as it has been fashioned within the scholarly study of religion. That is, we shall restrict the subject of this chapter to but one of the foci we have identified as being significant ways of executing the shift from singles to plurals, from the quest to identify a definitive core element to a descriptive portrayal of composite elements. We shall save the other possibilities for separate treatment in subsequent chapters.

Phenomenology of Religion: Two Dominant Strains

The first consideration is a qualification. Although a wide variety of scholars employ the word *phenomenology* to describe their methodological intentions, they do not always agree on what the label means. Nor do they always share a clear sense of the intellectual traditions out of which phenomenology of religion has arisen.

The reason for this lack of agreement is that there are at least two strands of thought—two intellectual points of departure—which can produce a phenomenology of religion. The most obvious is the one that stems directly from post-Kantian and post-Hegelian continental philosophy. Regardless of whatever else it includes, this strand always lists Edmund Husserl (1859–1938) as its primary inspirer, founding father, and intellectual catalyst. Thus, to this day, the phrase *phenomenology of religion* tends to evoke Husserlian interest, Husserlian techniques, and Husserlian devised conceptual terminology. So close are these associations that Maurice Natanson, in a lucid and perceptive study, treats the words *Husserl* and *phenomenology* as being virtually interchangeable.

We shall pay some attention to Husserl's phenomenology in this chapter, as is fitting, and also to major revisions of philosophical phenomenology as proposed by the French writer Maurice Merleau-Ponty (1908–1961). We are offering a description of Merleau-Ponty's orientation primarily to illustrate that there are ways of practicing philosophical phenomenology other than those strictly sanctioned in Husserl's work. Our overall interest, however, lies in trying to determine how philosophical phenomenology has affected the content, methodology, and direction of religious studies. It is necessary to point out immediately that the use of this form of phenomenology within religious studies has often been more tangential than direct.

Indeed, religious studies has taken more from examples of the ways Husserl approached things than from the substance of his philosophy. For, alongside whatever phenomenology of religion has proceeded from Husserl, there is a second more prominent point of phenomenological departure. This second form of phenomenology has been nurtured from within certain traceable developments within the history of religions. Many scholars, recognized to be phenomenologists of religion, have been trained first as historians of religion and not as philosophers. Many would also understand history of religions and phenomenology of religion to be complimentary and interchangeable undertakings, so closely related that they would be hard pressed to distinguish between them. Such phenomenologists of religion frequently admit to having no more than a surface understanding of Husserl's fundamental contentions. When they trace their intellectual roots, the genealogy they offer tends to reach back not to Husserl (who, nevertheless, is usually mentioned), but to such relatively obscure figures as Cornelius Petrus Tiele (author of *Kompendium der Religionsgeschichte*, 1877) and Pierre Daniel Chantepie de la Saussaye (author of *Lehrbuch der Religionsgeschichte*, 1877). These two are credited as being the first phenomenologists of religion, if only because they employed a descriptive system of classification in coming to terms with the particulars of religion. This strain of phenomenology of religion has moved from Tiele and Chantepie into the twentieth century through the influence of W. Brede Kristensen, Geraardus van der

Leeuw, Geo Widengren, C. J. Bleeker, Mircea Eliade, their students, and a host of others, some of whom have eventually come to disclaim most associations with any philosophical founding fathers.

The two phenomenologies share terminology, method, and conviction, yet their intentions can be remarkably different. Philosophical phenomenology is the product of a concerted attempt to give philosophy—and, sometimes, metaphysics—a more effective point of departure. Its strategy is to focus on the structure of *phenomena*, as distinct from earlier preoccupations with *noumena*. Phenomenology of religion, in its most common form, is ordinarily less ambitious epistemologically and ontologically. Being a particular development within religious studies, it simply regards concentration on religion's manifest features—the visible, empirical, and self-evident factors—as the most effective way of coming to terms with the subject. Both orientations qualify as phenomenology because each believes that attention to phenomena—to concrete form, immediate particulars, nonabstractable data—is the most appropriate way of approaching and discerning the truth.

We shall consider these two strands in order, beginning with the philosophical orientation of Edmund Husserl. Next, we shall work our way through some of the phenomenological orientations that have been developed within the history of religions. Finally, we shall examine the position of Mircea Eliade, a historian of religions who is also a phenomenologist of religion, and one who utilizes the products of both forms of inquiry to respond to some of the queries raised within philosophical phenomenology more specifically conceived.

Husserl's Philosophical Phenomenology

As we have already noted, the beginnings of Husserl's philosophical stance lie in the distinction between *noumena* and *phenomena* as this was recognized within the philosophy of Immanuel Kant. Instead of trying to unlock the dynamics of noumenal reality—by which he meant the world of pure intellection—Husserl proposed a radical and rigorous systematic turning to the world of phenomena (by which he meant the world of things apparent, perceptible, and sensible). He referred to this as a turn to "the things themselves."

Husserl knew the writings of Kant. He understood the sense and force of Kant's interest, and he appreciated the attempt Kant made to identify and disclose the dynamic structures of reflection. Husserl believed it important, too, to provide a rigorous description of rational consciousness. But he sensed that the philosopher could take an additional step. The philosopher could come to terms with experience more effectively and profoundly; could fashion the discipline to disclose the rudiments of something even more directly, immediately, and fundamentally real than Kant's world of rationality.

In short, it was Husserl's conviction that philosophical inquiry could focus its attention on "the things themselves," being dissatisfied with grasping anything more abstract than this. And he argued that phenomena are not unreal, illusory, or of a secondary importance, derivative state, or subordinate place. Instead they are real, perceptible, and, most importantly, primary. Furthermore, their reality does not derive, say, from some higher level of reality, as though such reality and status could be bestowed. In order to penetrate to the real foundations of human knowledge, Husserl believed it necessary to deal rigorously with the fundamentals of that world which is most immediate. This required rigorous concentration on phenomena.

To sense the radical quality of this philosophical turn, we must refer to the dispositions of selected previous philosophers, particularly on the question of the distinction between noumena and phenomena. As we have illustrated, the distinction was not new. Although he regarded it as being fundamental to all careful reflection about reality, Kant did not invent the distinction. He is not even solely responsible for its prevalence in modern philosophy. Even from the beginnings of classical Greek philosophical reflection, the distinction was made, though, of course, the precise terminology was cultivated later, particularly within the Enlightenment period. In the Greek period, the issue concerned the locus of intelligibility within the world. Plato's answer to the question, "What abides when all else passes away?" was a formulation in which the abiding reality—reality's permanent substance—was placed in a transcendent realm, the world of eternal forms. In Plato's philosophy, the eternal forms represent an intelligible order that constitutes and gives structure to the world of particulars. The world of transcendent forms is normative: it stipulates eternal truths; it provides the permanent structure that is reflected in the world of particulars. *Becoming* mirrors *being*, of which it is a dimmer and not always reliable reflection. Thus this earliest comprehensive treatment of the relation of noumena and phenomena—prior to the Enlightenment era—gives intelligibility a decided metaphysical ordering.

A significant change occurred when the basis of intelligibility was shifted from a transcendent metaphysical realm to an interior, mental, or even "metanoetical" place. The fundamental distinction stands, and intelligibility continues to be associated with the noumenal realm. But noumena is viewed more as a formal regulator of knowledge than as an abstract (or abstractable) level or dimension of reality. This shift occurs in Kant's attempt to describe the rudiments of intelligibility by analyzing, decomposing, and describing the structure of rationality. We have reviewed this procedure in the first chapter of this book, where we noted that Kant found reflection—or ratiocination—to be constituted in a particular manner through the workings of the categories and forms of intuition. As Kant conceived it, reflection is regulated by certain organizing principles. Such principles are implicit in the formulation of ideas, concepts, and in the apprehension of reality. But to divide phenomena and noumena this way is to approach intelligibility as though it were primarily mental. The product, appropriately, is a critical philosophy in which the powers of reason are identified and described. In short, thought is held up to thought; thinking is directed toward analyzing thinking; and the process of rationality comes to be better understood. All such activities occur within critical philosophical reflection.

Husserl believed it necessary to take the next step. He followed the shift from metaphysics to "meta-noetics," then urged the progression further to the "things themselves." This is the world of phenomena. It is also the "life-world" (or *Lebenswelt*), the realm that is most immediate. Having identified such a world, Husserl argued that it possessed discernible structure. He held that it was just as dependent on general rules, integrative and organizing principles, dispositions, patterns, and structures as are mental processes. In turning to the things themselves, Husserl believed he had moved away from abstractions and secondary qualities to the world of primary experience.

Significantly, Husserl turned to René Descartes' philosophy when specifying the point of departure for his own point of view. He regarded Descartes' *Meditations* as "the prototype of philosophical reflection," and entitled one of his own major works *Cartesian Meditations*. With Descartes, Husserl understood that the aim of philosophical reflection is to ground knowledge absolutely and indubitably. He also believed it methodologically correct of Descartes to turn from "naive objectivism to transcendental subjectivism" to make certainty accessible. Certainty, in other words, must be made dependent on the conditions of the subject. This makes it possible to construct "a genuine philosophy, a radical philosophy that begins with what is intrinsically first." It also implies that philosophy is self-knowledge, a way of giving signification to the Delphic motto, Know Thyself.

In his introduction to the English translation of Pierre Thevenaz's book *What Is Phenomenology?*, James Edie describes Husserl's intentions as follows:

> Philosophy is a rigorous science for Husserl in the sense that it is an investigation of the most radical, fundamental, primitive, original evidences of conscious experience; it goes beneath the constructions of science and common sense towards their foundations in experience. It studies what all the particular sciences take for granted and what we in "natural" everyday experience take for granted. A "presuppositionless" philosophy is one which will reach what is absolutely primary or most fundamental in experience.

This implies that the external world is not "the absolutely first basis for judgment." Hence, in turning from abstractions to "the things themselves," Husserl was not simply following lines of progression from idealism to empiricism. Rather, he was placing the basis of certainty within the subject: "certainty derives from a being that is intrinsically prior to the world." This means that the self, which Husserl described as "the mediating ego," is the "acceptance basis of all objective acceptances and bases."

The temper remains Cartesian. But the content and the context have been influenced by the subsequent history of thought from Descartes forward, and, particularly, by the fate of Kantian criticism, Hegelian idealism, and the ongoing development of empiricism. Yet, Husserl believed Descartes' hunches to have been confirmed: certainty in knowledge does indeed require a due and accurate assessment of the role of the subject in the cognitive situation.

This sounds like Kant too, whose elaboration of the subjective turn Husserl also found to be fitting. Husserl insisted that phenomenology sustain the dictates of the new "Copernican revolution" of which Kantian philosophy is a calculated celebration. The "revolution" signifies that certainty is made subject to the conditions of the knower. But Husserl—in keeping with his attitude toward Descartes—believed that Kant had not gone the full and necessary distance. Kant had concentrated on the formal components of knowledge, on the rudiments of conceptual knowledge. In Husserl's view Kant's evidence is not *first datum* but, instead, a construct. Indeed, as Husserl viewed it, neither Descartes nor Kant had given a full or sufficient account of subjectivity. Descartes had made the proper turn. Kant had provided a significant elaboration in conceptual terms. But neither had proceeded far enough. The truer access to *first datum* is not Kant's formal conceptual analysis, but disciplined sensitivity to the power of the *Lebenswelt*, the immediate human life-world.

Lebenswelt is described as the primary world, the world that is present even prior to reflection upon it. It is the world of primary experience: the prereflective, taken-for-granted world. As Maurice Natanson puts it:

> The cardinal consideration . . . is that it is within the life-world that all projection of more specialized realms—the law, government, the professions—takes place, and it is the life-world itself which becomes philosophy's theme: the search for self-knowledge coincides with the illumination of mundanity.

This is the basis, but it is just the beginning. From here the sequence of philosophical reconstruction proceeds as follows: *Lebenswelt*-consciousness is taken as the matrix of all phenomena; such consciousness is marked by an *intentional* character. Husserl referred repeatedly to "the intentionality of consciousness" in describing how the objects of thought are given "structure." This implies that "consciousness" is always "consciousness-of." Every act of thinking implies an object thought about, and is a structural act. Thus, since "consciousness" is always "consciousness-of," "reality" is always "reality as intended." The human subject exhibits an innate capacity for order—a capacity that expresses itself in the primary world, within the structure of *Lebenswelt*. This is the basis for proposing that consciousness is the matrix of all phenomena.

To discourage reductionistic interpretations, Husserl argued that the contents of the *Lebenswelt* must be considered in and of themselves—even apart from their ability to illustrate some abstract theory or general law, even apart from the place they might be able to assume within some more extensive system of meaning. The achievement of this goal belonged to the use of the methodological technique Husserl called *epoché*. The *epoché* involves a suspension of judgment: all presumptions about the ultimate nature of things are "bracketed" so that phenomena might be considered simply as phenomena. Husserl referred to this as the breaking of "the natural attitude." The goal is to gain access to the life-world in which persons live, feel, act, and think. The phenomenological *epoché* is a necessary means of access to the life-world because this world is often put beyond reach by theories about the world.

Then, once the life-world has been discovered—or, more properly, recovered—the phenomenologist goes about trying to identify its fundamental structures. Husserl employed the word *Wesenschau*—or "intuition of essences"—and sometimes "eidetic intuition" to describe the phenomenological task that follows upon a recognition of the life-world. This implies that the structures of meaning of *Lebenswelt* are to be made subject to an intuitive grasp. Husserl sought to employ this intuitive method in a rigorous philosophical manner.

Maurice Merleau-Ponty: Criticisms and Revisions of Husserl

We can probe this subject further by analyzing some of the criticisms raised against Husserl's viewpoint by other phenomenologists, notably the French thinker Maurice Merleau-Ponty. Merleau-Ponty's disagreements, while sharply raised, are based on a set of shared assumptions.

Fundamentally, Merleau-Ponty was critical of Husserl for not being radical enough. He believed that Husserl had started in the proper direction. But he thought he had penetrated to the real "things themselves" because of his unwillingness to abandon some rather persistent but old-fashioned idealist contentions. In specific terms, Merleau-Ponty was critical of Husserl's tendency—manifested particularly in the essays written early in his career—to meet the conflict between Kant's formal conceptualism and a more deliberately data-based empiricism by constructing a *via media* through "transcendental subjectivity." Passages such as the following, from Husserl's book *Ideas*, illustrate the focus of Merleau-Ponty's worry:

> [W]e direct the glance of apprehension and theoretical inquiry to *pure consciousness in its own absolute Being*. It is this which remains over as the "phenomenological residuum" we were in quest of: remains over, we say, although we have 'suspended' the world with all things, living creatures, men, ourselves included. We have literally lost nothing, but have won the whole of Absolute Being, which, properly understood, conceals in itself all transcendences, "constituting" them within itself.

"Pure consciousness in its own absolute Being," or "transcendental subjectivity"—such depictions of the primacy of consciousness, as understood by Merleau-Ponty, spelled a serious qualification.

Certainly Husserl intended to return to the "things themselves," and he had proposed to do so through a series of suspensions of unexamined expectations and presumptions. And yet, in Merleau-Ponty's view, the results of such phenomenological inquiries did not consist solely of isolated fields of data, completely detached from all schemes of interpretation. On the contrary, in addition to the "facticity" of what is immediately given, Husserl included a transcendent knowing consciousness—a kind of Cartesian indubitable ego raised to a metaphenomenological plain—through whose cognitional instrumentality the objects of consciousness become constituted. In *Cartesian Meditations* Husserl wrote:

> The objective world, the world that exists for me, that always has and always exists for me, the only world that can exist for me—this world, with all its objects, I said, derives its whole sense and its existential status, which it has for me, from me myself, from me as the transcendental Ego, the Ego who comes to the fore only with transcendental-phenomenological *epoché*.

For Merleau-Ponty, the orientation had to be refined. Opposed to Husserl's retention of emphasis on transcendental subjectivity, at least as these were enunciated in the *Cartesian Meditations*, he elected to give emphasis to Husserl's subsequent description of the *Lebenswelt*. In place of the Ego, Merleau-Ponty gave power to perception. He emphasized human's active involvement (as "body-subject") in the world through perception. He contended that the reality of perception in the lived-body makes pure consciousness unnecessary.

Husserl, in Merleau-Ponty's opinion, had not brought the world to a unity. By retaining a transcendental element, he gave the impression that there was still some additional "world apart." "To say that rationality exists is to say that perspectives blend, perceptions confirm each other, a meaning emerges. *But it should not be set in a realm apart*, transposed into absolute Spirit." Rather, Merleau-Ponty contended as follows:

> The phenomenological world is not pure being, but the sense which is revealed where the paths of my various experiences intersect, and also where my own and other people's intersect and engage each other like gears. It is thus inseparable from subjectivity and intersubjectivity, which find their present unity when I either take up my past experiences in those of the present, or other people's in my own.

In short, phenomenology simply "rests on itself." In Merleau-Ponty's view, it provides "its own foundation." This is in keeping with his attitude that "true philosophy consists in relearning to look at the world." Merleau-Ponty praised Husserl's intentions, but he believed he had not gone far enough or executed his principal convictions with appropriate rigor and daring.

Merleau-Ponty's response was assisted by his knowledge of the philosophy of Henri Bergson (1859–1941), whose position was also conceived, in part, as an alternative to Cartesian views. Whereas Descartes had said "Je suis une chose qui pense" ("I am a thing who thinks"), Bergson countered "Je suis une chose qui dure" ("I am a thing who endures"). And in according fundamental reality to duration and to processes of change, Bergson self-consciously opposed all philosophical tendencies to place "reality" in some transcendental world.

Merleau-Ponty acknowledged his appreciation for Bergson in his inaugural address on being appointed to the chair in philosophy in the College de France. Given the fact that body-spirit is integral, and that duration has large retentive and cohesive powers, the task of philosophy, Merleau-Ponty said, was "not to explain but to decipher life." It is possible to do this because fundamental agreement exists between the perceiver and phenomena. Rephrasing Bergson's contentions, Merleau-Ponty said: "It is necessary to rediscover 'the intention of life,' the simple movement which runs through the lines, which ties them to one another and gives them meaning." Then, referring to the correspondence and synchronization of body-spirit and duration, he suggested that "the intention of life" can be rediscovered "because we carry in our incarnate being *the alphabet* and *the grammar of life*." His point is clear: to decipher life, one need not make recourse to some transcendental level of insight or interpretation. All of this is unnecessary because the body-subject carries its own knowing capacities. Through perception, the incarnate self and duration "engage each other like gears." The mode of relationship with the world is "older than intelligence," Merleau-Ponty attested, for "lived experience" is consonant with duration.

Thus Merleau-Ponty believed he had fashioned a phenomenology in which consciousness and world were reciprocally interrelated in such fashion that dichotomies between subject and object ceased to exist. He also believed that the long-standing conflicts between rationalism and empiricism could be overcome. All of this belonged to a serious application of Husserl's proposal that philosophy had to find a way to return to "the things themselves." As Merleau-Ponty said:

> To return to things themselves is to return to that world which precedes knowledge, of which knowledge always speaks and in relation to which every scientific schematization is an abstract and derivative sign-language, as is geography in relation to the countryside in which we have learned beforehand what a forest, a prairie or a river is.

Then, to make the point even more vivid and forceful, he added:

> Truth does not "inhabit" only "the inner man," or, more accurately, there is no inner man. [Rather] man is in the world, and only in the world does he know himself. When I return to myself from an excursion into the realm of dogmatic common sense or of science, I find, not a source of intrinsic truth, but a subject destined to be in the world.

Before we go further, it is important to recognize the fundamental differences between Husserl's and Merleau-Ponty's phenomenologies. The differences are remarkably similar to those between *sine qua non* and origin-and-development orientations. Through the influence of Bergson, perhaps, Merleau-Ponty's position has a fluidity that is not present in Husserl's. Viewed from the other side, Husserl's phenomenology exhibits a stronger effort to identify permanence, an effort Merleau-Ponty exhibits little obligation to capture.

When the religious implications are plumbed, it turns out that Husserl's position is more popular than Merleau-Ponty's. Because the former carries a clear place both for a mediating Ego and for transcendence, it assists the effort to depict a world providing a place for a deity. By contrast, Merleau-Ponty's view appears "atheistic." It stands opposed to any retention of "transcendental subjectivity," and wishes to make the turn to "the things themselves" more rigorous and radical. Predictably, therefore, Merleau-Ponty has not received much attention among persons working in religious studies. Husserl has been considerably more prominent, for his position has created more conceptual possibilities for religion. The fact is worth studying. As a rule, it seems, *when persons in religious studies look to philosophical phenomenology for assistance, they are looking for a special sort of assistance.* They wish it to corroborate claims that might be offered in religious studies' terms. But we must approach this subject in more comprehensive terms.

Phenomenology of Religion: Origins within the History of Religions

The tendency to approach religion by describing its manifest features was established by Cornelius Petrus Tiele (1830–1902), a professor in Leiden. Tiele is remembered not only for his specialized work in Egyptian, Assyrian, and Mesopotamian religions, but, more importantly, for his attempt to treat the history of religion in a comprehensive and self-conscious manner, identifying its aims and methods as he proceeded. His literary legacy includes a one-volume *Outlines of the History of Religion to the Spread of Universal Religion* (translated into English in 1877) and a two-volume methodological work entitled *Elements of the Science of Religion*, the Gifford Lectures of 1896 and 1898.

In the earlier work, Tiele traced the development of religion from its animistic origins—which he expanded into the concept that "everything that lives is animated by a thinking, feeling, willing spirit, differing from the human in degree and power only"—to the formation of the Christian religion in Greco-Roman times. Then, having surveyed the origin and evolution of religion, Tiele turned to methodological concerns. His Gifford Lectures were devoted to analyzing the constitution of the science of the history of religion. He sought to identify the science's intentions, procedures, and scope. The result is an impressive exercise in phenomenology—indeed, phenomenology of religion. It is phenomenology in the sense that Tiele believed it necessary to engage in descriptive analysis of the manifest features of religion before trying to identify the subject's inmost core.

Tiele described the characteristics of the phenomenological method while proposing the intentions of a scientific approach to religion:

> First of all, it is necessary to state what we understand by science of religion, and what right we have to call it a science. We shall not begin, as is so often done, by formulating a preconceived ideal of religion; if we attempted to do so, we should only move in a circle. What religion really is, in its essence, can only be ascertained as the result of our whole investigation.

Then he proposed this working definition of the primary term:

> By religion we mean for the present nothing different from what is generally understood by that term—that is to say, the aggregate of all those phenomena which are invariably termed religious, in contradistinction to ethical, aesthetical, political, and others.

In Tiele's view, "the aggregate of all those phenomena which are invariably termed religious" is as extensive as the scope of religion itself. "The province of our investigation is sufficiently extensive—all religions of the civilised and uncivilised world, dead and living, and all the religious phenomena which present themselves to our observation." He recognized this to be a very different approach from one that begins with a conception of the essence of religion, then proceeds to examine the evidence in light of the conception already formed. Tiele wanted eventually to identify religion's essence, but he believed essences to be inaccessible until after careful phenomenological description had been carried out. Referring to the function of the science of religion (speaking of it in feminine terms), Tiele wrote:

> All she desires, and all she is entitled to do, is to subject religion, as a human and therefore historical and psychological phenomenon, to unprejudiced investigation, in order to ascertain how it arises and grows and what are its essentials, and in order thoroughly to understand it.

Then, with reference to the work of the scholar in the science of religion, Tiele added:

> He judges, in so far as his task is to compare the different manifestations of religious belief and life, and the different religious communities, in order to classify them in accordance with the stage and direction of their involvement. He criticizes in so far as he points out where there has been retrogression from a higher to a lower plane, in so far as he scrutinizes so-called religious facts which really belong to a different

domain—such as that of art, philosophy, or politics—and pathological phenomena—such as intellectualism, sentimentalism, or moralism—and distinguishes all these from sound and living religion. He takes up, if we may use the favorite philosophical term, an entirely objective position towards all forms of religion, but distinguishes them carefully from religion itself. Religion reveals itself in every one of these forms more or less imperfectly—and so he studies them all. No religion is beneath his notice: on the contrary, the deeper he digs, the nearer he gets to religion's source.

A two-stage approach is apparent throughout. Morphological description is a necessary antecedent to all attempts to identify religion's essence or source. That is the first task. The second stage—which Tiele called "ontological" to distinguish it from the merely "morphological"—is not to be initiated until phenomenological investigation has produced its own results.

Therefore, Tiele was quite willing to suggest a definition of religion, and to work toward refining it. But he insisted that all definitions must be based on morphological analyses. The essence of religion, he believed, could be found in the attitude of *adoration*. As he explained further:

> Now, wherever I discover piety, as manifested in different stages of religious progress, and particularly as exhibited in full beauty in the highest stage as yet attained, I maintain that its essence—and therefore the essence of religion itself—is adoration. In adoration are united these two phases of religion which are termed by the schools "transcendent" and "immanent" respectively, or which, in religious language, represent the believer as "looking up to God as the Most High," and as "feeling himself akin to God as his Father."

Then he elaborated:

> For adoration necessarily involves the elements of holy awe, humble reverence, grateful acknowledgment of every token of love, hopeful confidence, lowly self-abasement, a deep sense of one's own unworthiness and shortcomings, total self-abnegation, and unconditional consecration of one's whole life and one's whole faculties.

Further:

> To adore is to love "with all one's heart and soul and mind and strength." To adore is to give oneself, with all that one has and holds dearest. But at the same time—and herein consists its other phase—adoration includes a desire to possess the adored object, to call it entirely one's own, and conversely a longing on the part of the adorer to feel that he belongs to the adored one forever, in joy and in sorrow, in life and in death. . . . No pious man will ever rest satisfied until he can exclaim out of the fulness of his heart, "*My* Lord and *my* God!" Adoration therefore demands that closest communion, that perfect union, which forms the characteristic aim of all religion. . . . Further, the spirit of adoration affords a key to all the various manifestations of religion.

In Tiele's view, wherever religion is found, whether in earliest or subsequent form, "its vital principle has ever been adoration."

The particularly intriguing aspect of Tiele's thought is its suppleness. It gives evidence of a remarkable comprehension of a wide sweep of developments, both methodological and substantive, within the history of religions. As a result, Tiele's work bridges the paradigmatic distinctions we have sought to draw. To be sure, his work is one of the first comprehensive efforts in phenomenological description; thus, it deserves recognition among those approaches we have chosen to identify and examine in this chapter. At the same time, Tiele understood morphological analysis to be a necessary first step toward isolating religion's essence. Thus, his work also qualifies as a *sine qua non* approach. Eventually, via phenomenological portrayal, he wanted to identify religion's most characteristic inner core. Before working to do this, he also acknowledged that the primary morphological feature of religion is its capacity for development. He explained:

> All religions develop; but, like every form of social life, for a time only. All have their periods of birth, growth, bloom, and decline. . . . But we shall see that this transitoriness of religion is precisely one of the strongest proofs of the development of religion. Language, states, and peoples die, but mankind does not. Religion—that is, the forms in which religion manifests itself—die, but religion itself does not. Though ever changing in form, religion lives like mankind and with mankind.

Thus, when the *Outlines of the History of Religion* are placed alongside Tiele's later methodological work, the approach also qualifies as an illustration of the origin-and-development model. So integrated was his scheme and so versatile were his talents that the approach he fashioned can be seen to belong to all of the paradigmatic frameworks we have identified so far. Yet, if we must make a choice, we must view him first as a phenomenologist because of his conviction that all concerns about essences and origins must be suspended until after careful and painstaking phenomenological analysis has been conducted.

Chantepie de la Saussaye: Phenomenology Continued

The last sentence, with some refinement, would also describe the attitude of Pierre Daniel Chantepie de la Saussaye (1848–1920), a Dutch-born scholar who taught history and philosophy of religion at the University of Amsterdam from 1878 to 1899, then moved to Leiden to teach theology until his retirement in 1916. Like his countryman Tiele, Chantepie found the roots of phenomenology to lie in cultivated sensitivity to the various questions that are implicit in the science of religion. The introductory chapters of his *Manual of the Science of Religion* represent a self-conscious attempt to sift through the questions that were being raised by some prominent scholars at the time. Chantepie paid particular attention to questions regarding religion's origin and religion's essence, and he insisted that the two questions were not the same. It was necessary, he thought, to demonstrate that the matters of origin and essence could not be treated in the same way.

> [The] question as to the origin of religion touches closely on that as to the essence of religion, but the two questions are not identical; for primitive and essential are not synonymous, and though our opinion as to the essence of religion may strongly influence our views on its origins, it would be a grave error to maintain that the essence of religion must clearly show itself in the earliest forms under which it appears.

In Chantepie's view, the distinctiveness but interrelatedness of the two intellectual interests creates the occasion for a phenomenology of religion. Phenomenology of religion is necessary because the truly significant characteristics of religion do not reduce to questions about religion's origin or essence. He did not wish to imply that such questions were meaningless. His intention, rather, was to clarify the expectations. It was a mistake, he believed, to assume that identifying the origin of religion explains the meaning of religion. Similarly, to uncover the essence of religion—even if one could do this—would not explain the subject fully. Both interests would help one understand religion, but other inquiries into the nature of religion make considerable sense as well.

Initially, phenomenology of religion provides the vantage point from which the various sorts of inquiry are pulled together. It is phenomenology because it is descriptive and is designed to sort and classify components. But this is just the beginning, for there is more to phenomenology than sensitivity to the comprehensive makeup of religious studies. By phenomenology, Chantepie also meant concentration on the manifest features of religion. Taking all of these characteristics together, he described the discipline as follows:

> Phenomenology of religion is most closely connected with psychology, in so far as it deals with facts of human consciousness. Even the outward forms of religion can only be explained from inward processes: religious acts, ideas, and sentiments are not distinguished from non-religious acts, ideas, and sentiments by any outward mark, but only by a certain inward relation. We must leave the accurate definition of the character of religious phenomena to philosophy, and content ourselves with classifying the most important ethnographic and historical material connected with the phenomena of religion. We shall not therefore attempt here an analysis of religious consciousness, but only discuss the meaning of the most important classes of religious phenomena.

It is evident that Chantepie did not intend phenomenology of religion to be an identification of the essence or origin of religion. Instead, it deals with the "outward forms of religion." At the same time, those outward forms do imply something interior or inner. There are indeed "inner processes" of which the "outward forms are reflections or indicators." Thus Chantepie could not avoid dealing with inner consciousness—he even refers to "religious consciousness"—in treating manifest features. And with so many potential foci, phenomenology of religion has to be sure of its own starting point.

Here Chantepie offered a provocative suggestion. He believed that phenomenology could not even commence its work without having some basic understanding of the nature of religion. Phenomenology does not identify that starting point, but, instead, does its work after the starting point has been determined. Chantepie located the starting point by drawing upon evidence of another kind. From his knowledge of the scholarship that had developed on the subject, he proposed to place religion within the context of worship. "At all events, the phenomenology of religion must begin with the consideration of the different objects of belief and of worship." The same starting point is corroborated in the analyses of E. B. Tylor; namely, that religion has to do with belief in spiritual beings. Chantepie corrected Tylor's observation to read: "belief in superhuman powers combined with their worship." Having been given this starting point, phenomenology of religion was free to provide a more comprehensive descriptive account.

Morris Jastrow: Phenomenology and Academic Study of Religion

Morris Jastrow (1861–1921), professor of Semitic languages at the University of Pennsylvania, and recipient of a doctorate from the University of Leipzig, understood his work to have been inspired by Tiele. Indeed, Jastrow's best-known work, entitled simply *The Study of Religion*, published in 1902, was dedicated to Tiele. Jastrow self-consciously and deliberately wished to carry Tiele's phenomenology of religion forward. This entailed that he be interested both in the substance and content of religion and in methodological approaches that might make such substance intellectually accessible. His *The Study of Religion* is a veritable masterpiece, which deserves to be much better known than it is. It presents a history of the study of religion by focusing on the contributions of major thinkers and theorists, from the Greek era through the Renaissance into the Enlightenment period and into modern times. Along the way Jastrow provides a sketch of the sequence of historical interpreters of religion, noting that Johann Gottfried von Herder, Gotthold Lessing, Christoph Meiners, and Thomas Carlyle played significant roles, even before the scientific study of religion became an identifiable intellectual undertaking under the influence of Max Müller and Tiele. What makes Jastrow's chronicle all the more intriguing is that it includes American thinkers such as William James and Josiah Royce. At the time that he published *The Study of Religion*, Jastrow had good command of the scholarly work that had been done on the subject of religion throughout the Western world, and was even cognizant of studies in progress.

To his survey of intellectual approaches to the study of religion, Jastrow added a comprehensive classification of the religions themselves. Here he offered a modified evolutionary schema as his means of distinguishing the various religions. Without question he wished to develop contrasts between lower and higher stages of religious understanding, and he desired to separate the content of the religions according to their distinct emphases. From Tiele he had learned the distinction, for example, between nature religions and ethical religions. But, mindful of some of the difficulties involved in the imposition, he posited them lightly, as if always open to amendment and correction. He recognized that religions vary according to the distinct geographies within which they are situated. He was fully aware that some of them qualify as being monotheistic in orientation, while the majority of them do not. Some of them were intended to be universal religions, and others sought a more limited sphere of application. As Jastrow proposed potential systems of classification, he also involved himself in a careful and extensive evaluation of the systems proposed by other scholars. Thus his treatment of the subject of "classification" is filled with astute commentary on the work of virtually everyone who was involved in a similar venture, as if Jastrow were in conversation with all of them.

A related task was to lay out the intentions of the academic study of religion by examining the potential contributions and involvements of the various subject areas. Jastrow studied philosophies of religion, the relationships between religion and ethics, religion and psychology, religion and mythology, and religion and history. In each of these instances, he provided evidence of having good command of the primary occurrences within the fields themselves. He also draws upon such knowledge when he ventures some definitions of religion and examines a number of definitions that have been taken with considerable seriousness. At every point along the way, his discussion is marked by an almost encyclopedic understanding of the topics being examined. Thus, the section of the book on the study of religion employs materials that might well have been included in the section on the religions. The section of the study dealing with definitions of religion is filled with references to the most influential theorists, and the chapters on the theorists contain much that might well have been treated under definitions or under treatments of the academic study of religion. This is not to imply that Jastrow's own arrangement of materials was flexible and fluid, but rather to emphasize the multilayered character of his phenomenology of religion. It is a phenomenology of terms and categories that serves also as distinctive intellectual history that can also be employed as rationale for the study of religion in American colleges and universities.

Jastrow's thesis is that the historical method is the surest guide because it both assists in disclosing the facts and enables the scholarly inquirer to cultivate the necessary sensitivity to appreciate and understand religious ideas and traditions other than those with which he or she is most familiar. On the one side, Jastrow pleads for "a sympathetic attitude." From another side, not in conflict with the first, he argues that religion has nothing to fear from a rigorous scientific examination. Jastrow's rich and compact study stands as an example of what he is recommending. He pleads for a broad understanding of the subject in all of its aspects, observing that the contribution the specialist makes to the study "depends to a great extent upon the amount of knowledge he possesses not strictly belonging to his specialty." Describing the ideal he has in mind, Jastrow writes: "He gathers material far and wide, he constantly aims to enlarge his mental horizon, and the greater his general knowledge the better is he equipped for penetrating into the remotest corners of the restricted field in which alone he can become an authority." Truly Jastrow's phenomenology is as representative of religious studies as it appears possible for any one scholar to be at the beginning of the twentieth century. One reads *The Study of Religion* both for the information it provides and for the understanding of the subject to which it gives a powerful witness.

W. Brede Kristensen: Phenomenology of Religion as Descriptive Overview

Both Tiele and Chantepie engaged in phenomenology of religion while maintaining methodological interest in questions regarding religion's essence and origin. However, by the time of W. Brede Kristensen (1867–1953), a Norwegian who, following Tiele's death, taught at the University of Leiden, phenomenology came to be understood as a clear alternative to the search for origins and essences.

Kristensen also wished to approach the history of religion in something other than an evolutionist manner. The evolutionism in which he had been trained led, he believed, to misguided conclusions because it imposed a theoretical construct on historical and empirical data.

Thus, a refined form of *epoché* became a necessary methodological ploy. In this fashion empirical and analytical research in the history of religions could be undertaken for purposes other than the mere justification of the accuracy and comprehensiveness of some prior evolutionist schematic portrayal. In turning away from evolutionism toward "the things themselves," Kristensen wanted to ascribe an autonomy to the data he was investigating. As he put it:

> All evolutionary views and theories mislead us from the start, if we let them set the pattern for our historical research. . . . We are then dealing only with our own ideas of religion, and we must not delude ourselves that we have also learned to know the ideas of others.

There are lessons in this observation:

> The historian and the student of phenomenology must therefore be able to forget themselves, to be able to surrender themselves to others. Only after that will they discover that others surrender themselves to them. If they bring their own idea with them, others shut themselves off from them. No justice is then done to the values which are alien to us, because they are not allowed to speak in their own language. If the historian tries to understand the religious data from a different viewpoint than that of the believers, he negates the religious reality. For there is no religious reality other than the faith of the believers.

Kristensen's point can hardly be mistaken. The importation and imposition of interpretive—even speculative—theoretical schemes simply frustrates all attempts to grasp the data clearly, objectively, accurately, and in terms that those most directly affected by the data can understand and recognize. Too often, it seems, the product of analytical inquiry can hardly be recognized even by those persons who are most directly involved—"the believers themselves." To eliminate these contrivances, Kristensen wanted to accord an autonomy to "the things themselves," and to fashion scholarly inquiry in a manner that would support this primacy. This required that a true phenomenological approach should supplant all interpretations that function reductionistically. The same could be said against approaches that treat data primarily as examples or illustrations of imposed interpretive categories. Kristensen wanted to free the data to be what they are, and to be appreciated in this manner. He wished to approach religion through scholarly methods that protect phenomena from the imperialistic clutches of preformed theoretical schemes. And yet this was only the first step.

In Kristensen's view, there is also a synthetic—or synthesizing—dimension to phenomenological portrayal. Phenomenology is called upon not only to describe "the things themselves" in their intrinsic purity, but also to provide a kind of overview. In analyzing the data of religion, phenomenology differentiates categories according to which "the things themselves" can be classified. Commenting on this second aspect of phenomenological inquiry, Kristensen wrote in the opening chapter of his book of collected essays:

> Phenomenology of religion is the systematic treatment of the history of religion. That is to say, its task is to classify and group the numerous and widely divergent data in such a way that an overall view can be obtained of their religious content and the religious values they contain. This general view is not a condensed history of religion, but a systematic survey of the data.

Then, in distinguishing phenomenology of religion from history of religion, Kristensen proposed that the former deals in systematic as well as comparative inquiry. He was willing to conceive of phenomenology of religion as a kind of comparative religion, but he wanted it understood that comparative religion and phenomenology of religion divide their materials in distinctive ways. It is the intention of comparative religion to regard religions as units that can be measured against each other. Phenomenology of religion, in contrast, conducts its inquiries across cultural and religious lines. It works with the elements of religion that occur within the context of more than one religion or culture, or that seem typical of religious experience more comprehensively and systematically understood. As Kristensen phrased it: "Phenomenology does not try to compare the religions with one another as large units, but it takes out of their historical setting the similar facts and phenomena which it encounters in different regions, brings them together and studies them in groups." By contrast, comparative religion is described as follows: "The corresponding data, which are sometimes nearly identical, bring us almost automatically to comparative study. The purpose of such study is to become acquainted with the religious thought, idea or need which underlies the group of corresponding data."

Thus, in Kristensen's view, phenomenology of religion performs both descriptive and synthetic tasks. It seeks both to collect and then to arrange and classify the components of religion. It classifies materials according to distinctive patterns of similarity. But such classifications do not exist simply for and by themselves. Instead, the assumption is that knowledge of the type or category can illumine phenomena in other settings. Eventually, the phenomenologist is talking not only about this tradition or that culture, but about religion itself:

> The comparative consideration of corresponding data often gives a deeper and more accurate insight than the consideration of each datum by itself, for considered as a group, the data shed light upon one another. Phenomenology tries to gain an overall view of the ideas and motives which are of decisive importance in all of history of religion.

Kristensen's intention was to employ phenomenological description in such a manner that the systematic classification of data would not destroy the autonomy of the data. If that autonomy were diminished or qualified in any way, the scholar could not be certain that his portrayal is accurate, reliable, or compelling. On the other hand, without benefit of classifications and typologies, the scholar will not always recognize the significance of the data he uncovers. This is the tightrope on which all phenomenologists must walk, regardless of whether they are working in religious studies or in other fields. If they become too formalistic, they cannot be sure that they have not violated the autonomy of the materials they wish to describe and explain. But if they are not formalistic at all, they may be unable to name the patterns of arrangement that apply; in this situation, they would find themselves with little to say. The goal is to fashion only those formal structures that maintain the autonomy of the data. In proper phenomenological language, the goal is to lend "constitution" to the materials under scrutiny. But it must always be a disclosable constitution—one in full keeping with those necessary convictions about the power of "the things themselves." It cannot be a pattern of arrangement that is either extrapolated or read-in from some more general level of abstraction. Husserl discovered structure via the intentionality of the constituting consciousness. Merleau-Ponty found the same in perception. For his part, Kristensen wanted only those groupings and classifications that derive directly from the data considered in their own right.

Given all of these qualifications, the phenomenologist remains at liberty to view "the sacredness of the Greek and Roman kings," for example, "in light of the ancient concept of kingship." Similarly, the phenomenologist can utilize general notions about sacrifice while examining a particular instance of sacrifice. The phenomenologist can even employ the concept of deity, allowing for a wide range of variation, when approaching religious belief in high gods, or sky-gods, wherever this is appropriate. To proceed in this fashion is simply to recognize that the data can be typed, and that type, category, class and kind can be confirmed in the examples the phenomenologist uncovers and examines.

Kristensen's system of classification is both categorial and dispositional. Categorially, he perceived three sets of parameters according to which the data of phenomenology of religion can be grouped. Some of the materials that belong to the phenomenology of religion belong to a distinctively *cosmological* range, for they treat the cosmos, the sky, the celestial bodies, and the traffic of gods between heaven and earth. Another range of materials is more *anthropological* in orientation. It concerns human origins in all of its aspects, including humankind's place in the universe, purpose, destiny, attributes, capacities, the laws that govern human life, the ways in which societies and cultures are formed, the religious status of both society and culture, as well as relationships between human beings and God. A third set of materials pertains to the *cult* (described as "the sacred places, the sacred times, and the sacred images which play a role in the practice of worship"). Here Kristensen draws upon Rudolf Otto's conception of "the holy" in a manifestly phenomenological way to illustrate that holiness is implicit in the regulation of cult life and in interpretations and forms of worship. He offers this statement as a kind of summary:

> The subjects of phenomenology of religion may be classified into three groups: the conceptions or doctrines which we find in the various religions about the world, about man, and about the practice of worship. These three subdivisions are, in other words, religious cosmology, religious anthropology, and cultus.

The dispositional element is dual rather than threefold. Kristensen recognizes that the materials of phenomenology of religion reflect the fact that there are two dominant types of religion. The difference between the two is a dispositional matter. One type reflects the influences of a rationalist orientation. It is an orientation that has already subjected an earlier mode of religious apprehension to critical assessment. The second type, more mysterious or mystical, refers to a sense of life that the criticisms and judgments of rationality have not yet affected. Given this contrast, it becomes appropriate to call the rationalist form of religion modern, and to characterize the other disposition as being typical of ancient and premodern religious sensitivities. It is also appropriate to place the former in contexts that have come under rationalism's influence, and to refer to the latter as being prerationalistic.

Kristensen was unwilling to make unrestrictive distinctions between the two strands, recognizing that exceptions would abound were he to do so. Yet he felt compelled to call attention to the distinction. When religion is subjected to intensive critical reflection, its content becomes something that was not there before. The new rationalist and postrationalist religion is no longer characterized by an immediacy of apprehension: the mystical element and the mysterious components lose their original—some would say their *primordial*—spontaneity:

> That which is characteristic of the Ancient civilizations and religions is the vivid consciousness of the cooperation between, indeed a fusion of, the finite and infinite factors in all phenomena connected with the essentials of life. . . . Since the time of the Greeks, however, the conviction has dominated in Modern man that the unknown can and must be more and more limited and that it proves to be not essentially different from that which is already known. That which inspires this line of thinking is the sense of the autonomous and dominating activity of the human mind in subject nature to itself.
>
> But every value is won at the cost of another value; here it is at the cost of the awareness of the mystical background of existence. In the man of Antiquity there was dominant just this sense of the mystery that surrounds us, a feeling of the spontaneous forces and energies whose meaning he always understood in the form of myth.

Given this distinction, Kristensen's goal was to show that a sense of the sacredness of life can be captured even by persons oriented to the modern world, and that the same can be committed to phenomenological portrayal.

Geraardus van der Leeuw: Phenomenology of Religion with Larger Expectations

The best-known comprehensive phenomenological work in the history of religions is Geraardus van der Leeuw's *Phenomenologie der Religion*, published in 1933. This classic was translated into English and given the title *Religion in Essence and Manifestation*, published in London in 1938. It has since been revised and reissued in North America in 1963 under the editorial direction of Hans H. Penner. Through the years it has come to enjoy a status similar to

Rudolf Otto's *The Idea of the Holy*, a book with which it shares many formative contentions.

Geraardus van der Leeuw (1890–1950) was a literary craftsman. Consequently, one does not find detailed statements of methodological intentions in his writings. At the same time, it is clear to the careful reader that he was well aware of the principal contentions of the philosophical phenomenologists and carried out his own work within the phenomenology of religion in a way that capitalized on their methodological insights. That is to say, he wished his work to be above philosophical-phenomenological criticism. But such philosophical sensitivities are apparent without being either explicit or routinized. Thus, *Religion in Essence and Manifestation* is a comprehensive example of phenomenology of religion. It is a phenomenological performance, not a discussion of phenomenology.

Characteristically, comprehensive phenomenologists of religion tend to retain some hint of the matrix out of which they were conceived, even when they profess to be deviating radically from certain elements within that matrix. Van der Leeuw's phenomenology is no exception to this tendency. Professing opposition to reductionistic treatments of religion's essence, van der Leeuw's starting point is a definition of the concept of *power* in religion. This occurs in the first chapter of his book. Following the definition of power, all subsequent chapters stand as extensions or elaborations of the initial description. Van der Leeuw's approach is to look at the concept of power multiperspectivally. Then, having done this, the content of his book is composed out of a blending and interpenetration of the multiple perspectives.

Much of the background is formed by the work of Rudolf Otto and Martin Heidegger, the two in combination. Power, the central concept of religion, refers to the visible side, the tangible aspect, of human experience of the "other" (or *numinous*). But it is not simply the "wholly otherness" of the "other" that intrigues van der Leeuw. As distinct from Otto's treatment, van der Leeuw was interested in the ways in which human experience is connected or united with the "other." He wanted to describe and analyze the interrelationships between subjective and objective dimensions within human experience of the "other." Power makes the subjective and objective religious dimensions accessible because it belongs to both. It refers, on the one side, to the awesomeness, mystery, and majesty that Otto had associated with "the holy." And, on the other side, it refers to religious sensitivities that are evoked by a recognition of its presence. It has this dual aspect; it registers in both objective and subjective terms. Van der Leeuw was as much concerned to describe responses to power as he was dedicated to giving a full and accurate description to the concept of power. The concept cannot be enunciated except via the responses, and the responses are formed by awareness that power implies the reality of an "other." To describe the objectivity of power is to include the subjective response.

The recognition of the tremendous force and implicit compulsions of power led van der Leeuw to portray a variety of human responses. Human responses include attempts to define power, identify powerful things, mark out the range of the powerful, and regularize the patterns of emotional responses to power. The latter becomes formalized in worship and in the establishment of religious observances. From here, van der Leeuw proceeded to demonstrate that power and sacredness are intimately interwoven; both demand a separation and demarcation of special places and precincts. This subject led, in turn, to a treatment of the sacred environment. That environment cannot be described adequately without some more specific reference to its components, components that cannot be enumerated without attention to their function within the sacred environment. Similarly, a detailed treatment of sacred places and spaces implies some recognition of contrasting situations, since the word *sacred* implies a contrast with the word *profane*. The same topic is not exhausted unless attention is also directed to "regional distinctions" within the sacred environment. Thus, a treatment of the concept of power in religion leads to a phenomenological description of the relationship between "this world" and "higher worlds." And so the descriptive process goes.

The thematic unveiling is undergirded in *Religion in Essence and Manifestation* by an elaborate formal outline. One sometimes finds that the content of a phenomenology of religion seems to be based on nothing more than almost random selections of topics and categories. Sometimes, it seems, a phenomenologist of religion employs the table of contents as a list of creative opportunities, to suit chosen purposes. Because more is known about one subject than another, the phenomenologist might give one of them larger space than is accorded to other subjects. Frequently, the manner of arranging the materials in a phenomenological portrayal is simply ad hoc. Sometimes the table of contents is influenced by an approach to religion that phenomenology purports to make obsolete—as, for example, when the chapters on magic appear early in the list and those on high gods come near the end of the book. But van der Leeuw's outline is deliberate, logically consistent, and comprehensive. He drew upon the possible vantage points implicit in subjective-objective interdependence in devising a five-part outline. First comes treatment of the object of religion. This is followed by discussions of the subject of religion. Next, van der Leeuw treats the object and subject in reciprocal relationship. Then come the extensions and specifications: first, a description of the world viewed in religious terms; second, a descriptive examination of religious forms.

The central thesis of the book pertains to objective-subjective and external-internal interpenetration and interdependency. It was van der Leeuw's contention that the subject and object of religion stand together. This implies that there are both internal and external relationships between humans and power. Responses to power form inward and outward action—as, for example, in prayer and meditation and in human participation in sacrificial and other ritual ceremonies. But the reciprocity is to be felt in other ways too. "This world" and "the world above" are understood to interpenetrate. Thus, eventually, external-internal and object-subject distinctions should be understood as dimensions or perspectives within one and the same unitary "world." Van der Leeuw described it this way:

> [A] religious *Weltanschauung* is never merely a "point of view," but is always a participation, a sharing. For out of his own particular environment everyone constructs a world for himself which he believes himself able to dominate; there is therefore no one single world, but just as many worlds as there are human beings. The human spirit does not direct itself towards a world that is given to it, but allows what meets it to become part of itself, after it has sufficiently modified it.

This attitude helps define the ways in which the human being should respond.

> Accordingly, man does not conduct himself "objectively" towards the "world": he participates in it, just as it does in him. His path to the world, therefore, is neither that of contemplation, nor reflection, nor presenting himself as a subject and so forming a "substratum," but of existing as oriented towards the world. Man's domination of the world is thus a domination exerted always from within.

Having established an attitude to the world that was significantly influenced by the philosophy of Heidegger, van der Leeuw proceeded to describe the forms of religion. By *forms* he had reference, first, to the historic religions of the world, which he approached in a typological (but not sociologically rigorous) way. Second, *forms* refers to the founders of the religions, the religious personages, and to personal characteristics of followers of religious teachings. All such descriptive portrayals flow from van der Leeuw's fundamental analysis of power. The religions and the participants in them are what they are because of the dynamism and progressive unfolding of power.

Two editorial observations are in order. First, one cannot escape noticing that van der Leeuw was more intent than he always disclosed to describe the religious perceptions of so-called primitive peoples. The numerous references to the work of Lévy-Bruhl make this fact apparent. Many portions of van der Leeuw's book appear to have been written as if in conversation with Lévy-Bruhl. This tendency becomes even more explicit in another of van der Leeuw's books, *La structure de la mentalité primitif* (The Structure of Primitive Mentality), 1928, a book that was inspired by the orientation and interests of Lévy-Bruhl.

Second, it must be said that van der Leeuw's is phenomenology only in a "soft" sense. It does not display marks of the rigorous science Husserl envisioned, nor is it resolute in its apparent interest in "the things themselves." The Swedish scholar Åke Hultkrantz says that van der Leeuw's approach is "too speculative, in some places, even incomprehensible, to be of much use to the seriously working empirical religious researcher." Hultkrantz's comment highlights that van der Leeuw's work was not based on careful, precise, and methodical empirical analysis. Some empirical analysis is involved, to be sure—van der Leeuw did not make his subject up. But his goal was not to fashion as accurate and complete a portrayal as careful scholarly investigation is capable of. Rather, van der Leeuw cultivated insights and instincts, as well as personal religious sensitivities, of a dominantly aesthetic variety. He spotted connections and found analogies that are formal, poetic, literary, and artistic. It would be too much to say that his interpretations were posited rather than deduced. Yet it is accurate to say that van der Leeuw was a literary craftsman who worked under the conscious and deliberate influence of strong theological compulsions. For all of these reasons, Mircea Eliade is correct in pointing out that van der Leeuw "really never attempted a religious morphology or a genetic phenomenology of religion."

Hence, it is not surprising that the phenomenological tendencies in van der Leeuw's work are not methodologically rigorous. Certainly the book is a product of phenomenological description; but it also contains rather large vestiges of the *sine qua non* approach. Power virtually qualifies as "that without which religion would not be what it is." Seen this way, the two volumes can be read as illustrations of this fundamental contention. Hence the reader never really knows how to place the book, for the attempt to identify a single core element by grouping a collection of simples forces one eventually, it seems, to prefer one or the other of these interests. Van der Leeuw wanted to have it both ways. Hence, he has provided a descriptive account, with large poetical license and particular theological sanction, of a fundamental core element.

This reader concludes that the controlling disposition is neither methodological nor phenomenological. Nor is van der Leeuw's ultimate intention to present a descriptive portrayal. Rather, his work was influenced most significantly by his own devotional—shall we say liturgical?—attitude to the materials he treated. The aesthetic quality of *Religion in Essence and Manifestation* is the vehicle through which a phenomenological account became a doxology—a doxology to the God Christians worship. The same God rules the world, van der Leeuw believed, manifesting God's power in both objective and subjective terms.

C. J. Bleeker: Phenomenology of Religion Deciphered and Analyzed

The universities of Holland, as we have seen, have provided a setting for both early and intensive phenomenological inquiry into the nature of religion. They have also been places of considerable self-consciousness regarding the scope and practice of phenomenology in the study of religion.

Such methodological self-consciousness is most apparent in the writings of C. J. Bleeker (1898–1983). Although he is not a phenomenologist in the strict sense of the term, Bleeker deserves the attention of this chapter if only for his astute comments on the propriety of the phenomenological approach to the study of religion.

He has not tried to lay complete groundwork for his own phenomenological renditions. But he has been interested in assessing and clarifying the vast, multiform, and always somewhat complicated enterprise called the phenomenology of religion. Because of his interest in the subject, much of his efforts belong to what might be called a phenomenology of the phenomenology of religion.

Bleeker recognized, for example, that not everything called "phenomenology of religion" is the same in intent or design. Revising the classification first offered by Eva Hirschmann in her *Phänomenologie der Religion*, he observed that there are at least three distinctive kinds of phenomenology that belong under the large generic term. The first type engages in purely descriptive work and concentrates on a systematic classification of religious data. The second sort adds typological interests to descriptive classifications, and seeks to identify different types of religion. The third kind attempts to transcend mere description and typological portrayal by seeking to employ phenomenological techniques to make the essence and nature of religion accessible.

Bleeker believed that all three factors belong to a strong and resilient phenomenology of religion. He calls the first activity *theoria*, referring to the collecting and sorting of data. *Logos*, the second phase, denotes a deeper penetration into the internal structures of religious phenomena. The third motion, *entelecheia*, identifies a task that transcends the work of either *theoria* or *logos*. Bleeker explained that phenomenologists of religion have a propensity for focusing on "arrested pictures" or "moments of stopped action." He was suspicious of such tendencies, if the theorists allow phenomenology to be no more than this, because he believed attention was being restricted to static factors—or phenomena whose dynamisms are restrained by the very techniques of phenomenological inquiry.

He put it this way once, when commenting on Raffaele Pettazzoni's observation that methodologists frequently neglect the concept of *development* in their analyses of religion:

> It is clear that the task of the phenomenology of religion generally is taken as a static one. It is certainly true that the significance of religious phenomena can be clarified to a great extent if they are examined, so to say, as arrested pictures.
>
> But it should not be forgotten that they are also moving pictures, i.e., that they are subject to a certain dynamic.
>
> In order to do justice to this element I introduced the notion of "the entelecheia of the phenomena." In the course of my argument, it suffices to tell that *entelecheia* is taken in the sense which Aristotle assigned to this word, namely, the course of events in which the essence is realized by its manifestations.

The task of phenomenology of religion cannot be static, for the essence of religion is dynamic through and through.

Bleeker's proposal is subtle, and bears important ramifications. He was well aware that evolutionism, which builds upon concepts of motion and change, has held a prominent place in the history of religion. Yet he wanted to scrap this theory as a working operational principle in favor of a concerted attempt to appreciate the logic of narrative accounts. In other words, the attempt to find some sense in an "endless flux of happenings" is destined to treat the history of religion as a narrative.

There are good reasons, Bleeker believed, for shifting the focus. The concern to identify religion's origin, for example, is based on mistaken assumptions. The origin of religion is "beyond scientific comprehension," for, in his words, "religion appears spontaneously." Also, the quest for origins has led to a dissipation of interests that should have been devoted to appreciating and detecting "the historical logic" in the course of the history of religions. That logic is both more sophisticated and more complicated than the simple evolutionist theories are willing to admit. For example, nonevolutionary and antievolutionary factors serve important functions in development. Development is not the only course of history, however. Reformation, transformation, metamorphoses, and other designations of change also belong to the logic of history. These factors must become prominent, too, in any accurate narrative account. In addition, the narrative must be looked to to explain why some religions die and others survive, why some get stripped of alien features and others tend to be synthetic and are able to comprehend obvious aberrations. It must also come to terms with the multiple sorts of processes of transition and transformation that can affect a religion. This multiplicity is just the beginning of ways in which historical and phenomenological studies can be expanded and refreshed by the recognition of multiperspectival approaches. Such approaches are necessary to come to terms with complex change, real dynamism, and true spontaneity. In his remarks on the *entelecheia*, Bleeker has opened the windows to the creation of new designs of method and interpretation that may even carry phenomenology of religion beyond phenomenology. While the ramifications can only be sketched, the intentions are clear. In Bleeker's view, "religio-historical studies first get their full flavor when they show how religious conceptions and rites function in a texture of all kinds of non-religious ideas and forces." The stress should be placed on both ideas and forces, for the essence of religion, however one identifies it, is thoroughly dynamic.

Thus, Bleeker's contribution toward energizing the phenomenology of religion is expressed in at least three ways. He was concerned first of all to distinguish the several sorts of scholarly endeavor that are classified as phenomenology of religion. Then, turning his analyses toward the internal makeup of a phenomenology of religion that is regulated by an attempt to depict and characterize religious phenomena, he suggested certain focal objects that might be useful in lending rigor and discipline to phenomenological inquiry. These twin tasks in discriminating and sorting are tied to a larger objective that Bleeker hopes to insert into the phenomenologist's program. In addition to the two prominent intentions to which phenomenologists adhere and subscribe, Bleeker recommended a third purpose which, when its striking ramifications are traced, can lead to an updating and refurbishing of the method itself.

Bleeker's classification was based on an insight that phenomenology works at various levels or dimensions of penetration. Purely descriptive phenomenology is more surface oriented than the kind of phenomenology that seeks to identify underlying structures. Similarly, the *entelecheia* approach seeks for comprehensive explanation while the other two kinds are more content with reliable descriptive portrayal. Whether such a system of classification is useful in bringing order to a vast field is debatable. Those who draw up or respond to such schemes of classification exhibit a perpetual tendency to feel that all schemes, whatever they are, can be improved. But the table does illustrate the marked differences in method and approach among those who call themselves phenomenologists of religion. Their foci vary as well as their controlling interests. Perhaps the only link between them is provided by their shared intention "to detect the structure of a greater or smaller complex of religious phenomena." The means under which that detection occurs, and the uses to which it is put, as we have indicated, are markedly different.

Significant, too, was Bleeker's attempt to sort out the formal methodological components of phenomenology of religion. He recognized, for example, a kind of grammar to the enterprise: certain ingredients, elements, touchstones, or specific foci recur in structural inquiries into the function or nature of religion. He listed these recurrent structural characteristics, as follows:

1. *Constant forms* (or similar, analogous, or parallel features in the various religious traditions, regardless of their time or place of origin). Bleeker cites, for example, the high degree of similarity in the metaphors used within a wide range of religious and cultural contexts to describe the relationship between God and man. Another case in point is the almost common language employed in mysticism the world over to describe "the moment" in the ascent of the soul to God.

2. *Irreducible factors* (or the features of the portrayal of religious phenomena that are *sui generis*; namely, those that cannot be derived from anything else or reduced to any other line of approach to the subject). Bleeker was impressed with the uniqueness and originality of the subject domain of the phenomenology of religion. He insisted that phenomenology of religion is not a branch of another discipline, and that it does not derive from a more general field of study. But this is simply to say that religion must be approached by perspectives that are designed uniquely to treat religion. Other perspectives on the subject—be they sociological, psychological, anthropological, historico-cultural, theological, and so on—can replace the basic approach that honors the *sui generis* quality of religious phenomena. The method of penetration and analysis is designed to preserve the uniqueness and distinctiveness of the subject-field.

3. *Points of crystallization* (or the specific foci within a portrayal of religion that reflect characteristic genres of orientation). Here Bleeker made reference not so much to approaches to the subject as to how the materials of the subject are grouped. He recognized evident organizing principles within the data. When *nature* is that principle, for example, nature casts its formative powers upon whatever

is brought within its range of concern. Similarly, when *spirit* is that principle, the materials are arranged to give priority to spirit. When the religious orientation is toward cosmic life, the cult life is emphasized. Appropriately, "mundane existence" is given a lesser or derivative status, and, for the same "cosmic reasons," mysticism is given firm place. In other words, as Bleeker conceived it, phenomenology of religion classifies religious phenomena according to prevailing thematic tendencies.

4. *Types* (or inexplicable or incomparable fundamental motifs by which one religion is distinguished from another). Here Bleeker was referring to comparisons and contrasts of various religious traditions. He is impressed, for example, with the fascination with the mystery of death that is expressed in Egyptian religion. Greek religions exhibit a large interest in the relationships between the ideal form and creativity. A prevailing propensity toward law is found in Roman religion. Christians have always had a preoccupation with the harmony and order of the universe. Such fundamental motifs distinguish one religion from another.

Having identified some of the formal ingredients of phenomenology of religion, Bleeker added that the phenomenologist must find ways to bring all of them into his or her descriptive and analytical work. The phenomenologist must be concerned with recurrent features of religion, the uniqueness of the subject matter, the patterns according to which religious materials are arranged, and the differences between religious traditions. This is simply another way of saying that the phenomenologist of religion is dealing with a multiform reality that is accessible only when analysis is equipped to penetrate combinations of ingredients.

In light of this large list of methodological considerations, it is perhaps apparent why Bleeker did not write a phenomenology of religion in any full, comprehensive, and descriptive manner. Certainly philosophical modesty was a contributing factor. But even were this obstacle to be overcome, Bleeker would continue to have strong reservations. A phenomenological account can never be as comprehensive as it must be because of the dynamic character of religion. Hence, in pointing out this fact—ostensibly, to benefit phenomenology by insisting that its grasp be resilient—Bleeker actually made it more difficult to undertake the enterprise successfully. Clearly, in Bleeker's terms, phenomenology of religion is encouraged to produce a kind of symphonic portrayal, a rigorous science with all of the characteristics of *Verstehen* built in.

History of Religions Become Phenomenology of Religion: Geo Widengren

Something of the same spirit marks Geo Widengren's approach to phenomenology. Yet, unlike Bleeker, Widengren has written a comprehensive phenomenology of religion, which is resolute in preserving a grudging attitude to all theoretical extrapolations away from "the things themselves."

Throughout his career, Widengren has maintained a suspicious, critical, and openly skeptical stance toward theoretical free associations. He will not allow phenomenology to traffic in speculative and imaginative flights beyond the data. His inclination is to label all such elaborative tendencies "farfetched." For him, the initial overenthusiasm for phenomenology carried the new science recklessly beyond the proper limits of knowledge. Thus, phenomenology produced the same high-level generalizations—van der Leeuw's work is an example in point—that phenomenology was designed to overcome. Phenomenology's fundamental intention is to consider things in and of themselves, and not as examples, illustrations, or manifestations of some abstract theory, general law, or comprehensive system of thought. Widengren recognizes, too, that the very systematic and synthetic character of phenomenological elaboration creates content for religion that is not always historically or empirically justified. In other words, in Widengren's view, phenomenology of religion created some of the very characteristics of religion that it subsequently proceeded to describe. To be sure, this may have been done unwittingly, but it still makes the religion that registers within some phenomenologies of religion a construct. This, it goes without saying, is a questionable way of conducting a scientific inquiry.

Widengren's large, comprehensive manual is entitled *Religionsphänomenologie,* or, in its original Swedish, *Religionens Värld.* Both titles refer to the author's intention to identify, sort out, arrange, classify, cross-reference, and, to a degree, summarize the products of textual analyses and historical investigations. There are few other obvious signs—no reference to the work of philosopher predecessors, no evident utilization of the *epoché* or other formal philosophical terminology—that would identify the book as being phenomenological in anything other than a descriptive, classificatory sense. Indeed, the format and content of the book retain remnants of the evolutionist model, the approach to religion in which Widengren was trained as a student in Uppsala University. For example, the book begins with a chapter on distinctions between religion and magic. Distinctions between religion and magic have constituted the starting point in the history of religions in Scandinavia from their beginnings. This has been typical of the deportment of the discipline ever since Nathan Söderblom introduced C. P. Tiele's *Kompendium,* the outline of which was based on an evolutionist model. The treatment of this fundamental distinction is followed by a chapter on taboo, then a treatment of holiness—all of this before the author approaches the religions of primitive peoples. Even the chapter on deity follows the familiar evolutionist pattern: from pantheism to polytheism to monotheism.

Religionsphänomenologie is encyclopedic in scope. It is designed to group materials according to type, class, and kind rather than on the basis of geographical or historical considerations. Its author's competencies are primarily historical and philological. Hence, he approaches phenomenology of religion as a natural extension of rigorously empirical scientific work. Phenomenology of religion refers to an advanced summarizational stage in scholarly inquiry within which results are sorted out and implications are drawn. Phenomenology functions to identify, describe, and classify the positive features of religion. Agreeing with Kristensen on this matter, Widengren describes history of religion in the following way:

> While phenomenology treats all manifestations of religious life, from wherever they appear, the history of religion employs a purely historical method to investigate developments within individual religions. Phenomenology of religion tries to give a comprehensive account of all the various phenomena of religion in order to give a systematic summary of the history of religion. History of religion provides the historical analysis, while phenomenology of religion furnishes us with a systematic synthesis.

This reciprocity demands, in Widengren's view, that "the products of the systematic and the historical methods of approach must always complement each other." He is quick to acknowledge too that one takes certain risks in submitting the products of detailed historical research to systematic and synthetic phenomenological portrayal:

> [I]t stands to reason that a given phenomenon when taken out of its structure for phenomenological comparison will lose something of its real significance which it has only when serving as part of the total structure of the individual religion. Here, obviously, a real danger lies that a phenomenological investigation may lead to highly superficial comparisons and therefore be absolutely misleading.

Such statements imply that the normative context is "the total structure of the individual religion—each religion considered apart." Widengren does not think first in comparative-cultural terms, but rather approaches each religion as an integral unit, to which context every aspect of that religion makes reference. Throughout, the safeguards against excessive or extravagant elaboration are explicit. William of Ockham's dictum that multiplicity, or complications, ought not be posited without necessity (*pluralistas non est ponenda sine necessitate*) can be taken as a crucial operational principle within Widengren's version of the phenomenology of religion. Phenomenological depictions must always be judicious and economical. The phenomenologist must be temperate. Widengren's is phenomenology in a deliberately nonmetaphysical, nonontological and, especially, nonideological form.

This is simply another way of recognizing that for Widengren religious phenomena inhere in *sui generis* contexts. Religious phenomena possess their own particular manners and forms of determination. As a historian of religions, Widengren proceeds by fixing his attention on phenomena that are historically or textually accessible, and works to place these within their original, native contexts. In this setting, the historian can proceed to probe, explore, describe, cross-reference, and explain each item as fully, specifically, and minutely as the data allow. Then, when it becomes evident that one context has been influenced by another, or that an ingredient within one context actually derives from some other source, the historian can go on specifically to talk about borrowings, interaction, contact, influence, continuity, syncretism, and the like. But all such categories emerge from a careful scrutiny of native or natural contexts. They exhibit definite location and are not treated in an abstract, speculative manner. The rule is that one can treat a phenomenon by understanding where it stands, without transforming it, without reaching for some higher level of generalization, and without making that element ingredient in something else. Widengren does not feel comfortable with generalizations, for his interest is in the specific rather than in the generic. The same holds for the syntheses and systematic classifications that belong to phenomenology. Widengren recognizes that such ventures are necessary to bring order and design to the subject-field, but he is also well aware that the higher forms of generalization possess their own conceptual dynamics that transform data into something more elaborate.

For all of these reasons, Geo Widengren advises students and beginning scholars in the field not to begin with phenomenology. For him phenomenology is a field the historian of religion enters only after serving an appropriate apprenticeship (and not even necessarily then). The student does not begin training in the history of religion by studying phenomenology. Instead, phenomenological training is taken up after one has demonstrated one's ability in the necessary preliminary fields of investigation and research. One has to pass some qualifying exams first. All of this is consistent with Widengren's controlling temperament, his conviction that phenomenological adventures are engaged after one has been properly initiated into the field. The "initiation rites" are designed to strip the devotee of those baser intellectual appetites that, left to follow their own excesses, might easily lead to quick and premature syntheses.

As noted, Geo Widengren takes exception to the simplistic, excessive, and intemperate synthesis. He resists all transforming reinterpretations of the given. Thus his phenomenology is produced somewhat grudgingly, as if it can no longer prevent itself. But, for this very reason, it is also a phenomenology that assigns highest place to critical empirical and historical research. From this perspective, the links between Widengren's *Religionsphänomenologie* and typical philosophical or theoretical projects in phenomenology are always at least partially fortuitous.

Mircea Eliade: Phenomenology as Integrative Worldview

We initiated this chapter on phenomenology of religion by separating the various schools and approaches that go by that name. Our major contention, from the first, is that there is a phenomenology in a primarily philosophical sense that is different, in many respects and intentions, from the various approaches to religion that are also called phenomenologies. We distinguished two large versions of the philosophical form of phenomenology—Husserl's and Merleau-Ponty's—alongside of which we could have listed a wide assortment of others. Then we outlined and described several examples of phenomenology of religion in the more ideographic sense.

Before we leave the subject, we must focus attention on an example of phenomenology of religion that qualifies as phenomenology in both contexts. Certainly, it is not phenomenology in the fullest Husserlian sense; it makes no pretense at this. Yet it does indeed come to terms with Husserl's thought in a fundamental and direct way. And, in wrestling with Husserl's contentions, it has also served comprehensively and eloquently as phenomenology of religion in the second sense. We are referring to the distinguished work of Mircea Eliade (1907–1986), the scholar whose writings are referred to most frequently when phenomenology of religion is discussed, particularly in the United States.

So large, so suggestive, and so strategically comprehensive has Eliade's work been that many onlookers even attribute the definite and rapid growth of religious studies programs on college and university campuses in North America to its influences. Many students' first acquaintance with religious studies has come through Eliade's classic work, *The Sacred and the Profane.* This book may have as much influence on its generation of scholars and students as Otto's *The Idea of the Holy* had a generation or two before. In college after college, course after course, it has been employed as the textbook—in many instances the first book to introduce the subject of religion and religious studies. In addition to providing intellectual means of entry to the subject of religion, Eliade has also created his own phenomenology of religion, a portrayal sweeping in its scope and provocative in its suggestions. As indicated, it is phenomenology that purports to say something significant about the human being in relation to all that sustains humankind. When one becomes immersed in it, one is taught that phenomenology is a method that belongs to religious studies, and religious studies is a discipline that conveys important insights regarding the meaning of human existence—yes, even regarding the nature of reality.

As with other phenomenologists of religion, or historians of religion who employ phenomenological methods, Eliade's intention is to identify the prominent, influential, and formative patterns or structures of religious experience. His book *Patterns in Comparative Religion* gives good indication of his comprehensive life's work. To approach religion by concentrating on patterns or structures is to work toward identifying and describing some of the perennial aspects of religion, regardless of the specific contexts to which such phenomena belong. Eliade wants to do more than merely list these patterns, but he is not interested in providing an encyclopedia of them. Rather, as a historian and phenomenologist of religion, his intention is to demonstrate that the items he singles out for phenomenological portrayal contribute to an integrated rendering of the *morphology of the sacred*. In his understanding, "the sacred" (or, in Otto's words, "the holy") refers to a distinct modality, a modality of consciousness. Thus, his purpose as a scholar and writer is to lend characterization to that modality through an examination of its constitutive elements. In short, the morphology of a distinct modality of consciousness is approached by an examination of structures, patterns, and forms. Because the objective is to produce a morphology, and the method involves a systematic examination of structures, patterns, and forms of religious sensibility and behavior, the entire enterprise qualifies thoroughly as phenomenology of religion.

Eliade's work in this field is guided by two interrelated intellectual interests. The first, as already noted, involves the morphology of the sacred. In this respect, Eliade understands his work to have precedent in Otto's *Das Heilige*, whose purpose, its author acknowledged, was to identify, depict, and analyze "the modalities of the religious experience." Eliade was inspired by Otto's project, but he understands the focus of his own inquiry to be different from Otto's. The author of *Das Heilige* concentrated primarily on the irrational quality (the total otherness, or *ganz andere*) of the experience of the sacred. Without diminishing the significance of its irrational elements, Eliade wanted to provide a fuller and more comprehensive account. Thus, as he states it in *The Sacred and the Profane*, the intention of his own scholarly investigations is "to present the phenomenon of the sacred in all its complexity and not only in so far as it is irrational." He can say it in another way: "What will concern us is not the relation between the rational and nonrational elements of religion, but *the sacred in its entirety*." This gave him a sound starting point. As he puts it in the opening lines of *Patterns in Comparative Religion*: "All the definitions given up till now of the religious phenomenon have one thing in common: each has its own way of showing that the sacred and the religious life are the opposite of the profane and the secular life." The same point is made in *The Sacred and the Profane:* "The first possible definition of the sacred is that it is the *opposite of the profane*."

The sequence runs this way: To come to terms with religion, the scholar must concentrate on a subject that is fundamental, central, and decisive. The focal point of these studies must be the sacred, perhaps as Otto has shown. But having chosen the sacred as the fundamental point of focus, Eliade wanted not to demonstrate its centrality, but rather to describe, portray, and characterize it in all of its multiple dimensions. His purpose was not to prove that the experience of the sacred is fundamental to religion, wherever one finds it. Rather, within a perspective which acknowledges that fact, Eliade's goal was to engage in detailed and comprehensive morphological analyses.

The second major theme, possibly more temperamental than phenomenological, concerns the relationships between a worldview that is motivated by the religious attitude and those within which the same attitude is not given a regulative place. For example, Eliade perceived the vast ranges of difference between a perspective on the world that is formed by religious sensibilities and viewpoints within which the religious dimension remains unconscious or is deliberately obstructed. To a certain extent, he could make chronological, cultural, and even geographical sense of this difference. For example, the religious temperament seems to have been present early in human history, and the long ages of history seem to have constituted departures from it. Thus, the differences between religious and nonreligious ways of apprehending the world seem to correlate well with archaic and modern forms of society. The same can be said of differences between the East and West. Eastern religious temperaments seem to articulate best with what Eliade regarded as the religious mode, whereas Western views, infected by industrialization and technological incentives, tend to be displayed as nonreligious modes of apprehension. But the reader should be aware that this scheme never works simply, nor can it be applied with rigorous, unambiguous schematic precision. For, in addition to seeing a dichotomy between religious and nonreligious modes of apprehension, Eliade was aware too that the religious mode can remain implicit (unconsciously or as unrecognized) in nonreligious attitudes. Even the most obviously nonreligious form of human awareness always includes a vestige or a hint of the religious mode of apprehension. Thus, for example, whether modern man is aware of it or not, crossing a threshold—any threshold, for that matter—recalls the experience of passage in which a frontier was crossed that separates two spaces (wherein two spaces denote two regulative worlds). Similarly, the experience of a new year recalls the primordial experience of creation, wherein a new world is born, shaped, and given proper orientation. Likewise, settling a territory is equivalent to consecrating it. All of these common human experiences bear a deeper, primordial religious significance. Thus, while modern human beings may find it "increasingly difficult to rediscover the existential dimensions of religious man in archaic societies," the dimension of the sacred has neither been eradicated nor obliterated by nonreligious modes of sensibility. But with the passage of time and the onrush of civilization, the religious mode has become increasingly difficult to perceive.

The two themes are joined together by the differences Eliade perceived between the sacred and the profane, which are referred to frequently as "the two modalities of experience." The sacred mode is characteristic of the way in which human archaic societies viewed their experiences. The profane mode was a possibility in the archaic era, but it articulates most closely, as we have noted, with modern, technologized, industrialized, and postindustrialized humankind. "Religious man attempts to remain as long as possible in a sacred universe," Eliade observed, and this mode of existence must be contrasted with the total experience of life of "the man without religious feeling . . . the man who lives, or wishes to live, in a desacralized world." Desacralization is characteristic of modern times; it "pervades the entire experience of the nonreligious man of modern societies." Desacralization produces a profane mode of orientation to the world. And yet as pervasive as desacralization is, or may become, the profane mode can never become so separated from the sacred mode that the contrast between them no longer exists. Whether one is looking at the sacred or at the profane mode of existence, one must see both in terms of their fundamental opposition. The sacred is recognizable only in relation, contrast, or opposition to the profane, and the profane is known only in relation, contrast, or opposition to the sacred—regardless of whether one is examining the assumptions of a primitive, archaic society or viewing the Westernized modern world.

Against this background, Eliade's phenomenological intention was to "present the specific dimension of religious experience, to bring out the differences between it and profane experiences of the world." The binary opposition between sacred and profane, therefore, implies that a morphology of sacred existence will include, at least by contrast, a description of profane existence. For, at least in the modern setting, the profane and the desacralized are all but synonymous. The contrast is always there. Yet the mode of the sacred becomes accessible to the scholar not via the fundamental contrast, but instead through the presence of the hierophany. A hierophany, whether it be a stone, plant, tree, figure, symbol, or venerated object, is defined as that "which expresses in some way some modality of the sacred and some moment in its history." For the historian or phenomenologist of religion, the hierophany can serve two functions: (1) it has the ability to disclose something about the sacred; and (2) it lends typification to man's religious attitude. Accordingly, when working with a hierophany, the historian of religion has two tasks: "the religious historians must trace not only the history of a given hierophany, but must first of all understand and explain the modality of the sacred that that hierophany discloses."

What, then, is the expectation of the historian of religion? As Eliade saw it, after one has accumulated information about a particular sort of hierophany, the goal is to develop a "coherent collection of common features." Referring specifically to plant hierophanies (cosmic trees, agricultural ceremonies, the burning of logs, and the like), for example, Eliade made it clear that the intention of his morphological portrayal is "to formulate a coherent system of the various modalities of the vegetation cult." Thus, the meaning of such plant hierophanies pertains to "the rhythm of rebirth, the never-ending life that vegetation contains, reality manifested in recurring creation, and so on." On the basis of cumulative evidence, within which phenomenological data are employed to explain the modality of the sacred that plant hierophanies manifest, Eliade could conclude: "[A]ll these hierophanies point to a system of coherent statements, to a theory of the sacred significance of vegetation, the more cryptic hierophanies as much as the others."

Eventually, then, plant hierophanies will be seen as being but one modality of the sacred. What is done with vegetation must also be done with the sky (and its ingredients), water, the earth, sacred places, sacred times, myths, and symbols. All represent aspects of a coherent, interrelated system of modalities of the sacred. Taken together, the several hierophanal systems constitute what can be known and depicted of the sacred mode of apprehending the world, a mode which, from start to finish, stands in contrast to its appositional profane mode. The sacred mode describes a manner of living in the world in contrast to which profane existence manifests itself as "broken and alienated."

One wonders whether this is really phenomenology. Eliade offered brief but instructive comments on Husserl's project in a chapter on "Initiation and the Modern World" in his book *The Quest*. Here too he referred to the analogies between the religious function of initiation and Husserl's phenomenological endeavor. As Eliade saw it, what Husserl refers to as "the natural attitude" corresponds to "the 'profane' preinitiation stage." The function of initiation is to put one in touch with the sacred world. Eliade drew a comparison between the function of initiation in religion and the overcoming of "the natural attitude" (defined as "the everyday unreflective attitude of naive belief in the existence of the world") that Husserl sought to break down through bracketing, the employment of *epoché*, and phenomenological reduction. Thus, in Eliade's view, the profane mode stands to the sacred mode as the natural attitude stands to the perspective available to deliberate phenomenological disclosures. In both instances, the movement is away from what is illusory to what is truly real, and thus transforming. In other words, the phenomenologist, the historian of religions (as Eliade conceived of his task), as well as the religious person, seek access to what is true, fundamental, unmistakably reliable, and both primary and primordial.

Eliade's is not an approach that exhibits phenomenological aspects simply because it has incorporated some tested phenomenological techniques for making "the things themselves" accessible. Certainly, some of the same techniques are used by the historian of religions. But the real point of connection concerns the binary apposition that is present in both frames of reference. Phenomenology, in the philosophical sense, depends on the same distinction that is implicit in the relationship between the sacred and the profane. Thus, in both phenomenology and Eliade's version of the history of religions, emphasis is placed on the necessity of an unspoiled, immediate form of access to reality. Once the perspective has been spoiled—via the acquisition of the natural attitude, or, correspondingly, through the effects of desacralization—human recourse lies only in the possibility of reacquiring the primary, normative mode. While vital, education is not equal to this task, nor would it suffice that one became aware of previous and present errors of judgment. The chief problem is created by obstacles that have been placed in the way by the ease with which the alternative modality has become routinized. Such obstacles can be removed only when such acquired ways of apprehending reality are thoroughly arrested, then shocked into a new comprehensive form of sensitivity and recognition.

Ultimately, then, Mircea Eliade's morphological portrayal is designed to serve an important religious function. It is an instrument to enlighten human beings regarding the necessity of a mode of consciousness. This mode of consciousness is intrinsic to the experience of religion. In this respect, it has always been religiously normative. But it also gets lost easily, is rejected, goes unrecognized, or remains nonexplicit. The reintroduction of the primordial religious attitude into twentieth-century human experience carries the capacity, Eliade believed, of radically and positively affecting the conditions of both individual and collective experience.

Jacques Waardenburg: Phenomenology of the Phenomenology of Religion

After the explosion of interest in the subject that occurred in the Western world in the 1960s, with the development of new academic programs, new and resuscitated professional societies, and increased academic recognition, it was necessary that an inventory be taken of the scholarly work that attended such developments. Jacques Waardenburg, a specialist in Islamic religion, and then a professor of the history and phenomenology of religion at the University of Utrecht, took it upon himself to prepare such an inventory, a task he believed justified by virtue of the fact that it had been one hundred years since an identifiable subject had come into existence. In numerous respects, Waardenburg's goal in 1970 was akin to Morris Jastrow's in 1901: to create a volume (or two) on the study of religion that would identify the major contributors to theory on the subject, identify and analyze the fundamental points of methodological departure, and try to collect the findings and insights that such efforts had produced. Of course, Jastrow had created a type of study for which there were no clear precedents, while Waardenburg could take advantage of the efforts of others; but Waardenburg faced an enormously expanded range of data. Each, that is to say, was appropriately challenged.

Waardenburg proceeded by identifying the significant thinkers, theorists, and methodologists, then wrote summary statements of their work with specific reference to the contributions each one made toward understanding the subject of religion. Appended to this collection of essays are complete bibliographies on each of the writers selected. Prior to the summaries of each of the scholar/theorists selected is a set of analytical and interpretive essays on the study of religion itself. In one of them Waardenburg addresses questions concerning the interdisciplinary character of the study by showing how the various subfields (biblical criticism, anthropology, sociology, history) have made lasting contributions. In another of the prefatory essays, Waardenburg traces the development that found the academic study of religion emerging as an autonomous discipline. In another, he tackles questions concerning the future of the discipline and what practitioners within it can be expected to unlock and disclose.

His conclusions pertain primarily to the assessment of the field's strengths, weaknesses, vulnerabilities, and potential for the future. Waardenburg offers that it is vital to know and appreciate the social and intellectual circumstances out of which studies of religion emerge. He believes it important to recognize that Western openness to religions of other parts of the world was stimulated by the Enlightenment emphasis on reason and tolerance. Accordingly, a nineteenth-century interest in the dynamics of human nature spawned intrigue regarding religious experience. The desire to get some working sense of a "common history of mankind" has led to a desire to place the religious traditions side by side, in some meaningful historical or developmental order. The linkage of religion and culture presents challenges to understanding, particularly since both of these entities are dynamic and subject to change: Does religion change when the culture changes, or is it more useful to speak of the two as embodying interrelated and interdependent causal forces? Similarly, Waardenburg believed it important to examine the religions in contemporary as well as historical modes. Beneath it all, Waardenburg posits that the academic study of religion will enable the Western world to reduce or more effectively control its tendency toward self-absolutization. What the academic study of religion discloses is that religions are various, cultures are various, and the combinations between them are both numerous and ever-changing. Thus, at no time in world history are the religions simply situated in some permanent state, but all are in process of change. The relationships between religions, as well as between the cultures to which they are linked, are always changing and developing too. The layout of identifiable personages within the field, together with a brief discussion of their contributions to the study of religion, is looked to to achieve its own goals. That is, Waardenburg's phenomenology of phenomenology of religion provides impressive testimony that the field is characterized by considerable intellectual activity, the growth of which is producing an ever-growing fund of insights into the nature and function of religion.

Eric J. Sharpe: A Phenomenology of Religious Studies

At the beginning of this chapter the point was made that phenomenology of religion exhibits two discernible intellectual pathways, one that is substantively philosophical in nature and another that is committed to objective, descriptive portrayal and classification of the data of religion. The second of these pathways has also produced a "metaphenomenology," that is, an analysis and interpretation of what scholars committed to the phenomenological method have produced and achieved. Moreover, this metaphenomenology has tended to be developed sequentially; that is, the products and achievements of the scholars who have analyzed religious data this way have been attached to a chronicle that originates with the work of C. P. Tiele and P. D. Chantepie de la

Saussaye and exhibits representational examples from the time of methodological origins to the present. Consequently, most of the phenomenologists have studied other phenomenologies (that is, the available systems of classification) before advancing their own. And most provide some deliberate explication of the relationships between their proposed phenomenologies and the more comprehensive objectives of the academic study of religion. Many, as we have noted, tend almost to equate phenomenology of religion with the study of religion. A few others, like Jacques Waardenburg, treat the study of religion as phenomenology. His brand of phenomenology of religion involves providing objective, descriptive accounts of phenomenologists of religion in prescribed sequential order.

Something more is at stake when a scholar includes the phenomenologists within a comprehensive portrayal of the workings of religious studies. Moves in this direction can be found in Waardenburg's two volumes, and the precedent for the same was established in Jastrow's early twentieth-century book *The Study of Religion*. Yet, the fullest, most comprehensive example of this approach to the subject belongs to Eric J. Sharpe and his book *Comparative Religion: A History*, first published in 1975. Sharpe was born in England in 1933 and was educated there and in Sweden. He taught in both those countries before becoming chair of the religious studies department at the University of Sydney, Australia. Sharpe's study comes as close to being a comprehensive essay on the history and purpose of religious studies as anything that is yet available. As with Jastrow, Sharpe offers a brief history of the study by identifying significant antecedents. He reads nineteenth-century analyses and interpretation of religion with an interest in identifying those portions of it that stand as building blocks for a subject-field not yet sure of its own name. He chronicles the discussion through which the phenomenological categories were identified and tested. He places the pure phenomenologists—namely, those intent on providing objective description to the data of religion—within an intellectual context that also includes scholars interested in working with religious experience, other scholars whose preoccupation was the relationships between religion and culture, other scholars whose approach to religion came via probing the world of the unconscious, and other writers who stand as spokespersons for the various world religions. All of it, he attests, belongs to what he would prefer to call "comparative religion," a name that suggests there is no single privileged vantage point from which the whole of the subject can or should be approached. Sharpe allows that all of the activities he has identified and probed belong fully to the study of religion. Indeed, religious studies as it is known today would not exist were it not for the dynamic interaction between vantage points as well as for the intersection of interests and intentions by which the subject is both addressed and engaged.

As Sharpe views it, the challenge is to bring some order to this variety so that the subject-field called religious studies has certifiable content as well as scientifically respected methods of analysis and interpretation. This, of course, is the principal challenge that religious studies itself faces. There is a general acknowledgment that the varieties of intellectual pursuits to which religious studies gives encouragement are worthy of encouragement. But it is exceedingly difficult to discover the rules by which some activities are excluded and others given warrants. Sharpe observes that "the extent and variety of the available disciplinary options have increased to a bewildering extent," and there is little hope of discovering "a master key capable of opening every one of religion's innumerable locks, or some vantage point high enough to enable one to view the whole of the labyrinth." Therefore, Sharpe concludes that while the work that religious studies enjoins carries certain resemblances to both science and art, it probably comes closer to being *a craft*, given the fact that several interrelated and sometimes conflicting interests motivate a person to become a scholar. That is, the individual is at the same time analyst, critic, observer, believer, and unbeliever. It is appropriate that one recognize the particular disposition that is being exercised in any given analytical or interpretive act, but one and the same individual will exercise all of these dispositions when attempting to come to terms with religion. Thus, it should not be surprising that religious studies itself is characterized the same way. It is a body of discourse to which scholars have wide ranges of response and reaction, in which varieties of fields and disciplines own rightful place, and to which the most appropriate methods can hardly be scripted.

Since religion evokes such a wide assortment of reaction and response, it is no wonder that religious studies is reflective of this assortment. But Sharpe insists that the pathways toward intelligibility are not miscellaneous, but have been cultivated by venerable pathfinders, the record of whose successes and failures is worthy of serious study. This, too, occurs in religious studies. By extending phenomenology into religious studies, Sharpe intends that scholars recognize what others are about and how this relates to what they are about. Truly Sharpe's efforts qualify, in his words, as a "wide-angle approach to the study of religion and religions."

Structuralist and Poststructuralist Developments

When phenomenological methods were first conceived, they were touted as carrying the capacity to exercise the kind of scholarly impartiality and objectivity that was forbidden to methods that were either deliberately or tacitly ideologically dependent. Phenomenologists could claim that they had no other interest beyond providing an accurate portrayal of the phenomena or the data. Thus their penchant for descriptive accounts, and their reluctance to engage in speculation that might carry them beyond the range of their acknowledged competence, were well understood and almost uniformly admired. The problem is that some sort of rationale must be offered to explain why the descriptive account is written one way rather than another. As soon as such explanations are entertained—or if possible rationales are understood to be in competition with each other—the phenomenologist proceeds beyond purely descriptive work into justifications for categorial selections. Whether they admit it or not, all phenomenologists are forced to take this step—albeit, most frequently, reluctantly. But some phenomenologists make strong claims for the legitimacy of the categorial schemes they are advancing. When such claims are proposed, phenomenological description is carried beyond itself into one of the varieties of forms of structuralism.

The genesis of the movement reaches back into the nineteenth century to the methodological innovations of Ferdinand de Saussure, (1857–1913), author of *Memoire sur le système primitif des voyelles dans les langues Indo-européennes* (1878), whose catalytic structuralist work, *Course de linguistique générale* (1906–1911), was reconstructed from lecture and class notes by Saussure's students. Saussure was the first to treat language as a system of signs. In the new science of semiology (which treats the art of using signs in signaling or in expressing thought), Saussure not only included language alongside rites, customs, and other forms of social and cultural expression; he also argued that the other signs could be approached through the model of language analysis. It is significant that the structuralist method originated within the science of linguistics, and that, as a linguist, Saussure perceived connections and interdependencies between linguistic structures and conceptions of society.

Were we tracing the development of the movement further, we would cite the Russian formalist school, which focused on the form of works of art, the technical skill of the artist, and the interdependence of form and technique. Originating in the 1920s, the Russian school is known by a number of outstanding theorists, the most prominent of whom is Roman Jakobson (1896–1982), author of *Slavic Languages* (1955), *Phonological Studies* (1962), and more than four hundred other publications. Jakobson played a key role in the development of structuralism by creating intellectual and methodological bridges between linguistics and literary criticism. In so doing, he also motivated the Russian school from formalism to structuralism. Thus, while citing the achievements of the Russian school, we cannot neglect the significance of a single book, Vladimir Propp's *Morphology of the Folk Tale* (1968) as being instrumental to this development.

Consequently, wherever one finds it and however it is designed and executed, the disposition to approach cultures as well as their representative literatures with an interest in discerning their fundamental, underlying structural patterns is responsible for creating both a methodological orientation and a particular school of thought. Whether it qualifies as a school, a movement, or simply a loosely knit constellation of like-minded interests, the title given to the intention is *structuralism*.

Without question, the best-known practitioner of the school is the French social-anthropologist Claude Lévi-Strauss (b.1908), author of *Tristes Tropiques*,

Structural Anthropology, The Raw and the Cooked, The Savage Mind, and numerous other books, articles, and chapters in collections of scholarly essays. Indeed, Lévi-Strauss is as dominating within structuralism as Edmund Husserl is within the field of phenomenology. Both stand as formative thinkers. Lévi-Strauss is the one who gave the structuralist attitude systematic elaboration and extension.

Lévi-Strauss took Roman Jakobson's hypothesis to the next stage of elaboration and application. Jakobson concentrated on the procedures by which humans encode and decode sound patterns into meaningful speech forms. He proposed that the coding/decoding process relies on discrimination of sounds as bundles of binary oppositions. Lévi-Strauss took Jakobson's principle and applied it to the composition of culture, suggesting that the structural features—as represented in typical styles of art and architectural design, rules and regulations regarding marriage, rules and regulations regarding sanctioned eating practices, the layouts of towns and cities, and so on—manifest patterns of binary opposition. So too are the rules of binary opposition implicit (but explicable) in mythology. In the opening chapter of *The Raw and the Cooked,* Lévi-Strauss writes as follows:

> The aim of this book is to show how certain categorical opposites drawn from everyday experience with the most basic sorts of things—e.g. "raw" and "cooked," "fresh" and "rotten," "moist" and "parched," and others—can serve a people as conceptual tools for the formation of abstract notions and for combining these into propositions.

Such "categorical opposites" are reflected in the myths, tales, legends, and historical treatises of a culture, stories that are enacted in their ritual practices. Lévi-Strauss refers to the identification of such elements as being a kind of philosophical Kantianism in that the elements themselves are formal factors that function in regulative, organizational ways. Such forms of order, in Lévi-Strauss's view, are the "logic" or "code" whereby the human mind operates, the discernment and understanding of which make knowledge possible.

Perhaps the most serious defender of Lévi-Strauss among religious studies scholars is Hans Penner (b.1934) of Dartmouth University, author of *Impasse and Resolution: A Critique of the Study of Religion* (1991). Certainly Penner is not willing to accept all that Lévi-Strauss asserts, and he is far from being an enthusiastic proponent of structuralism. But he does believe that both Lévi-Strauss and structuralism should be acknowledged properly and studied carefully, for the latter, as he puts it, "may be the foundation upon which a well formed theory of meaning can be built." Penner underscores the potential fit between structuralism and the meaning of religion by utilizing the word *structure* in his definition of the subject: "religion is a verbal and nonverbal structure of interaction with superhuman beings(s)." Taking Lévi-Strauss' work as an updated version of Tylor's, Penner concentrates on *structure*, which denotes the manner according to which the system of elements is understood to cohere. In formulaic terms, "the relations that elements enter into define or constitute the system." Under religion as system, or systematic network, Penner urges his colleagues in religious studies to pay heed to critical analyses of structural dynamisms. No compelling theory of religion can be seriously advanced, he contends, unless its attention has been trained on the logics through which elements of the system are defined by the relationships in which they participate.

The spirit of Penner's injunctions are made explicit in E. Thomas Lawson's and Robert N. McCauley's *Rethinking Religion: Connecting Cognition and Culture* (1990), a study that applies Noam Chomsky's thesis that languages are sociocultural systems to religion. They understand religion to be "a symbolic-cultural system of ritual acts" accompanied by appropriate, culturally legitimizing conceptualization. Although Lawson and McCauley do not accept Chomsky's or Lévi-Strauss' contentions uncritically, they do regard them as having created the right setting for productive analysis and reflection.

In addition to Lévi-Strauss, prominent figures within structuralism include Roland Barthes (1915–1980), the keenest structuralist literary critic in France; Jacques Lacan (1901–1981), who approached psychiatry, neuropsychiatry, as well as psychoanalysis in a structuralist manner (arguing, for example, that "the unconscious is structured like language"); and Michel Foucault (1926–1984), who, despite his antipathy toward being labeled a structuralist, had heavy investments in such analyses in coming to terms with the development of culture in the West, from the seventeenth century to the modern era.

In the course of its development, structuralism has added to its range of application. Beginning as a method of analysis in the field of linguistics, it has expanded in the direction of analyzing myths, describing the unconscious life of human beings, and portraying structural formations within literary, artistic, and musical forms of expression. But, regardless of its focus, structuralism always works to penetrate the complex network of interrelationships of parts within a whole so as to provide a description thereof. Whether it is concentrating on the characteristics of a myth, the nature of consciousness, the structure of a musical composition, the form of plastic art, or the formal ingredients of literary expression, structuralism focuses on logical coherences; that is, relationships between necessary formal elements.

Georges Dumézil (b.1898) is not, strictly speaking, a structuralist. Rather he is properly identified as an Indo-European mythologist and folklorist who, in the course of his analyses, discovered a fundamental tripartite social and cultural pattern in the social organization and symbolic expressions of proto-Indo-European peoples. Dumézil suspected the pattern was also replicated wherever Indo-European language and culture cast their influence. Thus, Dumézil and his students and colleagues found the same pattern in German literature, Norse folklore, Greek and Roman mythology, and beyond. Tripartitism is reflected in the definition of the social stratum within each of the contexts these literatures reflect. The social stratum was determined by a threefold class distinction between warriors, priests, and the keepers of the herds. This, as has been pointed out, is characteristic of the social stratum of peoples throughout the known world, from India to the Balkans to the Black Sea to Scandinavia. Moreover, the threefold pattern is exhibited in conceptions of deity and in relationships that are understood to pertain between humans and divine beings.

Dumézil's portrayal is undergirded by Durkheim's insight that the way in which deity or divinity is conceived is reflective of societal organization, for both social facts are intertwined with supernatural facts. But Dumézil proceeded beyond Durkheim by proposing that the information about supernatural reality—namely, the content of myths—manifests deeply embedded ideological principles. He refers to this as "tripartite ideology," explaining that the cultures he has examined tend to organize their content according to three hierarchical principles: sovereignty, force, and fertility. As we have noted, the tripartite ideology is to be found in a wide variety of cultural settings. Among scholars of religion who make productive use of Dumezln's theories, we single out Bruce Lincoln (b. 1948) for the persistent attention he has given to an examination of the applicability of tripartite ideology. In *Death, War, and Sacrifice: Studies in Ideology and Practice* (1991), Lincoln provides a two-pronged appraisal of Dumézil's work. First, he uses Dumézil as guide in creating his own descriptive portrayal of Indo-European mythology. Then, he identifies the way in which Dumézil's preferred ideological position influences his rendition of the tripartite ideology. Clearly Lincoln is a disciple who has learned a great deal from the master and, as a clear sign of his respect, has decided to engage the master in a sparring bout over critical issues. Lincoln's other books, particularly *Myth, Cosmos, and History: Indo-European Themes of Creation and Destruction* (1986), are similarly cast as lively responses and vigorous reactions to Dumézil's contentions.

Religious studies has not yet made up its mind about the propriety and utility of structuralist methods, incentives, and interpretations. As already noted, Hans Penner and others have praised the work of Claude Lévi-Strauss as possessing disclosive abilities in identifying the ingredients of religion and the ways in which it functions in culture. Wendy Doniger's *Asceticism and Eroticism in the Mythology of Siva* is a vivid example of structuralist analysis that illumines a topic belonging centrally to the field of religious studies. Numerous scholars within the field have employed structuralist insights for purposes of textual analysis and interpretations. Whenever such methods and insights are employed, the discussion among French theoreticians is invoked. That is, these exploratory investigations cannot presume to go forward, even within the academic study of religion, without deliberate and conscious reference, for example, to Roland Barthes's analyses of literary form and semiology, Jacques Derrida's analyses of "signs" and "representations," and Michel Foucault's increasingly influential attempt "to uncover the deepest strata of Western culture." Prominent are Edmund Leach's (anti-Lévi-Straussian) structural analyses of myth and totemism, and Rodney Needham's technical defense and elaboration of Lévi-Strauss's analysis and interpretation of kinship relationships.

We have chosen not to pursue these developments here, for two compelling reasons. First, chapter 5 on "The Language of Religion" culminates in analyses of structuralist, poststructuralist, modernist, postmodernist, deconstructionist, and postdeconstructionist developments inasmuch as this entire body of interpretation originated in an effort to come to terms with *texts* and, consequently, then with hermeneutics. The second reason is that these developments do not progress in anything resembling a straight-line forward fashion. That is, much of the discussion concerning structuralism that has occurred within the field of religious studies concerns the propriety and utility of whatever it purports to stand for. Thus, before many of the anticipated returns were registered, and the method was given an opportunity for more extensive application, the approach itself was made subject to systematic criticism. Its vulnerability or flaw is that the patterns of order it is presumably equipped to identify are (or were) presumed to be of a homologous variety. This does not imply or intend that no distinctions are imposed, or that no differences are admitted. Rather, the patterns on which definition is based were understood to be of a homologous kind with respect to which all difference or distinction is comprehended within schema of harmony or symmetry. Even when there is binary opposition, the two components are understood to be ingredient in the formative relationship. When structural analysis unveils patterns that run contrary to such expectations, when distinctions imply prevalent, determined, or deliberate opposition and conflict, then all would-be harmonics are placed in jeopardy. And should it become apparent that structural difference is in fact real conflict, or that conflict rather than mediated difference is regulative, then the intentions of the analyst are altered too, and the implications of the inquiry point in other directions.

Suffice it to say here that phenomenology-become-structuralist eventually experiences deconstructionist influences. When this happens, methodological interest is focused not so much on how the pattern can be put together, but on why it happens that an intrinsic tension and conflict prevail. To understand this phenomenon, the analyst is encouraged to concentrate on examining the ways in which words (as well as sequences of words) function to put things in subjection as well as to carry out programs of subversion. But, as noted, this is a topic that properly belongs to a more comprehensive examination of the ways in which analyses of the functions of language, as well as the nature of linguistic construction, figure in the scholarly study of religion—a crucial topic that is reserved for the latter portions of chapter 5.

Summary Regarding Extensions of the Phenomenological Approach

Some of the intellectual enthusiasms attached to the structuralist approaches we have cited derive from the promise of greater definition, rigor, and solid footing that they are able to contribute to the method of phenomenology. Phenomenology, *per se*, always gives something of an impression of being unsure of its capacities. For example, phenomenology seems unable to tell its practitioners just how many characteristics of a subject must be included to provide an adequate portrayal. It has difficulty training its devotees in the art of appropriately identifying the nexuses of relationships and interdependencies that pertain between an entity's fundamental characteristics. Consequently, phenomenology seems vulnerable to the charge that its collection of ingredients is too random, or that its classification of phenomena is arbitrary, partial, one-sided, and static. Then, too, as a system of classification, phenomenology is not always sure of its proper range, or of the philosophical foundations on which its analyses rests. It seems to yearn for greater foundational coherence and more precise principles of operation and application. The tendency is there, from the outset, to look elsewhere for the authority on which sound investigative work depends. In other words, a descriptive approach to a subject possesses considerable advantages in that it need not wrestle with questions about essences and natures in order to proceed. But, what it was able to avoid at the outset, it almost seems predisposed to confront before it has finished, that is, if called on to explain why its descriptive portrayal can be trusted.

Husserl knew this, and came to terms with it by making his descriptions of patterns dependent on analyses of essences. Maurice Merleau-Ponty intended to mark in the ingredients of a "grammar of life," but to do so he had to contend with the age-old conflict between rationalist and empiricist forms of philosophical reflection. Ostensibly, what Mircea Eliade had in mind was a full and comprehensive account of "the patterns of comparative religion," but to accomplish this he had to employ the word *morphology* in a number of senses. Before he was finished, he had related a "morphology of the sacred" to a distinctly human "mode of consciousness." In other words, to complete the comprehensive portrayal of religious phenomena, he found himself engaged in a psychological and even a metaphysical inquiry. His conclusion is that there is no "morphology" without a distinctive "modality." An inquiry that was designed to come to intelligible terms with particulars—that is, with the specific components of a subject—begins to sound as abstract and theoretical as if it were about some transcendental reality. Many of the other classifications of the phenomena of religion that we have surveyed in this chapter—the ones that provide little if any rationale regarding the basis on which their selections of ingredients are made—seem random and arbitrary. Through what criteria should one prefer one over another? How could one persuade a phenomenologist of religion that his or her portrayal has omitted a vital element? From what vantage point can one argue that a particular phenomenological account is off base?

The force of such questions seems to be that if phenomenological portrayals are to be properly grounded, philosophically speaking, they would seem to require confirming authority that a descriptive method is not equipped to supply.

Hence, such an approach shows signs of wanting or having to reach out for such authority to resources that are always transmethodological. And, when it does so, it loses something of the precision of the rationale that belongs to the distinctiveness of its intentions.

This dilemma makes phenomenologies of religion susceptible to structuralist, Dumézilian, and a variety of other sorts of corrections and augmentations. Each example of augmentation is supported by the perceived need for greater definiteness. The Dumézilian approach finds the normative structure in mythology. Structuralism tends to look to language for its necessary definition. Other phenomenological accounts are rooted in the structure of consciousness, the structure of the psyche, the structure of human awareness, or even the structure of the modality of the sacred. The tendency in each case is to identify the whole of which the phenomena are characteristics.

The move beyond descriptive portrayal, while providing the means of confirming authority, also forces advocates of phenomenology to become "true believers." Previously they had been committed to the singular usefulness of a method; now they have also taken on a stance, or have acquired a position, or have become advocates of an ideology. Before long, the accoutrements can become so numerous and extensive that someone must declare that what is needed is the imposition of the single-minded rigor and modest methodological pretensions of the science called phenomenology.

Additional problems arise. In his book *Map Is Not Territory (1978)*, Jonathan Z. Smith has observed that there is a pervasive ideological element in the preponderance of scholarly approaches to the study of religion, an element that supports the disposition (or predisposition) to "lay prime emphasis upon congruency and conformity." Smith notes that this tendency is most apparent in phenomenological approaches to religion that build themselves upon the occurrence of repetition. He understands that the same tendency is present in "functionalist descriptions of feedback mechanisms" as well as in "structuralist depictions of mediation." Because of this preponderance, Smith has chosen to direct his own inquiries toward exploring "*the dimensions of incongruity* [emphases mine] that exist in religious materials." But the ramifications transcend Smith's own work. His suggestion is that the tendency in religious studies is to draw upon conceptual schemes, ordered by congruence and conformity, that actually frustrate the ability to understand much of what belongs to religion. He says it boldly: The search for patterns, repetition, and replication has had a devastating effect on the understanding of religion. The primary effect has been to project a presumed comprehension on data that elude the modes of understanding employed by the scholar. In such situations, the consequences of scholarship are no more than readouts of the mechanisms of analysis and interpretation that have been imposed under the sponsorship of a driving ambition to achieve congruence and conformity.

Charles H. Long (b.1923), who for years was Jonathan Smith's colleague at the University of Chicago, has also identified a pervasive ideological element, but for him it has less to do with formal and dispositional methodological factors and much more to do with how groups and peoples stand with respect to one another in specific cultural environments. In his book *Significations: Signs, Symbols, and Images in the Interpretation of Religion* (1986), Long gives evidence of detailed familiarity with the entire development of phenomenology of religion from its origins in Chantepie and Tiele to its current developments. In tracing this development, Long observes that most phenomenologies of religion are written from an intention to come effectively to terms with the religions or cultures of other peoples, and to do so in a manner that is objective (meaning fair-minded), accurate, and significantly illuminating. The stance that is assumed by the scholarly investigator is that what is out there to be interpreted is *other*. Very different conceptions result when the investigator is himself/herself *other*—other, that is to say, as defined or identified by the prevailing ideology under whose auspices the descriptive investigation is being carried out. What prevailing methodologies tend to do, in Long's judgment, is to endow the investigator with "privileged status." For some Americans, Long reminds his hearers, such ways of thinking are indeed "other," and for some, privileged status in America has never been experienced. "New discourse concerning the meaning of religion . . . will occur when Americans experience the 'otherness' of America." The discovery has been slow by virtue of the fact that prevailing cultural and ideological dispositions have protected stances that can avoid such realizations—paradoxically, under declared obedience to the principles of scholarly objectivity.

The discussion of this chapter was introduced via a distinction between two forms of phenomenology. The observation was made that religious studies has invested heavily in both of them. It was insisted that the roots of the two strands are distinct; the corollary had it that the history of the academic study of religion is replete with instances of conjunction and conflation. What has become apparent through this chapter is that the second form of phenomenology—the one that wishes to protect its extraphilosophical or theoretical independence—has looked to the other form of phenomenology, from time to time, for encouragement and support. When doing so, it has also requested complementation. The moral seems to be that, whether all advocates acknowledge this or not, both strands are necessary eventually. The most telling and crucial factor is the relationship that is understood to pertain between them.

THE FUNCTION OF RELIGION

Through the previous chapters of this book, we have been tracing a sequence of methodological development in religious studies. What began as a concentrated effort to identify a single, definitive core element of religion became challenged, along the way, by a series of attempts to provide religion's numerous characteristics with some perceptive and accurate pattern of organization. The approaches that we surveyed in the first two chapters are marked by a rigorous methodological single-mindedness: they are intent on identifying an *essence* or a *root cause* to make religion intelligible. The approaches that we examined in the third chapter are designed to come to terms with a multiplicity of characteristics, and their task is to bring such multiplicity to a perceptible and intellectually compelling order. We have noted that the move from single to plural focus is accompanied by a shift from normative definition to descriptive portrayal.

We also noted, in chapter 3, that phenomenology of religion (the methodological approach under whose auspices such descriptive portrayals are undertaken) has not always found it easy to provide an intellectually satisfying account of the basis for selecting its principles of organization. By temperament and disposition, phenomenologists would like to be able to contend that their schematic portrayals are reflective of religion's intrinsic orderedness. We have observed, however, that the same phenomenologists often reach out for criteria, sometimes external to "the things themselves," to bolster their claims. When they do, they involve themselves in additional kinds of theoretical reflection that invites the attention—sometimes praise, and sometimes scorn—of scholars working in other fields. This is not to say that the phenomenologist's approach to the subject of religion is seriously flawed. It is to observe, however, that each of the approaches we have identified carries built-in methodological challenges.

It is possible to bring intrinsic logical rigor to a descriptive portrayal of the phenomena of religion without having to appeal to external principles of verification: by linking the multiplicity of characteristics to the question of function. That is, instead of trying to bring order to the multiplicity as if it all existed in some fixed state, the inquirer can insert disciplined attentiveness to the teleological factors involved. To do so, following Aristotle's recommendations, is to treat the phenomena as being characteristics of an organism, and then to approach that organism as an entity that has an identifiable purpose or objective. Such an amendment carries the promise of lending rigor to a descriptive portrayal, since the organizing principle is not a product of some importation from outside. In addition, a teleologically focused phenomenological description carries safeguards that religion is being studied in terms of its social, cultural, and political roles. The analyst has specific social, cultural, and political considerations to keep in mind. Thus in this necessary concretization of the subject lies the prospect of a compelling descriptive account. Furthermore, a functional approach tends to improve the quality (while increasing the range) of access to the multiplicity of characteristics of religion. It is difficult to talk about religion *per se*, from this vantage point, since it is more appropriate to talk about the religions. Accordingly, one thinks less about society than about the specific societies with which the religions are in relationships of interdependence.

The founding fathers of this orientation are Emile Durkheim in France, and Max Weber in Germany. The two are not only the primary formative figures for approaching religion in sociofunctional terms, but, as might be expected, they also stand as seminal thinkers in the development of sociological theory. Each possessed the ability to formulate basic issues in provocative and resourceful ways. Both formulated methods and procedures that have been employed by generations of scholars who have followed them. As Immanuel Kant stands as the one who launched the inquiry regarding the religious *a priori*, so Durkheim and Weber stand as the initial patrons of that long, sustained, and ongoing attempt to understand the nature of religion by concentrating on the dynamics of social organization.

Emile Durkheim: Religion Is Eminently Social

We have encountered Emile Durkheim (1858–1917) before. In the second chapter of this book we observed that the interest in origin and development eventually joined forces with the treatment of religion as an organic system. We noted that this combination of intellectual interests was embodied in Durkheim's formulations. He weaved both models together, and his strategy was complex. He concerned himself, to be sure, with primitive thought, but he wanted to distinguish this interest from that of those who were tracing the lineaments of evolution. Thus, instead of focusing his attention on the ontogenetic factors of the primitive mind, he reached for morphological description. Next, he employed that morphology to demonstrate that there are exact (and not simply continuous) evolutionary correlations between elementary and contemporary forms of religious life. Eventually, he both created and inspired a comprehensive analysis of social systems. Thus, according to the categorization employed in this book, he devised an early version of religion as "a system of organic coordinates." In order to do this, he worked painstakingly to give definition to religion; and, in defining religion as "something eminently social," and in knowing precisely what this meant, Durkheim also offered a kind of *sine qua non* account. Hence, in partially detaching origin from evolution, and in approaching origin in collective social terms, Durkheim weaved together characteristics of at least three methodological approaches. The product was a contribution of such substance and worth that the book *The Elementary Forms of the Religious Life*, first published in 1912, still stands as a landmark in sociological theory as well as within the history of the academic study of religion. E. E. Evans-Pritchard, who disagreed with Durkheim on many questions, nevertheless referred to him as "perhaps the greatest figure in the history of modern sociology."

Durkheim's theory is both systematic and comprehensive. His methodological strategy was to identify, then describe and analyze, and, finally, to explain "the most primitive and simple religion." He wished to identify the least complex instance of the phenomenon so as to gain reliable and fundamental insight into, in his words, "the religious nature of man." He believed that religion is basic to human intelligence, so basic and primary that it carries a host of formative influences on the very structure of human life. The *sine qua non* interest prevails throughout. Primitive religions are instrumental to Durkheim's recovery of what is rudimentarily human. His intention was to uncover the indispensable. Indeed, he even employed the phrase with which we have become familiar: "that without which there could be no religion."

The proposal is that "religion is something eminently social." This means more than that religion has a social dimension, or that it registers in social terms. More profoundly, it is at this point that Durkheim's contentions regarding *collective representations* (from the French "collective conscience") come into strong play. By means of this concept, Durkheim called attention to the manner in which social groups form their respective patterns of conscious and articulable "we-feeling." Such collective cohesiveness always involves the articulation of ideas and symbols in terms of which the group understands its identity and gives expression to its sense of shared destiny. "Collective conscience" denotes the innate awareness or perception of the group or collective reality and is the basis for united action and cooperative endeavor at those times and in those circumstances when the group is functioning as an aggregate and not simply as a collection of individuals. Thus, "collective conscience" carries a representational capacity: it gives evidence of the way in which the group forms its conception of reality. In other words, reality is constituted by social order, and the "collective conscience" is the source and sustainer of moral values, cultural ideals, religious aspirations, and all other determinants of prevailing collectivity.

Durkheim's interest in religion, at least in part, was calculated to facilitate his quest for the rudiments of a universal collective conscience. As he views it, religion functioned—and still functions—to give formation to the intellect. Thus, in analyzing the characteristic features of primitive religions, Durkheim believed it possible to uncover some of the ideas by which the intellectual life is constituted. Of religion's formative intellectual capacities, Durkheim wrote:

> [I]t has been less frequently noticed that religion has not confined itself to enriching the human intellect, formed beforehand, with a certain number of ideas; it has contributed to forming the intellect itself. Men owe to it not only a good part of the substance of their knowledge, but also the form in which this knowledge has been elaborated.

He provided some examples:

> At the root of all our judgments there are a certain number of essential ideas which dominate all our intellectual life; they are what philosophers since Aristotle have called the categories of the understanding: ideas of time, space, class, number, cause, substance, personality, etc. They correspond to the most universal properties of things. They are like the solid frame which encloses all thought. . . .

Take time, for instance. Durkheim affirmed that the sense of time is composed collectively. All persons possess the capacity for time. Without this category, reflection is not possible. Yet, the particular content time is given derives from social life.

> It is not my time that is thus arranged; it is time in general, such as it is objectively thought of by everybody in a single civilization. This alone is enough to give us a hint that such an arrangement ought to be collective.

The calendar is the best clue, Durkheim holds:

> The divisions into days, weeks, months, years, etc., correspond to the periodical recurrence of rites, feasts, and public ceremonies. A calendar expresses the rhythm of the collective activities, while, at the same time, its function is to assure their regularity.

The same is true of space, and even of the ideas of class, force, personality, and efficacy. All of these reflect social conditions. The most telling feature, however, is that senses of time, space, class, force, and the others change through the centuries. This is further confirmation, Durkheim believed, that the rules by which intelligence is formed are significantly influenced by historical and social conditions.

His summary is that "religion is something eminently social," by which he means that "religious representations are collective representations which express collective realities." In other words, reality is constituted by social order, and the collective conscience is the primary constitutive factor.

Having located religion in this way, and having demonstrated its social and ceremonial origins, Durkheim proceeded to say something about how religion functions in society. Focusing particularly on religious belief, Durkheim offered that all beliefs, regardless of their historical and cultural circumstances, tend to invoke a primary distinction between the sacred and the profane. All of them, regardless of specific auspices, employ this distinction as their fundamental means of discrimination: "This division of the world into two domains, the one containing all that is sacred, the other all that is profane, is the distinctive trait of religious thought." The distinction between sacred and profane applies to the social function of religious myths, rites, and beliefs. Sacred things are always identified and protected in mythic story and ritual behavior. Profane things, contaminants that they are, are always kept at a safe distance. Furthermore, religious beliefs are "the representations which express the nature of sacred things." But, given the formative power of religion in society, the real function of the distinction between sacred and profane is to divide reality into two modalities. Durkheim noticed that "the whole universe" is viewed within a system of priority-setting that divides everything into "two classes which embrace all that exists, but which radically exclude each other." The representation of reality, formed by the religious imagination, consists of "two heterogeneous and incompatible worlds." Durkheim offers the following definition:

> A religion is a unified system of beliefs and practices relative to sacred things, that is to say, things set apart and forbidden—beliefs and practices which unite into one single moral community called a Church, all those who adhere to them.

On the basis of the primary distinction, one can appreciate why it is said that religion is aligned with the conception of the collective social vision. The conception of the ideal is born out of human aspiration and gives expression to a fundamental capacity inherent in human nature:

> [A]bove the real world, where his profane life passes, he has placed another which, in one sense, does not exist except in thought, but to which he attributes a higher sort of dignity than to the first. Thus, from a double point of view, it is an ideal world.

But, in attempting to form the content of aspiration, the ideal functions also to sustain society's present and actual situation. "The ideal society is not outside of the real society; it is a part of it. Far from being divided between them as between two poles which mutually repel each other, we cannot hold to one without holding to the other." In society, via the instrumentation of religion, the ideal is formulated. Thus society is always forming itself in light of the ideal it envisions, and the ideal is always in process of formulation. In the process, it becomes evident that the prime formative factor in religion is social. At the same time, religion also functions as the genetic root of social causation. Religion is the fundamental, formative germ of the "collective conscience," apart from which social context it cannot be understood. It is natural to the human. That is, its origins lie in something more universal than a particular capacity or idiosyncrasy of the earliest humans. Religion bespeaks a fundamental human tendency. It is a perennial and permanent feature of human nature.

Max Weber: The *Verstehen* Approach to Organic Coordination

We noted earlier that Durkheim shares with Max Weber (1864–1920) the distinction of being the primary formative figures, the seminal intellectual giants, in the sociology of religion. The approaches of each were not only comprehensive, they were also generative. Both asked questions in ways that invited answers, and additional questions, and corresponding answers for generations to come.

We must observe, at the beginning, however, that Weber's now famous analysis of the world's religions was tangential to his paramount interest. That interest was directed toward uncovering the reasons for the rise of capitalism in the West—a subject that belongs to the history and theory of economics. In trying to design a genetic account of the rise of capitalism, Weber undertook an examination of the characteristics of culture. In doing this, he involved himself in a careful examination of culture's religious and ethical components.

Had one asked Max Weber about his driving intellectual intentions, however, one would have been treated to extensive comment on the interrelationships between theoretical and empirical factors in the formation of a culture. Weber was steeped in Kantian theory and was keenly aware of the proposals that had been advanced regarding the conditions that make knowledge possible. His objective was to apply some of the same insights toward identifying the conditions that make culture possible. He believed that the key was to be found in the role of formal factors.

Recall that the neo-Kantian response to idealist criticism of Kantian theory involved an argument on behalf of the formative capacities of human intentionality in giving shape and order to the phenomenal world. Neo-Kantian revisionists, however, had no need of an ideal mind. Certainly, mental dispositional factors had to be acknowledged if the phenomenal world was to exhibit order. But this did not require, as the idealists had contended, that the world be a product of idea. Recall that for the idealists, reality itself is mental, and what is called phenomenal is regarded as a mere (and sometimes secondary) appendage of the fundamental noumenal reality.

The neo-Kantian response to the idealists intended to bring reality into the spatiotemporal manifold that Kant himself had referred to as phenomenal. Their goal was to remove the metaphysical encroachments of the idealists so that the "real world" could be delivered safe for rigorous scientific investigation. In other words, investigators could concentrate on making sense of "the real world" without being obligated to include some other (certainly transcendent) reality in their descriptions and interpretations. Scientific inquiry could proceed without having to pay obeisance to inappropriate considerations over which science had no intellectual or methodological control. Thus, when the phenomenal world was set free from noumenal reality, accorded its rightful self-existence, the methods of inquiry could become rigorous, and the inquirers could gain confidence that the results of their inquiries were thoroughly reliable.

We rehearse these various responses to Kant's philosophy because they form background to Weber's career. Weber's work belongs to the debate between the neo-Kantians and the idealists, and his discussion of the issues employs vocabulary that reflects this conversation. In this framework, Weber's intent was to find a way of reconciling the positive contentions of each of the several parties in the debate by extending the context to a range of subjects within which those contentions could be tested.

Against the strict positivists (those who regarded the spatiotemporal manifold, or Kant's phenomenal world, as the only world there is), Weber contended on behalf of a phenomenal/noumenal dual dimensionality. But with the positivists, Weber believed that the spatiotemporal world is open to strict, rigorous, analytical, scientific investigation. At the same time, against those who believed that scientific investigation could be reduced to empirical analysis, Weber sought to attribute scientific respectability to an extra-empirical, supra-analytical intellectual attitude. Weber referred to this form of intelligence as *Verstehen*, or understanding in the richest, deepest, most thorough sense. When defending the necessity of *Verstehen* in scholarly investigations, Weber came to give some shape and description to the noumenal dimension. *Verstehen* was not simply some fuller methodological ploy than what was exhibited in typical scientific approaches to phenomenal reality. In addition, it made noumenal content accessible, allowing and encouraging the researcher to cultivate rigorous scientific approaches to subjects the other approaches tended to avoid.

Weber's retention of revised idealist aspirations, however, should not lead us to suppose that he proposed arguments, say, on behalf of the reality of transcendent mind or spirit, or that he tried to populate Hegel's mental world. Here too he was much more refined and judicious. He retained a modified idealist multidimensionality so that valuations would register within rigorous analysis. For Weber, the noumenal world was populated with motives and intentions, all of which were implicit in mental acts. Thus, the only way to grasp phenomenal facts was to perceive them in meaningful relationships with a supraphenomenal range of human consciousness. But, because noumena consisted of motives and intentions, it could always be conceived functionally. Thus Weber paid attention to the interrelationships of motives and intentions with acts and events. In weaving neo-Kantianism and neo-idealism together, allowing each to modify the other, Weber sought to fuse scientific fact with cultural understanding.

The content of the noumenal world, in Weber's scheme, was constructed out of the typical dispositions of arrangement by means of which cultures are formed and meaning is rooted. In coming to terms with that content, Weber attempted to be thoroughly anti-aprioristic. He did not want to postulate noumenal content in advance of his investigations. Rather, he sought to uncover the real content through analytical syntheses of experiment and interpretation.

Throughout, an important distinction can be drawn between Weber's outlook and those of the theoretical philosophers. While the philosophers were treating and modifying distinctions between phenomena and noumena to come to terms with the nature of reality—or with the meaning of things, *per se*—Weber was concerned to give shape and interpretation to predominantly *social* reality. His scheme was not designed to map or explain the ways in which everything in the universe coheres, or even to identify the factors necessary to human cognition. Rather, he was seeking a reliable basis for social theory. Concerned with distinctively social reality, Weber used a contention that belonged to the wider context—namely, that knowledge is possible only through an integration of noumenal and phenomenal factors. But he revised, refined, and modified that contention so that it would fit the body of material with which he was working.

The application must be refined, but the task of integrating noumenal and phenomenal factors remains. Integration is necessary so that the empirical situation can be enveloped with meaning. And in drawing up an integrative scheme, Weber had to be careful not to violate the following principles: (a) that the content of the noumenal world is not produced in an aprioristic fashion; (b) that the constitution of the phenomenal world is not produced by the phenomenal world solely, but reflects the intentionality of the noumenal dimension; and (c) that the constitution of the noumenal world must be enunciated without violating the restrictions against apriorism or qualifying the dependence of phenomena on noumena.

Weber created a scheme of integration by drawing upon the constitutive abilities of a theory of "ideal types." This theory enabled him to sustain the ideological factor without diminishing the rigor and precision of empirical inquiry. Ideal types are described as configurations of meaning. They are conceived, framed, or postulated, but never created, by the researcher. They are considered as idealized examples. When Weber refers to them, he has in mind personalities, social situations, changes, revolutions, institutions, classes, and, of course, religions. They find confirmation in the empirical data they are called upon to interpret. They are hypothetical (that is, they have this formal status), but they also possess a concrete base. The researcher conceives of them in order to gain meaningful access to the social world. One conceives of them, but they are not created *ex nihilo*. Yet one can employ them without feeling obliged to account for their origins. Weber insisted on but two criteria in the postulation of an ideal type: (1) that it represent a situation that is objectively possible; and (2) that it possess a formative (causal) capacity. To demand that it be objectively possible is to insure that it not violate known fact. To require it to possess a formative capacity is to make certain that the researcher is dealing with a subject of significant consequence. The ideal type should be "causally relevant" to behavioral fact. If it is not, it leaves integration lacking. Thus, the causal relevance of the ideal type is consistent with the relationship between noumenal and phenomenal dimensions that Weber retains, while pointing its application to social reality. Under social refinement, the relationship of noumena and phenomena gets translated into the interdependence of motives and acts.

One can see a specific rendering of the interdependence of motives and acts in Weber's classic treatment of the relationships between Protestantism and capitalism. Weber's conception of this interrelationship illustrated his fundamental thesis that religious ideas (the formal, noumenal factor) possess an independent causal significance in any system of social action or process of social change. Thus, according to the manner of integration just referred to, Protestant religious orientation stands as the source of motivation from which the action of capitalism follows. To say that Protestant religious views are causally relevant to capitalism is to contend that without them capitalism may not have come to exist, or at least would not have become what it is. The interdependence of Protestantism (motive) and capitalism (action) is Weber's chief example of dynamic social integration.

But while noting that Weber found a direct correlation between Protestant religion and capitalist economic tendencies, we must also recognize that Weber usually employed the theory of ideal types in a comparative manner. His prime concern was not with the influence of religious ideas on personal and social motivation in the Western world, but rather with the integration of motivation and action in a cross-cultural perspective. It is from this vantage point that he approached a study of the world's religions. All of his many cross-cultural studies were ruled by a single contention: that the human conception of deity influences and shapes concrete actions and social relationships. This is another way of saying that the ideological religious conceptual system functions as a source of motivation within given cultures. Every specific social configuration of meaning has its ideal and its material counterparts. To put the same contention in more striking terms: Specific religious orientations are translatable into socioeconomic terms. The religious orientation supplies the socioeconomic situation with meaning and interpretations. *Verstehen*, it turns out, is an empathetic means of access to the dynamics of interaction. It puts the methodologist in touch with the motivational and actional components of integration.

We lack sufficient space here to trace out the content of Weber's cross-cultural religious comparisons. Suffice it to say that in every instance, he focuses on the manner in which the ideal and the material dimensions are interpreted. This prompted him to deal with specific conceptions of deity, conceptions rooted in specific cultural configurations. For example, the way in which deity is composed in Hindu religion both affects and is in keeping with the socioeconomic situation of Indian culture. Similarly, the way in which the cosmos is depicted in the Hindu sacred scriptures bears a causal relationship to the socioeconomic theory that prevails in lands where these scriptures carry influence.

Weber's insights were not construed, however, simply in the abstract. Rather, they are made precise in his projects in comparative cultural analyses. For instance, Weber cited the absence in Hindu religion of any need for ethical justification of the individual before God. It is only in the Western world, he noted, that ethical justification looms large in religious practices, for such practices rest on the conviction that the world has been created by God, as a reality that stands over against God. Consequently, Western thought has a tendency to hold that the world itself must be made acceptable to the deity. Looked at from another vantage point, in Western thinking the world (creation) stands under the perpetual threat of being rejected by God (the creator). Comparing the Western and Hindu attitudes on the subject, Weber wrote:

> All this was spared to Hindu mysticism. For the Asiatic the world is something simply presented to man, something which has been in the nature of things from all eternity; while for the occidental, even for the occidental mystic, the world is a work which has been created or performed, and not even the ordinances of the world are eternal. Consequently, in the Occident, mystical salvation could not be found simply in the consciousness of an absolute union with a supreme and wise order of things as the only true being. Nor, on the other hand, could a work of divine origin even be

regarded in the Occident as a possible object of absolute rejection, as it was in the flight from the world characteristic of the Orient.

The occidental view that reality is twofold, which follows upon the contention that God has created the world, introduces the need to justify the world. The Asian view contains a fundamental unity, rather than a duality, in the relationship between deity and the true order of things; hence, the need for ethical justification is absent.

This absence carries a tendency, too, toward world denial. In occidental terms, world denial runs contrary to deep-seated religious conviction.

Because cosmological schemes differ among the religious traditions of the world, so too do patterns of salvation. With different patterns of salvation, the religions treat personal religious functions in various ways. For the various religious figures—the prophet, priest, seer, magician, and so on—function within the context of schemes of salvation which, in turn, are correlatable with specific interpretations of the influence of divinity, deity, or transcendence within "the spatiotemporal manifold." The schemata are built out of fundamental attitudes toward "the discrepancies between normative expectations and actual experiences." A religion can be seen to dissolve the discrepancy by attempting to master or control actual experiences; when this occurs, the mode of religiosity is *asceticism*. On the other hand, resignation by adjustment, while carrying certain ascetical connotations, is the condition for *mysticism*. But both mysticism and asceticism can be undertaken in both this-worldly and otherworldly terms. All of these attitudes bespeak specific socioeconomic orientations. Otherworldly asceticism, for example, carried a disposition to organize persons denominated by the ascetic point of view into social collectivities. Innerworldly asceticism developed into a conviction that "monastic commitments" could be lived out in secular callings within this world. But in other sectors, where the basis of social organization is not selective collectivity, and where there is no radical disjunction between the conception of divine and human order, communities are construed in terms of the caste system (as in India).

Viewed in its comprehensive terms, Weber's interest in religion developed out of a systematic effort to find an effective and compelling alternative to Kantian, neo-Kantian, and idealist theory. As happens so frequently in the history of nineteenth-century thought, we are in the presence of a post-Kantian conceptual pattern that has been formed both in response and in opposition to the leanings of the dominant theoretical paradigm. That paradigm, we recall, was cultivated to root the various forms of human experience (ratiocination, ethics, and aesthetics) on a certifiable cognitive base. The cardinal insight was that one can distinguish the phenomenal from the noumenal dimensions in cognition. Knowledge is limited to phenomena but is made possible by the action of formal principles; such principles, since they are not empirically verifiable, are classified as noumenal factors.

When he got to the subject of religion, Kant began by distinguishing the natural from the revealed, and certified natural religion in human experience. Revealed religion was treated as a refined expression of natural human experience.

Kant did not involve himself in comparative studies in religion and culture. Indeed, when he thought of the specifics of religion, he had only the Christian religion in mind. Had his interest been of a comparative nature, he would have been under some compulsion to explain why one religion is a fuller or more accurate expression of natural human sensitivities than another, and this might have jeopardized his propensity to place Christianity in the highest place on the scale of comparisons. He was not criticized for failing to engage in comparative analysis because the force of his interpretation of religion was to identify it with one of the three certifiable forms of human experience. The quarrel, following Kant, concerned whether he had selected the right context.

The Kantian scheme left another possibility for religion wide open. Instead of working to root religion in the appropriate range of human experience, one could look to the distinction Kant had drawn between phenomena and noumena, or between the known and the unknown, and hope to give noumena religious content. This, as we have seen, became the idealists' project. Instead of restricting the content of noumena to the formal principles necessary to cognition, the idealists argued that the noumenal is spiritual, indeed, is spirit. Thus, according to their attitude, the phenomenal world is regarded as the arena in which the noumenal, spiritual reality gains expression. The idealist view has it that the phenomenal world stands as an expression of spiritual intention.

Weber, sensitive to all of the nuances of the discussion, sought a fresh starting point. He was not interested in certifying forms of human experience. He had little interest in protecting theology by contending on behalf of the spiritual content of the noumenal. Instead, he concentrated on the morphology of culture—how culture is shaped, how it is constituted, in what lies its fundamental dynamisms, and what makes specific cultures distinctive. He was concerned about the relationship between phenomena and noumena, but he approached that relationship through an investigation of social and cultural contexts. In doing so, he described and interpreted the compatibilities between many of the major religious traditions of the world and the cultural environments within which they are nurtured. In doing so, he gave the Kantian discussion of religion added sophistication, greater specificity, and a range of application that had not been envisioned before.

Ernst Troeltsch: Inspired by Weber

Ernst Troeltsch (1865–1923) was a German theologian who took Max Weber's insights and applied them both to identify the makeup of the Christian religion as well as to help explain why it is able to assume a variety of cultural shapes and social expressions. As a theologian, Troeltsch was also motivated by apologetic interests: he believed that a revised Weberian project was necessary if normative Christianity (he called it "traditional dogma") was to become, or remain, effectively related to the interests of the modern world. He was fully cognizant of the fact that original Christianity had undergone a variety of transformations to meet the requirements of the various periods in its history. Concentrating on the situation in his own time, however, he was not persuaded that the new formulation of the dogmatic tradition was in full accord with Christianity's initial ideological core. These discrepancies— the dynamic shifts that regulated both components of integration—forced Troeltsch to study the problem within the context of "the whole sweep of the history of the Christian Church." He couched his reply in modified Weberian fashion, by employing a set of ideal types. To do this without destroying the unity of the initial Christian vision, Troeltsch contended that the fundamental ideological core was susceptible to various sorts of refraction. It was amenable to expression in a variety of typical formations.

The theological dimensions of Troeltsch's query need concern us here only to the extent that they reflect a consistency with the Weberian approach. Troeltsch's formulation of the theological question made it appropriate to the sorts of sociological analyses that were prompted by Weber's contentions. But in every instance, whether Troeltsch was looking at the situation of the early church, medieval Christendom, or even the modern era, the two components of dynamic integration were present.

Theological issues aside, the important point to recognize is that Troeltsch's use of Weber's theory in coming to terms with "the whole sweep of the history of the Christian Church" led to his famous distinction between church and sect. The genesis of this distinction, for Troeltsch, was Weber's distinction between priest and prophet. The setting includes a consideration of differences between the time of initial religious enthusiasm and the effects of a routinization of charisma. Through the routinization of the charismatic element—which is in keeping with the tendency of institutions to adapt themselves to existing sociocultural and economic situations—the radical element of the religion's first occurrence is tempered. Thus, two types of institutional organization develop. The church (a product of the temporizing of history) tends to accept the social order as partner in its interest in achieving stability and universal applicability. The sect, on the other hand, in its attempt to be motivated by nothing other than the more radical religious impulse, tends to find disassociation from the accepted social order a requirement of existence and vitality. The attitude of the church toward the world is marked by accommodation, whereas the sect relates to the world through protest or rejection. For the same reasons, the church is much less discriminating in setting criteria for membership. By contrast, the sect must discriminate, since it is obliged to base voluntary association on common regenerative experiences, and must be willing to embrace a life of ethical commitment and ascetic rigor.

Troeltsch employed the distinction between church and sect to interpret the internal history of Christianity from its New Testament beginnings. His conviction was that both types of social organization were required. From this vantage point, the critical period in church history occurred in the late medieval period, when the two formal organizational types split apart. The split occurred because the church form of religious organization had come to dominate exclusively. But, since both types of social organization were required to meet the twin but conflicting social and cultural challenges, it was necessary for each to challenge the other, and for the original-enthusiasm orientation to contest established church. This occurred openly during the Reformation. From the Reformation forward, the dynamic interplay has continued to work itself out in socially expressible terms. At the same time, Troeltsch believed that a third type of organization, based on mysticism, was necessary to reconcile the opposition between the church and the sect.

For our purposes, it suffices to note that Troeltsch's sociotheological researches involved an application of Weber's treatment of socio-organic coordination to the kinds of organizations that belong to one religious tradition. Because of the predominantly theological cast of interests—that is, because he was almost exclusively concerned with the matter of Christian collective identity—Troeltsch did not engage in cross-cultural inquiry. But the Weberian temper, if not Weber's range of interests, was present throughout Troeltsch's analysis, and stands as a source of enrichment to his theologically sensitive inquiry.

Ferdinand Tönnies: Author of a Critical Distinction

Our survey of seminal theorists has identified individuals who have made significant contributions to an understanding of religion by virtue of the fact that they developed a comprehensive approach to the subject. Durkheim, Weber, and numerous others intended to examine the subject as a whole, and not simply in one or another of its aspects. From time to time, a scholar has made a formative contribution to an understanding of the subject not through a successful attempt at a comprehensive grasp, but because of a single distinction that was inserted into the discussion and remained for subsequent generations of scholars to consider seriously.

Such was the contribution of Ferdinand Tönnies (1855–1936), German sociologist, author of the highly regarded typological study *Gemeinschaft und Gesellschaft* (translated as *Community and Society*), published in 1887. Tönnies' intention was to distinguish two fundamental types of social organization, which he understood to be reflective of two fundamental types of human relationships. *Gemeinschaft* is reflective of the workings of "natural will" whose aspiration is to create bonds between persons and groups on the basis of instinctual and largely unconscious senses of solidarity. *Gesellschaft*, on the other hand, is reflective of the workings of "rational will," and refers to the intentional and sometimes impersonal pursuit of individual and group interests.

Tönnies contended that "natural will" intends to be integrative, while "rational will" allows all of the qualities of intellection (discernment, discrimination, segmentation) to have full sway. Tönnies himself believed that will carries a priority over intellect, and thus favored an organizational structure of a voluntaristic character. As noted, his distinction was a most influential one and earned a kind of permanent status within sociological theory. Not least, the American author William James paid high tribute to Tönnies, even associating him with the enthusiasm he had for his concept "will to believe."

Franklin H. Giddings: Founder of American Sociology

To this point in this chapter, we have been concentrating on the contributions of European thinkers who drew directly from the conversation stimulated by Weber and Durkheim, both of whom inherited problematics from the range of questions raised by Immanuel Kant and other Enlightenment thinkers. In turning to the proposals of Franklin H. Giddings (1855–1931), we are considering the first American thinker to be given place in this sequence, and we are moving away from Kant's essentialism and toward Auguste Comte's and Herbert Spencer's evolutionisms. Giddings was steeped in the writings of the evolutionists, including Charles Darwin and T. H. Huxley. He understood social evolution to inhere in cosmic evolution, which meant, specifically, that the social order evolves in accordance with the dynamics of human association, dynamics that were obedient to the sequence of differentiation, integration, segregation, and assimilation. Directing this ever-moving process is complex mental activity that is always dedicated to achieve an equilibrium of energy among individuals and groups, an objective that keeps the developmental process moving forward. Thus, for Giddings, powerful subjective factors are at work in the processes according to which social order is established and maintained. The structure of society is influenced by human behavior which, in turn, is determined in significant part by the communication that is necessary to maintain equilibrium between individuals and groups. Sociology, for Giddings, can rightly be defined as "the psychology of society." Throughout his portrayal, sociology is understood in thoroughly psychosocial terms. He utilized a heavily Spencerian evolutionary system as a basis to approach society in organic coordinative terms.

The implications for an understanding of religion are more indirect than direct. Giddings was himself the son of a Congregational minister, and both of his parents were direct descendants of the New England Puritans. In addition to schooling himself in the writings of the evolutionists, he was also familiar with moral philosophy. These sustained sensitivities are reflected in his recognition of the influences of emotion, feeling, and subjective inclination on the determination of the direction of the evolutionary process. He understood genesis, but he insisted that telesis (by which he meant the sense of direction and determination by which the process is compelled) must be properly acknowledged as well. Behind and beneath it all was Giddings' hope and desire that the social situation might be progressively improved. He understood that religion was one of the most powerful instruments available to humankind to effect this outcome.

Karl Mannheim: Exploring Ideology and Utopia

Following this brief American interlude, we return to Germany to consider the influence of Karl Mannheim (1893–1947), who was born in Budapest and educated in Hungary, France, Switzerland, and Germany before joining the faculties in Heidelberg and Frankfurt. Then, in 1933, with the coming of the National Socialists to power, Mannheim moved to England, where he taught at the University of London.

He concerned himself with two fundamental subjects: epistemology and the structure of modern society. He had inherited the first preoccupation from the German theorists in whose ideas he was immersed. He seems to have been prompted to pursue the second topic after experiencing the dramatic changes in European societal arrangements that necessitated his exit from the continent. Within the epistemological realm, he concentrated on sociology of knowledge, and, within this framework, on the manner according to which ideology is constructed and is intended to function. Within his studies of ideology, he tended to focus on the workings of *Weltanschauungen* (worldviews), which he understood to provide the perspective through which experience is placed, judged, and interpreted. He recognized that each age has its own intellectual challenges as well as its senses of truth and goodness. He also recognized that social status as well as vocational interests carry significant influences on the perspectives that become elevated into worldviews. Thus, in his last book, *Essays on the Sociology of Culture*, published posthumously in 1956, he provided evidence that personality plays a definitive role in cultural composition, and that intellectual fashions have clear effects on the objectives and ambitions of a society.

Having understood how ideology functions, and its relationship to world-building, Mannheim became something of an advocate for a system of social order that he believed his research efforts had qualified him to recommend. Here he placed emphasis on the necessity of collective planning, such as would be undertaken by social democrats who opposed totalitarian rule and yet sought to exercise self-restraint in their own collective efforts. Toward this end religion served to remind the collectivists of moral imperatives, imperatives that both focused activity and gave it validation. In the end, religion itself became part of the plan; that is, religion was required to be planned too, within the particularities of the social organization, a body that was also required to plan religion. Thus, in noting how ideology functions to give organization and constitution to society, Mannheim alerted sociologists to a factor that needed to be reckoned with. And when dealing with ideology, Mannheim underscored powerful religious factors that play both formative and teleological roles in the composition of both individual and collective life.

Joachim Wach: *Verstehen* Sensitivity in Intracultural Research

Among the most prominent historians and sociologists to treat religion as organic coordination is Joachim Wach (1898–1955), German-born scholar, who taught at the University of Chicago from 1945 to 1955. Unlike many of his predecessors, including Ernst Troeltsch, Wach practiced cross-cultural inquiry deliberately. Following Weber's lead, Wach was dedicated wholeheartedly to the *Verstehen* methodological approach. But, in this latter respect, Wach affirmed that *Verstehen* could only be appropriately practiced if the cross-cultural inquiry were conducted in a methodologically sensitive interdisciplinary and multidisciplinary manner.

To further his methodological cause, Wach found assistance and encouragement from a wide variety of thinkers. As noted, he was beholden to Weber and had studied Troeltsch. In addition, he had been influenced by Rudolf Otto, and conducted his inquiries as if in conversation with the author of *Das Heilige*. In addition, he had been heavily influenced by Wilhelm Dilthey, or, more precisely, by Dilthey's teacher August Boeckh, who inspired Wach to engage in a kind of *Geisteswissenschaf* that proceeded by means of a multidimensional inquiry into the varieties of expression of human experience. Like Dilthey, Wach was interested in virtually all forms of human expression, including music, art, dance, social movements, gestures, and the like. He understood that all of these were inherent in or interrelated with religion. Therefore, he sought to conduct sociology of religion with an emphasis on the varieties of human expression. He was convinced that this was also a suitable and effective way to engage in the history of religion. In other words, to study religion phenomenologically, or morphologically, was to focus on the sociological dimensions of the subject and to approach these dimensions through cultivated *Verstehen* sensitivities.

Wach's is an approach to the subject that keeps a constellation of foci everpresent in mind. His controlling assumption was that religion belongs to a dynamic human context that is formed by the interaction of history, culture, and society. Thus, when examining religion, he concentrated on forms of expression, divided into three types: (1) the *theoretical* (doctrinal symbolic, creedal, conceptual, and so on); (2) the *practical* (that is, those forms that belong to worship and cult life); and (3) the *sociological* (by which Wach referred to groups, community associations, and leadership roles played within such communities). A firm methodological principle that is never violated demands that no one of these components be treated in isolation from the others. A true perception of the phenomena demands that the analyst sense and appreciate the multiplicity of interrelationships and interdependencies of the various components.

Thus, when fashioning his approach to the sociology of religion, Wach took his formative cues from Max Weber. In this respect, he was not as interested in Weber's work on Calvinism (which he believed has already been properly acknowledged in subsequent scholarship) as he was in Weber's analyses of the religious traditions as well as the linkages Weber identified and only partially explored between religion and economics. Wach believed that Weber made a good start in each area, but it is both possible and necessary to go further. Indeed, it is even necessary to offer a corrective to Weber's rather exclusive emphasis on economics when addressing the subject of religion. Wach agreed that economics belongs in the analysis, but he also recognized that it is but one of the forms of social activity that any competent sociology must acknowledge in developing a more comprehensive and inclusive approach to the study of religion. Wach intended that sociology of religion examine all of the forms of human social activity, and that its focus include the "primitive religions" (which Weber left out) in addition to the wide range of identifiable religious traditions.

In desiring to expand both the range and the necessary detail in the study of religion, Wach did not delude himself into believing that his approach carried the key, say, toward understanding the nature and function of religion. On the contrary, his claims are rather modest. He did not believe that there is a single key, for example, and he was not looking to sociology of religion to "reveal the nature and essence of religion itself." His specific expectations can be stated in this succinct manner:

> We hope by an examination of the manifold interrelations between religion and social phenomena to contribute to a better appreciation of one function of religion, perhaps not its foremost but certainly an essential one. Through this approach we hope not only to illustrate the cultural significance of religion but also to gain new insight into the relations between the various forms of expression of religious experience and eventually to understand better the various aspects of religious experience itself.

Wach recognized too that his expectations regarding the work of sociology of religion may "supplement but can never replace phenomenology, psychology, or history of religion, to say nothing of theology." Moreover, the fact that the method he used produced results that are primarily descriptive does not mean that the conclusions to which he came will be merely academic. Neither can the sociology of religion be properly employed to make light, or cast suspicion on, the religious beliefs and attitudes of so-called primitive peoples. By the same token, Wach was unwilling to give in to the swinging of the pendulum to the other pole—toward cultivating nostalgia or longing for the "days gone by." On the contrary, his approach was designed to come to "a sympathetic insight into the meaning of religious experiences different from ours geographically and temporally with a critical awareness of its relevance to modern life and problems."

To the possibility that ideological biases are written into the approach to the subject of religion, Wach had this to say:

> There is no such thing as Christian or Jewish or Moslem sociology. But there are implicit or explicit Christian, Moslem, or Jewish social philosophies. The totally unwarranted confusion of social philosophy with sociology is evident in the normative concept of religion often styled "Christian sociology" which underlies most studies of the social implications of Christianity.

It follows from this that "it would be a mistake to assume . . . that the sociology of religion should be identical with definite programs of social reform." Such an assumption, according to Wach, would be "a betrayal of its [sociology's] true character as a descriptive science."

Then, if he had not already made the point with force and clarity, Wach described the tenor or spirit of the investigative enterprise. He wanted to insist, first, that the sociological approach to the subject will recognize "the vast breadth and variety of religious experience." This requires that the analysis cannot be limited to a single religion. Having established that the intellectual enterprise will deal with more than one religion and will involve insights and methods from the history of religions, anthropology, psychology, and sociology, Wach set some ground rules concerning the organization of his data. He wished to employ a typological approach so as to compare and contrast materials from numerous religions and cultures. And, finally, he wished that the gathering of data would be informed by the most resilient interpretive theories. "It would be helpful," he suggested, "if students of religion and philosophy and students of the social sciences could meet together at periodic intervals for reciprocal stimulation." This summary statement is indicative of the interdisciplinary quality of the descriptive and interpretive inquiry he had in mind:

> Sociologists given to the study of society, of political theory and the study of the forms of government, could develop one side of the subject, while students of comparative religion, aided by philology, archaeology, and the various theologies, might develop the other, both together successfully elaborating a sociology of religion.

The insight that pushed this multidimensional, cross-disciplinary analysis to an even more sophisticated level was Wach's contention that phenomena are in fact visible manifestations of an invisible reality. In other words, his entire schema was ordered to honor the conviction that varieties of religious expression testify to the universality of the religious reality. Wach could have phrased it in Rudolf Otto's terms, for, with Otto, Wach believed in the integrative function of the religious factor. In more proper Kantian language, Wach found religion to be identifiable neither with pure thought, ethics, nor aesthetics, but he placed it as the substratum on which all of these are dependent.

It is a multiplex assortment of ingredients that carries side benefits for theological self-understanding. The same approach also contributes methodology for interdisciplinary research in the humanities and the social sciences. But, if the distinction is fitting, Wach's method scores higher marks as a theoretical stance than as practical methodology. It does not easily translate into step-by-step procedures. The objective is to bring as much light as possible to a subject, and this enjoins the analyst to use a variety of methods and to make use of the insights from several fields and disciplines. Wach insisted that the sociological dimension belongs to any respectable treatment of religion. For him the sociological dimension gains content through the various forms of organization and institutionalization by which the religious traditions are characterized. It is to the same dimension that one can attribute the integration that the religious reality effects with respect to the wide variety of human cultural experience.

A theoretical line similar to Wach's has been pursued by the German scholar Gustav Mensching (b.1901). Trained at the University of Marburg under Rudolf Otto, Mensching was professor of the history of religions at Bonn for more than thirty years until his retirement in 1970. His orientation to the subject was prominently styled by Otto's conception of religion as "an experiential encounter with and response to the holy." Mensching contended that the encounter can take place in a variety of settings and in a variety of ways. Yet, behind all of these variations is a common religious factor. The scholar must examine religious traditions, approaching them as living organisms, by focusing on their integrated morphological characteristics. But the scholar must never lose sight of the common religious element around which all of them are organized. Mensching's approach, in short, is a modified *sine qua non* stance that treats religious traditions by focusing on the components of organic coordination. Only a multidisciplinary approach can make such a reality methodologically accessible.

One cannot mention Joachim Wach without referring to Joseph M. Kitagawa (1915–1992), his able interpreter and his competent successor at Chicago. Using Wach's methods and sustaining similar broad multidimensional interests, Kitagawa has refined, applied, and updated the same approach in dealing with the religions of China and Japan, particularly Buddhism and Shinto. Throughout his career, Kitagawa concentrated on the coordination of multidimensional factors in portrayals of religious traditions. In a paper delivered before a meeting of the

International Association for the History of Religions in Turku, Finland, in 1973, for example, Kitagawa described the work of the scholar of religion as being "compelled to examine both religious and nonreligious documents through literal source criticism as well as other types of form criticism, and to explore the meaning and structure of myths, legends, folklore, rituals, symbols, and the religious community itself." This, of course, is thoroughly true to the interdisciplinary and multidimensional approach of Wach. Then, showing how the historian of religions must expand on the treatment of literary texts, Kitagawa quoted Raffaele Pettazzoni, who said that the historian must study "religious data in their historical connections not only with other religious data but also with those that are not religious, whether literary, artistic, social, or what not." A statement to the same point is made in Kitagawa's recommendation that scholars of religion must learn how to "relate the study of religious documents to the study of symbols, rituals, institutions, etc." This is Wachian through and through, though without the complication of any aprioristic common religious element. But we need to back up a ways, and trace the development of another trajectory. This one also has roots in the work of Max Weber, and finds its genius in a merging of Weberian and Durkheimian orientations.

Talcott Parsons: Durkheim and Weber Linked and Updated

The direct line from Max Weber to present-day analyses of religious groups runs through social action theory, which, following Weber, was modified, tempered, and embellished by the work of such scholars as Thorstein Veblen (1857–1929), John R. Commons (1862–1945), Robert M. MacIver (1882–1970), Karl Mannheim (1893–1947), Alfred Marshall (1842–1924), Vilfredo Pareto (1848–1923), and others. From this group of influential scholars, we call particular attention to the work of Talcott Parsons (1902–1981), not only because of the distinctiveness of his contribution to social theory, but also because of the enormous influence he has had on persons who have become leaders within the field.

Parsons was a nestor in more ways than one. His translation of Weber's *The Protestant Ethic and the Spirit of Capitalism*, for example, may have been the single most important event in bringing the work of the German sociologist to the attention of the English-speaking world. In addition to this sponsorship of Weber, Parsons has also done impressive work to revive interest in Emile Durkheim's views, and to make of Durkheim something other than one whose work is restricted to analyses and descriptions of primitive societies. In this regard, Parsons is credited with detecting and enunciating the congruence between Weber's and Durkheim's interests. To bring these two large figures together involves establishing an association between German and French schools of social theory. Parsons achieved this by transferring both to American soil. By combining Durkheim's insight regarding the influence of social constraints with Weber's interest in discerning the way in which religious values become translated into social sanctions, Parsons was led to a new view of the structure of social action. His view carried the thesis that the social milieu possesses a set of conditions that are beyond the control of every particular individual, but not outside the mastery of human agency in general. Showing an interweaving of Durkheimian and Weberian stresses, Parsons offers this summary:

> Durkheim called attention to the importance of the relation of symbolism as distinguished from that of intrinsic causality in cognitive patterns. Finally, Weber integrated the various aspects of the role of non-empirical cognitive patterns in social action in terms of his theory of the significance of the problems of meaning and the corresponding cognitive structures, in a way which precludes, for analytical purposes, their being assimilated to the patterns of science.

Obviously, Parsons wants to give place to both.

But it was not enough for him to synthesize the views of Weber and Durkheim. He also borrows heavily from the insights of Alfred Marshall and Vilfredo Pareto, and believes that all four of these (Weber, Durkheim, Marshall, and Pareto) can be understood, by one who reads all four together carefully, to contribute to a resilient theory of social action. Parsons agreed with Marshall that economic life cannot be explained solely in terms of the satisfaction of wants. Marshall thought it necessary to add that the development of character functions as an incentive too. From Pareto's observations and proposals Parsons found support for the view that action carries "nonlogical" motivation. Indeed, in Pareto's understanding, the form of a society is determined by all the elements acting upon it, which, in turn, society reacts upon. Such elements are numerous and include natural conditions (such as climate, geological conditions, flora, fauna, and so on), the effects of other societies acting upon it, internal circumstances (such as race, natural aptitude, religious values, and the like), and the combinations of all of these forces acting in reciprocal fashion. The state of the society in any given moment reflects the equilibrium that has been achieved among and between these sets and conditions. Pareto wrote:

> The economic system is made up of certain molecules set in motion by tastes and subject to ties (checks) in the form of obstacles to the acquisition of economic values. The social system is much more complicated, and even if we try to simplify it as far as we possibly can without falling into serious errors, we at least have to think of it as made up of certain molecules harboring residues, derivations, interests, and proclivities, and which perform, subject to numerous ties, logical and non-logical actions. In the economic system the non-logical element is relegated entirely to tastes and disregarded, since tastes are taken as data of fact. One might wonder whether the

same thing might not be done for the social system, whether we might not relegate the non-logical element to the residues, then take the residues as data of fact and proceed to examine the logical conduct that originates in the residues.

In short, for Pareto society is a prelogical phenomenon, since individuals are possessed of sentiments, and sentiments (rather than the rationalizations of sentiments) determine the forms of social life. From Durkheim, Parsons borrowed the distinction between social constraint and natural causes.

For Durkheim, the activities of a society can only be interpreted with reference to the social milieu, that is, to the set of conditions by which the society is differentiated. Individual initiative retains some important place, but the social milieu is beyond the control of any individual. Meaningful action implies social sanctions, criteria that have been codified by some unwritten but yet normative social consensus. And from Weber Parsons learned much about the role of values, the place of metaphysical ideas, and even the influence of religious interests on the dynamics of action. From all four of these—working their insights to his own purposes—Parsons developed a new theory of action that came to terms with the place of the environment, the interdependence of logical and nonlogical elements, the power of collective sanction and constraint, and the motivational power of religious ideas and values. The product was a formulation that can only be explained and articulated through a reenunciation of the Aristotelian description of the role of the four causes. As Parsons explains:

> Evidently we have to acquire knowledge of the original causes . . . and causes are spoken of in four senses. In one of these we mean the substance, i.e., the essence (for the "why" is reducible finally to the definition, and the ultimate "why" is a cause and principle); in another the matter or substratum, in a third the source of the chance, and in the fourth the cause opposed to this, the purpose and the good (for this is the end of all generation and change).

The product is a conclusion that can be stated as follows:

> In any concrete system of action a process of change so far as it is at all explicable in terms of those elements of action formulated in terms of the intrinsic means-end relationship can proceed only in the direction of approach toward the realization of the rational norms conceived as binding on the actors in the system. That is, more briefly, such a process of action can proceed only in the direction of an increase in the value of the property rationality.

With respect to the ongoing history of the cultivation of methodology in social science, the significance of this insight is its insistence that the activities of a society are always multidimensional, intellectual access to which requires the employment of several systems of analysis and measure. The corollary is that social action theory retains its dependence on the wisdom of Durkheim and Weber. For religious studies, the key insight is that religion is an integral element of the social milieu, belonging as much to its character as it does to the object of its aspirations.

Clifford Geertz: Religion as a Cultural System

Talcott Parsons's reworking and fusing of Weberian and Durkheimian themes was so comprehensive, detailed, and painstaking that he inspired a host of students to take up the same or related investigatory causes. Indeed, one of the most significant paths of influence within religious studies is the multiplex trajectory initiated and instituted by Talcott Parsons and his associates at Harvard when they insisted that social thought be pursued in a methodologically sophisticated cross-cultural and interdisciplinary manner. One of the most impressive and influential of all of Parsons's students is Clifford Geertz (b.1926), an anthropologist, associated with the Center for Advanced Studies at Princeton, who has become well known within religious studies for the insightfulness of his proposal that religion is a "cultural system." Geertz summarized this proposal in an article, "Religion as a Cultural System," first published in a collection of essays on anthropological approaches to religion in 1966.

The pathway to religion is culture, and culture, in Geertz's formulation, is defined as follows: "[Culture] denotes an historically transmitted pattern of meanings embodied in symbols, a system of inherited conceptions expressed in symbolic forms by means of which men communicate, perpetuate, and develop their knowledge about and attitudes toward life." It is within this context that Geertz proceeds to describe the function of religious symbols, or, in his language, how "sacred symbols function within the cultural context." In approaching the subject in this way, Geertz registered some criticism of some of his own previous work as an anthropoloqist, and in being self-critical he was also being critical of the attitudes and assumptions of other anthropologists. In other words, in Geertz's mind, it is not enough that anthropologists examine the role of religion within selected cultures and societies, always concentrating on customs, rites, beliefs, and so on. The long and somewhat tiresome repetition of this interest has led to a situation that finds anthropological study of religion, in Geertz's view, to be in "a state of general stagnation." It is stagnant because it is disposed toward "producing more minor variations on classical theoretical themes." Geertz calls for an expansion of vision and an updating of anthropological interest. He proposes that the same can be achieved by concentrating on the role of sacred symbols in transmitting meanings in dynamic cultural contexts. His attitude has been influenced by Parsons, certainly, and the same influence is to be seen in Gertz's tendency to formulate definitions by integrating a variety of necessary components. Parsons, we recall, was unwilling to leave important factors unacknowledged. Inspired by the same ideal, Geertz defines religion as:

(1) a system of symbols which acts to (2) establish powerful, pervasive, and long-lasting moods and motivations in men by (3) formulating conceptions of a general order of existence and (4) clothing these conceptions with such an aura of factuality that (5) the moods and motivations seem uniquely realistic.

The role hereby assigned to religion befits the conception of culture as "an historically transmitted pattern of meanings." Putting the two definitions (namely, that of religion and of culture) together, Geertz writes:

> [S]acred symbols function to synthesize a people's ethos—the tone, character, and quality of their life, its moral and aesthetic style and mood—and their world-view—the picture they have of the way things in sheer actuality are, their most comprehensive ideas of order.

This agrees with his definition of religion as "a system of symbols" that carries certain functions. But the same thought can be stated succinctly:

> Religious symbols formulate a basic congruence between a particular style of life and a specific (if, most often, implicit) metaphysic, and in so doing sustain each with the borrowed authority of the other.
> [R]eligion tunes human actions to an envisaged cosmic order and projects images of cosmic order onto the plane of human experience. . . .

From here Geertz's analysis proceeds along two distinct lines. First, he takes each of the five components of religion, defines and describes them at greater length, providing examples of their influence. Then he demonstrates that they are organically interconnected because of the way in which religion, culture, and symbols are interdependent components of one and the same organism. It is appropriate that the word *congruence* should be employed often in this description, for the task is to demonstrate and illustrate how these various elements or components are congruent within one and the same organism. For example, when describing the composition of human thought, Geertz writes as follows:

> The perception of the structural congruence between one set of processes, activities, relations, entities, etc., and another set for which it acts as a program, so that the program can be taken as a representation, or conception—a symbol—of the programmed, is the essence of human thought.

Throughout the exposition the reader is made aware of Geertz's overall intentions with respect to the workings of anthropology of religion. He wants to breathe new and expanded life into the discipline, and he does so by making a subtle distinction. Previous anthropological investigations have approached religion through long-standing interests of anthropology. Geertz, by contrast, wishes to approach religion in its own terms. That is, instead of engaging the subject with a view toward drawing on its resourcefulness to illumine anthropological theory, or with an interest in making certain that it is included within any viable anthropological depiction of the workings of a society or culture, Geertz wants the subject to be able to stand on its own feet, as it were. It is necessary, in this respect, that religion be approached as an integral element within a society or culture—but other anthropologists have accomplished this. It is important, too, that the integral elements of religion be identified and their workings and functions described. But Geertz takes the matter even further in suggesting that there is a distinctive "religious perspective" on the world, alongside commonsensical, scientific, and aesthetic perspectives. Thus, before he has finished, Geertz has described religion in its own terms, in a self-referential manner; he has identified and described its functional role in society since it stands as an integral component of culture; and he has treated religion in worldview terms, namely, as a way of approaching the world or as a mode of engaging reality. And all of this is possible by virtue of the fact that the four causal factors, to which Geertz's teacher Talcott Parsons did obeisance, are also present as formal explanatory factors in Geertz's analysis.

In other essays, Geertz writes convincingly of the need for "thick" (detailed, narrative-based) description of the cultural context. In his view, understanding of the cultural system is gained by inspection; that is, by probing meaning that is publicly accessible. Thus, to study a culture is to study shared codes of meaning. We say that such meaning is publicly accessible, for, though he believes in "thick" description, Geertz is not suggesting that the ability to understand depends on the analyst's successes in trying to empathize with the peoples being studied. The interpretive task is not to share in the life of that which is being studied, but to comprehend the representations of that way of life through the symbolic forms that are integral to it. This is a revised *Verstehen* approach, but one in which specific methodological procedures have taken the place of empathetic feeling.

All of it enables Geertz to offer some suggestions regarding the importance of religion.

> For an anthropologist, the importance of religion lies in its capacity to serve (for an individual or for a group) as a source of general, yet distinctive conceptions of the world, the self, and the relations between them, on the one hand—its model *of* aspect—and of rooted, no less distinctive "mental" dispositions—its model *for* aspect—on the other. From these cultural functions flow, in turn, its social and psychological ones.

In cultural terms, religion is a system of organic coordinants belonging to cultures that are themselves systems of organic coordinants. Starting with an identification of religion's function within this context, Geertz proceeds to offer a commentary on religion's social and cultural importance.

Thomas Luckmann and Peter Berger: Cohesiveness between Religion and Society

A similar combination of interests is reflected in the work of Thomas Luckmann (b.1927) and Peter Berger (b.1929), both of whom have also been influenced by Karl Mannheim, Robert Merton, and developments within continental philosophical phenomenology, particularly the thought of Alfred Schutz (1899–1959). Both Luckmann and Berger are sensitive to the fate of the individual within a social context that has been preformed, or, as both Berger and Luckmann put it, a context that has been "socially construed." Luckmann views religion as "symbolic self-transcendence." This phrase refers to the ability that human beings possess to transcend all particularities by constructing objective, morally binding, all-embracing universes of meaning. And, for his part, Berger draws upon Weberian and Durkheimian insights when insisting on the projective character of "the social construction of reality." For Berger, all religious propositions are "projections grounded in specific infrastructures." Thus, religion itself can be defined as "the human enterprise by which a sacred cosmos is established." Apart from an awareness of the presence of the sacred, in Berger's view, it would likely not have been possible for human beings "to conceive of a cosmos in the first place." As he described it:

> It can thus be said that religion has played a strategic part in the human enterprise of world-building. Religion implies the farthest reach of man's self-externalization, of his infusion of reality with his own meanings. Religion implies that human order is projected into the totality of being. Put differently, religion is the audacious attempt to conceive of the entire universe as being humanly significant.

In addition to its rather obvious influence on social theory and its interweaving of large Durkheimian and Weberian themes, what precisely is the connection between Luckmann's and Berger's thought coordination? The answer is implicit in the title of Luckmann's book *The Invisible Religion*, and it involves a polemical contention. In the most obvious sociological sense, neither Berger nor Luckmann is willing to identify religion with church religion. Both acknowledge that religion is to be found in institutional form, but both prefer to root that social presence in the ongoing work of constructing symbolic universes of meanings. Neither can settle for an equation of the social form of religion with religious institutions in the more specialized and narrow sense. For both, it is a deception to take the social pulse of religion by concentrating on occurrences and developments within the church. Rather, the chief clues regarding the presence of religion are to be found in the processes of value legitimization within a society. These processes, in turn, reflect the dynamics according to which the "'transcendent,' superordinated, and 'integrating' structures of meaning are socially objectivated." Luckmann writes:

> Once the sociology of religion uncritically takes it for granted that church and religion are identical it blinds itself to its most relevant problem. It has prejudged the

answer to the question whether, in contemporary society, any socially objectivated meaning structures but the traditional institutionalized religious doctrines function to integrate the routines of everyday life and to legitimate its crises. It therefore fails to concern itself with the most important, essentially religious, aspects of the location of the individual in society.

Once the contrast is made, Luckmann can devote his efforts toward analyzing the interdependence of social institutions and symbolic patterns of sacred order.

Although Luckmann and Berger employ Weber's insights about the influence of symbolic and ideational sets of religious values on the structure of social reality, neither follows Weber in focusing on specifiable religious traditions when they carry out their own sociological analyses. Both of them shift away from religious traditions in order to talk more specifically about ways in which religious systems of value and meaning serve as principles of sanction and integration within the social order. Having established this focus, both theorists concentrate on the social constructiveness of special ideological convictions, and, by this means, on the interdependence of religious and social factors. In his book *The Sacred Canopy*, Berger explains the role of religion as follows:

> Religion legitimates social institutions by bestowing upon them an ultimately valid ontological status, that is, by locating them within a sacred and cosmic frame of reference. The historical constructions of human activity are viewed from a vantage point that, in its own self-definition, transcends both history and man . . . .
>
> To repeat, the historically crucial part of religion in process of legitimation is explicable in terms of the unique capacity of religion to "locate" human phenomena within a cosmic frame of reference. All legitimation serves to maintain reality—reality, that is, as defined in a particular human collectivity. Religious legitimation purports to relate the humanly defined reality to ultimate, universal, and sacred reality. The inherently precarious and transitory constructions of human activity are thus given the semblance of ultimate security and permanence.

Succinctly, in Berger's words, "religion thus serves to maintain the reality of that socially constructed world within which men exist in their everyday lives." But the best summary is the following definition of religion: "the establishment, through human activity, of an all-embracing sacred order, that is, of a sacred cosmos that will be capable of maintaining itself in the ever-present face of chaos." Berger insists that such a definition does not constitute grounds on which to criticize him for offering "a sociologically deterministic theory of religion." On the contrary, in his words, "the same human activity that produces society also produces religion, with the relation between the two products always being a dialectical one." Thus, the dependencies between religion and society run in both directions.

The other side of the picture is that whatever cooperative ventures link religion and society are vulnerable to the destructive powers of secularization. Thus, in addition to probing the ways in which religious and social factors interact and interconnect in the constructive intellectual activity by which legitimation is bestowed on human existence, Luckmann and Berger focus concentrated attention on the activities by which those cohesions and coalitions come apart. For secularization itself denotes a persistent undermining of the foundations of the human legitimizing process. Berger offers this definition of secularization:

> By secularization we mean the process by which sectors of society and culture are removed from the domination of religious institutions and symbols. . . . [W]e imply that secularization is more than a social-structural process. It affects the totality of cultural life and ideation, and may be observed in the decline of religious contents in the arts, in philosophy, in literature, and, most important of all, in the rise of science as an autonomous, thoroughly secular perspective on the world. As there is a secularization of society and culture, so is there a secularization of consciousness. Put simply, this means that the modern West has produced an increasing number of individuals who look upon the world and their own lives without the benefit of religious interpretation.

Put in even simpler and balder terms, the majority of human beings in the modern world do not accept (nor live in obedience to) the fundamental worldview to which traditional Western religion remains committed. It is not that these same persons are reprobate, or that they have chosen to exist in some state of rebellion against given religious authority. It is rather that they cannot accept religion's version of things as being plausible. In Berger's words, there is a "crisis" having directly to do with "the plausibility of traditional religious definitions of reality." The challenge before the religious institutions is "how to keep going in a milieu that no longer takes for granted their definitions of reality."

We will have to leave a treatment of the proposed outcome of this dilemma for another time and setting. Suffice it to say that the Berger-Luckmann approach is fascinated with the process by which cohesiveness is established between religion and society in given cultural settings as well as with the process by which the same cohesiveness comes unraveled. A collective spiritual crisis occurs when the cohesiveness is lost or when a presumed cohesiveness is discovered to lack sufficient plausibility. Luckmann's and Berger's work focuses on the "social construction of reality" as well as on processes by which that same reality is "deconstructed."

Robert N. Bellah: Social Construction as Civil Religion

What Berger and Luckmann divined in theory, with special reference to the dynamics of the interdependence of religious patterns of meaning and the social construction of reality, Robert N. Bellah (reference to whose work was made in chapter 2) disclosed as an undeniable and specifiable American fact. For, among his multifocused interest in treating religion in sociological perspective, Bellah (b.1927) is the scholar who most forcefully brought the concept of "civil religion" to prominence with the publication of an influential article in 1967. In so doing, Bellah lent specificity to Berger's and Luckmann's contentions that there is a discernible systematic, organic institutional alternative to church religion in American thought and life. The alternative is a living, functional civil religion that has been articulate in American consciousness since the founding of the nation.

> What we have, then, from the earliest years of the republic, is a collection of beliefs, symbols, and rituals with respect to sacred things and institutionalized in a collectivity. This religion—there seems no other word for it—while not antithetical to and indeed sharing much in common with Christianity, was neither sectarian nor in any specific sense Christian. At a time when the society was overwhelmingly Christian, it seems unlikely that this lack of Christian reference was meant to spare the feelings of the tiny non-Christian minority. Rather, the civil religion expressed what those who set the precedents felt was appropriate under the circumstances. It reflected their private as well as public views. Nor was the civil religion simply "religion in general." While generality was undoubtedly seen as a virtue . . . civil religion was saved from empty formalism and served as a genuine vehicle of national religious self-understanding.

In other words, "there actually exists alongside of and rather clearly differentiated from the churches an elaborate and well-institutionalized civil religion in America." Bellah called this phenomenon "the religion of the American way of life," noting that this religion is reflective of the convictions and attitudes of the American people *qua* American people.

The articulation of the same occurs through the speeches of United States presidents, particularly on ceremonial occasions. The moral principles that belong to the orientation are disseminated in the public schools. That is, the phenomenon is thoroughly American, and yet does not add up to "the worship of the American nation but an understanding of the American experience in the light of ultimate and universal reality." Similarly, it is thoroughly biblical, by which Bellah attests that "behind the civil religion at every point lie Biblical archetypes: Exodus, Chosen People, Promised Land, New Jerusalem, Sacrificial Death and Rebirth." Indeed, American destiny, by means of the instrumentation of the civil religion, is portrayed and explained in terms of biblical symbolism. The American citizenry—here Bellah quotes from Abraham Lincoln—is interpreted as being an "almost chosen people." The entire phenomenon can be understood as an example of organic coordination.

Thomas F. O'Dea:
Religion in Crisis

Once the Weberian-Durkheimian-Parsonian line of interpretation is established, and the fact of secularization is inserted into the dynamic process by which religious patterns of meaning are ascribed with institutional form, scholars can focus on a variety of intriguing issues. As we have observed, Luckmann and Berger concentrate on the implicit or tacit (Luckmann uses the word "invisible" and Berger refers to an overarching "sacred canopy") complex of religious meaning that attains concrete expression within the context of social reality. For his part, Robert Bellah attempts to make the implicit explicit in describing a particular network of religious meaning that has been influential in American civil, social, and political life. All such Parsonian-influenced efforts can be interpreted as refinements, extensions, and current applications of Weber's treatment of the interrelationship of motives and acts in the constitution of the world. They also register in Durkheimian terms, as examples of the law that religious conceptions always reflect and enunciate a prescribed pattern of social organization.

The same interdependence of comprehensive value-scheme and the formation of societal life can be approached from another side, especially if, as Luckmann, Berger, and Bellah indicate, it has been significantly affected by the secularizing process. Here, instead of focusing attention on the interdependence of motive and act, and rather than seeking to identify either the realm of action or the structure of motivation, the analyst can look at what happens when the meaning schema exists in a state of disarray. That is, the scholar can concentrate on the social and religious consequence of an ineffective pattern of meaning—ineffective because it no longer resonates with humanity's experience of (and within) the social reality.

Such is the focal point of the distinguished work of the American sociologist Thomas F. O'Dea (1915–1974), who, in addition, is the author of a highly regarded study of the Mormons. When one examines the titles of O'Dea's books, even if only superficially, one cannot avoid recognizing the prominence of stress-and-strain words like *crisis* and *dilemma*. One of his books is called *Alienation, Atheism and the Religious Crisis*. Another, focusing on post–Vatican II Roman Catholic life and thought, is entitled *The Catholic Crisis*. One of his prominent articles was entitled "The Crisis of the Contemporary Religious Consciousness." The final two chapters of his textbook, *The Sociology of Religion*, have the names "Religion and Conflict" and "Ambiguity and Dilemma." In every case, the pervasive "crisis" or "dilemma" is due to the fact that the prevailing pattern of religio-ideological meaning no longer functions appropriately as a viable source of motivation for social action or religious belief. O'Dea sensed that the mid-twentieth-century religious world was undergoing an experience of profound "uncertainty of what we are and what we want to be." He recognized, too, that this perplexity carries a widespread disorienting and distorting effect on the collective understanding of human meaning, value, and destiny. Previous motivational sanctions and sources of legitimization no longer held conviction. In short, the present period is a time of real "epochal change." The social transformations and the shifts in patterns and objects of belief are of such large-scale proportions that they threaten the very core of ideological intelligibility.

O'Dea recognized that religion functions to contribute "a sense of ontologically justified orientation," within which context he understands the word *ontological* to intend "that the orientation not only points out how man may locate and direct his life, but that such orientation is built into the structure of things." (Geertz, Luckmann, Berger, Bellah, and others have offered the same affirmation.) Yet, in times of crisis, this "ontologically justified orientation" seems difficult for its previous adherents to sustain. A series of attempts has been made to formulate it or sustain it, but all of them, from the Protestantism of the Reformation to Enlightenment liberalism (and its Marxist offspring) have failed. In O'Dea's view, this is all the more reason for taking the Second Vatican Council's attempt at *aggiornamento*—standing for the systematic updating of Roman Catholic teaching—with utmost seriousness.

Thus, the book *The Catholic Crisis* is devoted to an analysis of Catholicism's attempt at reform through the Vatican II period, and considers the potential ramifications of the success or failure of this reform movement by referring it to the more comprehensive and inclusive ideological-cultural crisis of meaning by which modern man is enveloped. The concern is twofold. First it is an inquiry into the sociological dynamics of institutional religious reform. Second, it is a question about the extent to which institutional reform plays into a reestablishment of coherence between motivation and action. O'Dea took the outcome of the Catholic reform movement as an index into Western culture's ability to survive.

In summary, the two processes—(1) the dynamism according to which the social formation of religious motivation meets and attempts to overcome "the internal strains and functional problems" of institutionalization, and (2) the ways in which specific forms of social organization are affected by metamorphoses at the more comprehensive ideological level—served as the interrelated foci of O'Dea's sociological analyses. Both foci carry the support of Weber's interest in discerning the interdependency of motive and act. Because disturbances and innovations are found at both points, the need to cope with strains, crises, ambiguities, dilemmas, and unresolved problems is ever-present. Thus, O'Dea's work stands as an approach to systematic social coordination within which organizational structures are regulated by organic growth, and organic growth is understood to carry both positive-developmental as well as dysfunctional connotations.

Melford Spiro: From Essentialist to Functional Theories

The constructive theoretical proposal of the American anthropologist Melford E. Spiro (b.1920) concerning the nature of religion first caught widespread attention when published in the Michael Banton-edited collection *Anthropological Approaches to the Study of Religion*, in 1966. Here Spiro tackled the problem of defining religion. He argued that definitions that purport to have made the "essential nature" of religion accessible are often difficult to understand, impossible to work with empirically, and ordinarily lack precise knowledge of what it is that is being defined. In place of such attempts to identify the "essential nature" of religion, Spiro recommended an ostensive definition that might support a formulation of empirically testable hypotheses. His definition is a vivid illustration of a transition from *sine qua non* to organic-coordinative methodological motivation.

Spiro's intention was to identify the core variables, the characteristic features that are present wherever one finds religion:

> On the assumption that religion is a cultural institution, and on the further assumption that all institutions . . . are instrumental means for the satisfaction of needs, I shall define religion as an institution consisting of culturally patterned interaction with culturally postulated superhuman beings.

The core variables in this statement (each of which is given specific treatment) are: institution, interaction, and superhuman beings. By explaining what is meant by each of the three variables—with many references to previous interpretations of the same within anthropological theory—Spiro went on to compare and contrast religion with other cultural phenomena that exhibit some of the same variables. He writes:

> This brief explication of our definition of *religion* indicates that, viewed systematically, religion can be differentiated from other culturally constituted institutions by virtue only of its reference to superhuman beings. All institutions consist of *belief systems*, namely, an enduring organization of cognitions about one or more aspects of the universe; *action systems*, an enduring organization of behavior patterns designed to attain ends for the satisfaction of needs; and *value systems*, an enduring organization of principles by which behavior can be judged on some scale of merit. Religion differs from other institutions in that its three component systems have reference to superhuman beings.

The last sentence bears repeating: "Religion differs from other institutions in that its three component systems have reference to superhuman beings." Thus, instead of looking for one underlying essence (an unambiguous simple element, for instance), Spiro has attempted to identify the "core variables" of all "culturally constituted institutions." Assuming that religion belongs to the class or genus of "culturally constituted institution," he worked to isolate religion's uniqueness within the more comprehensive but intrinsic context. He concluded that religion requires the same core variables as the other institutions, and its uniqueness pertains to its necessary (in his word, "compelling") reference to superhuman beings.

After finding an adequate definition of religion, Spiro proceeded to assess the various explanations that have been offered to explain the occurrence of religion, noting that the standard explanations are ordinarily of one of two kinds—*causal* or *functional:* "Causal explanations attempt to account for some sociocultural variable by reference to some antecedent conditions—its *cause.* Functional explanations account for the variable by reference to some consequent condition—its *function.*"

The distinctiveness of Spiro's approach is that it resembles the traditional *sine qua non* positions even while deciding for function against cause. Unlike portrayals of religion designed according to the Kantian model, Spiro's position does not call for the identification of an *a priori* element. But it does sort out the relationships between "core variables," and in doing this it enunciates a definite form of structural coherence.

The contrast between Spiro's position and those dominated more uniformly by the Kantian model can be put as follows. Under Kantian auspices, the usual way of accounting for structure was to reduce reality, in Cartesian style, to its essential elements. Next, an attempt was made to identify one of the elements as being religion's source, base, or root. After this was accomplished, the next step involved an analysis of religion through a description of the sense or content of the "religious core" (whether *a priori* or not). Spiro shares an interest in identifying the conditions of religion, but he proceeds functionally rather than causally, and he has greater interest in chronology than in ontology. Hence, instead of identifying roots or causes, this anthropologist looks for antecedents. Moreover, unlike those trained in the Kantian manner, Spiro feels no obligation to decide how many core elements there might be. His emphasis, instead, is on the composition of institutions, and, thus, methodologically, on the various variables in specific mixes. The same element can serve several functions, depending on its place within the organization of dynamic and systematic patterns of belief, action, and value. Depending on its place and function, one and the same element may be both antecedent and consequent. Yet the same element is a necessary feature within the set of conditions without which the institution—whether it be religion, culture, or society—would not exist.

Thus, in Spiro's account, there is a specific set of conditions without which religion would not exist. Such conditions are necessary to religion, and religion is necessary—as antecedent condition—to the other elements of the composition. For example, society cannot be explained except with reference to religion, for society is the manifestation of conditions that imply the presence of religion. But the same pattern is true of religion: religion has its own antecedent conditions. Specifically, that without which religion would not exist is human motivation. Without human motivation there would be no religion, for religion answers to certain aspirational-motivational drives. Technology is implicit in cognitive drives; expressive desires are satisfied by politics, art, and magic; aspirational-motivational drives, in turn, stand antecedent to religion. Throughout the schema, the composition is accounted for in functional terms. But Spiro is confident that what he is describing is indeed a composition.

J. Milton Yinger: Unitarial Comprehensiveness

One can hardly engage functionalist theories of religion without encountering the scholarship of J. Milton Yinger (b.1916), who is not only a theorist in his own right but has functioned as a kind of chronicler and analyst of the workings or achievements of sociology of religion as an academic field. Like Parsons, like Wach, and like so many of his colleagues who wish sociology of religion to take full advantage of the best insights from a variety of sources, Yinger constructs an outlook that is syncretistic and yet principled. Its ambition is to be as theoretical as it is empirical, and as empirical as it is theoretical, and this he understands to be a requirement of the sociology of religion because of the nature of its subject. That is, "because so much of religion is personal, unconscious, and dependent upon faith, the task of measurement and investigation of religion is exceedingly complex."

Yinger recognizes that sociology of religion, as an academic field, is long on theory—with the examples of Durkheim, Weber, Troeltsch, and others confirming this judgment—and even proficient in empirical analysis. The problem, however, is twofold: (1) Not all of the eminent theorists were careful researchers, nor were they in possession of techniques and skills of investigation that would have given them this ability; and (2) the field itself is characterized by a persistent disjuncture between its most astute wisdom and the rather inconsequential products of its most sophisticated empirical inquiries. As he states the dilemma:

> Most of the data available for use by the sociologist of religion . . . are lacking in comparability. This greatly hinders a study that is trying to discover generalizations. A related problem is that which were gathered without the guidance of explicit scientific concepts are often of limited usefulness for scientific purposes.

To make it explicit: "Ideally, empirical materials are gathered in direct reference to testable hypotheses. Very few of the data with which sociologists of religion have been working satisfy this requirement." The theoretical and empirical wings of the sociology of religion, in Yinger's view, are not effectively interrelated.

Being a student of the field itself, Yinger can offer specific examples of the disjunctures toward which he is pointing. He appreciates Joachim Wach's theoretical abilities, for instance, but he believes that it is far from satisfactory to certify findings upon the "authority" of an "outstanding scholar in the field." He is appreciative of the viewpoint of Max Weber, and knows that it appropriately carries large weight within the sociology of religion. But he wonders how far a theory should be allowed to reach if it developed as a means of explaining the rise of capitalism in Western Europe. Speaking directly of Weber's achievement, Yinger observes:

> This judgment of an enormously complex theoretical problem was based on examination of the few score written records—with very little possibility for checking them

for reliability and completeness. The present writer must confess—and thereby apply a little of sociology of knowledge to himself—that such research is insufficiently empirical for his American taste.

The problem is that the impressions of persons of large intellectual status are too frequently accepted as facts. But, from the other side, the accumulation of data, no matter how methodologically sophisticated, has not always influenced the prevailing sociological theories. Yinger urges the two sides to come together, to understand that their efforts are complementary and interdependent: hypotheses and data must always be correlated, for a worthy sociology of religion makes them integral.

Yinger's explorations include an additional important side. Not only is he insistent that the theoretical and empirical components of the sociology of religion be understood as reciprocal methodological factors, but he is sensitive to the roles scholarship plays in lending formation to the subjects under its scrutiny. That is, he is immensely interested in the relationships between sociology of religion and religion. He is concerned about the fate of religion in the Western world, and he is acutely interested in the affects sociology of religion may have on this process. He recognizes, of course, that intellectual inquiry studies values, and is not quite in position to create or construct them. At the same time, his own scholarly investigations have helped him understand what obstacles and challenges religion must encounter in the modern world. He perceives the outcome of that exchange to depend on developments to which scholarship is not simply a casual bystander. In this regard, the formula is the same, in principle, as what has been enunciated before. The problem of modern humans, as Yinger envisions it, is that the great truths of religion remain too abstract, lofty, and theoretical to be of immediate use. As he describes the situation:

> The twentieth century has been and continues to be a powerfully religious age—but its religions are partial and divisive. We are not lacking in world-encompassing values, but there are few structures through which they can be expressed and few procedures through which individuals can be trained to accept them at the deepest levels.

Note that the primary challenge facing contemporary religion can be described in virtually the same terms as the primary challenge to contemporary sociology of religion: Its theoretical and practical components are out of harmony (and, thus, out of effective reciprocal alignment) with each other. Just as earlier Yinger had lamented that the grand hypotheses were not consonant with empirical data, now he is observing that modern-day human beings are experiencing considerable difficulty in "ritualizing their behavior" in accordance with the truths and insights of the great religions of the world. Is it appropriate to ask whether these two necessary reconciliations were to be effected at the same time?

Does Yinger expect that the achievement of an effective methodological rapport between theoretical and empirical elements in scholarship will assist in a positive resolution of the contemporary religious dilemma?

For now, at least, the answer to all such questions must await further developments. Suffice it to say that J. Milton Yinger is a scholar who is motivated by a penchant for the unitary and comprehensive grasp of the subject, which unitarial comprehensiveness he recommends both on behalf of the greater vitality of an academic field and to give modern religious belief a heightened resilience.

Mary Douglas: Bringing Durkheim into the Current Conversation

Where anthropological approaches to the study of religion are concerned, one of the most intelligent and provocative is the one proposed by Mary Douglas (b.1921), former professor of social anthropology at University College, London, whose subsequent faculty appointments in the United States were to Northwestern University and Princeton. Douglas first came to widespread scholarly attention with the publication of her book *Purity and Danger: An Analysis of Concepts of Pollution and Taboo* in 1966. Douglas's own fieldwork was based in the Belgian Congo, where she studied the daily behavior of the Lele people, concentrating on implicit practices of etiquette and hygiene. Later, summarizing her discoveries, Douglas wrote:

> Among the Lele I found that rules of hygiene and etiquette, rules of sex and edibility fed into or were derived from submerged assumptions about how the universe works. It was evident that a very satisfactory fit, between the structure of thought and the structure of nature as they thought it, was given in the way that their thought was rooted in community life.

This matching of the structure of thought with the structure of nature is a principle to which Emile Durkheim was acutely sensitive. Indeed, his thesis that "religion is eminently social" stands as explicit recognition of the fact that the patterns of human knowledge of the universe are socially constructed; that is, what is known is a product of the generative powers of the mind. Knowledge of reality, in other words, is socially determined. When Durkheim proceeded to describe and explain how this collective cognitive process could be seen as being generative and determinative of religion, he concentrated on the distinction between the sacred and the profane. The concept of deity, Durkheim attested, is always socially determined and culturally dependent, and reflects the presence of dichotomy in the tribe's sensitivity to the power of the sacred. Thus, awareness of what is sacred is always bound up with awareness of what is profane. Neither of the two terms can be defined except in relationship to the other. Thus Durkheim's sociology of knowledge can be understood to be an elucidation of the implications of the distinction between sacred and profane. Since knowledge of the universe is always socially constructed, the same fundamental dichotomy should be reflected in the disposition and structure of social, behavioral, and attitudinal life. Thus, when Douglas focuses on *contagion*—which belongs to the category of impurity (versus purity), taboo (versus that which is not ritually prohibited), and uncleanliness (versus cleanliness)—she can rightly understand her inquiry and investigation to be supported by a range of intellectual insights that Emile Durkheim masterfully brought to widespread attention.

Douglas wishes, however, to press the insights further, and in so doing offers a compelling critique of Durkheim's conclusions. She contends, in brief, that he was unwilling to accept the full force of his own discoveries. Indeed, he was able to shield himself from the consequences of his insights on grounds that the primitive peoples he was studying followed rules of collective cognitive behavior that had been transcended by modern, scientifically influenced human beings. As Douglas asserts:

> If Durkheim did not push his thoughts on the social determination of knowledge to their full and radical conclusion, the barrier that inhibited him may well have been the same that has stopped others from carrying his program through. . . . he really believed that primitives are utterly different from us.

To be more specific, as Douglas paraphrases Durkheim's assumptions: "For him, primitive groups are organised by similarities; their members are committed to a common symbolic life. We by contrast are diversified individuals, united by exchange of specialised services." This distinction, in Douglas's view, enabled Durkheim to distinguish primitives from moderns on the basis that commitment to individual diversity, among moderns, matches up with allegiance to objective scientific truth.

Douglas believes Durkheim was mistaken in this regard. In her view, the principles by which primitive and modern societies are ordered are not so distinct, and even "a week's fieldwork would have brought correction [to Durkheim's assumption]." To illustrate that our ideas of contagion are similar to those of other peoples, Douglas focuses on concepts of dirt—namely, matter out of place (which denotes entities that must not be included within the range of things that can be sanctioned). Her contention is that implicit rules of pollution are at work in both contexts, and when examined carefully offer clues and indices into the society's understanding of boundaries, margins, and comprehensive order. That which is "unclean" is not simply judged to be out of bounds, as it were, but is also sensed to be dangerous, because it attributes power to disorder. Such entities attract ritual attention so that pollutants and the sources of dangerous and unclean (and thus disorderly) power might be appropriately jettisoned so that they cannot attain the ability to threaten or undermine the order of the world. Primitive societies are organized according to ritual processes that are designed to routinize such processes of purification. Modern society functions in the same way, in Douglas's view. In fact, all societies exhibit ritual processes by which abominations are distinguished, pollutants are identified, and dangers are exorcised so that the legitimate collective order is not destroyed by such dangerous and destructive forces. In the way in which the distinction between sacred and profane is effected within this ritual context lie the clues to the determinants of order and meaning by which both society and reality are constructed.

Durkheim's mistake, according to Douglas, was that he believed that his own cultural outlook was more rational than those of the primitive societies he was studying. This assumption, too, she believes, belongs to the generative activities of the mind: it is a cultural fact that persons "shore up their theory of knowledge by investing some part of it with certain authority." Here, in her view, Durkheim should have been more radical. He should have perceived that the creative intellectual activity by which the order of the universe is constructed is descriptive of his own theory of knowledge too. Here he would have been assisted had he the opportunity to encounter the insights of Ludwig Wittgenstein. In Douglas's words: "For, as Durkheim saw for the world of the primitive, and as Wittgenstein for all worlds, the known cosmos is constructed for helping arguments of a practical kind." That is, Wittgenstein understood that all schemes of societal order are constructed in the same way, and no one of them alone can carry the authority of being scientifically and objectively verifiable. Douglas believes that had Durkheim had the opportunity for a conversation with Wittgenstein, the latter "would have put it to him that even the truths of mathematics are established by social process and protected by convention." This is just the beginning of the insight, for, had Wittgenstein succeeded (as Douglas now wishes to succeed), "he would have shown him how much more elegant and forceful his theory of the sacred would be, stripped of exceptions made in honor of science." With such amendations, corrections, and extensions, Douglas proposes, "a new epistemology would have been launched, anchored to ongoing social reality and dedicated to developing a unified theory of consciousness." It is a powerful point, stated most appropriately in Douglas's own words:

If Durkheim's contribution was accepted only in a narrow circle, his friends have to admit frankly that it was his own fault. When he entered that great debate, he muffed his cue. . . . He could have been telling us that our colonisation of each other's minds is the price we pay for thought. He could have been warning us that our home is bugged. . . . Bane to those who claim that their sacred mysteries are true and that other people's sacred is false; bane to those who claim that it is within the nature of humans to be free of each other. Begging us to turn round and listen urgently to ourselves, his speech would have disturbed the complacency of Europe as deeply as the other two [Marx and Freud]. But instead of showing us the social structuring of our minds, he showed us the minds of feathered Indians and painted aborigines. With unforgivable optimism he declared that his discoveries applied to them only. He taught that we have a more genial destiny. For this mistake our knowledge of ourselves has been delayed by half a century.

Victor Turner: The Ritual Process and Social Change

Victor Turner (1920–1983) was born in Scotland, conducted his extensive anthropological fieldwork on the Ndembu tribe in central Africa, taught in Great Britain and in the United States (at Cornell and the University of Virginia), and is best known for his analyses of the ways in which religious symbols function in ritual contexts. The insights and theories of the Belgian anthropologist Arnold van Gennep, who is best known for his book *Rites de Passage*, were instrumental in helping Turner design a method of conducting cross-cultural research that concentrates on the dynamics of ritual action. Van Gennep had distinguished three aspects or phases within rites of passage: separation, threshold or *limin*, and reaggregation. Turner focused on the second of these three phases, on the dynamics of ritual liminality, and investigated the ways in which these functions both enable the group to lend expression to its fundamental social and cultural values as well as to subject those same values to transformation. Moreover, Turner was concerned about the ways in which such transformation affected the structure of social and cultural life—this interest he shared with van Gennep—but he was also concerned about the effects of the same transformations on the inward moral and spiritual lives of the participants in the rituals.

Turner's most lucid examples came from the world of religious pilgrimage. Understanding the pilgrimage to be a prominent example of rites of passage, he approached the phenomenon as being illustrative of the group's (as well as the individual's) social and cultural *raison d'être* as well as providing description of liminal ritual transformation. Turner understood the rite of pilgrimage to include both the experience of *communitas* as well as an encounter with the sacred.

A number of interpretive principles are implicit in his analysis. First, he was devoted to comparative studies, and he believed that the foci he had identified as well as the methodological interests to which he was committed would enable comparative cultural studies to thrive. As it happened, his work on the dynamics of pilgrimage inspired others to focus on specific pilgrimage rites that belong to a variety of religious traditions. Second, he selected ritual (instead of myth) as the means of coming to terms with Durkheim's proposals regarding the structure of social order. Turner affirmed the conviction that "religion is eminently social," while illustrating the same by tracing the morphology of ritual action. Had he achieved no more than this, his accomplishment would have been significant to anthropological and religious studies scholarship. But the distinctiveness of his approach is rooted in his conviction that social order and cultural patterns are never definitively set or fixed, but, on the contrary, are persistently and perpetually undergoing transformation. Turner believed that such transformation, *qua* transformation, is orderly, and not simply random or arbitrary. For there are constitutive "root paradigms"—axiomatic frameworks—with necessary reference to which all social and cultural change takes shape. Such axiomatic factors also make these transformations traceable.

In speaking this way, Turner found himself drawing on the language of the theater. His analyses are framed around words like *drama, dramatistic,* and *performance.* Indeed, when called upon to give labels to his own theory, he found it appropriate to employ the word *performance.* Such terminology became appropriate because he was intent on identifying, understanding, describing, and then explaining interruptions in expected sequences as well as disturbances regarding what had been expected. But this was just the point: social and cultural transformation, as well as the dynamics of spiritual insight, are reflective of the experience—as the word *limina* denotes—of crossing the threshold. If the structures of the universe were fixed, such action could only be conformist. The truth of the matter, Turner attests, is that the same action is performatory: its very occurrence effects changes in the environment within which it occurs, and it effects changes in the identities (both collective and individual) of those who participate in such action.

The social dramas that Turner first encountered when studying the Ndembu people he also saw reflected in theatrical productions, particularly in the experimental theater in the United States in the 1960s and 1970s. He became a student of the theater and urged his colleagues in anthropology to do the same. The dynamics of social and cultural life, he proposed, could be likened to dramatic performances. Such action carries constitutive and transformational functions. Like the experience of pilgrimage that stands, perhaps, as their most lucid example, they are responsible for compelling self-knowledge, both on the part of participants and on the part of awakened observers.

Erik H. Erikson: Religion and the Life Cycle

Another point of view that depends on an organismic outlook and bears certain resemblances to Weber's orientation has been proposed by Erik H. Erikson (1902–1994), prominent twentieth-century psychoanalyst and psychohistorian. Erikson's position, however, requires a modification or alteration of the fundamental Durkheimian thesis that "religion is eminently social." To this statement Erikson would add: "and also eminently psychological." His revised conception of the purpose and function of religion is nevertheless developed in organic-coordinative terms.

For Erikson, the fundamental organism is the human personality. The human personality is shaped and composed, as Sigmund Freud described it, by the organic coordination of ego, id, and superego. This is the starting point. But after introducing his analyses this way, Erikson proceeds to project the development of the personality according to distinct stages of the human life cycle. In so doing, he treats the developmental process as the working context through which organic coordination is effected. Religion is understood to be a factor that contributes to the formation of the personality. But this is just the beginning, for the human personality is involved in numerous relationships of interdependence with society as well as with history. Thus, within the context of a new academic field (or subfield) called psychohistory, Erikson has concentrated on the process by which the quest for individual identity involves the social matrix as well as perpetual ideological construction.

Personality development occurs within a framework that is formed simultaneously by social and ideological change. Erikson refers to these complex interconnections by describing the interdependencies between "identity" and "ethos." In illustrating how these factors coalesce and interrelate in specific instances, Erikson concentrates on individuals of remarkable religious sensitivity who also qualify as "cultural workers." The two most prominent of his studies of individual lives are his analyses of Martin Luther (in *Young Man Luther*) and Mohandas K. Gandhi (in *Gandhi's Truth*). Both of these individuals are interpreted as being "religious geniuses" who were also able to effect significant social, political, and ideological change. Both influenced the course of human history. Both provide classic, almost archetypal illustration of the necessary interweavings of personal history and social matrix. In both instances, the quest for personal identity played a larger collective and representative role. That is, the achievement of individual identity involved complex ideological innovation that also carried social and political connotations. Thus, Luther's struggles to find a benevolent deity resulted in a new cultural era—indeed, a new or revised way of understanding human nature. And Gandhi's insights regarding the sanctity of "nonviolent resistance" forced a change in the conditions of life for his people in India.

As has been indicated, some of the elements in Erikson's formula are similar to those suggested by Max Weber, although the psychologist attributes a much larger role to the individual in effecting a perpetual give-and-take between ideological structure and social matrix. In this sense, the individual—that is, the formative "religious genius" or "cultural worker"—functions in a way similar to the way the ego functions with respect to superego and id. Both ego and the formative individual human being become instruments of regulation between overarching patterns of meaning and the reservoirs of some primordial energy.

Erikson has concentrated on the cases of Luther and Gandhi. Others, influenced by his approach, have taken the same methods and sensitivities and have applied them to other candidates for psychohistorical interpretation: Saint Augustine, John Henry Cardinal Newman, Abraham Lincoln, Henry VIII, and Martin Luther King, Jr., to name some of the more prominent. In most instances, the approach is used not simply to gain in-depth insight into the dynamics of personality formation, but also, by that means, to illumine a period or segment of history. Thus, impressive and prominent psychoanalytic and psychohistorical translations have been created of the proposal that religion can be construed in terms of organic coordination.

Verstehen vs. Survey Research

In all of these fields—anthropology, sociology, and psychology—a distinction is frequently made between scholars who are engaged in careful analytical work and those whose work is informed by meta-analytical theoretical concerns. The former are sometimes described as "survey researchers" as distinct from those who are reaching for "more profound concerns" that are made accessible through *Verstehen* sensitivities. Considerable scholarship of both kinds has been directed toward items of keen interest to religious studies. Sometimes the two modes have informed each other. Sometimes they have overlapped. Sometimes they are allowed to coexist without being intermingled. It probably need not be added that representatives of the two dispositions have not always gotten along with each other. Survey researchers have occasionally been branded by *Verstehen* advocates as being engaged in surface (meaning superficial) phenomenona. From the other side, survey researchers have occasionally criticized *Verstehen* interpreters for attempting to explain weighty matters that are at best elusive, intangible, and carry the aura of being both philosophically and methodologically suspect. Either approach can be judged pejoratively by advocates of the other approach.

It is not our purpose in this survey of methodological variations in the academic study of religion to try to mediate or negotiate this persistent controversy. But it has become apparent that it seems easier for a *Verstehen* advocate to find representation in a study of this kind—at least, to this stage in the history of scholarship—than it is for one whose work is characterized as analytical, statistical quantitative analysis, although, as we shall observe, this predisposition is being called into question.

One of the reasons for this turnabout in academic sentiment and appreciation is the influence of a scholar, Gerhard Lenski (b.1924), and his best-known book, *The Religious Factor* (1961). Lenski's book stands as the first study to employ empirical methods to determine correlations between religious identity and social organization. Working at the time as a professor in the department of sociology at the University of Michigan, Lenski developed a questionnaire to which more than six hundred residents of the Detroit area responded. From this he was able to document that religion was indeed "constantly influencing the daily lives of the masses of men and women in the modern American metropolis." Moreover, through its impact on these individuals, religion also carries influence on the community as well as on the institutions and other forms of social organization of which communities consist. From this, Lenski was in position to predict both the behavior and the community impact of the various religious groups and denominations. In every instance, human behavior was perceptibly influenced by the religious groups to which individuals belong. And yet, it was not so much the conclusions to which Lenski was led (although, without question, these were impressive) as it was the success he displayed in employing empirical methods of quantitative research that established the seminal reputation of *The Religious Factor*. Lenski had taken revised and updated Durkheimian conceptualization of the functions of religion in society, and had developed empirical ways of testing theses as well as of gathering arresting information. Moreover, the methods he employed were eminently transferable to other research projects, and the investigation he conducted within the confines of the Detroit religious community could easily be transferred and extended to other communities of different religious composition. Will Herberg, in his well-known commentary on America's dominant religious communities, *Catholic, Protestant, Jew* (1955), had pointed to the powerful correlations between religious identity and social community. Lenski gave empirically derived content to Herberg's findings and made the latter's case more specific and compelling.

Charles Y. Glock (b.1919), who taught at Columbia University before moving to the sociology department of the University of California, Berkeley (frequently, in close association with Rodney Stark), demonstrated further the capacities of empirical inquiry. Whether probing anti-Semitism, inquiring into the reasons conservative churches seemed to be growing in membership, or asking questions about relationships between economic, psychic, social, and organismic deprivation and religious identity, Glock employed strict quantitative criteria, including polling, questioning, and other means of information gathering. From this vantage point, he also proposed working definitions of religion as well as statistically based interpretations of the ways in which societies, depending on their respective modes and complexities of social organization, tend to depict their deities and cohesive organizing principles. Glock contended that such an approach to the subject of religion was licensed by the insights of both Weber and Durkheim. In an article entitled "Images of God, Images of Man, and the Organization of Social Life," published in 1972, he examined the function of ideology in the organization of societal life by focusing on characteristic images concerning both deity and human nature. In this examination Glock affirmed that ideology and social structure are intimately related, and that "changes in one cannot occur without changes in the other." In specific terms, such "ideological changes involve a revision of what 'god' and man are understood to be like." He added that he believed Weber to be correct when noting that "a change in imagery may precede rather than follow a change in social structure." The implications are twofold. First, all such changes have now become measurable analytically, by quantitative research methods. Second, quantitative research has become an instrument by means of which both to critique and to confirm prevailing theories of large generalization. Trusting that he has demonstrated that the employment of the methods of quantitative research is in keeping with the long-established objectives of his subfield, Glock attested that the two sources that carried most influence with him are Max Weber's *The Protestant Ethic and the Spirit of Capitalism* and Emile Durkheim's *The Elementary Forms of the Religious Life.*

In asserting fidelity to Weber and Durkheim, Glock has brought the development of sociology of religion full circle. Weber's approach to religion as organic coordination was most sensitive to the formal and empirical components of knowledge as this interdependency had been treated by Immanuel Kant as well as in post-Kantian epistemological theory. Retaining the same combination of elements, Weber tended to approach religions as being suppliers of content at the ideological-motivational level. Such content became implicit in specific actual cultural situations. Accordingly, in his work with primitive societies, Durkheim followed a similar pattern—or at least one which, through the modifications imposed by such scholars as Talcott Parsons, could be conceived to be correlative with Weber's understanding. For Durkheim, societal groups always exhibit a certain representational capacity, and this representational capacity gives evidence of the ways in which the group forms its conception of reality. For Durkheim, reality is constituted by the collective consciousness of the group, and this collective consciousness is the source of moral values, cultural ideals, and religious aspirations. Given this range of common agreement, Weber and Durkheim could be fused together, as they were by many who had studied them together.

From these premises, as we have noted, the methodological paths lead in a wide variety of directions. There is sufficient material to work with at the purely ideological level, for example, to make it appropriate to undertake detailed analyses of ideational sets, whether these be embodied in the religions themselves (as Weber) or whether, with Luckmann, Berger, Bellah, and others, they are located somewhere other than in clearly institutionalized form. At the same time, there is sufficient material to work with at the more empirical and specific side to make it appropriate to undertake detailed analytical inquiries into the actual disposition of the social reality. This explains the interest of those engaged in quantitative research. But since the relationship between motive and act, ideology and social structure, is always rendered as something complex and dynamic, there is good reason to concentrate on the relationship itself. This would describe Talcott Parsons's emphasis. Within the more specifically religio-institutional context, the same interest seems to predominate in those who approach their study in the fashion represented by Thomas O'Dea. When analysis gives way to conclusions, materials abound on the basis of which one can make judgments, appraisals, proposals, and evaluative suggestions about the fate of the coupling of ideology with social structure.

The wide variation of emphasis and focus within the framework simply indicates that organic coordination is ruled by a dynamic interaction. Consequently, whatever the specific focus, the analyst must come to terms with realities in motion, and must therefore be prepared to deal with change. Process is comprehended within developmental stages, and these are most frequently conceived according to the analogy of the organism. At some point along the way, the analyst must decide what shall count as the principal organism, that is, how that organism shall be identified and named. Sometimes the organism is understood to be an institutional religion or a religious tradition. Sometimes it is identified as an extra-institutional phenomenon, such as "civil religion in America." And sometimes the organism is conceived to reflect on the reciprocity between motives and acts in a more comprehensive cultural setting. But however it is focused, the treatment of religion as an example of sociocultural organic coordination possesses these many sides. And the dominant purpose throughout is to identify the principle of organization so that the relationships between motive and act are never capricious and arbitrary, but intentional, as befits the teleology that regulates organic coordination.

New Directions in Quantitative Research

Once the attestation became convincing—namely, that the hypotheses of the pioneering theorists and the methods of quantitative research are congruent—there was virtually no limit as to where scholarly attention might be focused. That is, some twenty years after Lenski, Glock, Stark, and others launched the new (or amended) departure, there was no longer the need to make the case for the validity of survey research. Rather, it sufficed to make new applications, reap the intellectual benefits, and draw the appropriate consequences. It is to be expected, therefore, that the light of such multicommissioned research would be directed toward new investigative challenges.

In the introduction to his book *The Religious Dimension* (1979), Robert Wuthnow (b.1946) notes some of the changes that have occurred in sociological theory concerning religion since the Glock era. In the first place, the concept of religion that has become operational is one that transcends institutional frameworks; more recent theorists have been focusing on religion in a broader, more comprehensive range. Consequently, many of the descriptive and definitional terms that surfaced earlier—"civil religion," "sacred canopies," and so forth—can now be approached and assessed via quantitative research methods. Wuthnow also observes that quantitative research methods themselves have grown in sophistication and specificity. Consequently, much that is researched can be approached through multivalenced perspectives marked by "complex systems of variables." Thirdly, the use of the same analytical tools has been directed toward charting religious and social trends with a view toward cultivating the predictive capacities of quantitative research. And, finally, alongside the interest in predicting and forecasting, a trend developed toward the tailoring of quantitative research methods to the needs and challenges of comparative and historical studies in religion. Some of this comparative work has been directed toward developments on the international scene, while much of it has been focused on religious belief and behavior within narrower frameworks. But all of it represents the continuing fashioning of empirical methods of research for the development of reliable data bases, and, along the way, for the testing of applicable general theories and hypotheses.

Given these additional capacities, it is not surprising that much contemporary sociological research into the subject of religion has been directed toward charting religious and social change. Wuthnow himself has published a highly regarded example, *The Restructuring of American Religion: Society and Faith Since World War II* (1988), whose intention is to address the changes that have occurred in American religious comportment, principally in the 1970s and 1980s, and to make intelligible as much of it as possible. It is apparent that updated Durkheimian and Weberian sensibilities are at work in Wuthnow's tendency to correlate religious change with shifts in "the symbolic-expressive dimension of social life." Here Mary Douglas's insights become useful interpretive tools, particularly her application of the concept of "symbolic boundaries." Wuthnow uses the concept to assess the extent to which shifts in understanding of the presence of social matrices are reflective of new modes of religious interaction, revised religious identities, and shifting frameworks of moral obligation and ethical responsibility. Once again, changes in cultural orientation, public discourse, collective value, and societal organization are all reflected in changes in religious belief, attitude, and action. The interdependence between these factors is not causal, but perpetually reciprocal. Yet, by focusing on changes in conceptions of symbolic boundaries, Wuthnow proposes that sufficient tangible factors exist to enable carefully prescribed quantitative research to identify the constitutive themes in contemporary social, cultural, and public religious change.

Wade Clark Roof (b.1939), who shares much intellectual interest and methodological disposition with Wuthnow, has concentrated his attention on changes that have affected American Protestantism, then, within a broader intellectual environment, on the collective religious odyssey of what is most commonly referred to as "the Baby Boom Generation." The product of research on the latter subject has been published in Roof's book, *A Generation of Seekers: The Spiritual Journeys of the Baby Boom Generation* (1993), within which the author contends that the group he is describing finds itself caught in a variety of conflict situations. It is not possible in brief scope to review Roof's findings in detail, but it is important to point out that the empirical methods he employed were guided by theory concerning ways in which significant social change is linked to disruptions and discontinuities in collective senses of identity. Whereas Wuthnow's study of contemporary American religious change drew from Mary Douglas's insights regarding symbolic boundaries, Roof found illumination in Karl Mannheim's description of the manner according to which generations function in lending stability to the social order.

Finally, with an accelerating interest in identifying the dynamics of religion within the public domain, it should not surprise us to discover that empirical methods of inquiry and analysis are being rigorously applied so as to identify the characteristics of what is most appropriately referred to as "ordinary life philosophy." That is, if Weber's inaugural work was focused on the relationships between religious aspiration and economic incentives, and if Durkheim perceived reciprocity between religious belief and social organization, then it is entirely appropriate that researchers would eventually come to approach and interpret common belief as being worthy of the kind of scholarly attention that had formerly been applied to the functions of more formal ideologies. This, precisely, is the intention of a group of scholars who are members of the faculty of Uppsala University in Sweden, who approach "ordinary life philosophy" with the same circumspection that would be reserved for expressed articles of belief associated with any religion or religious organization. The difference is that "ordinary life philosophy" is reflective of the beliefs and attitudes of a group no more differentiable than "the people" or "the public." Employing empirical and quantitative research methods, however, these scholars—Anders Jeffner, Carl Reinhold Bråkenhielm, and their associates—have inquired as to the way in which the people establish priorities in life. For instance, does their concern for their own good health take precedent over their concern for the environment or their interest in the possibility of a future life? Again, it is not our purpose in such short scope to provide the details, or even to try to summarize initial findings. Were we to examine the orientation further, we would discover that implicit in the way in which "the people" establish day-to-day convictional priorities is a rather wholesale shift from a theocentric view of the universe to one that calls biocentrism normative. With this shift come alterations in the basis of moral authority as well as fresh understanding of the responsibilities human beings have for one another. Suffice it to say that the turn to "ordinary life philosophy" involves a specific application of a theoretical framework whose roots lie in the insights of Durkheim, Weber, and their followers and commentators. In this instance, however, the convictional set (that is, the faith or ideology) on which sociological methods have been trained is of a lowest common denominator variety. It is not that of a church, a religious organization, a generation of human beings, or of anything else specifically differentiable. It is simply that of people who have common convictions and express them in ordinary ways. Yet, the structure on which lucid interpretation rests is the shift in convictional foundations. When theocentrism gives way to biocentrism, moral decision-making ability can be sustained, but it is decidedly differently ordered. Yet, the methodological ploys utilized here are not very different from those responsible for the discernment of a "civil religion."

Persistent Challenges to Secularization Theory

When one examines functionalist discussion of religion in the 1980s, one cannot help but be impressed with the increasingly expanding range of subjects and topics that are brought under social-scientific scrutiny. When functionalist theory developed, the seminal theorists and their disciples participated in a shared conversation, and there was a sense that intellectual progress forward was a collective professional aspiration. In more recent times, the progress has continued—indeed, functionalist theory has at times seemed to leap forward as unexpected subjects and topics have been discovered, pursued, and explored. The rash of new religions, for example, has demonstrated that the previous church-sect distinctions cannot possibly account for the variety and range of phenomena that deserve serious attention. Similarly, the application of social-scientific research methods to the burgeoning field of cross-cultural studies in religion has manifested the methodological limitations of the founders' concentrated attention on Jewish and Christian religion. And the development of irreligion into indisputable religious fact, together with the incidence of comprehensive worldviews that are designed to call the legitimacy of religion into question, have forced scholars in this field to think in fresh ways.

Yet, were one to select one development that has had most pronounced influence on the formation of contemporary functionalist theory, that one factor would undoubtedly be the updating of theory regarding secularization. And if one were to select one functionalist theorist who can explain this transition—and its pertinence—lucidly, that theorist might be Bryan Wilson (b.1926) of Oxford University, who has kept close watch over the manner in which religion has been approached within a sociological perspective.

In a perceptive article included in Phillip E. Hammond's anthology, *The Sacred in a Secular Age*, Wilson has provided a concise, comprehensive review of the development of secularization theory from the period of Durkheim and Weber forward. Indeed, the roots of the presumption lie in the theory of August Comte, and are explained in the sequence of intellectual development that was chronicled in chapter 2, "The Origins of Religion." By this light, progress into the modern age has brought the increasing secularization of human society: the further removed humankind is from its original sociocultural state, the less it exhibits dependence on a theological framework or a shared religious bent of mind. With such progress came increased dependence on scientific knowledge and a consequent deemphasis on the influence of previously presumed supernatural factors.

At the same time, absolutes were progressively removed from moral decision making and the imposition of legal codes. The empirical world became increasingly accessible, and attained more and more legitimacy and integrity. A major consequence of these interrelated shifts was that religious institutions lost more and more of their influence over people's activities and behavior. As societies became increasingly secularized, religion's sphere of acknowledged influence was seriously diminished. This, at least, is how conventional secularization wisdom was presented and understood.

As Wilson has pointed out, however, the rise of new religious groups, the revival of traditional forms of religion, together with increased intense concern for the reestablishment of rigorous moral norms, appear to reflect a kind of resacralization of human life, at least in some locales, at least some of the time. Wilson has observed that numerous religious institutions have resisted the secularization process. Moreover, he is not alone in recognizing that religious sensibility has challenged modern technological consciousness on grounds that the latter insures shallow senses of identity and responsibility and leaves the inhabitants of the world in states of moral confusion while doing nothing to satisfy their deepest personal longings. Wilson recognizes that modern religion is pervasively subject to the secularization process, and yet he senses the resistance that religion is showing together with protections religion offers to individuals who seek alternatives to the secular and secularizing mindset. He describes religion as "an escape from the rigors of technological order and the ennui that is the incidental byproduct of an increasingly programmed world." Certainly one can find numerous impressive examples of the same not only in the restitution of traditional forms of religiosity, but also in the occurrence of "New Age" religion and the rise of highly eclectic forms of spirituality. In this regard, we can expect Catherine Albanese's pathbreaking *Nature Religion in America* (1990) to serve as precedent and invitation to nuance and reconceptualize both "religion" and "sacred" within "secular" environments in more extensive "cross-cultural" terms.

Quantitative Research and Religious Studies

Finally, in this chapter, we must provide brief description of the ways in which the use of quantitative research methods might influence and inform the academic study of religion. We have already provided some documentation of some of the ways in which the development of quantitative research is motivating the interest in identifying religion's societal functions. But it is something more to consider how such efforts belong to religious studies *per se*—that is, how they relate to the other components that belong to this academic undertaking.

For insight on this subject we turn to the writings of Phillip Hammond (b.1931), who studied under Charles Glock, then worked with his mentor on a number of projects. Hammond has also joined forces with Robert Bellah, Wade Clark Roof, and others in documenting shifts in beliefs and attitudes. He has done comparative crosscultural work on the subject of civil religion. He has focused specifically on Protestant Christianity and the specific challenges this dominant form of American religion has faced in the 1960s, 1970s, and 1980s. He has revisited the church-sect distinctions that were introduced by Ernst Troeltsch, and has worked for the expansion of interpretive categories that would encourage serious treatment of additional phenomena such as would be included in any comprehensive survey of the faiths, religions, and ideologies that mark the landscape in contemporary American life.

We choose to focus specifically on Hammond's recommendations concerning the inclusion of quantitative research methods in a vital understanding of the work of religious studies. He is not pleased, for example, with the narrow interpretation of religious studies that views it as a near equivalent to the history of religions, nor is he satisfied with concentration on historical data. Rather, religious studies is broader, more extensive, and more inclusive than history of religions, and the data on which its attention are properly focused are both historical and present-tense. Furthermore, Hammond affirms that the ability to employ quantitative research methods is as necessary to the vitality of the field as is the knowledge of other languages. He recognizes that the humanities have been directly involved in the composition of religious studies; his plea is that the social sciences be accorded equal status. The issue at stake is not competition over turf, but a recognition that the subject under scrutiny requires both avenues of approach and engagement if it is to be properly and effectively addressed. Hammond wonders if religious studies can convincingly lay claim to being interdisciplinary if these conditions are not met.

While it may appear that these methodological recommendations apply primarily to matters of investigative strategy and technique, Hammond recognizes that there are deeply substantive matters under consideration. The consequence of the Durkheimian and Weberian insights into the nature of religion requires that both formal and empirical factors be approached together since insight and discovery are dependent on a clear understanding of their necessary interdependence. If one side of this reciprocal methodological relationship is advanced without regard for the other, or if some working sense of balance is not achieved between them, analysis and interpretation can be badly skewed. That is, theory can be advanced without empirical justification, or data can be assembled without the benefit of guiding principles of organization. Students of religious studies need to be properly trained in all aspects of the task of putting theory and method into vital investigative and interpretative combination. Insight, discovery, and compelling results occur when there is an appropriate or striking match between these elements. And this, it seems, is simply to make functionalist studies more specific, rigorous, and reliable.

Increased precision and greater specification are called for by the direction that functionalist studies have taken since the beginning of the survey that has been chronicled in this chapter. Perhaps it was to be expected that the question about the uses and purposes of religion would never be answered in any simple, straightforward, singular fashion. For, as with the other questions that have been addressed in this study, singles have given way to plurals: the question about the function of religion turns out to be a multiplicity of questions about the functions of religion, the functions of religions, and the places, purposes, agencies, and uses of religious factors in societies, cultures, individual life-cycles, and so on. Thus, the attempt to answer a fundamental question teaches the inquirers that the comprehensive questions must be broken up and transposed into more discrete questions, which questions move analysis and interpretation forward because these questions too are capable of both refinement and multiplication.

The moral of the story might appear to be that functionalist inquiry has entangled itself in the trials and tribulation of infinite regress. It might seem this way, but considerable light has been shed along the way. Some of the discrete questions have been answered, and some new ones have been posed that would never have been entertained under an original devotion to single-minded purity. The discussion goes forward.

C H A P T E R · F I V E

THE
LANGUAGE
OF
RELIGION

The previous chapters of this study have chronicled a variety of ways in which a single intellectual paradigm, with roots in the philosophy of the Enlightenment, has directed and shaped inquiry regarding the nature, status, and function of religion. In the first chapter, we outlined and analyzed the construction of the paradigm and identified a number of theoretical approaches to the question about the essence of religion. In the second chapter, we observed the workings of the paradigm in its desire to account for the origins of religion. In the third chapter, we identified a specific transformation of the paradigm under the influence of phenomenology so that analysts might be equipped to describe religion accurately and compellingly. In the fourth chapter, we explored the modification of the paradigm under functionalist intentions. These four interests—about essence, origin, description, and function—have been fundamental to the study of religion. The responses that scholarship has yielded are significantly responsible for the intellectual substance and methodological shaping of the discipline we call religious studies.

The purpose of this chapter is to trace some typical theoretical responses to questions about the way in which religion is appropriately expressed. Therefore, we focus in this chapter on analyses of the language of religion. Here, as in each of the previous chapters, we will have opportunity to observe the intrinsic workings of the paradigm. The examples we shall cite, as was also characteristic of the examples cited in the previous chapters, are illustrative of intellectual interests that belong to the Enlightenment. Indeed, such interests can be referred back to the first of Immanuel Kant's critical questions, "How is knowledge possible?" While we kept this question uppermost in mind, our approach to the subject drew most of its inspiration from Kant's insights and proposals in his work on aesthetics, *The Critique of Judgment*. Thus, while the interest in epistemology remains, the responses we shall be identifying and analyzing are characterized by their fidelity to aesthetic consciousness. When a prevailing interest in epistemological issues is placed within the domain of the third critique, this mode of inquiry tends to focus on symbolic forms, on symbols and the process of symbolization.

Therefore, even before the treatment of epistemological issues in aesthetic form was directed specifically to the subject of religion, the intellectual connection between this mode of inquiry and the materials of religion had been made. For the materials (the data) on which this range of intellectual interests focused—symbolic forms, cultural symbols, and the process of symbolization—belong intrinsically to the world of religion and were acknowledged as such from the beginning. Myths and symbols, which form much of the content of religion, are appropriately approached as products or expressions of aesthetic consciousness. If the analyst wished to account for them in genetic terms, that is, by explaining how they happened to come to be, the analyst might propose that they have been produced through the powers of the imagination. Along the way, the same analyst will want to come to terms with the powers of intuition, with the manner according to which insights are effected, and with the creative process by which ideas are transposed into symbols and symbols are translated into ideas. When myths, symbols, cultural forms, and other examples of aesthetic consciousness are approached in this way, the description of their intentions and workings refocuses attention on the initial Kantian proposals and places these in previously unexplored combinations.

We wish to approach this subject, in this chapter, in two distinctive ways. Our intention is to chronicle the intellectual interest in approaching the question "How is religion expressed?" by distinguishing between those schools, movements, and theorists who concentrated on nondiscursive forms from those whose focus is discursive language. The first group includes Continental theorists, in the main, whose concern is with the workings of symbology.

Ernst Cassirer and the Marburg School

The response to Immanuel Kant to which we make repeated reference in this chapter was relatively slow in developing, perhaps because it was more delicate, more deliberately contrapuntal, and thus more difficult to discern. But once discovered and elaborated, it gained increasing prominence and came to bear large intellectual fruit. Those scholars who gave it impetus were operating self-consciously in the name of Immanuel Kant, though they came to be called neo-Kantians. We refer specifically to Herman Cohen (1842–1918) and Paul Natorp (1854–1924) of the University of Marburg. But the scholar who worked this perspective to the fullest benefit of the academic study of religion was Ernst Cassirer (1874–1945), also of the Marburg school, who is the author of the highly significant and influential three-volume work *The Philosophy of Symbolic Forms*, published from 1923 to 1929. Cassirer was indebted to the Kantian orientation, but in his readings of Kant's work, he noticed certain original suggestions that had remained undeveloped, and which, if developed, would extend Kantian insights to more specific ranges of discourse.

The intellectual and historical sequence runs as follows. The neo-Kantian emphasis—particularly in Cohen, who, in turn, influenced both Natorp and Cassirer—lay on "the unity of cultural consciousness." Cohen followed the pattern of Kant's activity by writing three related books in sequence: the first on pure thought, *System der Philosophie;* the second on ethics, *Ethik des reinen Willens;* and the third on aesthetics, *Aesthetik des reinen Gefühls.* In addition to showing that cultural consciousness displays a certain unity of apprehension, Cohen argued that the distinction between thought and being—on which distinction Kant based his observations and contentions about the *ding an sich* (thing-in-itself)—was based on a large misconception. Instead of viewing thought and being as dichotomous, Cohen (followed by Natorp) contended that they are inextricably and mutually related. Being exists only in the process of being grasped and determined by thought, he proposed. Thus, being and thought are closely interlocked, for thought is what most definitively lends determination to being. In Cohen's and Natorp's views, Kant's apriori-synthetic judgment describes more than the process by which knowledge is acquired. It is also the dynamic interplay by which being is formed.

Ernst Cassirer accepted these twin contentions about the unity of cultural consciousness and the mutual reciprocity of thought and being. The next task, he believed, was to extend the boundaries of the Kantian corpus so that other forms of consciousness might be included. In other words, he accepted the initial Kantian framework—pure reason, ethics, and aesthetics—but saw no reason to regard this as an exhaustive list. Furthermore, if additions were to be made, they need not be accorded a lesser status than the original three components. Nor need they be given a diminished or otherwise qualified function when it comes to lending constitution to the world. It is conceivable—so Cassirer argued—that reality is determined by means other than those modes of knowledge Kant clearly identified in the movement's initial statement.

Thus, Cassirer regarded his own project—a comprehensive philosophy of symbolic forms—as an extension and embellishment of the original Kantian critical philosophy. Writing in the introduction to his second volume (the one that deals specifically with "mythical thought"), Cassirer laid down some of the principles by which the original Kantian proposals could be extended and projected into heretofore unexplored areas:

> It is one of the first essential insights of critical philosophy that objects are not "given" to consciousness in a rigid finished state, in their naked "as suchness," but that the relation of representation to object presupposes an independent, spontaneous act of consciousness.

The cardinal principle carries a corollary, as Cassirer continues:

> The object does not exist prior to and outside of synthetic unity; it is no fixed form that imprints itself on consciousness, but is the product of the formative operation effected by the basic instrumentality of consciousness, by intuition and pure thought.

All of this is background to Cassirer's description of the intention of his own project:

> The philosophy of symbolic forms takes up this basic critical idea, this fundamental principle of Kant's "Copernican Revolution," and strives to broaden it. It seeks the categories of the consciousness of objects in the theoretical, intellectual sphere, and starts from the assumption that such categories must be at work wherever a cosmos, a characteristic and typical world view, takes form out of the chaos of impressions. All such world views are made possible only by specific acts of objectivisation, in which mere impressions are reworked into specific, formed representations . . . .

Then, Cassirer offered this preview of the conclusion of the project:

> Our investigation has already shown that this direction is by no means "simple" . . . that the ways in which the diversity of sensory impressions can be synthesized into spiritual unities can reveal the most diverse nuances. And this conclusion is strikingly confirmed when we contrast the mythical process of objectivisation with that of theoretical, pure empirical thought.

Note that the typical and familiar neo-Kantian themes are enunciated, with significant elaboration. The reciprocity between consciousness and the object is duly noted. The statement that the object is in "no already fixed form that impresses itself on consciousness, but is the product of the formative operation" shows that the Kantian disposition is being sustained, though restyled. In citing Kant's "Copernican Revolution," Cassirer is referring specifically to the fundamental insight and conviction that human consciousness determines whatever is reality for us. Cassirer's extension of the principle is that reality is formed by being apprehended through legitimate modes of consciousness. He understands himself to be reaffirming Kant's opposition to the viewpoints (1) that reality is already fixed or objectively self-contained prior to the process of cognition, and (2) that knowledge occurs when cognition is shaped to some external state of affairs. Cassirer wants to be corrective, but he believes that Kant's viewpoint is both more revolutionary and sweeping than its founder suspected.

Cassirer's overall thesis is that every symbol system bespeaks a fusion, a union, or synthesis of object and human consciousness. Such modes of consciousness are numerous and distinct, as numerous and distinct as the world of "reality" they inform. As he put it: "The ways in which the diversity of sensory impressions can be synthesized into unities can reveal the most diverse nuances." The modes are numerous, but they are also specific.

The next task is to identify these modes and to describe their inner workings. In our study, we cannot trace the project in detail, but we can and must focus on the mode of mythical consciousness—the framework that provides most illumination regarding the nature of religion—as Cassirer develops his analysis and description in the second volume of *The Philosophy of Symbolic Forms*. In Cassirer's view, mythical consciousness represents a comprehensive and self-consistent mode of knowledge, by means of which reality is determined and formed. It is a distinctive modality through which reality is determined, conditioned, and known, all through the workings of one and the same cognitive process. It is important, in this respect, to see mythical consciousness not simply as a legitimate perspective on the world, alongside a number of other legitimate perspectives, but, instead, as a distinctive mode of address, apprehension, and engagement by means of which "the world" is regulated, constituted, and given content.

Cassirer illustrates his contention by contrasting mythical with scientific consciousness. The two can be contrasted because each has the function of providing a schema of organization by which the world is both formed and known. But mythical consciousness lends a mythical form to reality, whereas scientific knowledge lends a theoretical form to reality. Although distinct in this respect, the two modes can be regarded, in Cassirer's words, as "a specific and peculiar index of refraction." By calling them specific and peculiar, Cassirer wants to avoid a situation in which he is asked or persuaded to give priority to one of them, or to provide some scale for rank-ordering. He avoids this as well as having to identify one of the modes with the status of being normative. Instead, each is regarded as a unique, useful, indispensable, and disclosive mode of engagement, for reality bears a kind of polydimensional character.

Although the modes cannot be graded epistemologically, they can (as we have shown) be compared and contrasted. Scientific consciousness, for example, presumes an ability to engage in abstract thought. Abstract thought is not typical of mythical consciousness. And the analyst can employ a temporal measure—a time line—in making distinctions between the functions of the various modes. Cassirer is acutely aware of the fact, for example, that it was in an earlier period of human awareness that self-consciousness was regulated by an immediate apprehension, or grasp, of reality. Such immediate apprehension relies on distinctive cognitive resources, clearly distinguishable from those that belong to scientific consciousness. As Cassirer explains: "Before self-consciousness rises to this abstraction, it lives in the world of mythical consciousness, a world not of 'things' and their 'attributes,' but of mythical potencies and powers, demons and gods." Scientific consciousness developed later, but did not thereby make mythical consciousness obsolete. In addition, scientific consciousness does not imply that a significant step closer to the truth has been taken. Rather, understanding of the world is formed out of the various legitimate modalities, each of which is shaped out of its own resources, each of which makes knowledge possible. Thus, though mythical consciousness was an earlier occurrence in the history of modes and methods by which knowledge has been acquired, it is neither made useless nor obsolete when, as Cassirer put it, "self-consciousness rises to scientific abstraction." From this recognition, the purpose of a philosophy of symbolic forms can be stated again. Such a philosophy, in Cassirer's words, "is not concerned exclusively or even primarily with the purely scientific, exact conceiving of the world." Instead, "it is concerned with all the forms assumed by man's understanding of the world." In summary:

> It seeks to apprehend these forms in their diversity, in their totality, and in the inner distinctiveness of their several expressions. And at every step it happens that the "understanding" of the world is no mere receiving, no repetition of a given structure of reality, but comprises a free activity of the spirit. There is no true understanding of the world which is not based on certain fundamental lines, not so much of reflection as of *spiritual formation* [emphasis mine] . . . . But, as we have seen, this articulation is not effected in the same way in all fields. . . . Thus, in particular, language and myth each reveal a "modality" which is specific to it, and which lends a common tonality to all its individual structures.

The range and scope of each modality are unique. Thus, the various modalities must be studied contextually. Thus there is reason for a philosophy of symbolic forms.

Yet, it must also be said that the various modes are interrelated. For example, not until the human spirit has acquired the ability to make abstractions does it recognize the characteristics of mythical awareness. It is through the acquisition of scientific awareness that one comes to discern mythical consciousness as a distinct modality. Through scientific knowledge, one is enabled to distinguish mythical knowledge. Scientific knowledge enhances modal self-consciousness. It assists one precisely to recognize the components and dynamics of the several modalities.

> For what distinguishes science from the other forms of cultural life is not that it requires no mediation of signs and symbols and confronts the unveiled truth of "things

in themselves," but that, differently and more profoundly than is possible for the other forms, it knows that the symbols it employs are symbols and comprehends them as such.

This recognition is implicit, of course, in the distinction between the immediacy of the mythical mode and the second-order reflective awareness of scientific consciousness.

Thus, while the scientific mode is not given a normative status vis-à-vis the mythical mode, it does own certain powers of discernment that give it insight into the configurations of mythical consciousness. This does not imply that scientific consciousness can sustain mythical consciousness by translating it into a scientific mode of awareness. On the contrary, the various modes of knowledge are distinct. Each has its own range. Each functions uniquely. Each forms reality intrinsically. Cassirer wanted to maintain all of the modes in their own terms. As noted, where knowledge of the world is the concern, Cassirer subscribed to a fundamental polydimensionality. Each of the modalities is a distinct way of lending form and pattern to the world, and apart from these formations the world is imperceptible and unknowable. Cassirer insists on the variety and distinctiveness of the several modes. At the same time, he understands the multi- or polydimensionality of the world to belong to "the unity of cultural consciousness." Thus, the diversity implicit in an enlarged, expanded, and embellished range of valid human experience does not mean that the several modes are discrete and unrelated. The polydimensionality of the world cannot destroy the unity of cultural consciousness, nor can modal variety violate the unity of the human spirit. In both distinctive and expansive senses, "the human spirit . . . advances beyond all the fixed boundaries we customarily draw between its various faculties."

Cassirer's polydimensionality really consisted of an effort to compose, in Hermann Cohen's words, a commentary on "the unity of cultural consciousness." It was Cohen's vision that Cassirer spelled out in detail. Both held that the expansion of the range of valid human knowledge does not destroy the unity of human awareness. In other words, when knowledge is distinguished by modes, the several modes need not be treated as discrete or disconnected entities. Instead, the modal polydimensionality contributes to richer, deeper, and more accurate conceptions of reality.

Amplifying the New Key: Susanne Langer

Cassirer's modal polydimensionality was illustrated, extended, made more accessible, and stripped of all remnants of Hegelian and Neo-Kantian metaphysical dependencies by Susanne Langer (1895–1985) in her influential book *Philosophy in a New Key*, published in 1942. Unlike Cassirer, Langer's orientation was not predominantly Kantian: her chief mentor was Alfred North Whitehead. Thus, through Whitehead's philosophy, she was already well acquainted with a schema for tracking "the continuous modality of the spirit" (in Cassirer's words) and did not have to contend for the same by seeking to reconcile it with an already prescribed index into valid forms of human experience. She expressed this tendency in the introduction to her *Philosophy in a New Key*:

> The study of symbol and meaning is a starting-point of philosophy, not a derivative from Cartesian, Humean or Kantian premises; and the recognition of its fecundity and depth may be reached from various positions, though it is a historical fact that the idealists reached it first, and have given us the most illuminating literature on non-discursive symbolisms—myth, ritual, and art. Their studies, however, are so intimately linked with their metaphysical speculations that the new key they have struck in philosophy impresses one, at first, as a mere modulation within their old strain. Its real vitality is most evident when one realizes that even studies like the present essay, springing from logical rather than from ethical or metaphysical interests, may be actuated by the same generative idea, the essentially transformational nature of human understanding.

On this basis, then, Langer could presume freedom, mobility, creativity, flux, spontaneity, transformation, metamorphoses, and the other products of Whitehead's thesis that *process is reality*. Her contribution registered primarily as an impressive illustration of the ways in which form influences content—as the two become reciprocally formative—in a variety of symbolic modes.

She referred to her approach as a "philosophy in a new key," a phrase that plays deliberately on modal vocabulary. The title indicates that the innovations to which she is calling attention pertain most of all to the placing of philosophical considerations in new tonal settings. As with John Dewey, Langer sees philosophy being reconstructed by being shifted onto new ground, whereupon even its fundamental questions have been changed. For her, the "disposition" of philosophical problems—the auspices under which issues are formulated, the intellectual horizon within which philosophical issues register, the "tacit, fundamental way of seeing things," the peculiar manner of phrasing curiosities—plays a crucial formative role in the cognitive process. For Langer, as for Cassirer, form and content always influence each other. The fundamental Kantian way of viewing the relation between form and content is never violated in *Philosophy in a New Key*. The same reciprocity is seen in the way human beings use and employ symbols.

Langer attested that symbol-making is "one of man's primary activities, like eating, cooking, or moving about." Such activity goes on at all times. Furthermore, symbol-making is the capacity that most significantly distinguishes the human from other animals. It represents the human's basic need. Symbolism is the prime stuff of thought. Thus, it follows that "the thinking organism must be forever furnishing symbolic versions of its experiences in order to let thinking proceed." In sum, "symbolization is the essential act of mind."

Symbolization functions to transform experiences for purposes of interpretation and communication. Speech is one form of symbolic transformation, but so also are myth, ritual (which includes magic), music, dance, art, and, in other ways, imagination and dreams. This view opposes the presumption that only linguistic forms of expression have cognitive value and that all nonlinguistic patterns of symbol formation belong to the realm of feeling and instinct. Instead, Langer extended the range of cognitive validity to nonlinguistic modes, but by making a crucial distinction first. For her, the true distinction is not between cognition and feeling, but between two sorts of symbolic modes: (1) those that function discursively, and (2) those that function presentationally. To say that linguistic forms of expression alone bear cognitive validity is to restrict knowledge to the discursive mode. This is also to regard the discursive symbolism as the exclusive bearer of ideas. Langer denounced this form of reductionism in favor of a view that honors nondiscursive modes of expression as unique avenues to truths about the world.

> I do believe that in this physical space-time world of our experience there are things which do not fit the grammatical scheme of expression. But they are not necessarily blind, inconceivable, mystical affairs; they are simply matters which require to be conceived through some symbolic scheme other than discursive language.

In other words, in Langer's view, there are various sorts of groupings—nondiscursive, nonverbal presentational forms of alignment—in which knowledge is formulated and articulated and meaning is acquired. The difference is that meaning is construed qualitatively rather than logically in the nondiscursive modes. Nondiscursive symbols function presentationally, for they express truths that cannot be verified logically. But this does not make them any less truthful. In Langer's view, intelligence cannot be restricted to the discursive forms, for nondiscursive, nonverbal formulation is also a product of serious and trustworthy mental activity. Both types of formulation give expression to "the basic human act of symbolic transformation."

Thus, Cassirer and Langer share the fundamental contention that knowledge of the world is not exhausted through the discursive, oftentimes scientific, logical mode of access. For both symbologists, the world is sufficiently multiform and pliable to allow for a variety of modes of access, each of which carries a formative capacity. Via each mode, the world is both apprehended and patterned. Because of his neo-Kantian leanings and his attention to ontological matters, Cassirer was more insistent than Langer in arguing that there is no reality apart from apprehension of reality, and that apprehension always occurs only through the instrumentation of one or another of the symbolic forms. The two share convictions regarding the multiplicity and richness of meaning that is available to a polydimensional modal approach to the world. It follows that for both of them any diminishing of the multiplicity and restriction of the modal richness of knowledge runs counter to the intrinsic mobility, fluidity, and fundamental large-heartedness of reality. Any restrictiveness would violate the adventuresome spirit by which the world is formed. On this point both theorists agree, and much of what each asserts is intended to support this central insight.

An attitude to religion follows due course. For both Cassirer and Langer, there are deep, natural, and intrinsic ties between religion and mythology. With morphological refinement, mythology functions as that without which religion would not be what it is. There would be no religion, presumably, if the mythological mode were discarded, or were replaced by some scientific, discursive, logical mode of address. Langer and Cassirer could not allow this to happen, for religion depends on mythology. Understandably, religionists have appreciated Cassirer's and Langer's philosophies, particularly because of their contention that meaning is neither exhausted nor regulated by scientific knowledge. This is particularly welcome news, especially during an era when scientific respectability tends to regulate all canons of verification. In Cassirer's and Langer's view, the scientific mode is but one way of giving pattern or structure to reality. Alongside scientific apprehension, there are other modes of access to the world as well as other worlds. In short, Cassirer and Langer stand opposed to the view that there is but one defensible way of approaching reality, a way that is defined by the scientific method. Within such a world, religious sensitivity is not without resourcefulness.

Some advocates of religion have found in Cassirer's and Langer's formulations another advantage. In their view, it is one thing to attest that the mythical mode is an authentic means of apprehending reality. But there is even more to be learned by attaching the various cognitive modes to distinct movements or activities of the human spirit. For example, if there is a logical distinction between *mythos* and *logos*, it may be due to the fact that the two have different cognitive functions, loci, and roots. Thus, if *mythos* is placed prior to *logos* within the cognitive process, religion can also be understood to have its roots in "prereflection" or even "precognition." From this perspective, the resources of religion are "preconceptual." And to claim that religion is "preconceptual" is to say something important about the nature of religion. To associate religion with mythology is in no sense to explain it away. To link it to the "precognitive" mental activity is not to make it obsolescent.

We noted earlier that Ernst Cassirer inserted an *élan* into the history of human consciousness. Movement forward is associated with a progressive tendency toward abstraction. The use of sign is conscious in the scientific mode, for example, while signs are not seen as signs in mythical awareness. Susanne Langer supports the same *élan*, but she adds an element that gives forward movement some additional dimensions. Some of these additional insights are borrowed from Alfred North Whitehead's rule for charting adventures of ideas. Through Whitehead's scheme, Langer develops a dynamic way of making the various modes interdependent. Furthermore, their interdependence is worked out chronologically and not simply logically. According to Whitehead, intellectual processes can be marked by their sequential moments of romance, precision, and generalization. These three moments form a sequence that is both cyclical and repetitive. Langer relates this pattern of interpretation to the sequence of development from ritual and myth to discursive language. Through the process, religion becomes elongated. It actually appears under new and various guises. It also becomes transformed into ingredients for new kinds of symbolic arrangement. Langer refers to philosophical thought, for example, as "the last reach of genuine religion, its consummation and also its dissolution." When something specific is gathered up into an abstraction, it is time for human understanding to embark on a new step in its adventures. In other words, modal apprehension is dynamic, for process is reality.

Symbols and Thoughts: Paul Ricoeur

Since World War II, the most impressive approach to religion based on a comprehensive treatment of symbolic forms (or cognitive modalities) is that provided by the French philosopher Paul Ricoeur (b.1913). Ricoeur's philosophy, which is formulated in an attempt to provide an extensive and systematic "phenomenology of the will," is conceived to refer to conversations of continental phenomenologists and existentialists—not only Edmund Husserl, Max Scheler, Maurice Merleau-Ponty, Martin Heidegger, and Gabriel Marcel, but also such lesser known figures as Pierre Thevenaz and Paul-Ludwig Landsberg. Hence, with Ricoeur the distinction between a philosophy of symbolic forms (à la Ernst Cassirer) and a phenomenological portrayal of the human condition (à la Husserl and Heidegger and Jean Paul Sartre) is elidible. Ricoeur approaches the latter through the medium of the former. His work on symbols is directed toward phenomenological descriptions of the human condition.

In some respects, Ricoeur's point of view could just as easily have been reviewed in chapter 3 of this volume, for its preoccupation with "modal parsing" is designated to make a comprehensive phenomenology possible. We have placed Ricoeur's approach here rather than in the earlier chapter, although either would have been fitting, because his phenomenological philosophy is based on distinctions he draws between cognitive modalities. (A chief case in point is his treatment of the relationship between mythological portrayal and conceptual representation, a relationship he sketches in his article "The Symbol. Food for Thought.") This placing of Ricoeur here is authorized too, we believe, by his repeated declaration that he is not preoccupied with the problem of the starting point in philosophy. For him it is sufficient to commence with language, and with the meaning that is inherent in language. Speaking about his approval of G. Bachelard's approach, wherein the attempt to establish the *primordium* is simply suppressed, Ricoeur writes:

> I should add that it is also an effort to bypass the thorny problem about the starting point of philosophy. We recall the tiresome backward march of thought seeking the first truth, and, more basically still, seeking a radical starting point which might not be a first truth at all. Perhaps you must actually experience the frustration involved in seeking a philosophy without presuppositions to appreciate the problem we are raising. In contrast to philosophies wrestling with starting points, a meditation on symbols starts right out with language and with the meaning that is always there already. It takes off in the midst of language already existing, where everything has already been said after a fashion. . . . Its big problem is not to get started, but, in the midst of words, to remember once again.

The significant line is the one in which Ricoeur refers to his own work as a "meditation on symbols" (in contrast to "philosophies wrestling with starting points") which "starts right out with language and with the meaning that is always there already." If this is phenomenology, it is not phenomenology done with revised Kantian objectives, but phenomenology in distinct modal keys. Its intention is not to establish a certifiable starting point, but to come to terms with the variety of substance of things made accessible through a modal parsing of the rhythmic interplay of literary and other symbolic forms of expression. This is not so much Kant's critical reflexivity as it is akin to Saint Augustine's mnemonic techniques for giving shape to subjectivity and content to introspection.

Ricoeur's starting point is an analysis of the human's situation in the world. This analysis is introduced by Ricoeur's contention that the human being suffers, at present, from a fundamental alienation, disproportion, a broken unity with respect to that by which the human being is sustained and supported. Approaching human experience in this way, Ricoeur takes advantage of the phenomenological rendering of the *natural standpoint.* The natural standpoint is characterized by its propensity toward distortion. Everything is distorted because it is viewed from a perspective within which human alienation is not yet self-conscious. Consequently, Husserl's program for *epoché* has strong redemptive connotations for Ricoeur in more than an epistemological or a cognitive sense. It is an instrument to assist the human to recognize his own disharmony.

In Ricoeur's view, the human is at odds with himself (we use masculine pronouns here merely for the sake of convenience). His capacities and performances, his intentions and acts, his ambitions and deeds, are distorted. Any phenomenological description of human subjectivity must recognize, as Ricoeur says, that "man is a flawed creature." He is marked by a "fault," a radical cleavage, that is manifested in the human passions and exemplified in ambition, likes, and dislikes. The condition is directly present to man in "the split which suffering introduces between me and myself." Ricoeur cites example after example to demonstrate that the human is a dual being despite his intention to be single. The human is a being divided against himself. Human existence itself is distorted. It suffers from a deep-seated constitutional weakness.

As with Søren Kierkegaard, Ricoeur's description of human subjectivity is correlated systematically with a series of descriptive literary essays. Furthermore, the several stages of the human dialectic, which are described in the literature, are also made accessible through specific hermeneutical modes. For each "stage," Ricoeur has developed a descriptive literature. Thus the first phase of Ricoeur's phenomenological program is called *eidetics*, and is described as a "phenomenological description of the essential structures of man's being-in-the-world," or a "study of man's fundamental possibilities."

In the first phase of the program, Ricoeur has attempted to depict human nature in its essential primordial wholeness, that is, apart from whatever consequences follow from the human's attempt to adapt to the conditions of actual existence. Since this depiction also describes what it is about the human being that makes him capable of fault, the title of the book in which this description is recorded is *Fallible Man*. The second phase of the program is introduced through the book *The Symbolism of Evil*. Here the focus shifts to a description of the human's actual existential situation. Phase one of the study was entitled *eidetics*, whereas phase two is called *empirics*. Phase three is *poetics*. Its purpose is to bring the analyses of the two previous studies together, to demonstrate how the human's actual situation can be reconciled with his essential conditions. In the third phase, Ricoeur becomes something of a visionary. Here he records his vision of a humanity reconciled with itself. The emphasis is on restoration, hope, collective self-realization. Thus, not until he reaches the third stage of his analysis does Ricoeur attempt to describe the dynamics of transcendence. Not until then is it appropriate to introduce promise and to speak of a definitive reconciliation of polarities. All three phases are included within a comprehensive and systematic attempt to engage in phenomenological description by tracing the intricate relationships and interdependencies between the voluntary and the involuntary. Ricoeur describes his own philosophy as a phenomenology of the will. It also registers as a phenomenology that provides an extensive and detailed description of the transformations necessary to overcome the "natural attitude."

We have indicated that Ricoeur's description of the subjective dialectic is correlated with a carefully conceived several-stage literary program. This correlation is Ricoeur's insight that literary modes are styled according to their intention. Myths and symbols make aspects of human subjectivity intelligible, whereas those same features are inaccessible through reflective conceptualization. In the same way, reflective conceptualization reveals aspects of human subjectivity that could not be reached through myths and symbols. The two spheres do not coincide, and yet they overlap and exhibit mutual ranges of interest.

Eidetics can be approached through careful and critical philosophical analysis, almost in the Kantian style. But when Ricoeur engages in empirics, he concentrates on myths under the conviction that humans gain consciousness of fault only through a mode of expression that, by analogy and figurative language, is equipped to sustain, corroborate, and come to terms with the fundamentally enigmatic character of human existence. That is, because they are designed to function suggestively and sometimes deliberately ambiguously, always indirectly, myths and symbols constitute a unique mode of disclosure. They also have a particular sphere of application. The experience of fault, which can never be brought to consciousness directly and objectively, can be mediated by the mythical and symbolic mode. Thus, whereas eidetics belonged to disciplined reflective analysis, empirics is reserved for myths, symbols, signs, rites, stories, and the other nondiscursive means of expression, communication, and disclosure.

This does not mean that once eidetics has been left behind—it is really never left behind—reflective analysis is finished. For, according to the rule that "the symbol is food for thought," and regulated by careful phenomenological principles, Ricoeur finds reflective analysis functioning even with the realm of empirics to interpret the myths and symbols and thus to formulate the meaning of the experience of fault. In this context, reflection is given a second-order function. The data of myths and symbols form the primary body of materials upon which reflective analysis and interpretation are exercised. Thus the meaning of the existential condition is derived through the content of myths, then the content is organized, synthesized, and even cross-referenced through second-order reflective tallies. In other words, thought elucidates the meaning of human subjectivity to which myths and symbols bear primary witness.

While Ricoeur approaches the human's essential nature in eidetics in an *a priori* fashion, his mythical account qualifies as an *a posteriori* approach. Reflection functions, as it were, on its own behalf in the first setting. In the second setting it is given a second-order function. In empirics, reflection works on the data and materials from myths and symbols. From this one can expect poetics to be formed by a reconciliation of the consequences of the straight philosophical reflection in eidetics with the mediated interpretative reflection of empirics. In poetics, Ricoeur will try to portray the consequences of subjectivity as this is projected through the singularity of human intentionality and mirrored in the duality of human affirmation. This stage is called poetics because it weaves intentional and expressive content together. But poetics is also consistent with the underlying structure that has been developed through eidetics and empirics. By means of a "meditation on symbols," which is also a fundamentally recollective endeavor, Ricoeur has engaged in a systematic effort at modal parsing which, at the same time, attempts to identify the declensions of human subjectivity. As noted, his comprehensive project is extraordinarily extensive.

Schleiermacher to Dilthey
to Gadamer

Another trajectory from Immanuel Kant forward also deals with symbols in an instructive manner. This trajectory moves from Kant through Friedrich Schleiermacher, then rests with Wilhelm Dilthey (1833–1911) for a time. In modified form it is brought into current conversation by Hans-Georg Gadamer (b.1900), author of the influential book of hermeneutical theory, *Wahrheit und Methode*. To refer it to Schleiermacher's revision of Kant's philosophy is to signal that the trajectory belongs to aesthetics. But this is something more than to give it a theoretical or disciplinary rootage within the humanities. The reference also implies that the best clues to the nature of reality are aesthetic. Reality is approached aesthetically: it is sensed before it is conceptualized.

The mood is Cartesian and Kantian in origin, at least initially, but the content of the mood, enunciated by Schleiermacher, was prompted by both Kant and G. W. F. Hegel. Kant supplied the interest in identifying a subterranean fundamental core. Hegel provided the contention that reality's core element is *Geist*, or spirit. To summarize the consequences neatly, what Dilthey sought was a nonidealist way of sustaining Hegel's criticism of Kant.

Dilthey's intention was to provide an alternative to the abstract character of Kant's analysis and to ground Hegelian motifs concretely. He was not attracted to Kant's categories of pure reason. The Kantian temper was too rigid and sterile, formed and inflexible, for Dilthey. In being stiff and erudite, in Dilthey's view, it violated the very suppleness of reality.

Critical of Kant's philosophy, Dilthey was only a little happier with Hegel's. In his view, Hegel's philosophy was too abstract, too theoretically rarified. He approved of Hegel's turning from formal epistemological components to devote concentrated attention to the dynamics of history and historical change. But he believed Hegel's preoccupation with the history of consciousness to be a concession to idealism and to involve flights of conceptual fantasy. Thus Dilthey wanted to be more precise and concrete than Hegel, and more flexibly expansive and less formalistically conceptual than Kant. He wanted to understand the workings of the human spirit in its utter concreteness. He was interested in tracing the movements of the human spirit in actual instances of specification. He was particularly interested in "lived experiences" and in "life relations." This meant working to identify the specific forms or modes through which the human spirit gains expression. Dilthey turned from the cold and abstract, and removed to *historical reason*. Historical reason provided him with a rationale. Historical reason implied that the *logos*—or principle of interpretation—could be located as being immanent in things. While it could be abstracted, it was not abstract. Finding, or locating, the rationale in things, Dilthey was able to identify specific instances of the objectification of the human spirit. Thus, Dilthey's alternative to the formalism of Kant and the speculative idealism of Hegel came in the form of deliberate attention to symbolic life forms. The symbolic forms were important to him because they function as indices into the workings of the process of understanding. In Dilthey's terms, "understanding is our name for the process in which mental life comes to be known through expressions of it which are given to the senses."

Dilthey referred to these expressions as "manifestations of life." These expressions, or manifestations, are of three kinds. Note the retention of the original Kantian scheme. The first class of expressions consists of *mental* acts. These include construction of thought, formation of ideas, creation and synthesizing of concepts, reasoning, processes, and so forth, all of which are the products of intellectual work. Words, sentences, paragraphs, essays, treatises, and books are the forms into which such intellectual work is shaped. The second class of expressions—again, in true Kantian style—consists of *practical* or *ethical* acts. Here Dilthey pays particular attention to the way in which purposes are achieved through acts. Purposes and acts are always interrelated (like *theoria* and *praxis*). Will and deed always go hand in hand. Acts are performed to achieve something specific and concrete.

In this regard, Dilthey's examples come from the worlds of private and social practical activity. He illustrated the power of this class of expressions, for example, by citing the acts of legislators in public institutions. He insisted that the examples not be restricted to individual efforts to fulfill personal ethical and moral obligations. Instead, he was interested in the public demonstration of the processes he had uncovered. By concentrating on the dynamism of acts, he believed it possible to penetrate to the basis of human purposes, and this would reveal something fundamental regarding the nature of the human spirit.

His third class of expressions was identified as *psychic* and *imaginative* acts (again, keeping the Kantian framework intact). Here Dilthey had in mind those manifestations of life through which the emotions are expressed. He gave prominence to art, for example, by which he intended that a variety of art forms be considered. And he had high regard for such phenomena as gestures, exclamations, tonalities, voicings, shadings, and nuances. Dilthey was particularly impressed with the content of this third class of expressions primarily because of its ability to disclose something rudimentary about the human spirit. It probably goes without saying that this is the point in his scheme wherein the aesthetic dimension is most apparent and prominent.

It is important to recognize, too, that Dilthey was not supremely interested in drawing up classifications, or in finding the interpretive key to enable him to know how one or another manifestation of life ought to be categorized. Rather, his prime attention was given to an attempt to write a morphology of human understanding. The symbolic forms were instrumental in helping him trace the logic of understanding. His goal was to make the human inner reality transparent. He focused on autobiographical materials, for example, because he thought they provided the opportunity for reexperiencing the mental processes of the autobiographers. A careful analysis of autobiographical materials promises to enable the analyst to reconstruct the mental processes of the text's authors. In reconstructing those processes, the analyst can also experience them for himself/herself. Throughout Dilthey's comprehensive organon of forms of interpretation, the analyst can reexperience the thought, act, and feeling that are implicit in the wide assortment of expressions or manifestations of life. By means of this interpretation, the objectification of the human spirit is enunciated.

Dilthey is important not only for his own rich accomplishment but because of his influence on subsequent theorists of interpretation. The intriguing contemporary hermeneutical work of the Marxist philosopher Jürgen Habermas, for example, was inspired by Dilthey's point of departure.

As we have indicated, the most promising line from Dilthey to contemporary work in religious studies flows through the hermeneutical ponderings of Hans-Georg Gadamer, author of the important book *Wahrheit und Methode* and scores of other books, articles, and monographs. Gadamer is quick to acknowledge that he belongs to Dilthey's tradition of scholarship. For instance, he shares Dilthey's interest in wanting to place and decipher the rudiments of human understanding. But he gives this subject new twists and turns. One can say, in brief, that Gadamer retains Dilthey's interest in concrete specifications of the human spirit. But, unlike Dilthey, he fails to give much attention to "historical reason." That is, Gadamer is more interested in what the forms of expression disclose about the nature of reality than in what they might say about the workings of the mental, ethical or emotional capacities of human beings. And Gadamer's concept of the nature of reality is Heidegger's through and through.

Still, the fundamental point of departure is Dilthey's. Gadamer's assumption is that the usual subject-object split between knower and external reality can and must be overcome through a dialectical interrelationship between "one's own horizon" and that of "tradition." In short, within human subjectivity there is a kind of "dialogue" between one's perspective on life and the perspective or vision that one possesses through transmission. Thus, understanding is formed via the encounter between "horizon" and "tradition." In addition, being—and not simply understanding—is disclosed through the same dialectical encounter. This disclosure occurs when one allows one's own horizon to be questioned by "the being of the thing so that the thing encountered can disclose itself in its being."

In Gadamer's view, cultural forms of expression are manifestations of life, as Dilthey had attested. Moreover, just as Dilthey hoped to be able to perceive the dynamic workings of life by examining the forms of expression, so too does Gadamer contend that cultural forms enable one to view and experience the world. For example, he can speak eloquently and persuasively of the way in which a work of art puts a question to the viewer, rather than the other way around. As he explains this:

In the presence of a great work of our whole self-understanding is placed in the balance, is *risked*. It is not we who are interrogating an object; the work of art is putting a question to us, the question that called it into being. The experience of a work of art is encompassed and takes place in the unity and continuity of our own self-understanding.

Thus, cultural forms of expression provide disclosures of reality as well as self-disclosures. They are the means through which reality is made accessible for us, and they are media of self-knowledge and self-consciousness.

Hans-Georg Gadamer's work can be understood to relate to the subject of religion and to the field of religious studies in at least three prominent ways. First, in his view, religion is a significant source of a host of cultural expressions through which reality is made known. Similar to art and other cultural constructions, religion is an influential medium through which the human spirit has achieved objectification. Because of this, religion serves as a means through which reality is disclosed.

Second, religion is an instrument of self-consciousness. It assists the process through which the conditions of self-knowledge are enunciated. To turn the matter the other way, whatever conditions are necessary to establish self-knowledge are also of religious importance. Self-knowledge is an important religious undertaking.

Third, Gadamer conceives the process of human understanding to be formed by a dialectical relationship between "personal horizon" and "tradition." This dialectic includes the possibility that religion might function as a reliable adjudicator of the relationship between "horizon" and "tradition." For example, religious traditions can be conceived as being party to the placing of questions to which the human self responds. Religious traditions have an important role to play in placing and prompting questions to which the human self responds. Religious traditions can also be assigned an essential role within the process of human understanding. They are significant components of that process, for, as mirrors on reality, they are also part of that accumulated body of wisdom that is handed on, through which encounters take place. And in the dialogue between the human spirit and religious traditions, certain important windows on the nature of reality are opened.

Cassirer's, Langer's, Ricoeur's, Dilthey's, and Gadamer's approaches to language and symbols are philosophical in nature and theoretical in temper. They are based on hermeneutical theory. As such, they are exercises in critical cultural reflection. They provide compelling collective testimony that theoretical analyses of symbolic and cultural forms must take religious factors into account.

Geraardus van der Leeuw: A Phenomenological Approach

Other avenues of approach to religion as symbolic form are rooted less in hermeneutical theory and more in iconography, history of art, as well as the history of religions. One of the best known of these is Geraardus van der Leeuw's classic *The Holy in Art*, which consists of combined phenomenological, historical, and theological insights. In his *Religion in Essence and Manifestation*, as we noted in chapter 3, van der Leeuw engaged in comprehensive morphological description of the subject of religion. In *The Holy in Art* he became more specifically focused. Citing illustrations from a wide variety of historical times and cultural situations, van der Leeuw contended that art is a consecrated means of religious expression. Thus, as the title of his book reinforces, religion and art are to be interrelated by means of the connector *in*. In other formulations, as we shall see soon, *and* is the connector chosen.

From the first page of his study, van der Leeuw makes it apparent that his intention is to offer a systematic, phenomenological portrayal of the complex interrelationships between religion and art. He approaches both as being valid forms of cultural expression. Indeed, he wishes to give each a prominent place within the catalog of various kinds of cultural expressions. His problem is that he does not want this high appraisal to violate or otherwise qualify the Christian understanding of divine revelation. He finds himself in a dilemma in this regard. From the one side, speaking as a cultural historian with evident religious sensitivities, he wishes to approach art—along with history and natural science—as a legitimate and effective medium of divine revelation. But, on the other side, he wishes to keep faith with the Christian teaching that the revelation of God through Jesus Christ is altogether final, complete, and definitive. How can he make both affirmations at the same time? How can he appropriately express what he knows to be true of artistic expression without qualifying his adherence to special revelation?

The dilemma is not easy to resolve, for he discovers some standard theological distinctions to be of little use. It will not help him resolve the issue, for instance, if he assigns art to "general revelation" in contrast to which are more specific and redemptive forms of divine disclosure. In his judgment, this distinction works inaccurately and unfairly against the world, and he is unwilling to participate in a devaluation of the status of art. At the same time, he is not happy with any proposed resolution that would ascribe to art more than is due, thus threatening the absolute priority reserved for the revelation of God through Jesus Christ.

The impasse can be overcome, van der Leeuw believes, through specific attention to a motif that belongs in both religion and art without violating their respective sensitivities. That same motif had already been identified by Rudolf Otto in his search to isolate the essential core of religion. The next task, for van der Leeuw, is to discover and decide how *the holy* and *the beautiful* might be interrelated. "We do not intend to pursue causal relationships, but rather to search for comprehensible associations. Further, we do not intend to investigate the truth behind the appearance, but we shall try to understand the phenomena themselves in their simple existence."

The product is similar in tone and format to van der Leeuw's *Religion in Essence and Manifestation*. It is a comprehensive collection, a veritable catalog of artistic materials of a religious nature. The author focuses on the human experience of beauty and holiness, as these expressions occur in dance, drama, rhetoric, the fine arts, architecture, and music. Its thesis is that religion and art are integrally interrelated since religion's core element is significantly reflected through and in art. The power of *das heilige*, in short, is implicit in art, and in all forms of art.

The next task is to illustrate the thesis more specifically by considering the various art forms. Van der Leeuw takes up these forms, one by one, attempting to establish precise correlations between religion and art as he proceeds. Always the goal is to identify "comprehensible associations"—art and religion belong together because they share common property. For example, when treating dance, van der Leeuw focuses on movement. Movement belongs to dance while giving expression to religious sensitivity. "The dance is the first discovery of movement external to man, but which first gives him his true actual movement. In the dance shines the recognition of God himself moving and thereby moving the world." Similarly, "holy play" functions within the context of drama as the connector between religion and art, for "holy play" expresses in dramatic form "the meeting of God with man, of man with God." Architecture is viewed in terms of "the well-built city of God's creation." Music is understood as "the echo of the eternal Gloria." Each form gives distinctive artistic expression to "the idea of the holy." This helps account for "the sacred in art."

Clearly, van der Leeuw's fundamental intention was to recover a sacramental vision of the world. He found this an appropriate task because of what modernity had done to deep-seated religious impulses. The means by which modern human beings interpret life to themselves, in van der Leeuw's opinion, has become impoverished and shallow. Feeling compelled to recall and recollect an earlier human vision—a view of things in which visible reality is an expression of an invisible reality—he set about to reconstruct the conditions by which an awareness of the transcendent dimension or plain can be restored. This is not a new vision, of course. Van der Leeuw attested that the integration of religion and art had been made explicit in the attitude of the world's first human beings. But the fundamental unity of that trusted human outlook in the world has been shattered. As a consequence, religion and art have become separated, and are even treated as unrelated subjects. So sharply have they become separated that they have even been judged to be antithetical to each other. The intrinsic compatibility between them cannot be reaffirmed, in van der Leeuw's view, until the fundamental unity of life is restored. Although complete restoration of that unity is no longer possible—this would require a reinstitutionalization of the sacramental vision—the Dutch theorist hoped that something of the original sense of things might be recaptured through the magnetism of the religious impulse. His book *The Holy in Art* was designed to assist this recovery. His intention was to re-create the setting and attitude and identify the human disposition that allows religion and art to complement one another within a unified picture of the world.

Of such intentions are theologies created. Van der Leeuw's study is neither art history nor history of religions strictly considered, but theology of art, heavily dependent on Barthian Protestant theological convictions. Thus mixed with declarations about how the relationship between religion and art ought to be, van der Leeuw cannot resist describing the process by which what was lost through sin is won back via redemption. The Christian, that is to say, is at least partially restored to the original human state, and hence can reenvision the sense of the wholeness of things that was characteristic of the earliest human beings' perspective.

The entire program is supported by a conviction that the living God is at work—mysteriously, ordinarily unrecognizably, always awesomely, as perceived by faith—in the transitions between form and image in artistic expressions. The dominant working model is provided by van der Leeuw's interpretation of the deity: form and image are analogous to Father and Son, the latter being the expression of the former as well as the concrete manifestation in which the former is reciprocated. Appropriately, van der Leeuw calls his work "theological aesthetics or aesthetical theology," and the designations are apt. To treat religion and art as harmonious cultural forms, he invokes the support of a theological worldview of premodern vintage.

Aby Warburg: Religion as a Component in Cultural Analysis

Another way of going about cultural history, based on an integrative view of the interrelationships between styles of art and reflection, has been proposed by Aby Warburg (1866–1929), the founder of the Warburg Institute, first in Hamburg, and now in London. Warburg's work belongs to an intellectual context that includes such personages as Johann Joachim Winckelmann (1717–1768), the first to write a comprehensive history of aesthetics by concentrating on form; Alois Riegl (1858–1905), who employed a formalist approach to make visual art studies rigorous; Heinrich Wölfflin (1864–1945), who sustained a formalist approach to the history of art in a conscious historically methodological sense, integrating insights from psychology; and Max Dvorak (1874–1921), who demonstrated the continuities between artistic form and philosophical and religious content, in its heritage. Equipped with such insight and inspiration, Warburg's dominant contention, though with significant variations, is that *art history is cultural history.* His own special interest was in making the dynamics of historical and cultural continuity and change accessible through comparative studies in symbolic forms.

While visiting and then living in Italy as a young man, Warburg was impressed with the recurrence of antique (both classical and pagan) forms and motifs in Renaissance art. Warburg had been trained to look for such phenomena by the influence of the classical philologist Hermann Usener (1834–1905). Usener focused on remnants and vestiges of primitive life in order to gain insight into the meaning of ancient, classical, and pagan texts. Warburg concentrated too on artifacts that testified to the "survival of antiquity." Thus, the recurrence of antique motifs in the Renaissance served as an emergent paradigm for using iconography as an index to the currents of cultural history.

Warburg was not naive. He recognized that the ancient world had been superseded by other forms of culture. He was aware too that a millennium separates the end of the classical age from the flowering of the Renaissance. He agreed that the Renaissance was a new age, but he was curious about the recurrence of classical forms, wondering how it could most fittingly be explained that a latent culture would reemerge in revitalized form. Such factors so impressed him that he worked his way toward a theory of cultural history that was chiefly cognizant of the repetition of ideal types.

Warburg's work had bearing on iconography, history of culture, and the relationship that pertains between them. In this latter regard, he concentrated on symbolic forms, having noted that when items from previous cultural eras reemerge in subsequent cultural periods they often do so in new or revised guise and forms. For example, consideration of deity in the classical era was closely associated with speculation about the planets and the significance of their rotations. But, later, when religious ideas gained some separation from cosmological speculation, the planets were no longer regarded as heavenly bodies. Appropriately, the religious functions once attributed to the planets were also transformed, though not lost. Eventually, for example, the "religious content" originally associated with the planets was internalized psychologically so that the forces which once ruled the world (from above) were construed as internal personal drives and temperaments. But the process continued, for, following this psychological internalization, another successive period occurred that was marked by a fresh burst of interest in astrology and the occult. Hence, the power once attributed to the planets as heavenly bodies was reassigned to those same planets. The religious, psychological, and cultural implications were drawn anew, a reconstitution that is the fundamental work of culture.

Aby Warburg's interpretive point was that the classical motifs do enjoy a certain durability as formative ingredients of Western culture, and while such motifs have undergone striking change and modification, they can be counted on to continue to function as prime instruments of cultural transmission and transformation. In this way, though the examples would fill a library (as they do), the survival of antiquity is employed as a comprehensive reference point to make the dynamics of historical and cultural continuity and change a methodologically accessible subject. Jean Seznec's book *The Survival of the Pagan Gods* is a vivid example of the sort of research that is inspired, conceived, and produced in the Warburg manner.

It should be obvious that Warburg's perspective has a bearing on the relationship between the various subjects that belong to the humanities, and even to the relationships between academic fields of study. Because of the perpetual inter-play of form and content, together with the dynamism that is characteristic of symbolic expression, the multivalent substance of both art and culture can never be uncovered through simple, one-tense, unidimensional, and static approaches to a subject. Rather, since the task is to seize upon phenomena in process of transition, transmission, and transformation, a wide variety of perspectives must be drawn upon simultaneously. This implicit "academic plan" is consistent with Warburg's conviction that reality usually falls into the "borderlands" between the academic fields. It also gives energy to his understanding that all of the disciplines that belong to the humanities and the social sciences must be accorded proper place. In principle, at least, none can be ruled out of an inquiry.

Commenting on Warburg's attempt to "tear down the barriers artificially set up between the various departments of historical research," Fritz Saxl, Warburg's associate and successor, has described the institutional vision this way:

> Historians of science were not to work independently of historians of art and of religion; nor were historians of literature to isolate the study of linguistic forms and literary arts from their settings in the totality of culture. The idea of a comprehensive "science of civilization" was thus meant to embody the demand for a precise method of interaction and correlation between those diverging scientific interests in the humanities which have shown a tendency to set up their subjects as "things in themselves."

Since its founding, the Warburg Institute has attempted to institutionalize a judgment against all forms of scholarly research that are neither interdisciplinary nor cross-cultural, and, in the words of Alfred North Whitehead, rigidify "selective attention." In treating the subject of cultural continuity and change, the Warburg Institute has discovered a way of conducting cross-cultural studies that allows the disciplines within the humanities to enter the discussion on their own terms, but then insists that they relate to each other.

In Warburg's perspective, religion does double duty. As an integral component of culture, religion is both a specific mode or form of cultural expression and the source of significant, formative cultural content. In other words, religion could be understood to be a significant "symbolic form," and it is also responsible for content belonging to other significant "symbolic forms." "Deity" or "divinity," for example, plays a prominent role in the articulation of a specifically religious cultural "symbolic form," but, under another guise, "deity" or "divinity" also becomes implicit in other specific cultural or symbolic forms. Thus motifs that may have a religious tradition as their source find their way into other forms and contexts. Such motifs are regulated by the dynamics of cultural transition and transmission. A particular theme or motif may have a special relationship with a particular religious tradition, but once it becomes ingredient in culture it can no longer be governed by the dictates of religion or the interests of the religious tradition. This is simply to reiterate that Western culture is composed of root elements that gain expression in dynamic and flexible ways.

Erwin Panofsky: Architecture and Reflection

Something of Warburg's spirit can be found in Erwin Panofsky's (1892–1968) researches, particularly in his book *Gothic Architecture and Scholasticism*. Here the attempt is not to develop a scheme that works for the integration of the cultural sciences, but to spot definite similarities between a specific art form and a specific pattern or style of thought. In *Gothic Architecture and Scholasticism*, Panofsky focused on a style of art and a pattern of reflection, both of which were characteristic of an era, then tried to explain why they occurred together and how they are interrelated. In short, he employed scholastic theology to help explain and interpret Gothic architecture, and Gothic architecture as a reflection of scholastic thought. His intention was to illustrate that since the medieval worldview was organic and unitary, one and the same article of religious conviction could be expressed symbolically in at least two symbolic modes. In the first place, it can be set to words and given expression in concepts. In the second place, it is also amenable to a visual structural portrayal. But it is the same affirmation that was articulated both in argumentation and in stone mortar, piers, and buttresses. The one is mirror image of the other.

The reason for this complementarity is that a single "mental habit" (or, in the phrase Panofsky also liked to use, "habit-forming force") is present in both contexts. This means that Gothic buildings were constructed according to scholastic principles. This made the medieval architect a kind of scholastic in his attempt to lend structural expression to scholastic principles. It also meant that the scholastic thinker engaged in a kind of architecture. Both theology and architecture were governed by the same structural principles. Both were characterized as theological systems and those responsible for their design as "system builders."

The mental habit implicit in both thought and architecture was also designed to create a "summary," a *summa*. Both scholastic theology and Gothic architecture were explicit summaries. Both sought to make the unity of truth visible. Both were deliberate announcements that reality itself is whole, unitary, and integral. Reality is not made up of disparate parts. It was not conceived as being atomistic or even dual or bipolar. Rather, the world is all of one piece. While there may be different places, realms, and regions within reality, these are all ingredient in the totality. Indeed, Panofsky's chief literary example, Saint Thomas Aquinas's major work, is appropriately entitled the *Summa Theologica*.

Both scholastic theology and Gothic architecture were constructed in accordance with three clear principles of design: (1) the structure needed to be comprehensive and include all relevant components and features within its total grasp

(Panofsky's requirement of "sufficient enumeration"); (2) the arrangement of parts within the structure was required to be orderly and systematic (Panofsky's requirement of "sufficient articulation"); and (3) the edifice itself, whether in thought or physical construction, was designed to exhibit distinctiveness and deductive cogency (Panofsky's requirement of "sufficient interrelation"). Drawing on these three examples, Panofsky identified the most prominent mental habit as "postulation of clarification for clarification's sake." In reflection the principle is called *manifestatio*, while in architecture it is referred to as "the principle of transparency."

Deliberate self-consciousness is present in both instances. In the structural design of the Gothic cathedral, Panofsky argued, every attempt was made to contain all of Christian truth in a reflexively self-conscious manner. The Gothic cathedral employed an architectural structural design to help "give voice" to motifs inspired by Christian teaching. This insight prompted Panofsky to observe:

> We are faced with what may be termed a "visual logic"... A man imbued with the Scholastic habit would look upon the mode of architectural presentation, just as he looked upon the literary presentation, from the point of view of *manifestatio*. He would have taken it for granted that the primary purpose of the many elements that compose a cathedral was to ensure stability, just as he took it for granted that the primary purpose of the many elements that constitute a *Summa* was to ensure validity.
>
> To him the panoply of shafts, ribs, buttresses, tracery, pinnacles, and crockets was a self-analysis and self-explication of architecture just as the customary apparatus of parts, distinctions, questions, and articles was, to him, a self-analysis and self-explication of reason.

Thus, the interest in maximizing explicitness is just as much a principle of architecture as it was of theology during the Gothic and scholastic era. The fully developed Gothic cathedral, corresponding to the fully developed theological system, is testimony to techniques and materials necessary to realize that interest. At each point along the way, from the formation of the mental habits to its culmination in the "high" period, correspondingly similar steps were taken in both fields. In both architecture and theology a definite style was being worked out according to one and the same set of structural principles. In both form and essence, then, Gothic architecture and scholastic theology are close filial expressions of an identical pervasive notion.

The mental habit Panofsky isolated is calculated to maintain a complementary relationship between faith and reason as well as the conviction that truth is one, whole and integrated. Alternative organizational principles were available, both to architecture and to theology, but their products were manifestly different from the interrelated styles Panofsky held up to scrutiny. For instance, mystical theology and nominalist philosophy are expressions of alternative organizing principles, neither of which is protective or illustrative of the scholastic mental habit.

Consequently, Panofsky saw both of them as threats to the unity of truth; that is, they do not measure up philosophically speaking. Neither do they maintain ways of keeping the relationship between faith and reason complementary. Scholasticism resisted these alternatives because they enshrined mental habits that lead to disintegration. Similarly, scholasticism successfully avoided the mistakes of the poets, humanists, and antirationalists, whose world tends to break up eventually, with its several components becoming disassociated.

The complementarity on which Panofsky focused scholarly attention is striking and instructive. One cannot be sure, however, that Panofsky's insights can be applied to other situations. It may well be that the scholastic-Gothic correlation is unique, and that similar conjunctions of art and thought are difficult to find. Panofsky himself was impressed with the possibility that a similar correspondence could be effected between the Carolingian revival in the arts and the philosophical work of John Scotus Erigena in the ninth century. Other potential examples come to mind. Albrecht Dürer, for example, might have done more for the cause of the Protestant Reformation with his art, so the case can be argued, than Martin Luther and Philip Melanchthon did with their books, treatises, and sermons. And yet the style that pervades both Dürer's art and Luther's theology may be one and the same.

Pushing the matter further, one can perhaps find parallels between the philosophers and artists of the Enlightenment era. Similarly, the early twentieth-century revolt against the post-Renaissance worldview seems to have taken the same structural, visual, and conceptual form in, say, the art of Dada, the philosophy of Friedrich Nietzsche, and even the poetry of Ezra Pound. German expressionist art, for another example, is matched by a corresponding German expressionist philosophy. The same kind of correspondence analysis seems to work well in other cultures too. Definite structural correspondences are found in Buddhist thought and Buddhist art. Classical Hinduism also developed its own art forms by means of which one can read the tenets of the worldview just as surely as one can discern them in the words of the sacred scriptures. In short, while Panofsky did not supply the transitional methodological steps, there is no doubt that the exercise he carried out can be conducted on other and additional cultural data that provide examples and candidates for parallel development. Panofsky's contribution to the discussion about styles and patterns in cultural history may register first of all as an articulation of a formal truth: namely, that once a descriptive name is applied to a culture (given all of the latter's complexities and its manifold comprehensiveness), inquirers and interpreters are prompted to find more and more precise ways in which that name or descriptive title is either apt or not.

In Panofsky's work we see a clear attempt to show the interdependence and interaction of religion and art in specific cultural settings. His work can be classified as intercultural comparative symbolics, for the intention is to identify correspondences between interrelated symbolic forms in a given place at a given time. The results are intriguing to scholars in religious studies because religion is made explicit party to a larger, more comprehensive cultural composite. In Panofsky's view, specific intrinsic ties exist between religion and other forms of human expression. Such linkages and correspondences can be demonstrated. They provide the touchstones that enable one to interpret a culture. Furthermore, it follows that unless the religion quotient is given due place, the composite cultural analysis is partial and, for that reason, impoverished.

The Jungian Attitude: Jung, Campbell, and Neumann

The ploy becomes fancier, more complicated, and considerably more pretentious when genre studies are examined to disclose (1) the fundamental characteristics, nature, or structure of human consciousness, (2) the fundamental characteristics, nature, or structure of reality, and (3) the fundamental characteristics, nature, or structure of both of these together. One finds this turn taken in impressive fashion, for example, by Carl G. Jung (1875–1961), the Swiss psychoanalyst and mythologist. Viewed from within an interest in the formation of religious studies, Jung's achievement lies in his ability to find corroborative evidence in mythology for his psychoanalytically derived indices into human consciousness. Thus, instead of identifying religion with a particular symbolic form or structural pattern, Jung took form and pattern as reflections and evidences of the dynamic workings of the human psyche.

Jung deviated from the position of Sigmund Freud, under whose psychoanalytic nurturing his attitudes had been formed in Freud's school in Vienna. Indeed, it was his disagreement with Freud that led him to the attitude toward religion that we are attempting to summarize here. The divergence between the two focused on the definition and function of what Freud called the libido (which, with ego and superego, was taken as one of the three formative components or motivational factors of the personality). Freud saw libido as raw motivational power or energy, which he identified closely with sexuality. Jung could agree with Freud that the unconscious consists of drives and energies, but he was unwilling to give sexuality such large priority and exclusive control. He conceded that some unconscious processes have the characteristic of Freud's id-system, but then asserted that other unconscious energies and strivings are the sources of positive and creative activity. These same energies and strivings are instrumental in the growth and maturation of the individual.

It is clear that the disagreement was not simply conceptual or definitional. The two really had different conceptions of the place and function of psychoanalysis. Freud was interested primarily in uncovering the basis of neurotic and psychotic behavior; he was concerned about deviations from the norm. Thus he approached libidinal energy in attempting to identify mechanism of repression. As Freud understood human nature, libidinal drives were in conflict with acquired and established cultural sanctions; the same conflict was mirrored in the psychological makeup of individuals. As Jung saw it, Freud was concerned primarily to treat the aberrations, the neurotic and psychotic by-products of this fundamental conflict. Jung understood himself to be more ambitious. It was not enough to neutralize the negative. In addition, he sought to identify and express the role of the unconscious life in positive, constructive terms. The difference between Freud and Jung consisted largely of differences in intention coupled with large differences in temperament. Simply put, whatever assumptions and standpoints they shared were directed toward markedly different ends.

Jung distinguished between two systems of unconscious processes. The first, personal or individual unconscious drives, could be depicted in the terms Freud selected. These drives are highly idiosyncratic and deeply personal and individual. As Freud discovered, the unconscious is formed out of infantile urges, some very animal like in nature, all of which carry the capacity to develop pathological expressions. But Jung discerned an additional side or dimension, the *collective unconscious*, by which he referred to cumulative human resourcefulness in generic terms. It is as though the long, accumulated, corporate experience of the human race had been gathered into one, then transmitted through deep-seated unconscious mental and psychological processes. The principles that are derived from this accumulated collective experience provide the basis for action and reaction. Jung drew upon the phrase "archetypal tendencies" to refer to the disposition "to react and to apprehend or experience life in a manner originating from the remote past of the human race." He defined "archetypes" as "congenital conditions of intuition." They are conditions of intuition because they influence the ways human beings receive, place, organize, and interpret their perceptions, feelings, aspirations, and experiences.

These interests placed Jung in immediate contact with the worlds of mythology and symbolism. In his view, archetypal unconsciousness is implicit in the images and symbols that belong to mythology. Mythology provides a visible disclosure of the rudiments of human consciousness, indeed, on a universal scale. The assumption is that the structure of the psyche is determined by the force and character of archetypal awareness. Because human consciousness is remarkably the same the world over, one and the same myth or mythological theme will occur in the folk literatures of peoples of very different cultural settings and from very different times. This fact brings strength to the thesis that the archetypes are present to human experience, universally considered. The mythological figures of Prometheus, Zeus, Hermes, or Proteus, to cite a few examples, are born over and over again, not only as cultural artifacts but as elements within self-consciousness.

Thus, the strong linkages that Jung discovered between religious and psychological realities have been explored, expressed, and illustrated by Joseph Campbell

(1904–1987), among others, particularly in his book *The Hero with a Thousand Faces*. The intention of this book is to assist the process of individual self-discovery; that is, to facilitate individuality, or to enable one "to become aware of the hidden totality of the self." Campbell portrays the coming to self-awareness as a journey, an interior pilgrimage, which, like religious pilgrimages of all times, involves the successful meeting of obstacles, hurdles, and crisis points along the road of trials.

The process is made up of three significant stages, which Campbell enumerates under the names *departure* (separation from the world), *initiation* (a penetration to some source of true power), and life-enhancing *return*. Although depicted as a three-stage journey, the process is also described as a "coming to terms with one's own inner center."

Departure denotes "the sounding of the ego-centric system," a turning into the darkness to face the unknown, the passage into the realm of night which, by interpretation, indicates the first determined step away from *persona* toward recognition of one's true self. The second stage, *initiation*, refers to being subjected to the road of trials. Such trials, if successfully met, culminate in the experience of enlightenment. The third stages includes the *return* to the initial point of departure after the pilgrim (or hero) has experienced self-realization. The implication is that contact with eternity helps redirect one back to influence one's native surroundings. Campbell explains:

> The battlefield is symbolic of the field of life, where every creature lives on the death of another. A realization of the inevitable guilt of life may so sicken the heart that, like Hamlet or like Arjuna, one may refuse to go on with it. On the other hand, like most of the rest of us, one may invent a false, finally unjustified, image of oneself as an exceptional phenomenon in the world, not guilty as others are, but justified in one's inevitable sinning because one represents the good. Such self-righteousness leads to a misunderstanding, not only of oneself but of the nature of both man and the cosmos. The goal of the myth is to dispel the need for such life ignorance by effecting a reconciliation of the individual consciousness with the universal will. And this is effected through a realization of the true relationship of the passing phenomena of time to the imperishable life that lives and dies in all.

The account is intriguing, not least for the reason that Campbell can interpret a large range of stories, fables, and myths in light of the chronicle. Drawing upon folklore and mythological accounts from cultures east and west, ancient and modern, Campbell makes a convincing case that it is the same fundamental account that is being rendered each time the story is portrayed. Thus "the hero with a thousand faces" is really each person, each one who senses the need to effect a passage from *persona* to realization of a truer self.

> The aim is not to *see*, but to realize that one *is*, that essence; then one is free to wander as that essence in the world. Furthermore: the world too is of that essence. The

essence of oneself and the essence of the world: these two are one. Hence separateness, withdrawal, is no longer necessary. Wherever the hero may wander, whatever he may do, he is ever in the presence of his own essence—for he has the perfected eye to see. There is no separateness. Thus, just as the way of social participation may lead in the end to a realization of the All in the individual, so that of exile brings the hero to the Self in all.

A related Jungian posture is enunciated in the writings of Erich Neumann (1905–1960), particularly in his book *The Origins and History of Consciousness* (1949). Neumann was born in Berlin, and after studying with Jung in Zurich in the mid-1930s he sought to apply Jungian insights to the history of consciousness. The thesis of his major work is that the history of human consciousness as a whole mirrors the same archetypal stages of development that characterize the process of progressive individuation. In other works, Neumann turned his attention to symbolic mythological portrayals of femininity as disclosures of the fuller nature of the human psyche.

The extension of psychoanalytic structures from individual to collective application can also be undertaken in Freudian terms. In fact, Freud himself introduced this line of inquiry in the works *Civilization and Its Discontents* and *The Future of an Illusion*. More recent versions of the same extension include the works of Norman O. Brown, David Bakan, Robert Jay Lifton, Erik Erikson, and run to Gananath Obeyesekere's *The Work of Culture* (1990). There is not sufficient space here to outline Brown's attempt to recast Western intellectual history in terms of a repeated compulsion to abolish repression, nor even to sketch Obeyesekere's provocative use of updated Freudian categories to decipher culture change and stability. Similarly, we can only point to Bakan's interpretation of biblical narrative as giving expression to the fundamental psychic and psychological interplay between father, mother, and children as Freud enunciated this in his interpretation of the Oedipus myth. But these brief pointers should indicate that the use of psychoanalytic categories for purposes of tracing the development of self-consciousness on a collective basis can be effected under Freudian auspices too.

The Debate about Structures: The French School

At a certain point in the development of this point of departure, however the interest in structure tends to surpass the interest in mode and genre. This occurs, for example, when genre comes to be regarded merely as a contextual framework, and when patterns expressed within frames become normative. We return to the example of structuralism. Structuralism is more an effort at pattern discernment than a desire for genre morphology. Structuralism seeks more to penetrate the content within a genre than to let the contours of genre unfold. It is more interested in the structure, pattern, or even cycle of myths, for example, than it is in the nature of myth. It tends to approach myth more as being instrumental to unlocking the rhythms of archetypal order than for its own intrinsic worth.

But we must quickly add that this distinction becomes more difficult to make when structuralists claim to be able to discern the same fundamental pattern in a variety of contextual settings, and when the same pattern is regarded as being able uniquely to disclose the rudiments of "reality" and of human nature. This turn is taken by structuralists who regard literary structures as being representative analogically of cultural structures, then take both to be characteristic of the way in which human consciousness is ordered. When this occurs, it is clear that we are no longer treating a genre issue, but, instead, a sophisticated refinement of the implications of pattern formation in a comprehensive sense.

The most compelling and significant recent examples have come from the work of a group of influential French thinkers who have carried structuralist insights to the next stages of articulation and amplification. Although such developments have attained sufficient distinctiveness and individuality to qualify as identifiable approaches and movements in their own terms, they retain their commitment to Ferdinand de Saussure's original proposal that language is a system of signs. Furthermore, these new and fresh points of departure within the structuralist camp acknowledge the truth of the insight that specific forms of grammatical order function as indices into the workings of social myths, literary works, and even modes of human consciousness. As has been noted earlier in this study, the structuralists affirmed that such grammatical order is coherent, systematic, and analytically penetrable. As has also been noted, the work of Claude Lévi-Strauss stands as the most prominent example of the employment of this method of gaining access to the explicit organization and workings of selected cultures.

In the 1960s and 1970s in France, however, strong reaction arose against certain features of the structuralist approach, which eventually came to assume the banners of "deconstructionist" and "poststructuralist" schools of thought. The world's leading "deconstructionist," Jacques Derrida (b.1930), who teaches philosophy and the history of philosophy at the École Normale Supérieur in Paris, as well as at the University of California at Irvine, undertook to "deconstruct" the metaphysical theories of Western philosophy. Derrida's principal contention is that all of Western philosophy is characterized by a "logocentrism," which he identifies as a persistent "metaphysics of presence" in which everything of any significance is understood to possess the quality of being present. According to this perennial assumption, whatever is real is real by virtue of the fact that it is present. And the category of being present, or possessing presence, is made applicable to the West's understanding of existence, essence, transcendence, and even God. Reality is ordered this way; therefore, any component of reality can be confirmed as being real—that is, if the case can be made successfully—because that entity enjoys presence.

Derrida's counterproposals became identified as deconstructionist because they functioned to dismantle this fundamental underlying thesis. In Derrida's view nothing is simply present. Hence, the category of presence cannot be the basis for the meaning that something has. Rather, as Derrida views it, meaning is to be found in the relationship of one thing to another thing and to other things. Furthermore, as he put it, "there is nothing outside the text," which means that all understanding is mediated by language. Since language consists of rules of procedures and of words, the definitions of words depend on their differentiation from other words. But the meaning of the same is not penetrable in any straightforward manner since differentiation between words (from which definitions come) implies contrast and, therefore, a reversal of meaning. In the viewpoint of deconstructionism, words never mean what they seem literally to mean, and texts are not to be interpreted so much as "deconstructed," since meaning is an elusive linguistic construction.

Derrida's primary insight pertains to the relationships between word and referent, signifier and signified. In proposing that this relationship is arbitrary and conventional—an attitude he shares with Ferdinand de Saussure, the founder of structuralism—Derrida criticizes the cardinal assumptions of Western thought. Western thought is constructed out of a series of distinctions that are hierarchically ordered—distinctions between origin and derivation, central and marginal, literal and figurative, to cite some of the most prominent ones. Derrida's strategy is to illustrate that these oppositional relationships are reversible since they reflect the duplicity of the medium of language. And, as philosopher, he illustrated his contentions by analyzing texts by Plato, Jean Jacques Rousseau, and Friedrich Nietzsche. Subsequent deconstructionists have applied the same strategic procedures to the works of Percy Bysshe Shelley, John Keats, Herman Melville, George Eliot, and, most significantly, Karl Marx and Sigmund Freud.

The consequences for the study of religion are being explored at present, and the findings are both partial and tentative. At the expository level, however, religious texts are seen to be characterized by the same hierarchical ordering of fundamental distinctions, the patterns of which can be interpreted as being indicative of conflicts or contests of power. In short, the deconstructionist strategy is eminently employable by interpreters who are sensitive to political consequences. Michael Ryan, author of *Marxism and Deconstructionism*, understands Derrida's proposals to be apt grist for the revolutionary mill: "The deconstructive criticism of absolute concepts in the theory of meaning can be said to have a political-institutional corollary," Ryan writes, "which is a continuous revolutionary displacement of power toward radical egalitarianism and the plural defusion of all forms of macro- and microdomination." In other words, the direction of force and emphasis within the hierarchical distinctions can be reversed. And since it can, deconstructionist insights can be made the basis for revolutionary action—say, on behalf of Marxist causes, perhaps even more particularly to lend a greater credence to the feminist movement. All of this flows from the insight that the primary relationship between word and reference, or signifier and signified, is not simply a matter of functional equivalents, but involves subversion and subordination. Noting that such conflict pertains, deconstructionists can also point to alternative formulations should the outcome between these warring factions be decided in other ways. The application of the same to primary texts within religious studies remains an embryonic venture, but the philosophical possibilities hold sufficient promise to encourage such analyses to take the next necessary steps.

One of the most astute analyses of Derrida's proposals is that provided by Giles Gunn in his book *The Culture of Criticism and the Criticism of Culture.* Gunn is quick to acknowledge that the deconstructionist proposals carry considerable intellectual force:

> According to poststructuralists, the freight of our expressive life, particularly in the West, has been carried since the time of Plato by a metaphysics of substance—Derrida calls it a metaphysics of presence—that has now collapsed under the weight of three centuries of philosophical criticism.

What has collapsed is the confidence that "our assertions, like our actions, are supported, if we could but dig beneath them deep enough, by an ontological bedrock called reality whose structure they must reflect or mirror in order to be true." Gunn paraphrases Derrida's alternative to imply that "our conceptions of the thing called reality, no less than the statements we make in an effort to define it, are cultural constructs whose veracity or validity is wholly restricted to what our linguistic equipment permits us to know and say about it." Gunn recognizes the force of this insight, and in his lucid treatment of it he provides numerous examples of ways in which it carries influence. And yet he raises a large question:

> If all epistemic standpoints, as deconstructionists argue, are equally privileged and biased, if there is no secure epistemological or ontological ground anywhere, then on what, it must be asked, can the deconstructionist stand as he or she mounts an assault on our specious habits of fabrication?

In other words, would not the criticism that Derrida has directed against previous formulations be applicable as well to the revision he offers? Is not his own deconstructionist program subject to deconstructionism?

Gunn recognizes that Derrida is acutely aware of the problem and that, in wanting to offer an effective response, he takes refuge in phrases that sound much like religious language. Derrida gives evidence of wanting to penetrate beyond the logic of the concepts, even into a "transcendence beyond negativity," even to "the point whether neither no nor yes is the first word, but an interrogation." Gunn comments:

At this point Derrida seems, but only seems, to save himself from self-contradiction by insisting that this total question posed by the failure of our concepts, our language, to encompass and include the "transcendence beyond negativity" is experienced "not as a total presence but as a trace."

In a provocative but still unpublished paper, W. Richard Comstock accepts Derrida's conclusion, while pushing it further. For him, the relationship between word and referent, signifier and signified, involves tension and, thus, separation. But he understands the conflict between the two to be but one (albeit an important) element, and harmony to be the other. Both pertain. The imagery of "warring factions" is appropriate, but so too is that conveying harmony, balance, symmetry, and homology. As Comstock summarizes it: "The world is based on relation which both separates and unites the signifier and the signified. Signs are based on difference which is both separation and deferred union."

Jacques Lacan's (1901–1981) point of entry into the discussion comes through psychoanalysis; more specifically, via extended commentaries on and reinterpretations of Sigmund Freud's understanding of the nature and function of the ego. The framework is created by intellectual interest in the relationship between psychoanalytic understanding and the dynamics of culture. Lacan was well aware of the numerous portrayals of contemporary culture that called attention to the narcissistic disposition of its inhabitants, or that pit the cultivation of psychological life against collective cultural vitality.

Lacan takes "desire of the Other" as the focus of his analysis, observing that relationships create the occasion to come to terms with the way in which individual identity is fashioned in the conjunctions between intersubjective psychodynamics and relationships with other persons in a social and cultural context. Why the focus on desire? The answer is to be found in Lacan's insight that desire develops from a psychological event that occurs early in the life of an individual: the recognition that there is a split or rupture between an experienced fragmentary self and the image of being whole or unified. The situation would be easy, in Lacan's judgment, were it sufficient that a whole, unified self needed to make effective rapprochement with a society or culture, or, to turn it the other way, were a society or culture called upon to give proper place to the individuals that are nurtured by means of its collective ministrations. The difficulty is due to the greater complexity: the self that is called upon to live within society is itself neither whole nor unified, and thus is assigned a double task, the achievement of each phase of which must occur simultaneously. There is not space enough in this brief survey to do justice to the details of Lacan's viewpoint. Suffice it to say that he understood psychoanalysis to be a linguistic science that is devoted to a study of the speech that is appropriate within this multivalent environment. To catch the significance of this reinterpretation of the function and placement of psychoanalysis, one need only recall that Freud did not understand himself to be discussing linguistics, but medicine. Whereas Freud employed a medical model to describe the workings of psychoanalysis, Lacan assigns it to the science of linguistics.

How then does this relate to the study of religion? That is, what is the point of connection between Lacan's revision of Freud's psychoanalytic theory and the scholarly attempt to understand the nature and function of religion?

A chief clue to the appropriate answer to these questions is to be found in Lacan's preoccupation with Saint Augustine, the author of *The Confessions*, which has been hailed as the Western world's first autobiography. Lacan understands Augustine's text as the document wherein discourse between God and psyche became normative; a document, that is to say, that both certifies and illustrates paradigmatic Western understanding of the relationship between psychology and religion. *The Confessions*, not unexpectedly, describes the workings of desire. When Saint Augustine confesses, "our hearts are made for thee, and have no rest until they rest in thee," he has provided illustration of the very life force that Lacan has identified as being constitutive of human behavior. Indeed, for Lacan, Saint Augustine stands as the significant case study that tends to legitimate the necessary criticism of Freud while demonstrating that the challenge most fundamental within human experience is most effectively accessible linguistically. In other words, Saint Augustine has allowed Lacan most dramatically to make his point.

Scholars of religion have undertaken some work on this subject, notably American scholars who placed themselves in conversation in 1986 and then commissioned essays to be shared with one another. We refer specifically to the American Academy of Religion 1986 plenary session in which Charles Winquist, Mark C. Taylor, Carl Raschke, Charles E. Scott, Edith Wyschogrod, David Crownfield, and Robert Scharlemann participated. Subsequently, Wyschogrod published her own essay, *Saints and Postmodernism: Revisioning Moral Philosophy* (1990), which is heavily dependent on Lacan's insights. Indeed, Wyschogrod's starting point for re-thinking ethics and moral philosophy is Lacan's revision of the relationships between "the self" and "the cultural matrix" according to the manner that we have sketched.

The most provocative and influential of the French thinkers is Michel Foucault (1926–1984), who employed his multiple skills to penetrate to the core of Western culture. As has been noted, Lacan worked with psychoanalytical theory; Roland Barthes was a literary critic; and Jacques Derrida concentrated on linguistics. Foucault, by contrast, committed himself to Western intellectual history with special attention to the grammars by which the sciences and arts developed as elucidations of the composition of culture. Thoroughly influenced by the iconoclasms of Friedrich Nietzsche, Foucault carried out a detailed polemic against historical objectivity. That is, instead of approaching history as harmonious, congruent, uniform monolithic progression, he trained his attention on discontinuities, breaks, and ruptures, prompting more than one commentator to suggest that Foucault's intention was "to make the past unfamiliar." His publication program stands as testimony to his intention to identify aberrations, phenomena that do not conform to the norm and are not obedient to some prescripted rule. From the new archaeology of the human sciences that he published in 1970 under the title *The Order of Things*, he moved to studies of specific topics: the history of insanity (*Madness and Civilization*, 1971), the study of medical knowledge (*The Birth of the Clinic*, 1973), a study of mental illness and how it is identified and portrayed (*Mental Illness and Psychology*, 1976), a study of prison life (*Discipline and Punish: The Birth of the Prison*, 1977), and, finally, a three-volume treatment of the way in which sexuality has been understood in the Western world (*The History of Sexuality*, 1978, 1984). In every such instance Foucault rewrote Western intellectual history by demonstrating that the histories that had attained authoritative status were primarily reflections of the cultural outlooks that such histories made more fully explicit. Consequently he offered his own defamiliarized historical interpretations as a ploy in the necessary act of grasping modern cultural identity.

Religious studies scholars have been teased by Foucault. Yet, once again, it seems premature to try to digest what the eventual fallout might be. Clearly, Foucault's polemic against historical objectivity will stimulate both dehistoricization and eventual rehistoricization as attention is focused on discontinuities, ruptures, and breaks in sequential development, and this is to put the matter mildly. His interest in the methodological reciprocities between the ways in which archaeologies of knowledge are fashioned and cultural identities are known carries profound implications with respect to the manner in which both religious understanding and understanding of religion are shaped. Further, his provocative commentaries on the influence of Christianity within Western culture will prompt historians of dogma (as well as ecclesiastical institutions) to take a fresh look—indeed, even to the point of holding many formerly accepted interpretations and judgments in suspense. But his influence, like Nietzsche's, goes much further. While he did not present himself as an expert in comparative cultural analysis, his portrayal of the culture with which he was most familiar has given comparative cultural inquiry bold incentives. For example, Foucault's concentration on confession as the fundamental epistemic modality of Christianity, which, *ex hypothesi*, distinguishes a special type of religion, invites comparisons with religions for which the truth about oneself is derived in other ways. The ways in which understanding of reality is reciprocated in the modalities by which such truths are acquired also provide promising avenues through which such comparative work might be carried out. The deeper implications of Foucault's insights are even more dramatic. Were one to take his defamiliarization polemic seriously, one would find oneself under a necessity to rethink virtually everything that one assumed one had already satisfactorily understood.

Mark C. Taylor: System, Structure, Difference, Other

The last line in the previous paragraph describes both the challenge and the program of Mark C. Taylor (b.1945), a prolific author whose every topic is addressed through a comprehensive understanding of Hegelian and post-Hegelian philosophical commentary, especially as this pertains to the complex interplay of religion, literature, art, architecture, and theology. Taylor, like the majority of others who belong to his generation, was trained in the intellectual history that informs our study. That is, his essays tend to begin with explicit reference to Descartes's *Meditations*, then give large place to Kant (particularly to *The Critique of Judgment* and other treatments of aesthetics), and then concentrate on the discussions raised by Hegel and extended by the French phenomenologists, and, of course, the structuralists, poststructuralists, modernists, and deconstructionists. Thus, he offers a steady sprinkling of citations from Heidegger, Husserl, Merleau-Ponty, de Saussure, Sartre, Derrida, Foucault, and important lesser-known thinkers such as Emmanuel Levinas, Maurice Blanchot, Georges Bataille, and Philippe Lacoue-Labarthe. Then, after having narrated Western intellectual history in this fashion, Taylor returns to the late eighteenth and early nineteenth centuries to give fresh interpretation to the "theo-aesthetics" of Johann von Schiller, Friedrich Schelling, Friedrich Schleiermacher, Johann Gottlieb Fichte, and others who were drawn to the small town of Jena in the duchy of Weimar.

This is the framework within which Taylor has set his analyses of the relationships between religion and the visual arts. The temper of his analysis, however, is set by the close attention he pays to Søren Kierkegaard's critique of Hegel's philosophy, the respect he accords the theology of Karl Barth, and the pervasive manner in which he has been influenced by Friedrich Nietzsche. Thus, Taylor's writings tend to concentrate on subjects that cannot be included within comprehensive conceptual systems. He writes repeatedly of the challenge "to think what philosophy leaves unthought." He shares Heidegger's interest in that which "has always remained unasked throughout this history of thinking." He applauds Kierkegaard's critique of Hegelianism, and is cheered with Bataille's preoccupation with what Hegel excludes. He contrasts Hegel's working "from the unknown to the known" to Bataille's "slips and slides from the known to the unknown," slips that culminate in what is "incompletely experienced in absolute nonknowledge." All of this, Taylor contends, requires that one "think both *with* and *against* reason," a program that stands diametrically opposed to the desire to "overcome nonknowledge by dispelling illusion and correcting error."

In applying these principles to the study of religion, Taylor is assisted by parallels/nonparallels and analogs/nonanalogs from the history of the visual arts. In a brilliant study, *Disfiguring: Art, Architecture, Religion* (1992), he traces the challenges that all three of these subject areas must address, and encourages insights and implications from each of the fields to assist understanding/nonunderstanding in the others. Such is appropriate by virtue of the fact that the major developments in the various art forms (religion included) running throughout the twentieth century are reflective of each other. Of course, the powers of deconstruction are operating with all of these frameworks. Consequently, when Taylor approaches religious studies, he takes the initial task to be to identify what religious studies would not be, and this is to think what reasonable religion leaves unthought.

Origins of Analyses of Discursive Language

Where expressivist approaches to religion are concerned, many of the significant insights and developments have occurred within the framework of discursive language, much of it to the seeming total disregard for nondiscursive symbolic forms. The fact is brought about by the revolution in philosophy implicit within positivism, linguistic analysis, the Vienna Circle, the fresh insights of Bertrand Russell, G. E. Moore, Ludwig Wittgenstein, and their students and successors. In the remaining sections of this chapter on religious language, we shall focus on the fundamental proposals of the "linguistic school," sketch some of the principal contentions of Wittgenstein, and then provide a sampling of the implications of this work with respect to the methodological aspirations and self-conceptions of religious studies.

Taken on its own terms, linguistic analysis originated within the school of philosophical positivism, and positivism derives from the contentions of Auguste Comte. Recall that in the Comtean trilogy (see chapter 3), the scientific mode is given highest priority in the evolution of human thought. It is marked by a critical self-consciousness of which both theological and metaphysical modes are incapable. Scientific knowledge increases clarity of knowledge. It also enables the world to be principled, controlled, and mastered. Because of these several capacities, science can be looked to to supplant and replace both theology and metaphysics as the normative mode through which the world is apprehended. Science has been assigned this role because its cognitive sense is sure, and thus its knowledge is exact.

Recall, too, that Comte understood sure knowledge to be restricted to verifiable *phenomena*. Repressing all tendencies to concern himself with noumena, or even to make the noumenal realm a focus of inquiry, he disciplined himself, limiting his inquiry to that to which knowledge has appropriate access. This implied that he would forego speculation about *why* things happen the way they do since he could only explain *how* things happen.

Logical Positivism: The Vienna Circle

The Comtean positivistic attitude was carried forward by a number of influential thinkers, among them Ernst Mach (1838–1916), a mathematician and physicist in both Prague and Vienna. Because of his scientific expertise, Mach was even more rigorous (though no more eloquent) than Comte in discarding metaphysics. He conceived of philosophy to be something other than an explanation of eternal verities or the ultimate explanation of the nature of things. Proper philosophy—namely, positivist science—was to be employed as an instrument of organization and control. It was to be *used* instead of simply being conceived. It was to be functional and operational, to enable its practitioners to gain a firmer hold on the dynamics of things. This meant that the scope of philosophy was severely reduced. Instead of engaging in speculative system-building, whether in the classical or in a revised Kantian or Hegelian style, the philosopher was obligated to concentrate on the data of sense experience. Such data are manifestly available. Via rigorous methods of investigation, the data can be rendered trustworthy. Thus, under the program of logical positivism, the philosopher defines and analyzes the concepts and principles employed in scientific investigation, that is, when the latter is conducted with respect to subjects and interests that admit some possibility of clarification.

Mach's views were taken up in the 1920s in the work of the famous Vienna Circle philosophers, notably Rudolf Carnap (1891–1970), Moritz Schlick (1882–1936)—the group's acknowledged leader and successor to Mach in empirical philosophy in the University of Vienna—Otto Neurath (1882–1945), and Friedrich Waismann (1896–1959). These Vienna thinkers were joined by Hans Reichenbach and Walter Dubislay in Berlin as well as by other scholars of an obvious mathematical, scientific, and antimetaphysical philosophical bent. Through the concentrated efforts of the Vienna Circle, philosophy was given a fresh departure and compelling new sets of issues. Philosophy of the Vienna Circle kind was understood to be most akin to the field of mathematics.

G. E. Moore and Bertrand Russell: Revolt against Idealism

Similar currents of thought were and had been in the wind elsewhere. In England, G. E. Moore (1873–1958), together with his contemporary Bertrand Russell (1872–1970), were leading a revolt against idealism. In the British case, the specific version of idealism was less Kant's and Hegel's than F. H. Bradley's. Moore, known best for his *Principia Ethica*, published in 1903, was especially interested in resolving long-standing dilemmas within the fields of logic and epistemology. A prominent way of treating knowledge was to try to bring the knower into a cognitive relationship with the object to be known. The rationalist approach, that is to say, was to focus on the manner according to which mind lends form to whatever is to be known. The empiricist way, on the other hand, was to emphasize the importance of sense impressions, or what might be called the facticity of empirical data. Thus, the rationalists were lined up on one side and the empiricists on the other. Both sides shared the conviction, however, that truth was regarded as being the product of an established correspondence between the knower and what is to be known. In both versions, correspondence was established on the basis of the relationship between the knower and that which is knowable.

Moore turned the tables on these assumptions. According to his view, *truth is a quality of propositions.* The truth of propositions is decided on the basis of something other than correspondence between the proposition and some external state of affairs. Propositions are not looked to to provide accurate readings or perceptions of things. Rather, propositions establish specific relationships between concepts. Thus, truth pertains to linguistic form. As Moore put it: "the only objects of knowledge are concepts," and propositions consist of "concepts standing in a specific relation to one another." There is no possibility of transcending the relationships that are established within propositions among the appropriate ingredients of propositions to establish the truth. That is, there is no possibility of appealing to some alleged "higher authority," as if truth is a property of some reality that lies beyond propositional accessibility. Although Moore found it necessary constantly to revise and amend his proposals, particularly on the question of the relationship between concepts and things, he never wavered from his defense of the common-sense view of the world. Thus, in breaking ranks with idealist philosophy, he was committed resolutely to the reality of the everyday world. As he saw it, it is impossible to have certainty regarding anything that "lies beyond" what is accessible through propositional truth.

For Bertrand Russell, philosophy was to be constructed and styled according to the models of logic and mathematics. As with Moore, Russell associated himself with propositional truth. Propositional truth derives from the specific relationships that pertain between components of a proposition. Such relationships are reducible, in Russell's words, to "properties of the terms between which they hold." For Russell, too, there is no reality to be made accessible beyond the components of relational propositions. Relational propositions possess the quality of being irreducible.

Russell's most significant contribution to the field of philosophy lies in his attempt to construct a mathematics strictly on the basis of logical form. His analysis of propositions is related to perceptions regarding the coincidences of logic and mathematics. Put even more simply, the meaning of a proposition is inherent within the proposition: meaning is thus implicit within the arrangement of the ingredients of the proposition. Put even simpler, the meaning of a proposition is not constructed by the person who reads it in, for example, or who finds it necessary to do something with the proposition. In sum, each meaningful proposition is an instance of specific logical relationships. Formal concepts (those of kind, class, number, and so on) may be logical constructions, but neither logical relationships nor logical constructions are products of human inference or construction. Truth, Russell (with Moore) insists, is a quality of propositions.

Ludwig Wittgenstein: The Limits and Function of Language

Moore and Russell are significant figures in the development of analytical philosophy, particularly at Cambridge and Oxford universities, the early centers of such intellectual development in Great Britain. But where language analysis is concerned, both stand in the shadows of a thinker many regard as the greatest philosopher of the twentieth century: Ludwig Wittgenstein (1889–1951), an Austrian by birth, who first came to England in 1912 to meet and study with Russell, and who then became a Cambridge University philosopher.

During his lifetime, Wittgenstein published but one book, the *Tractatus logico-philosophicus* (first in German in 1921, then in German and English, in parallel columns, in 1922), a book that influenced Russell, and whose title was contributed by Moore. Wittgenstein's technique was to break reality down into elementary and rudimentary bit parts, referred to as atomic particles, or irreducible simples. Such particles or things receive names, and in names words signify objects. Names, words, and then concepts are interrelated in propositions.

Wittgenstein shared Moore's and Russell's conviction that truth is propositional. He understood truth to derive from arrangements within propositions, but not quite in the way Moore and Russell had said. The propositional arrangement of names, in his view, provided a "picture" of a possible or ostensive state of affairs. In the end, language was conceived to function as a picture of reality.

The ramifications are noteworthy. Wittgenstein's thesis that "what can be said at all can be said clearly, and whereof one cannot speak thereof one must be silent," can be pointed directly at the nature of religious discourse. For, as the *Tractatus* indicates, truth is a quality of propositions, and "a proposition is a description of fact." But most religious discourse pertains to things that fall outside the range of fact. Taken as propositions, such discourse registers as being nonsensical. This is not to say that there is no place for such discourse, or that it is meaningless to engage in it. Wittgenstein can give credence, though no verifiability, to the world of mysticism, and there is an appropriate language of mysticism. Yet, none of the positive hints, suggestions, or comments that he directs toward mystical attitudes can violate his dictum that "whereof one cannot speak thereof one must be silent." Indeed, when it addresses religious issues directly, philosophical interest focuses on the status of religious belief. And here Wittgenstein contended that religious belief must be distinguished from the kind of truth claims that issue from factual evidence. Their sources are distinctive. Religious beliefs are not born of the same conditions through which knowledge is established. Thus, in the technical philosophical sense, they carry no truth quotients.

In his second book, *Philosophical Investigations*, published posthumously, Wittgenstein disagreed with some of the proposals he had presented in his *Tractatus*. The *Tractatus* was devoted to a methodical circumscription of the limits of language;

its subject is the function of language. Thus, in the *Tractatus* language is treated as the product of the coalescence of atomic particles. When language is properly ordered in sentences, the product is propositional truth. In the *Tractatus*, Wittgenstein made most frequent reference to the model of the proposition that functions as a picture of fact, because it properly represents the atomic particles. As we have seen, those subjects—particularly religion, but also ethics and aesthetics—that are not formed from factual discourse were placed outside the range of topics to which propositional truth had access.

In *Philosophical Investigations*, however, Wittgenstein relaxed his strict devotion to the logical-mathematical model. With this tempered epistemological relaxation came some modification of the rigorous restriction that truth is a product of propositions that are made normative by conformity to the logical-mathematical standard. That is, Wittgenstein allowed for greater flexibility in his assessment of the function and accomplishments of factual discourse, and in assessing the function and accomplishments of discourse that does not count as being factual. In the earlier *Tractatus*, he had approached all other-than-factual forms of discourse, by definition, as being transgressions against the truth. But in the subsequent *Philosophical Investigations* he showed a strong eagerness to account for the transgressions too. In short, in *Philosophical Investigations* Wittgenstein tried to come to terms with forms of linguistic communication that could not be regularly verified by the criteria by which truth is ascribed.

Another way of putting the same point is to observe that the influence of Bertrand Russell is prominent in the *Tractatus* but is muted in *Philosophical Investigations*. In Russell's likeness, the Wittgenstein of the *Tractatus* sought *a priori* conditions for propositional truth, expecting to be able to invoke logical and mathematical rigor. The Wittgenstein of *Philosophical Investigations* was more flexible on the matter of paradigmatic exactness, much more empirical, and, thus, more interested in *a posteriori* and synthetic modes of validation. While the early Wittgenstein seemed preoccupied with the formal conditions of propositional truth, the later Wittgenstein was impressed with the workings of ordinary language. Thus, his *Philosophical Investigations* inquires into the particular nuances of language that are evident in actual linguistic practices. The irony is that once Wittgenstein made the transition from the formal conditions of propositional truth to linguistic practices that give shape to ordinary language, he came to recognize that the logic of his analysis in the *Tractatus* did not really give expression to actual cases.

This recognition also encouraged him to modify his "picture theory of truth," again because he needed an analog that would allow for multiple and flexible viewpoints. Accordingly, as he worked his way from the position of the *Tractatus* to the position of *Philosophical Investigations*, he moved from the analogy of picture-making to the analogy of game-playing. As he put it, in ordinary language a wide variety of games are played. These games have multiple purposes and, consequently, multiple rules. Whereas the *Tractatus* gave the impression of setting forth rigid criteria, *Philosophical Investigations* is more flexible. It is pervaded by a willingness to acknowledge the credibility of a number of actual language games. Thus, the latter book gives evidence of its author's interest in observing the ways in which language functions in particular instances of actual usage. This leads to his conclusion that language is designed and constructed for us; thus a word has as many meanings as it has uses. No longer, as in the *Tractatus*, is Wittgenstein obligated to establish truth on formal *a priori* propositional grounds. Rather, sentences are understood to carry a wide variety of functions.

This leads Wittgenstein to propose the purpose of philosophy. Philosophy exists, he attests, to clarify misunderstandings, confusions, and errors in the use of language. In the *Tractatus*, philosophy was understood to function this way when it uncovered logical errors and the misuse of language. In the *Philosophical Investigations*, Wittgenstein contends that misunderstandings arise when one language game is confused with another, when several language games are regarded as being identical, or when a single language game is regarded as being the only legitimate kind.

Although the philosophy of Wittgenstein's *Tractatus* is recognized for its radical character and for revolutionizing the intention and materials of philosophical reflection, it can still be viewed from within the perspective of enduring intentions of Enlightenment philosophy to which this book has made repeated reference. For, like Kant, Wittgenstein was concerned to probe and fix limits. In Kant's case, the aim is to assess the limits of reason. In Wittgenstein's case, the focus is on the limits of language. In both instances, limits are fixed so that the analyst can circumscribe the context within which it is meaningful to register truth claims. Immanuel Kant achieved this objective by describing how reflection is constituted. Wittgenstein did the same by showing how language functions. For both, once the area of circumscription was fixed, religion was assigned a position outside the perimeters. Kant assigned boundaries to knowledge, as he put it, "in order to make room for faith," but, for him, faith and ratiocinative knowledge were assigned distinctive contexts. Similarly, Wittgenstein placed "those things whereof one cannot speak" outside ordinary linguistic perimeters. The place outside the ordinary perimeters was described as a large, expansive, and even mysterious sphere to which silence is appropriate. Thus, the intentions of the two programs are similar, and the respective treatment of religion follows the paradigmatic pattern that has been established. Because religion lies outside the bounds of regular cognitive sanction, the certification of religion is dependent on extraregular criteria.

Consequently, it is appropriate to use the word *grammar* when describing similarities between Kant's and Wittgenstein's approaches. Both were involved in assessing the workings of particular grammars. Kant sought to write the grammar of the ratiocinative process. Wittgenstein approached thought by trying to identify the way in which thought is captured and expressed within the formal network of language. Both attempted to describe the rudiments and inner workings of a formal cognitive system. And both contended that the system is something more than a mere instrument within the cognitive process. The network is not simply a means of expression and communication. Rather, the network is ingredient in thought (for Kant) and in language (for Wittgenstein), lending formation to thought and language. Indeed, the network's function is so crucial that, in both instances, truth is regarded as being the product of the network's intrinsic activity.

It follows, too, that the interest in fixing boundaries with precision and without qualification is expressed as a shared mistrust of metaphysical speculation. Metaphysics, as Kant and Wittgenstein view it, traffics in areas of philosophical excess that tend to transport thought beyond the perimeters of the formal network. Metaphysical speculation tries to extend the network to an area over which it can exercise no control. It provokes the formal network to consider matters of inquiry that exceed the capacities of the network. It uses the network in an inappropriate manner, teasing it to reach beyond its proper domain.

In short, for both Kant and Wittgenstein, metaphysical speculation is deceptive and extravagant. Frequently it is criticized as being an overextension, a conceptual exploitation. Kant explains such metaphysical excesses as having been inspired by the transposition of regulative into constitutive ingredients of reflection. By this he means that the formal ingredients of cognition are accorded an extraformal status, as though they made reference to things. Wittgenstein makes the same point on the basis of the use of language, that is, when language loses contact with that which can be verified. And since religious statements often appear much like metaphysical statements, they are judged to be incapable of producing legitimate truth claims. They may be expressive or emotive, but, in epistemologically or linguistically certifiable senses, they are not true propositions.

A. J. Ayer: Religious Statements Belong Outside the Range of Propositional Truth

Wittgenstein's formidable insights and proposals stand as a watershed in Western philosophy. Behind them lie the powerful influences of Moore, Russell, the Vienna Circle, and the other positivists and analysts throughout the world. It was a movement within philosophy with which everyone involved needed to come to terms. As we have seen, it was inevitable that the implications of this philosophical revolution would one day affect the understanding of the nature and function of religion.

One of the earliest, clearest, most forceful, and most compelling efforts at drawing these religious implications came in Alfred J. Ayer's book *Language, Truth and Logic*, first published in 1936. Treating religious affirmations as though they could be classified like metaphysical assertions—for, as we have indicated, the two seem to have much in common—Ayer (1910–1989) contended that both were nonsensical. He was quick to clarify that they stand as being nonsensical in the technical rather than pejorative sense: they simply lack verifiable factual content. Religious affirmations, in short, must be understood to be communicating something other than facts.

In drawing this conclusion, Ayer was confident that he would have the support of both the advocates as well as the disclaimers of religion. As he wrote:

> [W]e are often told that the nature of God is a mystery that transcends human understanding. But to say that something transcends the human understanding is to say that it is unintelligible. And what is unintelligible cannot significantly be described. Again, we are told that God is not an object of reason but an object of faith. This may be nothing more than an admission that the existence of God must be taken on trust, since it cannot be proved. But it may also be an assertion that God is the object of a purely mystical intuition, and cannot therefore be defined in terms which are intelligible to the reason. And I think there are many theists who would assert this.

Indeed, Ayer believed that his observations were ones with which the most avid supporters of the legitimacy of religion would agree, even with his conclusion, namely, that "if one allows that it is impossible to define God in intelligible terms, then one is allowing that it is impossible for a sentence both to be significant and to be about God."

At this point, Ayer's rendition becomes more religiously specific. "If a mystic admits that the object of his vision is something which cannot be described," he continues, "then he must also admit that he is bound to talk nonsense when he describes it." Throughout his portrayal he pleads that he does not intend his analyses to be antireligious. In treating religious affirmations as he did, he thought he was simply repeating interpretations (and placing them within specific contexts wherein they might be accorded greater rigor and exactness) that advocates of religion—believers and mystics alike—had been suggesting for a long, long time. He believed there was consensus, in his words, that religious statements belong outside the range of propositional truth.

Language Analysis and Religion: Responses from Religionists

Much of the analysis of the implications of linguistic analysis for an understanding of the nature and function of religion has been by the "Falsification Controversy" that was introduced in a book called *New Essays in Philosophical Theology*, edited by Antony Flew and Alasdair MacIntyre in 1955. Since 1955, responses to the issue have become more refined and elaborate, and the implications have been traced into fields and subject areas that were not envisioned in the beginning. Nevertheless, the discussion continues to revolve around the question: What is the logical status of religious affirmations? As we have seen, the initial interest lay in distinguishing religious assertions from other forms of language in which other sorts of truth are claimed. In the initial group of essays, co-editor Antony Flew formulated the problem like this:

> [T]o assert that such and such is the case is necessarily equivalent to denying that such and such is not the case. Suppose then that we are in doubt as to what someone who gives vent to an utterance is asserting, or suppose that, more radically, we are skeptical as to whether he is really asserting anything at all, one way to try to understand . . . his utterance is to attempt to find what he would regard as counting against, or as being incompatible with, its truth.

Flew believed that these were appropriate and realistic expectations since, "if the utterance is indeed an assertion, it will necessarily be equivalent to a denial of the negation of that assertion."

He explains:

> And anything which would count against the assertion, or which would induce the speaker to withdraw it and to admit that it had been mistaken, must be part of (or the whole of) the meaning of the negation of that assertion. And to know the meaning of the negation of an assertion is, as near as makes no matter, to know the meaning of that assertion.

He follows with the assertion: "And if there is nothing which a putative assertion denies, then there is nothing which it asserts either, and so it is not really an assertion."

In other words, unless one can state the alternative, an assertion is not a genuine claim to truth. Unless a state of affairs exists that could count against the truth of a religious affirmation, such an utterance does not qualify as a genuine assertion: it is not a statement about a given state of affairs.

From this starting point, the responses divide along traceable lines. R. M. Hare, among the first to respond to Flew's "challenge," identified the distinctiveness of religious assertions by identifying them as "bliks." A "blik" is a nonfalsifiable belief that is not based on empirical evidence. The truth or falsity of a "blik" cannot be negotiated by empirical testing, nor are "bliks" the products of observation. "Bliks" need not correspond to anything that happens in the world. Neither is a "blik" to be treated as a hypothesis or as an explanation of events, for it cannot be undermined by counterevidence. In Hare's mind, however, it is through our "bliks" that we are able to say what does indeed count as valid explanation. Two persons holding different "bliks" may not be asserting anything different about the world, but there would be large differences between the two persons as well as different limitations on the range of things that are conceptually accessible. In Hare's view, religious assertions are like "bliks." There is no reason why they should not be taken seriously; at the same time, they do not qualify as assertions about a given state of affairs.

Basil Mitchell, another participant in the original discussion, maintained that religious affirmations do make significant factual assertions. In Mitchell's view, religious claims allow certain states of affairs to count against their truth, but the grounds of refutation are never conclusive. Mitchell wants faith or belief to be given proper place. Faith—real, vibrant faith—must stand firm, resisting all evidence to the contrary. The counterevidence can be admitted, but, by virtue of the nature of faith, such evidence is never powerful enough to refute the affirmations of the believer.

The nature and disposition of religious affirmations and convictions were studied by another analyst, I. M. Crombie, whose attitude is decidedly Christian. In offering a genetic account of religious beliefs, Crombie argues that religious affirmations are statements of fact which, because of their special characteristics, can never completely meet the requirements of most ordinary factual statements. In Crombie's formulation, the context within which religious affirmations are meaningful is distinguished from other contexts. This enables Crombie to defend the view that what is factual from within a religious context may be inaccessible and incomprehensible from the outside. The critic and the believer, in other words, are not standing on the same ground.

Another writer and scholar, R. B. Braithwaite, concedes that religious statements do not normally fall under the classification of statements for which regular methods exist for testing truth values. But, writing under the title "An Empiricist's View of the Nature of Religious Belief," Braithwaite also recognizes that religious statements are not the only expressions that fall outside the range of ordinary propositional truth. The same place must also be assigned to ethical and moral assertions. In fact, ethics and religion are compatible with each other—indeed, belong together. Braithwaite contends that religious affirmations really belong to an ethical context, within which context they carry a dispositional influence with respect to the conduct of life.

John Hick, like others whose positions have been summarized here, also wishes to have it both ways. On the one hand, Hick argues that religious affirmations are indeed factual assertions and therefore must conform to the ordinary standards of meaningfulness required of all such statements. In some way, religious affirmations must be tested by reference to actual experience. At the same time, the testing ground for religious affirmations is an intrareligious context. That is, their factual basis can be sustained only within the religious context by which they are nurtured. The affirmation of life after death, for instance, is not to be empirically tested except within the context of a religion's teachings on this subject. Referring to this principle as "eschatological verification," and illustrating his point by drawing upon the content of the Christian religion, Hick writes:

This eschatological element is quite inseparable from any conception of God and the universe which is to be recognizably Christian, and it is at this point that the corpus of Christian belief lays itself open in principle to experiential verification—though not, in virtue of the peculiar asymmetry of predictions concerning continued existence after death, to falsification. If one is willing to allow experience itself to show what different kinds of experience there are, one cannot dismiss *a priori* the Christian prediction of a future experience of participation beyond death, in the Kingdom of God.

Although such a statement does not argue for a standard "logical certification" of the truth of a religious affirmation, it does serve, in principle, to "leave no grounds for rational doubt as to the validity of that faith." In Hick's view, theistic faith can be verified "by one who holds it to be proved beyond rational doubt." But he adds that the same faith "cannot be proved to the non-believer." As noted, Hick's view comes close to that of Crombie, though the former's framework of verification is more religiously specific.

D. Z. Phillips, an articulate spokesman for a viewpoint commonly referred to as fideism, finds his starting point in Wittgenstein's remarks about "grammar," "language games," and "forms of life." Phillips's point is that there is no way to get outside of language to see whether the concepts one is using "match up" to "the facts." Instead, language and concepts assist in determining what is and is not "factual." Therefore, for Phillips, fundamental religious affirmations cannot be described as factual statements. Instead, they are to be considered as "grammatical remarks." They do not certify that whatever is being referred to exists, but they indicate what kind of an entity is being referred to, and what it makes sense to say of it. As he explains:

> It makes as little sense to say "God's existence is not a fact" as it does to say "God's existence is a fact." In saying that something either is or is not a fact, I am not describing the "something" in question. To say that X is a fact is to say something about the grammar of X; it is to indicate what it would and would not be sensible to say or do in connection with it. To say that the concept of divine reality does not share this grammar is to reject the possibility of talking about God in the way in which one talks about matters of fact. I suggest that more can be gained if one compares the question, "what kind of reality is divine reality?" not with the question, "is this physical object real or not?" but with the different question, "what kind of reality is the reality of physical objects?"

From these sets of analogies, D. Z. Phillips offers this conclusion: "To ask a question about the reality of God is to ask a question about *a kind of reality*, not about the reality of *this* or *that*, in much the same way as asking a question about the reality of physical objects is not to ask about the reality of this or that physical object."

Thus, in Phillips's view, the reasons believers give for their religious beliefs presuppose the context from within which such beliefs issue. This does not mean that such beliefs are misguided or baseless, though the same beliefs cannot claim external justification. There can be no appeal to an "objective reality" outside the world of discourse or a "form of life" to which religious affirmations belong. This is not to say that only a believer can understand something about religious language. Rather, Phillips's point is that any responsible account of religion must view it from within the context of belief and resist the urge to assess it according to alien criteria. Phillips explains: "So . . . I distinguish between religious and philosophical understanding. What I wish to urge is that one can only give a satisfactory account of religious beliefs if one pays attention to the roles they play in people's lives."

One of the sharpest criticisms of fideism has come from the pens of Kai Nielsen and Alasdair MacIntyre. Nielsen, in a book entitled *Contemporary Critiques of Religion*, offers that "to understand religious discourse, one must have a participant's understanding of it." This, so far, sounds like a statement on behalf of fideism. But Nielsen adds that the participant's understanding of religious discourse does not give that discourse immunity against philosophical criticism. Moreover, to give religious language a use and function no other segment of language can perform is not necessarily to insure the validity of logical coherence of religious language.

In Nielsen's view, the "fideist" position is vulnerable precisely for supposing that distinct "form of life" implies "autonomous criteria of rationality." Nielsen proposes that it is not a contradiction to speak of the possibility of an "ongoing but irrational form of life," and he cites belief in witches and fairies as denoting "forms of life" that have come to be rejected as incoherent. He also argues against treating religious language as being protected from such inquiry because it is somehow understood to be sacred: "Religious discourse is not something isolated, sufficient unto itself; 'sacred discourse' shares categories with, utilizes the concepts of, and contains the syntactical structure of 'profane discourse.'" The same objection against approaching religious affirmations as though they belong to a separate language is expressed sharply in the following statement:

> "Reality" may be systematically ambiguous, but what constitutes evidence or tests for the truth or reliability of specific claims is not completely idiosyncratic to the context or activity we are talking about. Activities are not that insulated.

Nielsen's point is that it is altogether proper and fitting that questions about the meaningfulness of religious language be raised. Moreover, the inquirer has every right to examine the conceptual structure and implicit reasonableness of religious discourse: ". . . the fact that there is a form of life in which God-talk is embedded does not preclude our asking these questions or our giving, quite intelligibly, though perhaps mistakenly, the same negative answer we gave to witch-talk." Thus, Nielsen's antifideism is based on the contention that standard forms of intelligibility exist by which one can judge diverse forms of activity and discourse. For him it would not be enough to say that religious affirmations are *sui generis*. Or, if one says this, the declaration does not place such affirmations above criticism.

Alasdair MacIntyre offers a similar objection to the attitude that intelligibility is always contextually based, that understanding is directed by the activity or form of discourse in question. MacIntyre's point is that norms of intelligibility and criteria for measuring truth own a history: they can and do change. Even the contexts to which fideists make appeal undergo change through social and cultural influences. With this change come shifts in what is considered to be rational and coherent. McIntyre also believes, with Nielsen, that the practices of a society, or a mode of social life, may not be coherent. In other words, even if one could rely on *sui generis* references, there are no assurances that the intrinsic pattern is self-consistent. It is entirely possible that standards of intelligibility, within a framework or context, are manifestly incoherent.

There is another important side to MacIntyre's observation. He is not thinking simply about social and cultural patterns in the abstract; he has specific examples in mind. His primary reference, in this respect, is to Christian belief, and he is intrigued by changes in attitudes toward the articles of Christian faith. He observes, for example, that even at the time of the church fathers, many theologians had noticed inconsistencies in the pattern of Christian belief. None of these was regarded as being an insurmountable difficulty because all were compatible with a comprehensive way of viewing the world, a viewpoint articulated with the social, cultural, and intellectual life of the era. But this does not describe the contemporary situation. The modern secularized view of the world unmasks incoherent and contradictory religious beliefs because they are removed from the social and cultural contexts from which they originally drew nurture. This separation of the articles of belief from the context within which they were generated leaves them unable seriously to affect contemporary religious life. MacIntyre therefore finds it futile to try to make the same articles of belief invulnerable to philosophical criticism. As he puts it:

> If I am right, understanding Christianity is incompatible with believing in it, not because Christianity is vulnerable to skeptical objections, but because its peculiar invulnerability belongs to it as a form of belief which has lost the social context which once made it comprehensible.

In other words, in MacIntyre's view, the very fact that religion can be viewed as an autonomous form of life may make it incomprehensible to modern, secularized human beings. Moreover, the fact that the skeptic and the believer do not share whatever bridging concepts have been offered to create common discussion is simply confirmation of the differences between the two contrasting orientations to life.

MacIntyre has expanded on this point of view in a subsequent study, *After Virtue; A Study in Moral Theory* (1981), which traces the progressive disintegration of the language of morality from the Enlightenment period to the present. Here, too, the problem is that secularization has placed the world in a disjunctive situation: religion no longer possesses the capacity to provide the background and framework of moral discourse. The absence of an effective, resilient language of morality, in MacIntyre's view, is a "grave cultural loss." Informed by MacIntyre's historical and philosophical analyses, Charles Taylor has charged that secularization has transposed religion—which, at one time, was central to the whole life of Western societies, public and private—into sub-cultural status. Explaining this situation in his book *Sources of the Self: The Making of the Modern Identity* (1989), Taylor also charges that contemporary philosophers are ignoring questions about how human life ought to be lived, have directed less than adequate attention to issues concerning a common good, and have diligently tried to avoid all subjects that are understood to have belonged to the province of religion. Perhaps it is accurate to say that religious affirmations are *sui generis*, in MacIntyre's and Taylor's views, but this is not due solely to the fact that they were intended to be.

It would be impossible, in brief scope, to trace even the most prominent ways in which analyses of religious language translate into social and cultural theory. Accordingly, we cannot even begin to city the theorists, the books, articles, and monographs that deal with this immense subject. But we can trace a pathway that uses linguistic analysis as a instrument of cultural interpretation, the first example of which is the work of the British philosopher and anthropologist Peter Winch, who employs Wittgenstein's insights when conducting comparative anthropological studies.

Agreeing that cultural conceptions of "reality" are reflected in language, Winch proposes that the anthropologist pay close attention to the operating "limiting notions" of a given society or culture. By "limiting notion," Winch refers to the fundamental keys of understanding and interpretation by which a culture or society is formed. These include conceptions of birth and death, human destiny, the difference between right and wrong, the establishing of conditions through which possibilities for good and evil are determined, and so on. All societies exhibit such "limiting notions," which possess a categorial status in their apprehension of reality, though the contents of same differ markedly from culture to culture. Winch writes:

> The specific forms which these concepts take, the particular institutions in which they are expressed, vary very considerably from one society to another; but their central position within a society's institutions is and must be a constant factor. In

trying to understand the life of an alien society, then, it will be of the utmost importance to be clear about the way in which these notions enter into it.

Such "limiting notions" function, for Winch, as modes through which personal and societal life is ordered. Their contents reflect specific ways in which "reality" is experienced and conceived. Winch understands that "reality is not what gives language sense." On the contrary, "what is real and what is unreal shows itself *in* the sense that language has." Even "the distinction between the real and the unreal and the concept of agreement with reality themselves belong to our language." Therefore, it is "*within* the religious use of language" that conceptions are shaped, outside of and apart from which context they cannot be judged. The principle is that reality is determined by its actual use in language. Winch believes that this interpretation of the function of language lies in fullest keeping with Wittgenstein's proposals as outlined in the latter's *Investigations*. Noting that Wittgenstein's understanding of this issue had progressed between his *Tractatus* and the *Philosophical Investigations*, Winch explains:

> In the *Tractatus* Wittgenstein sought "the general form of propositions": what made propositions possible. . . . [He said that] the proposition was true when there existed a corresponding arrangement of elements in reality. The proposition was capable of saying something because of the identity of structure, of logical form, in the proposition and in reality.
>
> By the time Wittgenstein composed the *Investigations* he had come to reject the whole idea that there must be a general form of propositions. He emphasized the indefinite number of different uses that language may have and tried to show that these different uses neither need, nor in fact do, all have something in common, in the sense intended in the *Tractatus*. He also tried to show that what counts as "agreement or disagreement with reality" takes on as many different forms as there are different uses of language, and cannot, therefore, be taken as given *prior* to the detailed investigation of the use that is in question.

The implications for the academic study of religion are extensive. Winch proposes that one can only begin to understand the life of another society by recognizing that the concepts used by that society "can only be interpreted in the context of the way of life" of that society.

> To say of a society that it has a language is also to say that it has a concept of rationality. There need not perhaps be any *word* functioning in its language as "rational" does in ours, but at least there must be features of its members' use of language analogous to those features of *our* use of language which are connected with our use of the word "rational." Where there is language it must make a difference what is said and this is only possible where the saying of one thing rules out, on pain of failure to communicate, the saying of something else.

Such insights regarding understanding the life of another society derive from appreciation for the place of language games.

Language games are played by men who have lives to live—lives involving a wide variety of different interests, which have all kinds of different bearings on each other. ... Whether a man sees point in what he is doing will ... depend on whether he is able to see any unity in his multifarious interests, activities, and relations with other men; what sort of sense he sees in his life will depend on the nature of this unity.

The implications for cross-cultural studies in religious studies, as well as anthropology, can be stated as follows:

> What we may learn by studying other cultures are not merely possibilities of different ways of doing things, other techniques. More importantly we may learn different possibilities of making sense of human life, different ideas about the possible importance that the carrying out of certain activities may take on for a man, trying to contemplate the sense of his life as a whole. ...
> We are confronted not just with different techniques, but with new possibilities of good and evil, in relation to which men may come to terms with life.

But in whatever society one is studying, regardless of circumstances, regardless of time of origin, the scholar will encounter those fundamental concepts—Winch's "limiting notions"—that determine the possibilities for good and evil within the society. In providing explication for what is intended by "limiting notions," Winch quotes a passage from *The New Science* by Giambattista Vico:

> We observe that all nations, barbarous as well as civilized, though separately founded because remote from each other in time and space, keep these three human customs: all have some religion, all contract solemn marriages, all bury their dead. ... For by the axiom that "uniform ideas, born among peoples unknown to each other, must have a common ground of truth," it must have been dictated to all nations that from these institutions human began among them all, and therefore they must be most devoutly guarded by them all ....

Winch's objective is to translate Vico's insight into an effective investigative principle. He understands that the pathway toward doing so involves employing Wittgenstein's proposals regarding the uses of language.

Hajime Nakamura: Language Analysis as Method of Cross-Cultural Comparisons

Another way in which linguistic analysis can be used effectively in religious studies has been illustrated by the Japanese scholar Hajime Nakamura (b.1912), principally in his book *Ways of Thinking of Eastern Peoples* (1964). Not only has Nakamura cultivated a way of conducting modal analysis within the context of cross-cultural studies, but he also employed this analytical technique to increase understanding of religion. Indeed, he proposes that the distinctive modes of thought of a people can be identified so as to differentiate their outlook on the world. When one engages in this kind of analysis, one should focus on the matter of linguistic, grammatical, and syntactical construction.

Nakamura is highly trained. Influenced by Bertrand Russell, he also found himself gravitating toward the *Verstehen* approach to ideological identification and analysis as he encountered it in the writings of Max Weber. Thus, his intention in conducting cross-cultural analyses of selected cultural traditions is to understand how persons in various societies come to acquire their characteristic philosophical viewpoints, or, as he calls them, "ways of thinking." His method is to examine the processes of judgment and inference that are implicit in the uses of language and in the inherent operations of linguistic forms. Specific language usage, and the abilities that are resident in language, have a strong influence on the attitudes of a society or people in engaging, addressing, or otherwise conceiving of or relating to reality.

Nakamura puts his central assumption in the form of a question: "Are not the expression-forms of judgment and deduction which we adopt as the cognitive means for studying the characteristic ways of thinking, working at the same time as an *existential basis?*" He then answers his own question:

> Generally speaking, since the grammar and its syntax, which regulate the expression-form of judgment and deduction do not easily change, they are not only expressive of the characteristic ways of thinking of a nation, but in return they also regulate them for some time. In other words, it is probable that the ways of working of a thought-form might in turn be qualified by its language form.

From which the conclusion follows: "Therefore, the expression-forms of thought employed in language are the existential basis for the characteristic ways of thinking of a people."

In the learned analyses that follow in *Ways of Thinking of Eastern Peoples*, Nakamura describes the "modes of thought" of four East Asian peoples, those of India, China, Tibet, and Japan. The result is a comprehensive morphology of linguistic and grammatical preferences. One can expect it to stand as an impressive first in a developing series of methodologically rigorous cross-cultural studies.

In addition, because Nakamura is well versed in the philosophical writings and religious texts of both Western and Eastern cultures, he is able to suggest points of contact that would not always be apparent. Consequently almost every page of his book is an exercise in cross-cultural comparisons, since references are made to Greece, to India, to China, to Japan, to Mediterranean cultures, all within the same paragraph. Yet the direction of his interpretations is provided by a sustained interest in the function of language. Grammar, linguistic patterns, and syntactical order both affect and are embodied in the outlook of a people and in the disposition of its culture. Self-consciousness regarding grammar, linguistic patterns, and syntactical order is also embodied in the outlook and the disposition.

Their presence makes it possible to study all of these elements together, and to have a reliable basis on which to conduct cross-cultural analyses in the process.

D. Z. Phillips: Fideism as a Way of Recovering Evolutionist Intentions

We encountered D. Z. Phillips earlier in this chapter. We noted that he is known for championing the position commonly referred to as fideism, so named because Phillips affirms that there is no way to get outside of language to judge the reliability of the concepts. This corroborates the conviction that there is no way *outside of the attitude of faith* to make certifiable sense of religious affirmations.

It is one thing to declare all of this. Something else is involved in reinterpreting the sense of significant anthropological inquiries into the nature of religious experience in light of it. This is precisely what Phillips does in returning to the nineteenth-century theories of such thinkers as E. B. Tylor, Sir James Frazer, Herbert Spencer, and others considered previously in this study.

Under the title "Are Religious Beliefs Mistaken Hypotheses?" Phillips focuses on the tendency within interpretations of the behavior of primitive peoples to regard their orientation to life as misguided and mistaken. Phillips believes that such appraisals are imprecise. Whereas primitive peoples engaged in rituals that have been taken as evidence of their own superstitions—and thus, by nineteenth- and twentieth-century standards, of the pervasive irrationality of their point of view—Phillips would like to offer an amended interpretation. Such behavior is not irrational, but is supremely rational within the context of the attitude and outlook of those who are engaged in it. Using Wittgenstein, Phillips adds that the same rituals "can be seen as a form of language, a symbolism in their own right; a language and a symbolism which are expressive in character." Again the rituals "express values concerning what is deep and important for the people concerned—birth, death, hunting, cultivation of the crops, personal relations, etc." Supported by sophisticated analyses of the nature and function of language, Phillips is confident that he stands on firm ground when he asserts that the attitudes and behavior of primitive peoples are just as rational as those of anyone else, in spite of the fact that modern interpreters frequently find much of it difficult to take seriously.

The Language of Religion: A Summary Statement

At the beginning of this chapter, we indicated that analysis of religious language has developed along two distinct lines. From the one side, it has focused on nondiscursive forms: symbols, symbolic forms, images, modes of consciousness, and products of the imagination.

From the other it has concerned itself with discursive language, as in propositional truth, assertions, declarative statements, articles of faith, creedal formulations, and the like. In the preceding pages we have examined a number of prominent examples of elucidations of both points of departure. On the nondiscursive or symbological side, we selected a sampling: the work of Cassirer, Ricoeur, Langer, van der Leeuw, Gadamer, Panofsky, and others. From the discursive side, we attempted to trace a trajectory forward, starting with the work of G. E. Moore, Bertrand Russell, and Ludwig Wittgenstein (frequently via the influence of the Vienna Circle) to the work of more recent theorists such as D. Z. Phillips, Peter Winch, and other British- and American-trained analytical philosophers of religion.

At the beginning of the chapter, we argued that the two groups really belong together. We noted that despite large differences in manner as well as in specific focus, the two sides share the conviction that knowledge is dependent on the capacities of distinct modal sets. On the nondiscursive side, modal set has reference to the various symbolic forms. On the discursive side, modal set has reference to propositions. Those who work with discursive language assumed, at least in the beginning, that propositional truth could be formed and assessed according to the canons of logical-mathematical truth. Propositions were understood to make truth claims when they adhere to the standards of logical consistency and strict mathematical order. The second phase of the linguistic analysts' era is characterized by an obvious relaxing of logical-mathematical criteria, and a shift toward recognizing the propositional legitimacy of ordinary language. This transition, as we noted, is most evident in differences between the positions of the early and the later Ludwig Wittgenstein—differences reflected in the contrast between *Tractatus* and *Philosophical Investigations*. In moving from the earlier work to the later, Wittgenstein can be interpreted as paralleling the most striking difference between Bertrand Russell and G. E. Moore, the latter of whom was committed to the validity of ordinary language. But throughout the long cycle, regardless of particular emphases, the focus remains on the workings of discursive language. And the contention is that conditions for registering truth claims are isolatable when one discerns how language is formed in actual practice, that is, in its actual usage.

Strikingly, in both discursive and nondiscursive cases, the formal conclusion is the same: the ability to acquire knowledge, as well as to express and communicate it, depends on the internal workings of the modal set in question. Accordingly, much emphasis is placed on the matter of propriety; that is, detailed attention is given to distinctions between subjects that belong properly to the modal set in question vis-à-vis those which, modally speaking, are out of bounds. The proposal is that subjects which really do not belong to the modal set should not be approached as though they do. To proceed inappropriately in this regard is to commit errors of judgment and categorization. A category error occurs when a topic alien to the symbolic or linguistic framework is inserted there, under the pretense or mistaken assumption that it actually belongs. When this occurs, someone needs to discern the proper range of applicability of the modal set, then specify its actual boundaries, perimeters, and radial axes. This involves analysts in setting limits and fixing capacities, so that substance and content are properly conjoined. Such determinations are apparent in Kant's limitation of knowledge "in order to make room for faith," as well as in the early statement in the *Tractatus* that "whereof one cannot speak thereof one ought to remain silent." The same sort of boundary determinations are made in Paul Ricoeur's distinction that "myth provides food for thought," though, of course, without becoming thought or being translatable or reducible to thought. The same kind of discernment is implicit in Aby Warburg's speculations about the sorts of metamorphoses of content that take place when distinct modal sets are interchanged. In all such instances, a conviction is registered that truth is a product of discernment and discrimination. That is, truth—sustainable truth—cannot be indiscriminate. Regardless of whether one is referring to discursive or nondiscursive language, the approaches we have surveyed agree that truth belongs to the interworkings of formal components within specifiable modes of communication and expression. And religion, it seems, has invested heavily in all of them.

CHAPTER • SIX

THE COMPARISON OF RELIGIONS

John Hick, the noted British theologian and philosopher of religion, has pointedly expressed what many others have suspected all along: that a person's religious preferences are heavily influenced by personal biographical circumstances. Hick stated it plainly: "in the great majority of cases, the religion in which a person believes and to which he adheres depends upon where he was born." He explains:

> If someone is born to Muslim parents in Egypt or Pakistan, that person is very likely to be a Muslim; if to Buddhist parents in Sri Lanka or Burma, that person is very likely to be a Buddhist; if to Hindu parents in India, that person is very likely to be a Hindu; if to Christian parents in Europe or the Americas, that person is very likely to be a Christian.

The rule, Hick proposed, applies in about 98 or 99 percent of the cases: "Whether one is a Christian, a Jew, a Muslim, a Buddhist, a Sikh, a Hindu— or, for that matter, a Marxist or a Maoist—depends nearly always on the part of the world in which one happens to have been born."

Given the power of this fact, Hick believed it essential for devotees of one religious tradition to become familiar with the teachings and practices of the other traditions. This viewpoint is shared by Wilfred Cantwell Smith, the distinguished Canadian historian of religion, who observed as early as 1961 that

> the time will soon be with us when a theologian who attempts to work out his position unaware that he does so as a member of a world society in which other theologians equally intelligent, equally devout, equally moral, are Hindus, Buddhists, Muslims, and unaware that his readers are likely perhaps to be Buddhists or to have Muslim husbands or Hindu colleagues—such a theologian is as out of date as is one who attempts to construct an intellectual position unaware that Aristotle has thought about the world or that existentialists have raised new orientations, or unaware that the earth is a minor planet in a galaxy that is vast only by terrestrial standards.

Smith noted that up until the mid-twentieth century, "philosophy and science have impinged upon theological thought more effectively than has comparative religion." But he knew that this pattern would not continue. Indeed, some twenty years after he made the statement quoted here, Smith wrote a book with the title *Towards a World Theology.*

Readers may wonder why such observations, mostly about theology, are given prominence in a book about religious studies. In this regard, it must be noted that questions about the relative truth of one religion versus others arise within the self-consciousness of every religion. The responses evoked, similarly distinct in tone and intent, and markedly different from causal accounts, descriptive portrayals, functional renditions, and the like. Characteristic of the responses is the protection and privileging of the tradition from within which the questions are raised. That is to say, everyone expects the responses to be value-laden. The questioner intends that the protections and privileges will be maintained, but asks that some policy of fairness (the terms of which are determined internally) be extended to the other religions being acknowledged or referenced.

Are all religions true? Some have answered emphatically. Some have responded decisively. And some, if not most, have sought reasonable accommodation. *Does the question belong to religious studies?* No, if a yes answer means that religious studies is there to adjudicate the answer. Yes, if it is the work of religious studies to make the questions that are asked about religion intelligible.

As has been our custom in preceding chapters, we shall start with the analysis of religion that was conceived in the Enlightenment period, and trace the development of the interest in negotiating pluralism to the present time. To proceed in this way is no methodological contrivance. We recall that the cardinal Enlightenment paradigm, within which our subject was placed, was designed in the first place to secure the distinction between natural and revealed religion. In this respect, the analyses we are tracing in this chapter share a common starting point with those we have identified in previous chapters.

Natural vs. Revealed, When Revealed Is a Given

We recall that the Kantian approach was initiated to give religion a certifiable basis within human experience. There was a profound discontent with the prospect that the only possible certification lay in divine revelation, or in teachings prescribed and authorized by the church. The same lack of satisfaction carried over to the claim that religious beliefs were true because they had been transmitted by reliable authorities from one generation to the next. Unwilling to allow religious truth to be certified circumstantially, the patrons of Enlightenment intellectual sensitivities sought more rigorous canons or standards of legitimation and confirmation. Thus, by distinguishing between natural and revealed religion, and by attempting to defend the intellectual validity of the first only, the Enlightenment theoreticians thought they had uncovered noncircumstantial evidence for the claim that religion is a valid form of human experience. This was their paramount intention. The corollary was that revealed religion would be supported—if, indeed, it could be supported at all—only on the same natural grounds.

We have traced the way in which this argument worked when we examined the interest of Immanuel Kant, Friedrich Schleiermacher, Rudolf Otto, and others in identifying religion's *sine qua non*. We noted that Otto was drawing from this tradition when he described Christianity as religion par excellence. His explanation carried implications for comparative analyses of religious traditions:

> These conceptions . . . characterize it [Christianity] sharply and definitely as a religion of redemption par excellence, setting it in this respect on a level with the great religions of the East, with their sharp dualistic antithesis of the state of liberation and bondage, nay, justifying its claim not to fall short of these, but to surpass them, both in the importance it gives to these conceptions and in the richness of meaning it finds in them.

Out of the same enthusiasms, Otto wrote: "[I]n applying to the Cross of Christ the category 'holy,' Christian religious feeling has given birth to a religious intuition profounder and more vital than any to be found in the whole history of religion." In speaking this way, Otto was following the intrinsic disposition of the Enlightenment paradigm from whose resources he was drawing. If revealed religion is to be approached on the basis that its enduring content is rooted in natural experience, then the Christian religion must be approached from this vantage point too. And if the Christian religion is to enjoy an eminence when the various religious traditions are compared with each other, it must be on the grounds that it equips natural religious experience with the fullest possible expression. Analogously to the role a symphony plays with respect to innate and instinctual musical talents, revealed religion is an impressive integrated cultivation of natural human capacities.

The tendency from the beginning in Western scholarship was to make Christianity the favored religion. Though one can find serious criticisms of Christian orthodoxy, these hardly translate into arguments that any other religions are profounder and more articulate expressions of the natural human religious spirit than one could find in that religious tradition that most powerfully lent formation to Western culture. It would be difficult indeed for an advocate of religion to direct the analysis toward any other conclusion, for the paradigm was established to bring reciprocity and compatibility to the relationship between faith and reason as persons of Judeo-Christian persuasions understood it. Thus, the chronicle gives evidence of repeated efforts to support the claim that Christianity enjoys premier status among the religious traditions of the world—a claim that was bolstered by the theological conviction that belief in Jesus Christ is necessary to salvation.

One finds this pattern explicitly laid out in Allan Menzies' book *History of Religion: A Sketch of Primitive Religious Beliefs and Practices, and of the Origin and Character of the Great Systems*, which was published in 1895. Menzies (1845–1916), who was a professor of biblical criticism at the University of St. Andrews, was very much influenced by C. P. Tiele and P. D. Chantepie de la Saussaye. Therefore, his intention was to employ a descriptive approach to the entire history of religion, viewing this history as an organic whole, so as to lay a strong intellectual foundation for comparative religion. True to evolutionist form, Menzies started with animism, then moved through the religions of the Mediterranean world into Persia, India, and beyond. In the course of his survey he acknowledged three groupings of "human piety," namely, those of the Semitic tradition, the religions of India, and the third category simply called "Aryan Religion." From this threefold system of classification came a concluding chapter on "Universal Religion," which is immediately preceded by a description of Christianity, the last of the traditions to be examined.

Menzies' thesis is clear and concise. The religious experience of humankind is an organic whole the ingredients of which require time for their development and expression. Christianity stands as the highest form of identifiable institutional religion by virtue of the fact that it encompasses the previous developments. Yet Christianity, in Menzies' view, was not intended to be the final stage in the series, but, rather, to usher in a "universal religion" that might serve in the same capacity for the other religious traditions as well. That is, while the Semitic, Indian, and Aryan religions are in position to recognize the advances Christianity embodies, all of them together are understood to be propaedeutic to the universal religion that, based on Jesus' teachings, is destined to become "the faith of all mankind." As Menzies saw it, Jesus' teaching was "the living embodiment of the true religion," by virtue of the fact that it was identifiable with "the cause of freedom in every land," which is motivated by the desire of all peoples to live in brotherhood and harmony under the authority and benevolence of a "loving God who is the Father of all alike" and, as the history of religion attests, is "the desire of all nations."

Thus, in Menzies' formulation, comparative religion brings articulation to a progressive human religious history that begins with tribal religion, moves to national religion, then to individual religion, and finally to a universal religion within which all human beings are accorded a rightful place. Menzies' viewpoint stands as a depiction of evolutionist religious history that is made the basis for the kind of comparative religion that validates Christianity's alleged superior status.

A portrayal similar to Menzies' in intention was offered by J. A. MacCulloch (1868–1950), who was rector of St. Columba's on the Isle of Skye, in a book with the straightforward title *Comparative Theology*, published in 1902. Like Menzies, MacCulloch contended that Christianity is the universal religion to which all of the others point. But instead of working off the evolutionary model, MacCulloch examined the other religious traditions for glimmers and analogs that are more fully articulated, in his judgment, in the Christian religion.

MacCulloch asserted that the human fall into sin somewhat thwarted a providentially intended development of religious understanding, but, nevertheless, foreshadowings of subsequent realizations are found in prior expressions. For example, "pagan religion" gives evidence of a kind of monotheism that finds fuller articulation later on. Roman and Scandinavian religion provide subtle, clear, if not yet satisfying "glimpses of the Saviour," and there is even a kind of nascent belief in the "communion of the saints" in Vedic and Persian religion. MacCulloch understood that each such glimmer or foreshadowing carried the status of a "prefigurement" that found explicit fulfillment in the Christian religion. He believed that the inner logic of the world's religious history would become better known as these developments became more fully realized.

MacCulloch's disquisition follows the pattern established by Frederick Denison Maurice (1805–1872), professor of divinity in King's College, London, who published an influential book, *The Religions of the World and Their Relations to Christianity*, in 1854. Maurice had been influenced and inspired by Thomas Carlyle's *On Heroes, Hero-Worship, and the Heroic in History*, published in 1841, in which the author includes a chapter on Mohammed when seeking to identify human beings of evident personal strength who understood themselves to have been given a divine mission. Indeed, Carlyle placed Mohammed within a collection of strong persons including Dante, Shakespeare, Martin Luther, John Knox, Samuel Johnson, Oliver Cromwell, and Napoleon, Mohammed being the only one of "the heroes" from outside the Christian world. Maurice used Carlyle's portrayal of Mohammed as his own launching point for providing a comparison of the religious traditions on a point-for-point basis. It is clear from the outset that Christianity will defeat all competitors, since the theologian attests that his own religion is "the religion of truth, meant for all peoples, here and everywhere." But Carlyle was willing to accord some truth value to the insights embodied in the other religious traditions. These too can be received as manifesting a divine witness, but the witness is primarily to the fact of human need. With respect to this need, Christian revelation serves as antidote. Thus, the point-for-point debate is followed by a point-for-point application of Maurice's fundamental thesis. While the author of *The Religions of the World and their Relations to Christianity* knew in advance how his inquiry would culminate, he did acknowledge that other religions at least possess "facticity."

Many other theorists, working from within Christian bias or preference, have not been even this flexible. In most extreme form, their position has been championed by Hendrik Kraemer (1888–1965), a Dutch theologian and mission theorist, who labored to reverse the paradigm's sequence. That is, instead of allowing natural religion to stand as the guarantor of revealed religion, Kraemer wished to have it the other way around. "I put it fairly and squarely," he wrote, "that for me, the measure of what is true and what is real, and this not only in a religious context, is Jesus Christ, the Truth Himself." In Kraemer's view, regardless of the extents to which natural religion might constitute a powerful spiritual force—even a force for good in the world—the only reliable standard of judgment is Jesus Christ, whom he describes as "the absolute rule by which all religions, including Christianity, must be judged." He made the point explicitly and forcefully, asserting that Jesus Christ is "the critic of all religions as of everything else." In his view, "it is not Christian belief which is absolute, but the source and object of that belief, namely, God's self-revelation in Jesus Christ." The corollary is that only Christianity can be regarded as a true, authentic, and authoritative product of revelation, since Christianity is the institutional channel through which Christ, the Truth, is made known.

Kraemer regarded Jesus Christ as the absolute norm, and judged the religious traditions on the basis of their ability to make Christ known. Since this is not their purpose, their devotees must be converted to the true faith if they are to enjoy personal salvation. It is significant in this respect that Kraemer repeatedly draws upon the vocabulary of single-mindedness: "in Christ alone" and "only Christianity is the *one* true religion" are frequent phrases in his books and articles. Kraemer's position illustrates how relationships between religious traditions are understood when one religion—in his instance, the Christian religion—is understood to be the norm against which all others are contrasted and negated.

When degrees of truth and authenticity are acknowledged, however, and are ascribed to the various religious traditions of the world, the schematic arrangement becomes more complex. That is, if more than one religion represents the truth, no matter to what degree, it is more difficult to specify the relationships between them.

To describe and explain how several (or all) religions can all be at least partially true at once, comparativists tend to employ hierarchical or linear schemes. Since the inquiry we are tracing has been inspired and informed by Enlightenment philosophical considerations, the Christian religion, *ex hypothesi*, has been placed in the privileged position. When this proposal is presented according to a hierarchical scheme, Christianity is placed at the top of the ladder, as the highest or most fully developed form of religion, and the other religious traditions that are understood to count are arranged subordinately, according to the degrees to which they reflect the ideal. Or, when the linear scheme is imposed, Christianity tends to be placed at the culmination point, representing that stage of religious development toward which the other religious traditions may be moving. From this linear vantage point, the other religious traditions are described as having a "pre-Christian status," or to belong to preliminary stages of religious development that have been superseded by subsequent developments. This schematic arrangement enables the scholar of comparative religion to propose that exposure to or contact with the Christian religion either nullifies such pre-Christian states or stages of religious awareness, purifies them of pre-Christian or sub-Christian elements, or transforms them into orientations far richer and more authentic than they could have become had they simply been left in their original state. The same attitude is open to the interpreter who believes that the Christian religion may be the highest or fullest expression of natural religious sentiments to date, but that its own sensibilities will also be surpassed in some religious state of awareness that lies ahead in some glorious future. The same assumptions and principles apply: the transformational capacities the Christian religion may have exercised over previous religious orientations can also be exercised upon the Christian religion. In other words, just as the Christian religion might be regarded as a synthesis of divergent and emergent religious tendencies, so also can it be understood as material for some subsequent religious synthesis wherein it is also transcended. Proposals of this kind can be presented and illustrated in both hierarchical and linear schematizations.

Instead of tracing these schematic possibilities in logical and conceptual form, we will turn to examples of formulations that are available on the subject, and watch the story unfold as we review the work of those theorists who have made contributions to this range of intellectual interests. For this purpose we have chosen to retrace the narrative account by starting with the twentieth century; specifically, with the work of the Swedish theologian and historian of religions Nathan Söderblom. Then we shall work our way forward into the present era, saving a summary of the implications for understanding the nature of religion until we have surveyed several typical and prominent examples.

Nathan Söderblom: Revelation Made Expansive

History of religions is involved in this inquiry, and Christian theology perhaps even more so. But it was the dawning of the ecumenical age that brought the issue to the forefront. It is within this context that Nathan Söderblom (1886–1931) made a significant contribution.

Söderblom was a man of far-flung interests and enormous energies. After serving as professor in the history of religions at Uppsala University, he became Archbishop of the Church of Sweden from 1914 until his death. From both vocational vantage points, he developed a conception of the status and place of the Christian religion within the context of humankind's more extensive and expansive religious history. This subject intrigued him throughout his scholarly and ecumenical career. He gave it his fullest treatment in his Gifford Lectures in 1931, lectures published subsequently under the title *The Living God*.

Söderblom approached and portrayed humankind's religious history as representing an amalgam, a concatenation of instinct and training, not all components and products of which could be coordinated with systematic consistency. A major influence on his view was his strong adherence to the unqualified primacy of the Christian scriptures. He was a Lutheran whose intellectual work occurred during a time when the Scandinavian universities were championing a Martin Luther renaissance. As one who was loyal to his Lutheran heritage, Söderblom was committed to the normative status of biblical revelation. So strong was this element in his writings that his approach to the religious experience of humankind was guided by his understanding of the function of divine revelation. His aspiration in this respect was to understand revelation as a dynamic and flexible source of divine truth.

Thus, in his book *The Nature of Revelation*, Söderblom depicted the Christian religion "not as the end of the journey of religion aided by culture, but as the full completion of a special revelation of God." Note the linear schematization implicit in this statement. Note too that Söderblom speaks of "a special revelation" instead of "the special revelation," thus allowing for additional possibilities, when identifying Christianity's source.

The next step in Söderblom's interpretation involves working with the idea of degrees of quality. The difference between the Christian religion and the other religions of the world manifests itself as a matter of quality:

> The special relation in which this revealed religion stands to the general development of culture is matched by the inner character it possesses, which, in comparison with any corresponding religions, marks it as superior not only in degree, but essentially differing from them in those qualities which are common to all religions.

The difference in quality refers to a "special revelation of God" which, as far as Söderblom knows, is unique to Christian experience:

> The difference between the general science of religion and Christian theology is that, for the latter, faith in revelation is essential. For Christian theology, the history of religion is at the same time a divine self-disclosure. The general science of religion leaves the question of revelation open.

Or, to put the matter more explicitly: "In the biblical faith in revelation there is indeed included the conviction that one part of the history of religion constitutes revelation in a more real and richer sense than in the history of religions in general." This is part of the story, and it assures that Christianity will be accorded a distinctive and unique character, a quality that guarantees its normative religious status.

At the same time, Söderblom was imbued with a strong sense of the presence of God (the source of divine revelation) in the natural evolution or progression of human consciousness. He believed that the same spirit of God who was responsible for inspiring the biblical writers continued to influence the course of world history and to inform the development of a more inclusive human (perhaps universal) religious sensitivity. "There is a measure of revelation," he suggested, "wherever there is found a sincere religiousness." Thus, his convictions on this subject prompted him to try to sketch out the entire universal history of religious experience. In doing so, his objective was to do justice to revelation in both special and general terms.

Söderblom was assisted toward this end through the influence of two French thinkers, Auguste Sabatier (1839–1901) and Henri Bergson (whom we encountered in chapter 3). Both were process thinkers, and both employed evolutionist-sounding conceptual categories. Both proposed that interpretation employ the language of process and development. For both, progress and development regulated the entire course of human understanding, including religious understanding. Sabatier's crowning work, *Religions of Authority and Religions of the Spirit*—which, though unfinished, was published shortly after its author's death—gave expression to a fundamentally developmental attitude toward Christian doctrine. Hence, Söderblom was surrounded by influences and intellectual orientations of a progressive variety. It was to be expected that he would find a way to utilize the same insights to approach the history of religions, yet without diminishing his adherence to the centrality of divine revelation in establishing and protecting the uniqueness of Christianity.

The expression of the accomplishment of this intention came in his Gifford Lectures, in which he attested that there is a fundamental complementarity between the development of religious understanding, in the more general sense, and the truths of revelation, in the more specific Christian sense. In Söderblom's view, divine revelation has been present throughout the entire history of human religious awareness, but this fact does not diminish the uniqueness of Christian revelation. The reconciliation of these two proposals is not easy to achieve. Again, when speaking of the uniqueness of Christianity, Söderblom made reference to "special qualities" like "dignity," "greatness," and even "genius." Yet, he also wanted to affirm that the Christian religion is "more congruous with the cravings of higher human intellect and human aspiration." He had no hesitation in calling Christianity "the highest religion." And the reasons given are theological through and through: general revelation reflects a situation that finds man searching for God—everywhere in the world, wherever one finds examples of religious aspiration—while special revelation testifies to the dynamics of God's search for humans.

He wanted to add a corollary, however. If divine revelation (in both general and special aspects) is continuous, and encompasses all of human history, the activity of divine revelation can be expected to continue on into the future. "God's revelation is not finished—it continues," he affirmed. "All of human history," he attested, "is in God's hand." Furthermore, history itself has a goal, one that surpasses the capacities of human understanding.

These convictions led the Swedish archbishop to commend the following stance to Christian believers: "To the task of Christian thought it belongs little by little to make history understood in a religious sense, that is, to make men learn to see in the whole of history, in a prophetic way, God's miracle, his revelation." This implies a distinctive view of the nature and purpose of God:

> God is ever revealing himself. God's continued revelation is history. Of course, I hold that the Church is God's work and God's instrument. But God's revelation is not confined to the Church, although the Church, in the scriptures and in its experience, has the means of interpreting God's continued revelation. The Church ought to open its eyes, more than it does, to see how God is perpetually revealing himself.

Söderblom was confident that the attitude and stance he was recommending was thoroughly compatible with the most fundamental teachings of the church. "We often fail to learn the lesson of the Bible," he observed, "that our God is a living, a still living God, who has not become older and less active than in earlier days."

Bengt Sundkler, Söderblom's able biographer, reports that Söderblom did not decide on a title for his Gifford Lectures until July 12, 1913, the day he died. After deciding on the title, as Sundkler reports, Söderblom confided to his wife and children, "There is a living God, and I can prove it by the history of religions." The conviction that made this confession possible was that the long process of developing religious understanding can be interpreted as a persistent search for God, a quest that is a response to the compelling nature of that same God.

Karl Rahner: Natural Religion Perfected, Not Destroyed

Söderblom was only one among numerous Christian theologians to be fascinated with the conceptual possibilities inherent within evolutionism for schematizing the relationship between the Christian religion and the major religious traditions of the world. Wherever this developmental approach was cultivated toward this end, two axioms were always implicit: (1) that divine revelation is universal in scope; and (2) that special revelation (which is responsible for the occurrence of Christianity) and general revelation are complementary. At the heart of Söderblom's portrayal was a distinctively Lutheran theological principle. It held that Christianity testifies to the ways in which God seeks human beings while all other religions are motivated by humans seeking God. Whatever tension was present in this formulation was understood to have been modulated through the dynamic quality of evolutionist progression.

There are other ways of utilizing a developmental scheme to speak to the same issue. One of the most prevalent among them holds that "grace perfects nature without destroying it," which, by application, means that the Christian religion perfects the other religions without destroying them.

One can find this position expressed in the writings of numerous Catholic theologians. For illustration, we have selected Karl Rahner (1904–1984), one of the most influential and respected Catholic theologians of the twentieth century. Rahner's evaluation of "non-Christian religions" (it is telling that he identifies the major religious traditions of the world in this way, as not being Christianity), like Söderblom's, has been informed by a combination of theological conviction and advocacy of developmental categories. We have included exposition of it here because of its strikingly rudimentary character. Not only are the working hypotheses transparent; in addition, Rahner makes a point of identifying them and assisting the reader in coming to terms with them.

Rahner's attitude to the subject was developed in conjunction with his systematic attempt to provide the tenets of Christian belief with a refreshed and updated formulation. In undertaking this task, he was influenced by a Belgian philosopher, Joseph Maréchal, and by the German philosopher Martin Heidegger (1889–1976), among others. His position was intended to build an intellectually respectable place for religious faith by associating it with the prereflective capacities of human intelligence. This inclination is in evidence too as he worked out his scheme by which to relate Christian and so-called non-Christian religions. We cite as chief source Rahner's treatment of "Christianity and the Non-Christian Religions" in the fifth volume of his *Theological Investigations*, which is offered as an argument for "openness in Catholic teaching and practice." In this context, openness refers to a willingness to recognize that other religions do exist, and, even from a Christian perspective, have some measured utility and validity. It would be naive for Christians to suppose that they live in something other than a pluralistic religious context. One of Rahner's objectives is to help Christians understand how they can or should regard persons of other religious persuasions.

The first thesis states that "Christianity understands itself as the absolute religion, intended for all people, which cannot recognize any other religion beside itself as of equal right." The justification for this attitude rests in the conviction that the Christian religion is the product of "God's free self-revelation" to human beings. But Rahner adds a significant qualification to the thesis. He recognizes the difficulty in attributing an absolute status to a religion that has precise historical origins. This leads to some sophisticated distinctions concerning the span of time

Christianity has been in existence. He distinguishes the period of time from the birth of Jesus forward from the preceding era, then argues that, strictly speaking, the absolute status of Christianity pertains to the *destination* of the world. This says something different than claiming that Christianity possesses an absolute status, say, from the beginning of time. Rather, Rahner's view is that past and present religious pluralism will yield to a more monolithic situation one day, but in a day reserved for the future. Only then will it become apparent that all of human history has been moving toward a common religious destiny. More importantly, only in terms of history's ultimate destination can Christianity be conceived as an absolute religion. This status derives from the goals toward which humanity is moving. Whatever implicit absolute status the Christian religion possesses now lies in an anticipation of the final or ultimate meaning of human history.

In his second thesis, Rahner turns toward a specific evaluation of "non-Christian religions." The second thesis contends that from a Christian theological perspective, non-Christian religions can be recognized as lawful (or proper) religions because they have been formed by natural knowledge of God. This is another way of saying that "non-Christian religions" are not illegal: they do not exist in violation of the Christian's conception of God's will. On the contrary, all religious traditions, Christian and non-Christian alike, are recipients of supernatural grace. Supernatural grace is in evidence in the very fact that religion exists. This does not mean that "non-Christian religions" are valid, even in part. It simply means that the fact or presence of "non-Christian religions" is not a violation of divine providence. When all things become known, it will be better understood how providence can sustain a variety of religious points of view and still sustain a preferred one. Thus, to call "non-Christian religions" lawful is to intend the following:

> A lawful religion means here an institutional religion whose "use" by man at a certain period can be regarded on the whole as a positive means of gaining the right relationship to God and thus for the attaining of salvation, a means which is therefore positively included in God's plan of salvation.

Rahner's third thesis, an expansion of the second, suggests how Christians are to respond to "non-Christian religions." In Rahner's words: "Christianity does not simply confront the member of an extra-Christian religion as being a mere non-Christian, but as someone who can and must already be regarded in this or that aspect as an anonymous Christian." The response is dictated by the conviction that all persons have been touched by divine grace (recalling that Rahner gives grace a precognitive place within human experience). Thus, the emphasis on the word *anonymous*. What is precognitive may also be preconscious. Rahner proceeds to talk about the process by which the anonymous Christian (that is, any person not consciously and deliberately Christian) is transformed into "someone who now also knows about his Christian belief in the depths of his grace-endowed being by objective reflection [pre-cognition's counterpart] and in the profession of faith which is given a social form in the church." The situation Rahner describes is the setting for missionary activity. And the Christian missionary should go forth under the conviction that the non-Christian world is inhabited by an anonymous Christianity.

The fourth thesis refers to the Christian's expectation in the age between now and the culmination of human history. In keeping with the emphasis Rahner has given to precognitional factors, he sees the time from now to the end of time as being devoted more and more fully to an explication of religious awareness:

> The church will not so much regard herself today as the exclusive community of those who have a claim to salvation, but rather as the historically tangible vanguard and the historically and socially constituted explicit expression of what the Christian hopes is present as a hidden reality even outside the visible church.

Given this contention—Rahner would call it a vision—the Christian is free to view all hostility to Christianity not as essential resistance, but as a sign that the explication process has not yet worked its way. When all things become known, it will become apparent that "those who oppose are merely those who have not yet recognized what they nevertheless already really are." In that day, differences and antagonisms between Christian and "non-Christian religions" will disappear. Gradually, then finally, the implicit will be made explicit; all things anonymous will acquire name and place. Because of this wonderful expectation, the Christian has a perfect historical and religious right to regard the "non-Christian" as being "a Christian who has not yet come to himself reflectively." From start to finish, the evolutionary process works to make the preconscious conscious, a conception that articulates fully with Joseph Maréchal's revision of Kant's critical philosophy.

When one reads between the lines, one can detect the workings of the Enlightenment paradigm—the one that can be employed to give supremacy to the Christian religion. Rahner makes changes and adds a variety of flourishes here and there, but the outcome is the same. The reader will recall that the paradigm in question functions to secure a firm basis for religion (and not for any specific religion) by treating it as a valid form of human experience. Having done this, it proceeds to define the nature of religion, then defends all relevant examples of religion as being expressions and articulations of this fundamental, underlying core element. In this way, Christianity is linked with natural religious experience and can be valued as the best, fullest, and most representative expression of the fundamental religious disposition. In the paradigm—as well as in Rahner's portrayal—the Christian religion is treated as explication of inherently human religious sensitivities.

Rahner works with the same ingredients but arranges them in different ways, with the outcome being about the same. Having established the normative status of the Christian religion, he insists that everything valid religiously is also anonymously Christian. Thus, working with sets of contrast—for example, between conscious and unconscious, knowing and unknowing, awareness and lack of awareness—he approaches "non-Christian" religious experience as being comprehensible within the Christian context. The confirming theological principle for this is the time-tested Thomistic conviction that "grace perfects nature without destroying it." Thus, everything natural—including "non-Christian religion"—can be affirmed, although judged as significantly lacking completion. The process of transposing what is unconscious into vivid consciousness, and of bringing the imperfect to perfection, is covered by the category of *explication*. For Rahner, normative Christianity is gaining progressive explication in "non-Christian" religious experience.

All of this is included in Rahner's impression that advocates of other religious persuasions, whoever they are, wherever they may live, are "merely those who have not yet recognized what they nevertheless already are." He wishes to be friendly and generous toward all of those persons and communities who do not see the world the way he does. He wants to be positive toward them, and not judgmental. He has found a way to certify such desired rapprochement with them; that is, on his own—albeit expanded—terms.

Jean Danielou: Historical Applications

The same attitude and approach are much in evidence in Jean Danielou's (1905–1974) treatment of the relationship between Christian and other religious traditions. We need not go over the ideological ground Danielou shares with Rahner. There are differences in background, training, and emphasis. For example, whereas Rahner has concentrated on systematic theology and philosophy of religion, Danielou has directed his attention toward early Christian history. Furthermore, whereas Rahner belongs consciously to a school of thinkers influenced by the neo-Kantianism of Joseph Maréchal, Danielou cannot be identified with any one school of thought so particularly. But given differences and variations of this kind, Danielou nevertheless shares the same fundamental attitude with Rahner: that Christianity can be regarded as the transformer of the other religious traditions because it was uniquely formed by revealed truth. Danielou's task is to formulate this conception in such fashion that it does not exclude the value of other religions or imply either contempt or disdain. He writes: "What we are saying here should not be misunderstood. In no way is it a question of deprecating the examples of the interior life which we find in non-Christian religions."

Because Danielou was more of a student of the religious traditions than Rahner, however, he can be more specific in his attitude toward them. For example, he noted that Christianity must always give emphasis to precise historical events; other religious traditions, by contrast, can rely on the cultivation of the interior life of individual persons. By emphasizing historical events, the Christian religion subscribes to "the intervention of the eternal in time." Danielou believed that other religions argue for an eternal world but show no propensity for divine intervention into the present world. In his view, Christianity understands Jesus' role to be both decisive and essential; other religions elevate other religious figures or understand Christ merely in an archetypal, symbolic fashion. Danielou was also distressed by the prospect that the fundamental Christian doctrines are implicit, though in disguised or inexplicit form, in the other religions. He was aware of the real differences in this respect. Yet even after he could find no real analogs to Christianity elsewhere, he was unwilling to write them off:

> Does this mean that the natural religions have not attained certain truth concerning God? Such a statement would be inaccurate. St. Paul himself teaches that "since the creation of the world, the invisible perfections of God are known through visible things." The non-Christian religions have been able to grasp that which human reason left to itself is capable of discovering, that is, God's exterior, his existence, and his perfection as these are manifest through his action in the world.

In another place Danielou adds that "compared with Christianity, the pagan religions seem out of date and distorted," noting that "still, they contain some worthwhile elements."

Danielou's is an ambivalent attitude toward religions other than his own. He cannot give them full status, and yet believes that their complete disappearance from the world "would constitute an impoverishment of the human spirit." But, believing that his attitude, as attitude, is orthodox, he reminds his readers of the wisdom of papal teaching on the subject: "The church has never treated the doctrines of the pagans with contempt and disdain; rather, she has freed them from all error, then completed them and crowned them with Christian wisdom."

The formula Danielou utilizes is the same as the one that informs Karl Rahner's position: *Grace perfects nature without destroying it.* In translation, the principle holds that Christianity brings complementation and perfection to the other religions and religious persuasions, without asking or forcing them to be completely other than they are. The most vivid examples come from Danielou's own field of scholarly expertise:

> Thus we find early Christianity integrating the values of Greek philosophy after having purified them. Thus shall we be able to see in the future Christianity assuming all the values contained in the asceticism of the Hindus, or the wisdom of Confucius, after having purified them.

Raimon Panikkar: The Religious Traditions as Co-contributors to Cross-cultural Understanding

The suggestions made by Danielou have been applied and illustrated in significant detail by Raimon Panikkar (b.1918), Spanish-born theologian of

Spanish-Indian parentage. Because of that lineage, Panikkar seems to live and breathe within a Catholic-Hindu environment. He is distinguished too for being one of a few Christian theologians who possess large firsthand familiarity with the Asian religions they speak and write about, as well as knowing the languages of their primary texts.

Thus the advance Panikkar has made upon former Roman Catholic efforts to come to terms with the other traditions is attributable not solely to his academic training in the history of religions, the history of Christian theology, and the philosophy of science. It also derives from his native affinity for at least two diverse and sometimes variant religions. These are different qualifications from those of Karl Rahner, for example, who approaches non-Christian religions primarily out of Christian theological principles. It is a different approach too from that of Jean Danielou, who brings a historical dimension to theological considerations while restricting his scope to the formative era in Christian history. This focus allows Danielou to concentrate on those religions and philosophies that competed directly against Christianity and were to be found in the same geographical locale and cultural milieu. As a historian of religions both east and west, and as a Christian theologian, Panikkar's interests cover a wider territory. His attitude is also distinctive in that he views Christianity as something other than a competitor in an arena filled with other aspirants toward cultural, religious, and intellectual respectability. When Panikkar thinks of the non-Christian religions, he is thinking both comprehensively, precisely, and in a fundamentally noncombative way. Hence, the form and spirit of his response bear structural similarities to the attitude of Rahner and Danielou, but the detail is more precious, and the arguments are cast in a manner that invites other historians of religion to take them seriously.

Many of the themes we have encountered before are enunciated in Panikkar's writings. From the beginning, he wants to accord and sustain Christianity's normative status. But in doing this he also tries hard to find a way of maintaining normative status in a nonexclusive way. His approach to the distinctiveness of Christianity is via qualifiers that carry a "both-and" rather than an "either-or" set of inferences. Similarly, according to the pattern to which we have become accustomed, Panikkar approaches "non-Christian religions" as being carriers and containers of actual, implicit, and not always conscious religious truths. Where implicit, such truths need to be explicated. Where unrecognized, such contentions need to be brought to consciousness. Rahner approached the issue this way; we saw evidence of the same in the attitude of Danielou. The products of Panikkar's nonpolemical synthetic efforts sound very Christian—witness the title of his best-known book, *The Unknown Christ of Hinduism*. But complexities are always present to keep the comparisons from becoming superficial and to frustrate the interpreter's suspicion that Panikkar's contentions stand as a superb example of a highly cultivated but nevertheless rather traditional Roman Catholic position, similar in disposition to Rahner's and Danielou's.

The uniqueness of Panikkar's perspective derives from the way he envisions the explicative process. In other formulations, the Christian religion is assigned an explicative function with regard to the convictions and beliefs of non-Christian religions. The assumption is that the other religions contain bits and pieces of religious truth, and the task of identifying these truths is left for the Christian interpreter. This familiar pattern of interpretation works to assign the Christian religion the task of explicating the implicit truths of the other religious traditions. The theological warrant for this is to be found in the conception of the relation of grace to nature: "Grace perfects nature without destroying it." In explicating the truths of non-Christian religious traditions, Christianity seeks to bring them to self-realization as well as to a conscious recognition that they must be transcended (perfected) by formulations containing Christian truths. With precedents in such abundance, one would expect this attitude to be prevalent too in Panikkar's writings, especially given the fact that he builds upon explication. But once again, the familiar category is transformed. In his view, it is not simply Christianity that acts as the agent of explication on behalf of a "non-Christian religion." Rather, both the Christian and the other traditions conspire to explicate each other. Both have something substantial to contribute to the dialogue. Each can make a positive contribution to the greater welfare of the other. The religions of the world can affect Christianity as Christianity affects the world's religions. Both sorts of religion are active participants in the explicatory process.

There are additional distinctions in Panikkar's view. Each of the religions can affect the other because both are subject to a process of explication that intends the transformation of all religious traditions. All religions need to be edified, embellished, and transformed into something that none of them alone is capable of representing. Christianity continues to be Panikkar's preferred religion—though perhaps not his favorite one—but he understands that Christianity must also undergo change and reformulations if it is to survive in the situation toward which present religious experience is being directed.

Panikkar is very much devoted to the evolution of religious consciousness, even in corporate terms. Within the history of religious consciousness, the Christian religion has assumed the role of transforming other religious traditions. In transforming them—as, for example, in the third and fourth centuries C.E., when the new religion engaged the religions and philosophies of the ancient Greco-Roman world—Christianity also led them to a stage of development which, in Panikkar's view, they could not have achieved on their own power. But, given the transforming function of Christianity, the history of religious consciousness also points forward to a time—and it may be either present or imminent—when similar transformational enactments will be exercised on all of the living religious traditions, including Christianity. The entire history of religions points to a culmination in which the particular and often exclusive claims of the various religious traditions will be suspended in favor of a total universal outlook to which all of the religions can make a significant contribution. It is not religious eclecticism that Panikkar argues for, but rather a form of collective creative religious work that is dictated by the human family as it moves into the future.

Some of the stresses referred to above were present in Panikkar's position as this was enunciated in his early book, *The Unknown Christ of Hinduism*. Using language appropriate to a pre-Vatican II era, he sought to identify a "hidden force" moving through Hinduism that was tending toward "full disclosure." As could have been expected, Panikkar identified that hidden force as the Christ—the underlying Principle—that also motivates Hindu religion, even though this fact had not yet been made apparent either to Christians or Hindus. Against this background, Panikkar was pleased to announce that the dramatic disclosure is occurring in the present encounter between the two religions. He saw his own task to be one of assisting to help lift the veil, as it were, so that "the unveiled truth may be ready to receive the revealed fullness of Christ." The basis for this view is the contention that Christ is "the fullness of religion and thus the real perfection of every religion." Thus, one of the functions of Christianity is to help "fill out"—as Panikkar himself wants to "lift the veil"—Hindu religious truths. Hinduism needs this. Christianity needs it too. Christianity is dependent upon it in striving to be genuinely universal and fully catholic. The complementarity that the Christian religion offers not only lends extension and coherence to Hinduism, but is also necessary to the development of a nonparochial self-identity.

Panikkar conceives part of his task to be similar to Saint Thomas Aquinas's when the latter had to work through the tenets of the Christian faith in Aristotelian categories of thought. Of course, for Panikkar the challenge is not Aristotelianism, but Hinduism; but the task, nevertheless, is to show the compatibility of the Christian gospel with a previously hostile or alien universe of discourse. Panikkar's thesis is dramatic: The Hindu religion is more compatible with the Christian religion—if for no other reason than that both of them are religions—than Aristotelian philosophy is compatible with Christian theology. The same principle would hold true, we suspect, were the tested example Platonic rather than Aristotelian philosophy. Furthermore, the conjunction of religion with religion might just as well concern Buddhism rather than Hinduism, though each case would offer significant deviations in compatibility. Each religion or philosophy exhibits constellations of materials with which the Christian religion can interact for purposes of a sharpened self-identity, mutual enrichment, and reciprocal edification. It is from this background that Raimon Panikkar is in position to propose large global projects in crossreligious and cross-cultural comparative analysis. His conviction is such that dialectical engagements are uniquely beneficial to the individuals nvolved. Further, they can lead to a significant increase and deepening of human understanding. Beyond this, they provide the most promising instrumentality for a world that chooses global harmony over global disaster.

R. C. Zaehner: Evolution in Teilhardian Form

Raymond Charles Zaehner (1913–1974), who shares certain tendencies both toward catholicity and evolution with Raimon Panikkar, also differed from him in a number of important respects. An Indologist and Sanskritist by training, Zaehner was Spalding Professor of Eastern Religion and Ethics, and Fellow of All Souls College, Oxford. He made his reputation through translations of Upanashadic and Vedic scriptures, careful philological studies, and comparative studies in mysticism. *Mysticism Sacred and Profane* (1957) and *Hindu and Muslim Mysticism* (1960) are just two examples of extensive distinguished scholarship in this area.

Something additional happened to Zaehner after 1955, when he was introduced to the writings of Pierre Teilhard de Chardin (1881–1955). For Zaehner, Teilhard was able to supply the insights, language, and conceptual framework necessary to think sensibly about the contemporary religious situation. As Zaehner put it:

> The appearance in 1955 of Pierre Teilhard de Chardin's *Le Phénomenè humain* and its English translation in 1959 as *The Phenomenon of Man* amounted almost to a revolution in Christian religious thought. . . . For what Teilhard de Chardin has done was to situation the Christian religion within its evolutionary context. This was new and exciting.

Zaehner was captivated by Teilhard's perspective, for he shared the view that humankind has entered a new historical era, an era characterized by "the convergence of mankind in upon itself." This convergence implies that the world's religious traditions are encountering and confronting each other and forcing alterations, revisions, and emendations in their own perspectives, as well as creating intellectual and spiritual opportunities for the sharing of insight and conviction. Clearly, in Zaehner's view, reinforced by the inspiration he received from the writings of Teilhard de Chardin, something new has arisen on the religious horizon, and it will compel the major religions of the world to acknowledge the presence of each other.

> Now for the first time the religions of the world confront each other directly, and it is to be assumed that just as, on the purely secular plane, world unification cannot be long delayed, so, on the religious plane, the present melting pot of religions must, in the long run, simmer down into a coherent whole.

Zaehner believed that religion will follow the pattern whereby political nationalisms eventually yielded to effective international order. Eventually, in his judgment, real religious unity will prevail throughout the world.

As Panikkar did, Zaehner believed that he could already perceive the embryonic form of this religious convergence through eyes that had been trained under Roman Catholic intellectual influence and spiritual nurture. The final convergence of the religions is uniquely tied to the growth of Catholicism toward fullness. Hence, in this capacity, Catholic Christianity functions as the first sign of a much larger explication of natural religious tendencies. The fuller realization of these tendencies also requires an expansion of the Catholic religious edifice. Yet, the convergence is complicated by virtue of the fact that in no conceivable way can it ever be said that the major religious traditions of the world are making identical affirmations. Zaehner recognizes that the differences between them are real and abiding. In his book *Hindu and Muslim Mysticism*, for example, he reminds his readers "that the Hindus entirely differ from us in every respect," and he offers a number of confirming examples. Moreover, Muslims and Hindus differ radically from each other. Consequently, whatever true religious convergence means, it can never be equated with uniformity, or with an eradication of the substantial and prevailing differences between the religions.

Given the addition of a Teilhardian thought pattern, the similarities between Zaehner's and Panikkar's attitudes to the evolution of a universal religious consciousness are obvious. Both find Catholic Christianity to be the source of the principle of inclusion and exclusion. Both see the relationships between the Catholic Christian tradition and the world's religions to be reciprocal: in the growth of the religious traditions, in the tendency toward convergence and mutuality, Catholicism itself is becoming more and more what it is finally intended to be. As the Catholic vision is progressively articulated, it carries transformative abilities both with respect to traditional Catholic teaching and toward the totality of humankind's religious experience. Thus both Zaehner and Panikkar see the present coming together of the world's religions to be guided by the familiar Catholic theological principle that grace perfects nature without destroying it. Both view the meetings, dialogues, and exchanges between religious traditions as being guided by a sacramental view of the universe: visible events and occurrences testify to the workings of an invisible reality. And both identify with the conviction that the invisible reality is becoming better known and more fully expressed through the visible events and occurrences.

But, given these similarities, serious differences of opinion divide these two Catholic theorists. For example, Panikkar depicts the present religious situation as being ripe for dialogues between the major religions. The parties to dialogue are always the representatives of the large religious collectivities—the major religious or cultural *isms*, chief among which are Hinduism and Christianity. Once the parties have been brought together for dialogue, Panikkar focuses on the similarities between the doctrinal or convictional attitudes characteristic of the various religions. As we have noted, frequently such similarities are not discernible until after a series of analogical reinterpretations have been applied to the textual material. Panikkar has a penchant for citing a phrase that typifies one religion's stance, and then showing how the same phrase could be reinterpreted so as to be sponsored by the other religion. Also, as we have noted, his reinterpretation follows the pathway of thesis, followed by threatening antithesis, followed by a relieving and joyful synthesis.

Zaehner works in a much different manner. He shows only incidental interest in the ism-blocks as such, and consequently does not rely on the dynamics of dialogue to effect religious syntheses. For him, the crux of the issue is not necessarily served if Hindus and Christians find a useful language or a range of shared attitudes and convictions. Nor are the large collective entities construed as components of a larger ideological (and, certainly, metaphysical) dialectic that is working itself out in an evolutionary process.

Instead, Zaehner comes to seize on the conviction that in religious matters truth is not the product of patronage. One may find expressions of the truth in a variety of textual loci, but this need not imply that all texts are speaking the truth. Nor does it mean that everything said in any one religion is true. Hinduism, for example, is not necessarily a true religion—Zaehner would have a difficult time speaking about "true religions"—simply because it gives expression to a variety of religious truths. It may be authentic. It may exhibit a variety of religious truths. But it cannot be viewed as being comprehensively true. It is also full of falsehoods, but is certainly not comprehensively false. Religions are neither true nor false but sometimes express truths and sometimes express convictions that are short of the truth.

Furthermore, the history of religions consists of topics of interest regarding which there is a flexible and growing understanding. It may very well happen that the commanding insight into the topic was generated in a particular locale at a given time, and flowed from there to another religious climate. Perhaps on another range of issues a particular religion will have insights of which none of the others are capable. But these occurrences need not signify that one religious ism is more collectively advanced than any of the others. It is the case, instead, that religious truth is not negotiated in terms of systematic collective wholeness. Ranges and subjects of religious interests exist, and there is an increase of insight regarding some of these subjects and interests, but not all at one time, nor in every place or any one place. Religious truth has a self-validating capacity, regardless of the identity or station of its sponsors.

Speaking about the Hindu Vedantic concept of the absolute unity of being, for example, Zaehner notices that it builds upon a "monistic metaphysics on the psychological experience of the absolute oneness of each individual soul in its ontological essence." In recognizing this, Zaehner has placed the notion with a larger conceptual framework where it can be treated as a subject for critical discussion. By referring the Vedantic concept to this larger monistic framework with its attendant history of criticism, Zaehner can state both that the basic idea is "irrational" (by which he may not be saying anything pejorative) and "naive." Then, as is his custom, he cites an authority (in this instance, Buber, the Jewish writer and thinker) who, in Zaehner's view, had unusual insight into both the force and the deceptions of the religious concept. Again, Buber is recommended on his own merits, and not because he is Jewish, or Hassidic, or because of any other collective religious representational ability he might claim.

By means of an application of such critical insights to typical religious formulations, Zaehner addresses the matter of truth and falsity in religion. This also gives him the basis to contend that some religious views (as well as some religious collectivities) cannot survive much longer. As a matter of fact, many of them have not survived into the present. And some existing religions find the present very hard going. The survival factor is regulated by the correlation between the pattern of definiteness that characterizes a particular religion and specific religious and conceptual needs. For example, Indian Yogic mysticism is formed by a desire for self-integration and self-realization. Christian mysticism, however, is formed by the desire for union of one spiritual essence (humanity's) with another spiritual essence (God's). Both attitudes qualify as mysticism, but the two are saying very different things. Rather than contending simply that both strands are necessary to either fullness or true catholicity, Zaehner judges them on the grounds that religion must ultimately secure a place for both body and spirit. This is in keeping with his conviction that it is not enough for religion to concern itself exclusively with individual salvation, as Indian Yogic mysticism seems to do, or with corporate salvation exclusively, as religions that sustain the reality of things physical tend to do. Instead, both tendencies must be honored in any ultimately viable religious stance. Those religions that honor only one of the two necessary tendencies must find the complementarity available to them through the other tendency. Otherwise their deficiencies will be unmasked by the consciousness-effecting religious convergence.

Eventually the onrush of evolution will force true catholicity (Zaehner's norm) to expand toward greater and clearer universality. As this happens, the Christian church will be attaining its full stature, and the twin tendencies, spirit and matter, will be enunciating the reconciliation between themselves that has been inherent and implicit in creation since the beginning. The ultimate goal is a "solidary mankind reconciled to God in Christ and Christ's body, the church."

[T]he Church will continue to grow quietly and perhaps all but unperceived; but she will grow nonetheless slowly attracting to herself all the craving toward unity that lies deep down in the heart of every individual man. The Church herself, . . . proclaiming ever more insistently the indissoluble marriage of Spirit and matter in Christ, and rejecting as emphatically all private attempts at personal spiritualization, will appear ever more *solidaire*—so "solidary" indeed so centered on her divine Founder that all other organizations, because they lack such a center and because they are strangers to a sacramental system that nurtures each individual with the lifeblood of the whole and the blood itself with the Spirit, must inevitably feel the strange attraction she cannot help exercising.

Finally, then, it is the Catholic theological principle, "grace perfects nature without destroying it," that serves as the principle of inclusion and exclusion. This dictum is also applicable to the relationship between spirit and matter: spirit perfects matter without destroying it. The principle is also applicable to the ongoing *élan* by which truth is distinguished from inauthenticity, as collective consciousness comes to greater and more effective self-consciousness. This is the Teilhardian vision, attached to extensive historical inquiry into the genesis and history of religious traditions both east and west.

Paul Tillich: Systematic Theology and the History of Religions

So far in this chapter, with some qualification, we have paid attention primarily to formulations of the relationships between the major religions of the world that have been proposed by Roman Catholic Christian theorists. We have made reference to Hendrik Kraemer and to Nathan Söderblom too, and have suggested that Kraemer understood his approach to be consistent with the theological position of Karl Barth. But we need to explore Protestant Christian alternatives in more detail. To do so, we shall consider the influence of Paul Tillich (1886–1965), Barth's clearest rival, who has also stimulated considerable interest among both theologians and historians of religions. In fact, one can make a strong case for the contention that the academic study of religion gained sufficient intellectual stature to enter the world of the state or public university within the United States and Canada in the late 1950s and 1960s largely because of the Tillichian conceptualization of the theological enterprise. Tillich approached Christian belief in a manner that allowed Christians to develop an openness to religions other than their own, and to approach the devotees of those religions as being something far more than candidates for conversion or proselytization. This historical note can be verified, at least partially, by analyses of the commanding convictions of those who were responsible for establishing academic programs and curricula in religious studies in colleges and universities during the same period of time. In institution after institution, from Bloomington to Tallahassee to Missoula to Santa Barbara, many of the scholars and teachers who took the initiative in organizing religious studies were of a perceptible Tillichian mind. Most of them had been trained in Christian theology in seminaries and divinity schools. Consequently, the curricular models that became operational when such programs were inaugurated gave expression to intellectual transition: Tillich's theology gave its adherents forceful and clear access to the more inclusive cultural worlds, and in ways that could be sanctioned religiously and theologically.

The Tillichian model, as we have described it in the first chapter in this study, was formed by a compelling interest in identifying religion's *sine qua non*, which, as we have also recognized, Tillich called "ultimate concern." Such a principle was useful in establishing that religion was a valid form of human experience. Its formulation and expression were also easy to chronicle in humankind's ongoing religious history. In fact, the principle was so apt that religious traditions of the world can be approached as having been formed and organized around one or another way of identifying and lending expression to "ultimate concern." The student and scholar can address each major religious tradition of the world as having taken responsibility for the identification and protection of something that qualifies as the object of "ultimate concern."

As it turns out, the stance we have outlined is not the one, without refinement, that Tillich stayed with throughout his career. Rather, shortly before his death in October 1965, he gave indication of having undergone same fresh thinking on the subject. The occasion was a lecture on "The Significance of the History of Religions for the Systematic Theologian," which he presented at the University of Chicago. In this now-famous lecture Tillich sketched an emerging approach that was based on the assumption that "revelatory experiences are universally human." It was a new development for him, but one that he understood to be an extension of his previous thinking on the matter, particularly that which he had already presented in his three-volume *Systematic Theology*. The difference was that he had had limited exposure to the world's religions before writing his systematic theological treatises; that exposure had been increased by the time of his October 1965 presentation. In addition, he too had come under the influence of Mircea Eliade, with whom he jointly taught a graduate seminar at the University of Chicago, and this had caused him to look for fresh interpretive perspectives on the matter.

Several theoretical principles, he offered, need to be identified and carefully scrutinized. First, revelation is not unique to Jewish and Christian experience; rather revelation is a universal religious phenomenon. This means that the familiar classification of religions under the two categories "natural" and "revealed" simply does not work. It is a naive distinction. Its bias toward Christianity is blatant. The truth of the matter, Tillich would like to think, is that revealed religion is much more extensive than Judaism and Christianity: it describes humankind's religious experience in its totality. Second, wherever and whenever it occurs, revelation is always received within specific social, cultural, and historical circumstances. It is always apprehended and expressed in a manner reflecting and incorporating actual lived conditions. Such circumstantial conditionality implies that revelation is vulnerable to the distortions that affect all human modes of knowledge. Revelation, as such, is never pure, but must be purified. Third, revelation does not occur simply in isolated instances, here and there, in this instance and in that, at this time and at that time, and so on. Rather, revelation is more process than episodic occurrence. In Tillich's words, "there is an ongoing sequence of revelatory experience." And this ongoing process also includes refinements and correctives of the inevitable distortions and miscommunications. Fourth, Tillich sought to describe the nature or morphology of the revelatory process. In entertaining the possibility that "there *may* be a central event in the history of religions" that blends corrections of distortions with ongoing revelatory experience, Tillich was really pointing to the inner dynamism of the process. But, before enunciating this, he states that ongoing revelatory experience implies continuity and universality. Thus, it is conceivable that revelatory experience can be unified, that it does lead to some culmination, and that it possesses universal scope. Fifth, he identifies the process's fundamental dynamism as the presence or reality of the sacred. The reality of the sacred is also fundamental to the history of culture: "The sacred does not lie beside the secular," he attests, "but it is its depths." Said in another way, "the sacred is the creative ground and at the same time a critical judgment of the secular." In other words, the sacred is the name for the dynamic reality that motivates the ongoing process of revelation. But Tillich was able equally well to refer to the Holy, or to identify that fundamental core element as "the Holy, or the Ultimate, or the Word." The Holy, the Ultimate, or the Word is implicit wherever revelatory experience occurs.

Given these suppositions, Tillich's next responsibility was to provide larger clues regarding the direction and intention of the revelatory process. He initiated this subject by contrasting his position with others that are well known. First, revelation conceived as a dynamic process does not imply progressive development. Thus, he disagreed with G. W. F. Hegel, and with Teilhard de Chardin, regarding the inevitably progressive development of religious consciousness. By contrast, his own view is that the same elements in the experience of the sacred occur again and again. Wherever the sacred reality is implicit, it gives expression to some common fundamental elements: "There is no progressive development which goes on and on, but there are elements in the experience of the Holy which are always there, if the Holy is experienced." These various components are present because the process of revelation plays out a perpetual dynamic tension. The dynamic tension is necessary so that the concrete embodiments of the sacred—or the Holy, or the Ultimate—are not mistaken for the ultimate reality itself. This requires that the dynamic tension include a self-corrective process to insure a constant, recurrent transcendence of all concrete expressions of the ultimate:

The Holy as the Ultimate lies beyond any of its embodiments. The embodiments are justified. They are accepted but they are secondary. One must go beyond them in order to reach the highest, the Ultimate itself. The particular is denied for the Ultimate One. The concrete is devaluated.

Three necessary elements exist in all religion, according to Tillich: (1) the sacramental; (2) the mystical; and (3) the ethical components. The sacramental element is necessary initially so that the Holy will be experienced within the finite. The mystical element is necessary to correct the sacramental tendency toward idolatry; this occurs whenever the sacred is equated or identified too closely with any of its concrete, finite manifestations. And the ethical division is necessary to correct the less-than-positive products of sacramental religion: "the third element in the religious experience is the element of 'ought to be.' This is the ethical or prophetical element. Here the sacramental is criticized because of demonic consequences like the denial of justice in the name of holiness." The product—or creation—of this ongoing sequence of checks and balances is what Tillich called "the religion of the concrete spirit." This religion both posits and denies itself as its intrinsic tension is articulated. Just as the words "the Holy" or "the Ultimate" could be interchanged for "the Sacred" earlier, so too the words "inner *telos*" are equivalent to "concrete spirit." Both designations refer to "that toward which everything drives," that is, the fundamental intrinsic disposition of the revelatory process that testifies, in turn, to the dynamism of sacred reality.

> We can see the whole history of religions in this sense as a fight for the Religion of the Concrete Spirit, a fight of God against religion within religion. And this phrase, the fight of God within religion against religion, could become the key for understanding the otherwise extremely chaotic, or at least seemingly chaotic, history of religions.

This is as far as Tillich could go. This, his "inaugural address" on the relation of theology to the history of religions, was his last lecture. One can only speculate about how he might have articulated his new approach had death not come when it did.

But what does the formula say about theological interpretations of the history of religions? It is clear, initially, that Tillich was simply laying the groundwork. His ideas were not fully formed. Some of them were presented tentatively. All of them were offered as being provisional. Instead of trying to evaluate humankind's religious experience theologically, he was interested simply in establishing rapport between theologically trained interpretive sensibilities and the larger world of global religious experience. It was enough that he stipulate a context or framework within which such evaluations might be conducted later on. Thus, instead of taking religious traditions—or religious truth claims—one by one and examining their interrelationships, he was content to develop a sketch or description of the expressions of the sacred in historical and cultural process terms. His work here too was preliminary and provisional. It could be likened to the initial insight that inspires a prolegomenon. Its function is to point to something that needs to be explored further and to provide some tentative suggestions as to how the approach might be conceived. Tillich recognized that the fuller development would require a new career, if not for himself, at least for systematic theology. But he had been able to establish the foundations.

Earlier he had attempted to offer insightful comments on the nature of the Christian religion by analyzing the contemporary cultural situation. Initially his was a theology of culture—a distinctively and explicitly Christian theology of culture. His method of correlation had worked to bring Christian theology and contemporary culture into working contact with each other. But shortly before his death, he took on something additional which, by his own admission, possessed much larger stakes. His new intention—if not for himself, at least for systematic theology—was to analyze religion by probing the context of humankind's collective religious history. This time through, his intention was not to try to correlate theology and culture but, instead, to bring theology and religious history together. This required new rubrics, a fresh methodological strategy, and the cultivation of unique interpretive categories:

> . . . I must say that my own *Systematic Theology* was written before these seminars [the ones with Mircea Eliade], and had another intention, namely, the apologetic discussion against and with the secular. Its purpose was the discussion or the answering of questions coming from the scientific and philosophical criticism of Christianity. But perhaps we need a longer, more intensive period of interpenetration of systematic theological study and religious historical studies. Under such circumstances the structure of religious thought might develop in connection with another or different fragmentary manifestation of theonomy [the inner aim of the history of religions] or of the Religion of the Concrete Spirit. This is my hope for the future of theology.

This was a new intellectual environment, and it carried the prospect of placing Christian theology on newly resourceful grounds. As Tillich perceived it initially—his remarks were provisional and embryonic—theological interpretations of religious history needed to penetrate the dynamics of the universal revelatory process. When it did this, it would discern that the process is dynamic and contains specific components. These components refer to a certain fundamental intrinsic disposition that characterizes the way the Sacred—or the Holy, or the Ultimate, or the Word— is expressed in concrete terms. The older distinctions between natural and revealed religion have been undercut. The theological interpretation of humankind's religious history is given new terms, but continues to belong, despite its tentativeness, to an idealist Hegelian mold. And, as a consequence, the normative revelatory process looks much like the unfolding of the Christian consciousness of God.

Robert D. Baird: A Tillichian View Made Current

A more traditional Tillichian approach—more dependent on his earlier, less tentative, and less embryonic views—has been made succinct by Robert D. Baird (b.1937) in the preface to his chapter on "Indian Religious Traditions" in an anthology edited by W. Richard Comstock. Baird writes: "If the study of religion is characterized as the study of what is ultimately important to persons and communities, then the study of Indian religious traditions is the study of what has been and is of ultimate importance to Indians." This statement illustrates how Tillich's emphasis might be employed as a way of giving focus to comparative studies of religious traditions: religions are studied in terms of that which they regard as being of ultimate importance. Each of them, that is to say, is characterized by what is identified in both subjective and objective terms as Ultimate Concern.

Baird's elucidation of this methodological point of departure is reserved for a subsequent book, *Category Formation and the History of Religions*, published in 1971. Here Baird refines and extends Tillich's approach, using "ultimate concern" in functional terms. He believes that historians of religions must sidestep the question as to whether there really is an object of ultimate concern somewhere. This, for Baird, is a matter of theological interest, but not a question that historians can appropriately address. It suffices for the historian of religion to be aware that persons and cultures exhibit ultimate concerns, and to recognize that attitudes and behavior within cultures can be explained in no other way. Moreover, it is entirely appropriate that such ultimate concerns be identified; under certain circumstances it is even proper for the scholar to investigate them. Baird explains:

> Hence the study of religion will include the study of the ultimate concerns of persons and communities as well as the subordinate phenomena which are significantly related to such concerns. If the focus of the history of religions is ultimate concern, then the religious dimension of subordinate ideas, symbols, rites, etc., must all be understood in the light of their relation to ultimate concern.

This focus can be exercised with respect to a single religious tradition, or it can serve a cross-cultural function when several religious traditions are analyzed, compared, and contrasted. The study of Chinese religion, for instance, might focus on what has been and remains of ultimate importance to the people of China. The study of primitive religion might attempt to identify what appears to have been of ultimate significance to primitive cultures. Whatever the specific focus, this approach rests on the assumption that wherever religion is present, ultimacy is ascribed to something or someone. Thus, the category of ultimacy is given content wherever there is a religious tradition. The content will vary since a variety of religious traditions exist, but ultimacy will be implicated in every instance. The stipulation of what is identified as being ultimate is what most characteristically gives a religion its shape and specifiable range of interest and concern.

In approaching the purpose of comparative religion studies in these terms, Baird could invoke the authority of Paul Tillich. Indeed, even in his famous last lecture, Tillich subscribed to the belief that the various religions could be approached in terms of their characteristic responses to what he called "the question of the intrinsic aim of existence." It is in relation to this question that Christianity attempts to describe something of the Kingdom of God and Buddhism resonates towards nirvana. The religious category is single: the question is the same regardless of the religion that is being interrogated. But the answer will vary from religion to religion because the content differs, and because the historical, cultural, and religious circumstances are distinctive.

Baird can approach the subject of comparative studies this way, and can offer useful distinctions to describe differences and similarities between the major religious traditions of the world. Indeed, using "ultimate concerns" as a means of conducting comparative analyses of the religious traditions need be nothing more than careful descriptive work. But analytical work becomes something additional when the analyst checks each religious tradition to see if it makes an idol of what it has identified as the Ultimate Concern. To take an expression of ultimacy as if it were ultimacy itself, in Tillich's view, is to fall victim to a conceptually mistaken and religiously idolatrous equation. The ultimate—the real Ultimate—resides beyond all expressions of ultimacy, and, by maintaining their concreteness, prevents them from being taken for more than they really are.

Christianity is authentic, Tillich would say, because it testifies to the reality of "the God beyond the gods." In other words, Christianity is normative because its conception of ultimacy actually frustrates the prescription of ultimacy to anything that is less than ultimate. Other religions and world philosophies become "quasi-religions" because they fall victim to an idolatrous equating of the ultimate with objects or ideals obviously specific, literal, and transitory. Tillich referred to the Christian religion as being normative on the basis of its fullness, richness, and accuracy of expression. (In so doing, he was simply following the intellectual tendency identified in the first chapter of our study—Rudolf Otto's presentation comes immediately to mind.) Yet, in Tillich's use of the paradigm, there are built-in safeguards to prevent the Christian expression of ultimacy from functioning specifically and literally. When greater specificity is required, Christianity possesses a unique status among religions because it recognizes that two necessary and fundamental tendencies must be honored together: (1) the tendency to remove the conditions of idolatry absolutely; and (2) the "need for a balance between the concrete and the absolute"—a need that, according to Tillich, "drives man toward trinitarian structures." Christianity finds a place for both tendencies.

Baird, on the other hand, did not use the Tillichian approach to ascribe a normative status to the Christian religion, or even to what is sometimes referred to as "the Judeo-Christian tradition." His objective was simply to create a method of comparative analysis that was equipped to come to terms with the formative and definitive features of a religious tradition, and to be able to provide principled assurances that this method did not place any of the religious traditions in any privileged place. By focusing on inherent "ultimate concerns" as a way of coming fundamentally to terms with the primary characteristics of selected religious traditions, Baird believed that he had given religious studies scholarly sanctions and freedoms to conduct its work in ways that were above criticism. Such methods could not be criticized on grounds that scholars were focusing only on surface—and therefore superficial—features of a religion, for the identification of a religion's "ultimate concern" penetrated to the core: a religion's ultimate concern qualifies as that without which a religion would not be what it is. And, from the other side, Baird's approach could not be criticized on grounds that it had favored one of the religious traditions—for example, by deciding which rendition of ultimacy is most authentic and compelling. Rather, because what is truly ultimate lies beyond any and all expressions of ultimacy, all religions enjoy the same status. Baird believes that the approach he is recommending performs two essential tasks at once: it penetrates to the heart or core of the religion in question, and it does so in a way that cannot be criticized for being religiously or theologically preferential.

Sarvepalli Radhakrishnan: East Viewing West

Sarvepalli Radhakrishnan (1888–1975), Indian statesman and Hindu philosopher, has cultivated an approach to this subject that is somewhat similar, at least in spirit, to that of Paul Tillich, while being representative of an attitude that has been influenced by Indian philosophy. This attitude refuses to approach the world's religions as participants in the conflict between truth and falsehood, or even as competitors to truth. In Radhakrishnan's view, no religious tradition has an exclusive right to truth. No religious tradition, by itself, is the normative religious tradition. Rather, the approach to truth in religion is motivated and regulated by a more generous spirit.

For Radhakrishnan, humankind is one—a single family—and the fundamental teachings of the various religions of the world can be reconciled with each other. In fact, Radhakrishnan was bold to proclaim the advent of a universal religion toward whose realization he finds the separate traditions groping to find their way. As he puts it: "If we do not bring together in love those who sincerely believe in God and seek to do his will, if we persist in killing one another theologically, we shall only weaken men's faith in God." This requires cooperation instead of competition between the major religious traditions of the world: "If the great religions continue to waste their energies in a fraticidal war instead of looking upon themselves as friendly partners in the supreme task of nourishing the spiritual life of mankind, the swift advance of secular humanism and moral materialism is assured."

Radhakrishnan desires unity and cooperation between the religions of the world so that peace might be given an opportunity:

> [W]e cannot afford to waver in our determination that the whole of humanity shall remain a united people, where Muslim and Christian, Buddhist and Hindu shall stand together bound by common devotion, not to something behind but to something ahead, not to a racial past or a geographical unit, but to a great dream of a world society with a universal religion of which the historical faiths are but branches.

He can speak of "a universal religion" to which all of the religions of the world are connected since he affirms that all have sprung from "the same generic tradition."

Thus, for Radhakrishnan, any partial or self-possessed truth within the religious domain must be regarded with suspicion, for abiding truth is always impartial as well as being universally applicable. This thesis becomes the rule by which the validity of all religious traditions is judged. In principle, no religion is valid if it claims special or exclusive access to the truth. Validity can be ascribed only to the *unity* of religious experience—a unity that transcends all finite, temporal, concrete, and partial formulations. For Radhakrishnan, as for Tillich and Panikkar, truth is a property of the ideal. When the ideal is qualified, truth has been tampered with. To qualify or modify the ideal is to reduce truth to something less than truth. Thus, all contentions regarding the qualified ideal are misleading, for they describe a state of affairs that has already become defective. Indeed, it was by virtue of the fact that religions sometimes ascribe normative status to partial and parochial insights that Radhakrishnan found it necessary and appropriate to sound his alarm. His universal religion is antidote to the parochializing tendency.

Ewert H. Cousins: Global Religious Unity and the Progression of Axial Periods

Similar in spirit to the proposals offered by Raimon Panikkar is the vision of Ewert H. Cousins (b.1927), an expert in medieval Christian theology at Fordham University in New York. Cousins takes as starting point the argument that any global assessment of the future of religion must be global from the beginning, and this requires the analyst to think carefully of the consequences of the long sweep of human consciousness to which religious understanding must be correlated. Taking cues from suggestions and proposals offered by Karl Jaspers in his book *The Origin and Goal of History*, Cousins distinguishes between two great axial periods. The first period, to be dated approximately between 800 and 200 B.C.E, witnessed the dawning of the mode of human consciousness that produced the great religious traditions; it was informed by the teachings of such personages as Socrates, Plato, and Aristotle in Greece, the prophets in Israel (principally Elijah, Isaiah, and Jeremiah), Buddha and the seers of the Upanishads in India, and by Confucius and Lao-tse in China. All of the major religions of the world were formed at this time, so too theological reflection, so too theological reflection within an intellectual context that included the arts and sciences. And one of the primary products of the first axial age, in Cousins's view (as influenced by Jaspers), is that human beings developed individual consciousnesses and were able personally to experience the truths of their respective religions.

With the second axial age, the period prevailing now, human needs shifted. Instead of being preoccupied with the cultivation of individuality, human beings are now looking for opportunities for cooperation and convergence. Cousins finds that human beings are exhibiting a desire to form a human family so that the human race might be drawn together "into an organic whole." This is the new global consciousness as differentiated from the individual consciousness that characterized the previous stage or state of human awareness and sensitivity:

> [T]he diverse peoples of the earth are being interrelated on the surface of the earth through an organic network of communication. This complexity on the surface of the earth is producing a new collective interiority, which constitutes the essence of the new global consciousness. It is global . . . because a deep sense of relationship, arising from the center of the person, links the person primarily to the human community as a whole—not primarily to the historically divergent cultures, nations and tribes.

Cousins is optimistic about the outcome: "This sense of relatedness to the whole human race in its organic interconnectedness around the earth can radiate out to establish new concrete relationships among the countless individuals and groups that make up the global community."

What has all of this to do with the relationships perceived between various religious traditions of the world? Cousins's response is that the consciousness that has emerged with the dawning of the second axial period has encouraged the religions of the world to engage in dialogue. Instead of viewing themselves as competitors, or as offering rival claims to some single-minded construction of the truth, the religions are encountering one another in an atmosphere of mutual trust and respect. Greater understanding is occurring between them than has ever been present before, and this understanding is growing through continued and increasing contact. As Cousins puts it, "Instead of defending their beliefs and refuting the opposition, religions are striving to understand each other, to determine what they share in common, and to respect their differences." Evidence of this is found, for example, in the interest Christians are exhibiting in the philosophies and ways of life of India and China, and in the growing number of comparative studies of Eastern and Western theoreticians. In addition, devotees of the various religious traditions are reading each others' sacred scriptures, and are approaching their truths seriously in the spirit of openness. Cousins believes that these dialogues are more of a spiritual than of an academic nature, and yet he remains confident that scholarship will assist the endeavor. So hopeful is he that he approaches the emerging dialogue of the world's religions as representing "the distinctive spiritual journey of our time."

John Dunne: Faith Seeking Understanding in a Global Religious Context

While Ewert Cousins approaches the emerging cooperation between the religious traditions of the world as a spiritual journey, the American Catholic theologian John Dunne (b.1929) prefers to treat pilgrimage as an occurrence involving individuals primarily. His proposals are offered in the book *The Way of All the Earth*, published in 1972. Written from an Augustinian standpoint, the book understands that "faith seeks understanding" within a comprehensive religious environment. Dunne is well aware of the fact that the religions of the world cannot possibly agree on every issue, even though they are able to establish some compelling interrelationships. But he makes no attempt to offer a scheme that might explain these relationships. Instead, he describes the distinctive qualities of the various religious traditions as a pilgrim might encounter them were they conceived as stations or orientational points along the pathway of pilgrimage. Similar to the structure of Joseph Campbell's *Hero with a Thousand Faces*, Dunne's odyssey reflects a sequential ordering of departure, initiation, and return: a journey away from home territory leads to a series of new encounters with accompanying self-discoveries, and these are followed by a return to the starting point with fresh appreciation. In Dunne's view, it is helpful for the Christian to walk out of his/her tradition, to "pass over" into another cultural or religious tradition. But the "passing over" is followed by a "coming back" to the familiar territory with pilgrimage-awakened perceptiveness.

Thus *The Way of All the Earth* is religious autobiography. Its author both recommends the pilgrimage and illustrates it by identifying some of the insights the pilgrim might acquire in "passing over" to a religion or culture that had been unfamiliar territory. In the course of his journey, the Christian pilgrim learns that guidance can be received from luminary figures in other religious traditions. The Buddha and the prophet Mohammed are mentioned prominently as trustworthy companions of the pilgrim. The pilgrimage is rich, variegated, and long enough to enable the pilgrim to encounter most of the inspirational figures in the religions of the world as fellow travelers on the way. Dunne does not wrestle with whatever philosophical or theoretical problems are involved in wanting to make the cardinal truth claims of the religions of the world compatible with each other. To do so would be contrary to the spirit of the journey. In fact, if one could do this in advance of the journey, the journey itself would lack the appropriate anticipation and excitement. Dunne is motivated by the potential culmination of the pilgrimage, and much less so with the specific terms of entry. In this respect he proposes that the pilgrimage is destined, perhaps, to create new religious orientations. This is not something that can be programmed, however. It is a prospect that is "dawning" rather than being constructed. But as it happens, its configuration promises to be unlike any of the religious traditions that have been formalized before:

> Although it has been many centuries since a great religion shook the world, maybe one is rising now out of the meeting and confluence of the religions of the past. Gandhi's "experiments with truth" are perhaps an indication of what this religion may be like. Its truth need not be simply the common ground of the previous religions. Rather it may be a more comprehensive truth like that to which Gandhi was led by trying to live both the Gita and the Gospel.

Dunne is able to maintain this elastic view because of the way the pilgrimage functions. The pilgrimage is comprehensive enough to take in everything that is instrumental to its formation. Thus it can even contain the interreligious distinctions and contrasts that tend to defy all attempts at conceptual systematization. It does this because its fundamental goal is self-knowledge. In Dunne's view, the teachings of the great religions of the world are not first of all arguable ideas, to be accepted, approved, or rejected. Instead, they function as potential sources of insight, to be gathered and appropriated by the pilgrim in that ever-developing odyssey toward increased human understanding. In the typical Augustinian pattern, one "goes abroad" in order to turn more profoundly inward. The spiritual life of the individual person is cultivated through explorations in interior space and time. The journey of "crossing over" and "coming back" is a journey toward self-identity. Nowhere is it suggested that the pilgrim should approach the teachings of the great religions as being alien or dangerous to religious understanding. These teachings are never placed in an adversarial relationship to each other. Nor must they be sanctioned before they can be incorporated into the ever-widening perspective that Dunne portrays as being decidedly Christian. He simply assumes that the pilgrimage is positive and nonthreatening. Hence, inquiry into relationships between Christianity and the religions of the world—and the same would be true, in principle, were the origin of the pilgrimage in Buddhism, or Hinduism, or in any of the other religious traditions—can be rid of all polemics.

Jacob Needleman: Eastern and Western Religions in New Fusions

In the writings of Jacob Needleman (b.1934), comparative studies in religious traditions are blended with sustained interest in the occurrence of "new religions" and new religious movements that blend insights from Eastern and Western cultures.

Trained in philosophy at Yale, Needleman found himself obliged to teach courses in philosophy of religion when he became a member of the faculty at San Francisco State University in the middle 1960s. Accordingly, he set out to deepen his knowledge of the subject by observing and studying prominent "religious phenomena" within the state of California, only to discover that the phenomena were regulated by a series of exchanges between Eastern and Western religious currents. Needleman sensed that the exchanges implied something more than increased awareness of the presence of other religions. But it was happening informally and unofficially, without being sanctioned or even encouraged by professional organizations, and it appeared to involve dimensions and components of development that reached far beyond what was intended by the ecumenical movement.

As he looked into the matter further, Needleman became convinced that the fusing of Eastern and Western religious currents belonged to the gradual and progressive unfolding of the religious mood or sensibility of the time. Within this context, he concerned himself less with cross-cultural comparisons of the religious traditions, and much more with the distinctive hybrids that were being formed by the coalescing of these various religious and cultural strains. In time, he came to focus on the "new religions"—the synthetic, syncretistic hybrid forms of religion that had been created out of the fusing of these religious currents. Of course, he took note of the growing number of Westerners whose religious self-consciousness had been affected by Asian religions. And he is well aware of ways in which that same self-consciousness can be nurtured by depth psychology as well as by the aspirations of the counterculture.

Thus, rather than approaching religious traditions as being clearly identifiable constructs, Needleman concentrated on current examples of fusion between Eastern and Western religious tendencies. Within this context, he is particularly intrigued by the innovative, idiosyncratic, and often unusually irregular manner in which such religious enthusiasms are bundled. Yet, while he recognizes the informal manner in which such fusions have occurred, he firmly believes that the teachings of the "new religions" carry the power "to change the religious life of the western world."

Eventually he took his knowledge of this innovative syncretistic activity as a way of reconsidering the dynamics of historical religious traditions, particularly Islamic Sufism and early and medieval Christianity. On the latter subject he wrote a book, *Lost Christianity*, to identify a rich strain of spiritual nurture that has been underemphasized in the history of Christian theology but is thoroughly compatible with contemporary religious currents. Indeed the subtitle of *Lost Christianity* is *A Journey of Rediscovery to the Center of Christian Experience*. Along the way, he also sought to bring modern scientific knowledge in line with ancient philosophical truth. In all of these endeavors he suggests that contemporary rediscoveries of the essence of the religious life can also be employed as avenues into the richness of ancient wisdom, wisdom that would include the abiding truths to which the religious traditions testify.

When we relate Needleman's work to that of others chronicled in this chapter, we notice, significantly, that the element of vested interest is absent. This makes Needleman's work fundamentally unlike that, say, of Aelred Graham, whose book *Zen Catholicism* (1963) strives to sanction fusions between Christianity and Buddhism on Christian theological grounds. For Needleman, the next step is not sanction or apologetics, but a sustained interest in identifying rudimentary religious factors, regardless of their sources and cultural environments.

As noted, Needleman has been fascinated with the fusing and blending of Eastern and Western religious currents. But he is also intrigued by the attempt to identify an underlying fundamental religious substratum. Thus his inquiries mediate between expressed present religious need and the world's religious traditions. He emphasizes that human beings have an obligation to learn, and relearn, how to appropriate authentic religious truths. He is also taken with the possibility that something like a primordial religion functions at the base of all cultures, whether Eastern and Western or ancient and modern. In this respect, Needleman is much intrigued by the proposals of the French scholar René Guenon, who has influenced a number of thinkers to consider the possibility of a primordial religious tradition. Needleman summarizes Guenon's position as follows:

> Writing in the 1930s and 1940s, Guenon posited the existence of what he called a Primordial Tradition, a body of the highest universal truths, or Principles, as he called them, that lie at the heart of every authentic religion. The various traditions are each a manifestation of this Primordial Tradition, and each is a path toward the practical realization of these Principles in the life of man.

At the heart of each authentic religion, in Guenon's view, are these deep-seated, primordial, and perhaps archetypal religious elements, which gain expression in culture, and which are also responsible for the vitality of the religious traditions. Accordingly, cultures serve as the vehicle through which the primordial elements flow to influence contemporary life. Needleman explains: "For Guenon, all civilization worthy of the name serves a spiritual function: to act as a channel for the influence of tradition upon every sphere of human life."

Within this framework, given this pervasive cultural dynamism, it is conceivable to Needleman that much of the current religious ferment in the world can be interpreted as a search to identify true, lasting, and authentic religious roots.

Even the phenomenon called "the new religions" can be placed this way. The interest in Eastern religious currents on the part of Westerners may be a sign that Western religion—and Western culture—is no longer cognizant of its sustaining forces. These developments are evidence that modern humanity is detached from its most fundamental, sustaining root factors. Needleman summarizes this possibility as follows:

> In cutting himself off from Primordial Tradition, modern man cut away the only hope he could ever have to struggle for that individual transformation of being that is both the highest potentiality of human life and the one goal that justifies all the burdens and sufferings of man on earth.

The next question concerns the possibility of recovery. Is it possible for this contemporary human being, now separated from those fundamental roots, to rediscover them? Or is the distortion consequent upon alienation so pervasive, so deep, that no chance of rediscovery is available? Needleman asks:

> Is the eternal energy that created the revelations of old incapable of manifesting anew in these conditions? What forms would this new "revelation" take? Or, is the fact that we feel ourselves called upon to choose—to choose in the absence of understanding and cut off from that in ourselves that is connected to the force of will—is this fact itself a sign not that we have removed ourselves from tradition, but that on the contrary the established traditions have removed themselves from us and have lost sight of the shifting balance of strength and weakness peculiar to our time and place?

Suffice it to say that Needleman is hopeful about the outcome but does not regard any positive resolution of the dilemma as a foregone conclusion.

We have traced enough of the orientation within this chapter to be able to illustrate that Needleman's and Guenon's approaches to the subject of religion are motivated by a different spirit than prevails in many of the methodological points of departure that we have surveyed. Many of the other examples of comparative inquiries in religion have regarded one single religion as being normative, and then have examined the others in relation to the norm. Or, should it happen that the norm does not reside in any one religion, a variation on the approach might propose that all of the identified religious traditions, at least at bottom, are regulated by the same normative element. And a variation on this theme would have it that if the norm has not been articulated yet, it will be someday. To this latter interpretation can be added the conviction that the history of humankind is progressing toward the time of full disclosure.

Needleman and Guenon are intrigued by the single norm proposal, and yet both believe that the task of enunciating this normative principle is frustrated by a multilayered distortion process. The human apprehension of the roots of religious experience is inexact because of these distortions. The further contemporary social and cultural experience moves away from their abiding and formative roots, the greater the distortion—indeed, the greater the spiritual blindness. But, no matter how difficult to discern, the primordial substratum is the measure, sanction, and occasion for any and all religious traditions. All of them are nurtured by it whether they recognize this fact or not. And the religious ferment within contemporary cultural experience is a powerful sign that human beings need and want to reestablish appropriate rapport with the deepest wellsprings of resilient religious life.

Frithjof Schuon: Unity among Religions and Temperamental Casts

Similar in intent is the work of Frithjof Schuon (b.1907), who, like René Guenon, has worked to identify common or universal characteristics of religious traditions, all under the supporting auspices of a comprehensive theology. Schuon's large contribution to the subject has been assisted by Huston Smith, who is outspokenly impressed with Schuon's vision and perspicacity, as he indicated in his introduction to the English translation of *Schuon's De L'Unité Transcendante des Religions.*

Schuon's preoccupation is with the "unity and diversity of religious traditions." His goal is to maintain differences between traditions while demonstrating their deep and intrinsic underlying unity. His thesis is that "religions are alike at heart or in essence while differing in form." That is, the distinctions between religions are referred to the distinctions between essence and form. The difference between essence and form is no simple distinction. It takes into account that reality is characterized by levels or grades, that human temperaments differ, and that the classic philosophical distinction between essence and accident can be modulated into (though never equated with) the distinction between exoteric and esoteric. In effect, the distinctions between religions are interrelated with distinctions between temperamental casts of mind, which, in turn, are undergirded by gradations within the nature of reality.

In Schuon's view, religions divide the way human temperaments are distinguishable, and human temperaments can be distinguished this way because of the character of the nature of reality, and reality is this way because it functions to comprehend diversity within an overarching unit and coherence. Thus, to say that "religions are alike at heart or in essence while differing in form" is to recognize that differentiation applies only to that level or domain of reality where it is possible to distinguish between subject and object, knower and known, and human and divine. At some less differentiated place on the scale of gradations, the same distinctions become transcended; and at the highest point there is undifferentiated unity. The various religions testify together to the several stages or levels that are comprehended by the scale. So also do religious temperaments. Some persons, for example, display a fascination for the specific, the concrete, the exoteric, while others of a more metaphysical bent take their religious orientation from "undifferentiated unity." Exoteric temperaments tend to be attached to a specific set of historical circumstances, a definite creed, uniquely sanctionable religious texts, and particularity in its many visible forms. The esoteric are less dependent on special circumstances, specificity, objectivity, historicity, and concreteness, and tend to be motivated by infinite, eternal, and formless essences. Religious traditions reflect these same temperamental distinctions; but all of them are comprehensible together because of reality's fundamental unity and coherence. Such unity and coherence are apparent, Schuon believes. They are given, implicit, enjoying an *a priori* status. Thus, the interaction between religious traditions can be likened to the workings of *grammars of discursiveness.* Discursiveness breaks up what is also unified and coherent. Discursiveness presupposes an abiding permanence to which it stands in contrast.

Schuon's scheme, in short, is based on obvious Neoplatonic leanings and enthusiasms. Not only are reality graded and human temperaments distinguished, but the same gradations and distinctions are also implicitly evaluated. Thus, the esoteric is not only different from the exoteric, but it is also placed at greater distance away from the undifferentiated unity.

In some of the other formulations we have encountered in this chapter, one of the major religions of the world (most often Christianity) was regarded as the normative instance, and the other religions were judged in comparison with it. But in Schuon's outlook, "mystical religion"—that is, the religious posture most devoid of concreteness, specificity, objectivity, and so on—is accorded highest place.

One wonders if the religious traditions have actually been distinguished from each other, or if, instead, all of them have been assigned some appropriate place within a hierarchically ordered Neoplatonic-influenced intellectual schematism. And yet, for those who have been influenced by them, the power of Schuon's suggestions lies in their author's in-depth familiarity with the specifics of the major religious traditions of the world.

Huston Smith: The Primordial Tradition in Religion

Any recitation of the proposals of René Guenon and Frithjof Schuon must include repeated reference to the work of Huston Smith (b.1919), the American philosopher of religion whose readable survey of the religious traditions, *The Religions of Man,* has functioned as a primary introduction to the subject for countless undergraduate students over the years. This little book was inspired by Smith's recognition of the distinctivenesses of the major religions of the world. In describing their individuality and variety, he focused on their respective intentions and their underlying motivational factors.

Readers of *The Religions of Man*, including students who are introduced to the subject via this text, come away with a tutored sense that the major religions of the world differ from each other because they respond to distinctive questions in characteristic ways. This is a markedly different approach from one that says that religions differ by virtue of the fact that they respond to the same question in distinctive ways. In *The Religions of Man*, Smith illustrated that the philosophical environments are distinctive too, and that the major religious traditions of the world represent distinguishable orientations within a world that includes a multiplicity of religious interests and aspirations.

Eventually, however, Smith published a companion volume to *The Religions of Man*. In this book, *Forgotten Truth: The Primordial Tradition*, he examined the other side of the same issue. While previously he had presented the truths of the religions of the world in their variety and multiplicity, he employed *Forgotten Truth* as an instrument to explore their convergences. His thesis is presented in a straightforward manner: though there is evident variety among the religious traditions of the world, beneath that variety is "a remarkable unity." The primary analogy is that of the human body: "When we look at human bodies, what we normally notice is their surface features, which of course differ markedly. Meanwhile on the insides the spines that support these motley physiognomies are structurally very much alike." Applying this distinction between "inner" and "outer" to the situation in religion, Smith continues: "It is the same with human outlooks. Outwardly they differ, but inwardly it is as if an "invisible geometry" has everywhere been working to shape them to a single truth."

To lend intellectual force to his claim that there is an "invisible geometry" that stands as the intrinsic basis of unity between the religions of the world, Smith offers several proposals. In the first place, he believes that scientific investigations apply only to those realms of existence to which science possesses reliable access, beyond which realms there are a number of others. In other words, science represents a viewpoint, indeed, a rather restricted viewpoint, which needs to be complemented by other viewpoints. Smith explains:

> Taken in its entirety, the world is not as science says it is; it is as science, philosophy, religion, the arts, and everyday speech say it is. Not science but the sum of man's symbol systems, of which science is but one, is the measure of things.

Secondly, Smith does not believe that the general conception of things that developed from the Enlightenment period is necessarily normative, or even that it represents progress (for Smith, there is a basis for hope, which is markedly different from confidence in progress) over previous orientations to life. In fact, Smith wishes to affirm that the fundamental attitude of those human beings frequently denigrated as "precivilized," and certainly the attitude of those who lived prior to the dawn of modernity, possessed a multivalent sophistication that has been lost in the reductionistic dispositions of post-Enlightenment human beings. The ability to conceive of the world hierarchically, which was too quickly displaced by nearly blind obedience to the dictates of the scientific method, carried certain cognitive and spiritual capacities that enriched the religious life of those so oriented. This ability, in Smith's view, seems to have been prevalent the world over until a particular point in human history.

To be able to think hierarchically enables one to appreciate the intentions of classical Greek philosophy. It also provides reliable access to the world of the mystery religions. And, without question, it stimulates sensitivity to depth psychology, the writings of Carl G. Jung, the fundamental teachings of all of those religious traditions that distinguish levels or dimensions of selfhood, and to all religious, philosophical, and psychological orientations that correlate levels of selfhood with dimensions of reality. This is the key for Smith. By rekindling the spark of sensitivity to the intellectual and spiritual environments within which the ancient traditions arose, he believes he has done something to reestablish the conditions by which apprehension of those same truths and insights can be reborn. It is to this body of insight that the religious traditions of the world bear witness. The knowledge they both protect and transmit is authentic self-knowledge, for the environment they are both probing and reflecting is altogether continuous with "the stuff of which the mind is composed."

Therefore, Smith both makes and illustrates his point by drawing upon the literature of a variety of religious traditions. Here he can demonstrate that Buddhist insights, for example, are reflected in Sufi insights, which in turn are reflected in Jewish and Christian insights—that is, if one knows where to look. And the same insights that are shared by the major religions are also reflected and enunciated in the literature of depth psychology, in certain metaphysical interpretations and extensions of scientific discovery, in dream analysis, in the experience of the mystics, and, not least, in the fundamental teachings of the first philosophers. Therefore, Smith can attest that the primordial tradition is not simply some recent theoretical construct, nor is it an esoteric development that at all times runs in contrast to whatever viewpoint has prevailed. On the contrary, the primordial tradition is both the most venerable and the most universal viewpoint the world has known, which, for moderns, has been obscured from view. In his words: "That there have been in this world, and are today in lingering pockets, metaphysical doctrines that are complete along with means for their realization—this is a notion that for moderns is barely conceivable, but it has emerged as [our] thesis."

Ninian Smart: Religion as Multidimensional Organism

The most straightforward of comprehensive and systematic attempts to compare and contrast the major religious traditions of the world according to criteria proposed by phenomenology of religion is Ninian Smart's textbook study *The Religious Experience of Mankind*

(1969) and successor portrayals. We refer to it as being straightforward because it is specific, detailed, and, most importantly, self-possessed. Unlike Max Weber, for example, Smart (b.1927) does not arrive at the religious traditions after engaging in complex theoretical analyses of the components of larger sociocultural ideological stances. Nor does he treat the religious traditions as testing ground for more extensive methodological or cultural issues. Unlike Talcott Parsons, Smart does not turn to religious traditions to illustrate how patterns of social integration work. And, unlike Joachim Wach, he can specify an approach to religion's multidimensionality which argues for more than that religions should be approached in a multidimensional way. He is not searching for the alien factor within the religious context, or for the religious factor in some other context.

Instead, without flourish or methodological brocade, Smart contends that religions consist of strands or dimensions—John Henry Newman might have called them "notes"—that are present in various degrees of emphasis in the various traditions. The strands or dimensions are six in number (though Smart never insists that his list is intended to be taken as exhaustive): doctrine, mythology, ethics, ritual, social institutions, and religious experience.

> To sum up our account so far of what religion is: it is a six-dimensional organism, typically containing doctrines, myths, ethical teachings, rituals, and social institutions, and animated by religious experiences of various kinds. To understand the key ideas of religion such as God and nirvana, one has to understand the pattern of religious life directed toward these goals.

As noted, not all dimensions are present in the same degree in all religions. But the crucial factor is that the manner according to which they are present, interrelated, and juxtaposed gives a religion its internal dynamism as well as its morphological character. As an example of the interrelatedness and interpenetration of the dimensions, Smart employs the language of organism, referring from time to time to "the anatomy of religion." The intention is to demonstrate that doctrine is related to myth and both are related to ethical stance. In the author's chosen phrase, the several strands "hook up" with each other because they belong to a unified organism. Within the context of that organism, they own a reciprocal relationship to each other.

In *The Phenomenon of Religion*, Smart elucidates and adds some flourishes to the schema that were not present in the original treatise. Here the author proposes that there are both "external and internal explanations" of religious phenomena. The six-dimensional account qualifies as internal explanation, which "involves trying to show the explanatory connection of an item or items in one dimension with an item or items in another dimension." But there is another large perspective on the subject that attempts to do something other than identify, as it were, the components of an anatomy. Smart refers to this as "external explanation" because it attempts "to show how religious items are shaped by structures not in themselves falling wholly within the territory marked out by the definition of religion." He cites several crucial examples:

> For instance, the shape of a particular myth may be in part determined by the exigencies of the kinship-system in the society in which it is recited. More sweepingly, the dominance of mother-goddesses in certain phases of religions might be at least partially ascribed to the emergence of agriculture. Conversely, some features of a society may be heavily influenced by religion itself, in which case the direction of the explanation runs the other way.

Such differentiating elements do not belong to the category of "internal explanation" because they cannot be reduced to the intrinsic interaction of the components of the organism. Rather, they are outside, or "external explanations," because they belong to the particular characteristics of the environment within which the religion has arisen, and in terms of which it achieves specification and definition.

By virtue of internal and external characteristics, religions are formed in and through the interaction they have with the social environments through which they are nurtured. And this is why, in Smart's view, the scientific study of religion is dependent on the contributions of a variety of fields and disciplines. The reciprocity between internal and external factors can neither be identified nor understood apart from the methods and insights of sociology of religion, psychology of religion, history of ideas, history of art, history of music, literature, and so on. Indeed, the range of disciplines that can contribute to the depth and integrity of religious studies is virtually as wide as the range of the arts and the sciences. But this tendency, too, is in keeping with Smart's devotion to Aristotelian methodological sensitivities. Religious studies consists of a large panoply of subjects and academic courses—to which the approach is always "polymethodic"—because the subject, religion, is understood to be an *organism*.

With the publication of *Worldviews: Cross-cultural Explorations of Human Beliefs*, Smart added detail to his approach while enunciating what can only be referred to as a humanitarian program. The detail that has been added derives from the proposal that it is appropriate to approach the religions as representing worldviews, namely, "the systems of belief which, through symbols and actions, mobilize the feelings and wills of human beings." Smart's intention is to talk about religions within the same context within which it is appropriate to talk about ideologies, all of this having reference to the ways in which beliefs and symbols "form a deep part of the structure of human consciousness and society." Smart believes it important to consider these matters not simply so that religious studies will be conducted properly, but because of dramatic recent developments within the human community. Smart recognizes that "human civilization is now so tightly knit that its every crisis sends ripples around the globe." Coupled with this is the fact that human beings remain fundamentally religious. As he puts it:

> We are all to some degree or other political animals, because power is a fact of life; and we are all economic beings, for financial exchange is a fact of life. But we are also religious beings, for orientation to life itself is a fact of life; and we are all in one way or another so oriented.

The combined testimony, therefore, is that if human beings are going to live in harmony with one another, they must understand each other's distinctive orientations to life, their worldviews; that is, "the systems of belief which mobilize their feelings and wills." Thus, "a main part" of the academic study of religion, in Smart's view, is "worldview analysis," which he explains as "the attempt to describe and understand human worldviews, especially those that have had widespread influence." Within the list of these Smart includes not only the major religious traditions of the world, but also ideological orientations like Marxism and philosophical orientations like Platonism. The same is indispensable for the student of religion, of course. But Smart affirms that its indispensability reaches much further: "An educated person should know about and have a feel for many things, but perhaps the most important is to have an understanding of some of the chief worldviews which have shaped, and are now shaping human culture and action." And it carries significant personal consequences:

> [B]eyond knowing the geography of human consciousness, a person may wish to explore his own orientation, to try to articulate his own beliefs, to reflect about life and the world: to form or clarify the basis of his own worldview. Such a goal goes beyond the comparative study of worldviews: it is itself a quest. This too can form a living part of the modern study of religion, for once we have traveled into other minds and times we may want to return to our own lives. What do these symbols mean to me? Toward which orientation should I set my own soul's face? . . . Here the student of worldview analysis becomes the self-explorer, the quester.

By the time he has reached the final pages of his portrayal, Smart has combined a number of the key ingredients of his ongoing analysis. Yes, the religions of the world are approached in terms of the dimensions or strands that they exhibit. Yes, the religions of the world are understood to have been formed by influences and forces both internal and external, some of them belonging to the intrinsic dynamism of the organism itself, and some of them having been contributed by formative environmental factors. And yes, the religions of the world are approached as being representative of resilient worldviews, thus belonging to an ideological environment to which they are not the only contributors. And, yes, the purpose of the study of religion in this way is not simply to make religious studies intellectually vibrant, but also to contribute substantially to understanding the world. And yes, such study carries useful and vital personal dimensions:

> I think a sensitive understanding of worldviews is a marvelous preparation for life in our world, and it is a substantial ingredient in proper reflection upon the ways to move our societies forward. So a wish to explore the field more, to voyage inwardly and outwardly through the symbols, experiences, and thoughts of human beings, is not a luxury. It is an exciting quest and there are many valuable things to discover. But it is also a crucial part of any person's self-education.

Wilfred Cantwell Smith: Cumulative Traditions and Personal Faith

As we have noticed, scholars have approached the religious traditions of the world from a variety of standpoints and vested methodological interests. Some of the time the dominant intent has been to give focus to sociological theory. Some of the time religions traditions became the object of study because larger or more comprehensive cultural analyses could not fail to account for them. And frequently religious traditions became the focal object through a kind of essence-instance logical entailment. In the latter case, the religious tradition was looked to as the empirical and visible manifestation of the nature and essence of religion.

Within this variegated context, the work of Wilfred Cantwell Smith (b.1916), past director of the Center for the Study of World Religions, Harvard University, is particularly important. In the first place, Smith's writings reflect methodological self-consciousness, sophistication, discernment, and perceptiveness regarding the variety of interests through which scholars approach the study of world religions. He recognizes, for example, that insight in these matters is a product not only of theoretical formulation and empirical investigation, but also of grammatical order and syntactic and semantic construction. In other words, *religion* is a word that can be denominated as a single or plural noun (*religion, religions*) and as an adjective (*religious*) that modifies other nouns (institutions, traditions, and persons). Its syntactic and semantic position influences not only its function but also the methods and interests under which it is approached. Smith recognizes, in other words, that religious studies is a complicated enterprise because its subject is multiple. In the second place, Smith's own approach to the subject concentrates on the interrelationship between religion and the religions; but he does this in a way that updates previous formulations of that interrelationship because it seeks to discard the familiar essence-instance model.

To say that Smith seeks to discard the essence-instance model is to note that he is absolutely opposed to defining religion before one approaches or examines the religious traditions. The scholar does not work from the definition to illustrations of the definition. Furthermore, it is not simply that the essence-instance sequence needs to be modified; it is also that a definition cannot (and need not) be given. But, at the same time as he abandons the logical priority of definitional efforts, Smith is unwilling to settle for merely descriptive, empirical accounts of religions traditions. As the title of his best-known book illustrates, Smith is concerned with the *meaning* of religion, not simply with a morphology or a classification of religions.

Can one have it both ways? For Smith, the reconciliation is based on a recognition that religion pertains primarily and finally to persons. It is ultimately a personal matter: "fundamentally one has to do not with religions, but with religious persons." Illustrating the prominence of the personal dimension by drawing on his knowledge of Islamic religion, the religion in which he has specialized, Smith writes:

> "Islam" comes alive for the Muslim through faith, which is not an item in a religion but a quality in some men's hearts. . . . Once it has come alive, it is *ipso facto* no longer what it appears to be to him for whom it is not alive. . . . Those of us on the outside who would interpret to ourselves the Muslim must understand not his religion but his religiousness.

The same attitude prevails when the religion in focus is not Islam but Judaism, Christianity, Buddhism, or Shinto. Always, the scholar must acknowledge the presence and force of the intrasubjective dimension: how the religion is appreciated by the insider.

Smith believes so firmly in the necessity for a new departure that he urges a discarding of both the words *religion* and *religions* in treating these matters. In place of *religions*, he prefers to refer to specific *traditions*; and rather than speak about *religion*—which gives the misleading suggestion that there is religion in general—Smith prefers to speak about *faith*.

> By "faith" I mean personal faith. . . . For the moment let it stand for an inner religious experience or involvement of a particular person; the impingement on him of the transcendent, putative or real. By "cumulative tradition" I mean the entire mass of overt objective data that constitute the historical deposit, as it were, of the past religious life of the community in question: temples, scriptures, theological systems, dance patterns, legal and other social institutions, conventions, moral codes, myths, and so on; anything that can be and is transmitted from one person, one generation, to another, and that an historian can observe.

Smith claims that anything of any importance within the subject-field can be approached through the rubrics of *tradition* and *faith*. For him, these terms are clearer, less troublesome, and conceptually more economical than the misleading systems of classification others have used.

Several strategies are implicit in Smith's recommendation. In the first place, the shift enables the inquiry to be empirical at both focal points. Smith believes this preferable to treating at least one of the foci as something metaphysical and the other as an expression, or as a metaphysical implicate. Both *tradition* and *faith* are observable facts that can be explored by the scholar, using specifiable and repeatable methods.

But this strategy possesses more radical implication, which involves a shift from a single to a dual focus. In previous formulations, the word *religion* was frequently used to apply both to what Smith prefers to call "traditions" and to some deeper or more essential reality that religious traditions were regarded as expressions of or within which they were thought to participate. Smith writes:

> The proposal that I am putting forward can, at one level, be formulated quite simply. It is that what men have tended to conceive as religion and especially as a religion, can more rewardingly, more truly, be conceived in terms of two factors, different in kind, both dynamic: an historical "cumulative tradition," and the personal faith of men and women.
>
> I have proposed my pair of concepts, tradition and faith, to replace the currently established single one, without inquiring at length into the nature of the two. This is partly in line with my concomitant thesis that the "nature" either of religious traditions or of faith is not an intellectual desideratum nor a metaphysical reality; we are dealing here rather with historical actualities, which must be explored as such.

As noted, both foci are observable. Cumulative tradition refers to the "growing congeries of items" of which a specific corporate religious history is composed. Smith admits that the words "the cumulative tradition" is a conceptual construct by means of which coherence is inserted or imposed upon a mass of detail for purposes of intelligibility and recognition. Smith refers to cumulative tradition as "a device by which the human mind may rewardingly and without distortion introduce intelligibility into the vast flux of human history or any given part of it." The polar concept, faith, too, has its observable side. To the analyst, faith may not be visible, but its expressions certainly are, and in a variety of forms. "Without . . . knowing what it is, we may nonetheless affirm with confidence that there is some personal and inner quality in the life of some men and to it we give the name faith, in relation to which overt observables are for those men religiously significant." Accordingly, the expressions of faith can be seen in belief, art, religious community, personal character, ritual, moral sensitivity, ideas, and words. Given this variegation, Smith can conclude: "Faith, then, is a personal quality of which we see many sorts of expressions."

In concentrating on these two foci, Smith wanted to formulate an approach that would "serve simultaneously both observer and participant—for these two attitudes are coming more and more to coalesce." He wanted to guard against interpretations that mean much to the analyst but are unintelligible or insignificant, once again, to religious persons. In other words, it would be improper to interpret a tradition except in a manner that fits a representative self-interpretation of faith. The foci are dual, but they are always interpenetrative.

An intriguing side to Smith's contention involves something more than his suggestion about how religious traditions ought to be approached. It is even more special than his treatment of the relation between religions and religion—both of which terms he dropped, as we have noted, in favor of subjects that are more precise. We refer to the evolutionary dimension of Smith's portrayal. His approach is undergirded by convictions regarding the progressive development of human religious understanding. In Smith's view, the cumulative traditions are never static phenomena, but are living, dynamic, are perpetually regulated by strong growth factors. This developmental tendency makes it necessary to find new, more viable terminology to speak about religion. It is even more apparent in the mid-twentieth-century compulsions that the various cumulative traditions feel to recognize each other and to formulate their own destinies in intertraditional terms: "Men of different religious communities are going to have to collaborate to construct jointly and deliberately the kind of world of which men of different religious communities can jointly approve, as well as one in which they can jointly participate." This is in keeping with Smith's view that

> the future progress of one's own cherished faith even within one's own community, depends more largely than most of us have realized on the ability to solve the question of comparative religion. Unless a Christian can contrive intelligently and spiritually to be a Christian not merely in a Christian society or a secular society but in the world; unless a Muslim can be a Muslim in the world; unless a Buddhist can carve out a satisfactory place for himself as a Buddhist in a world in which other intelligent, sensitive, educated men are Christians and Muslims—unless, I say, we can together solve the intellectual and spiritual questions posed by comparative religion, then I do not see how a man is to be a Christian or a Muslim or a Buddhist at all.

In other words, the various cumulative traditions are coming to a realization that they are participants in a common human religious destiny. They also sense more and more that this destiny is taking shape progressively. Smith finds it appropriate to utilize the word "convergence" (both Teilhard de Chardin and R. C. Zaehner employ the same word frequently) to speak of such matters. Current religious consciousness testifies to the fact that a religious convergence is occurring, and that its opportunities and demands are being increasingly felt. This is yet another reason why previous formulations of the relation of religion to religions must be regarded as being obsolete. Both tradition and faith are affected by the dynamisms and compulsion of emerging human self-consciousness.

For Smith, then, the problem is not just a theoretical one; nor is it simply a concern of the scholar—or of the scholar alone:

> We need new ideas, certainly, that will allow us to live in this new phase of human history into which we are moving. . . . [But] the basic question of comparative religion in the modern world is not solely an intellectual question, requiring some neat theoretical formula—those of us who are theoreticians can handle that, at least if enough good men will join in the search. No, the basic question here is an historical one and is a question for all men—large, urgent and deeply involving us every one. . . .
>
> I call it an historical question because it is a matter of what is actually going on in our century in world affairs, and of the direction in which civilization is to move, and of our capacity to enter a new phase of human history. It is a question of our recognizing new trends and new goals, and of our constructing here on earth over the next hundred years, or, perhaps, less, the new kind of world that alone can be viable today.

Smith elaborates this vision in his book *Towards a World Theology: Faith and the Comparative History of Religion*, published in 1981. Here the intention is to explore such concepts as "the unity of religious history" and "universal self-consciousness" to examine ways in which the particular insights, for which each of the several religious traditions is known, might contribute to collective and cooperative world understanding. Here also is an invitation to adherents of one or another of the religious traditions to view the others as being their own, for, as he puts it, one is "in principle heir to the whole religious history of the race thus far." Moreover, "the community of which one is a member is in principle the human community, and that to which one gives one's final loyalty is in active relation with all one's fellows." In exploring the religious experience of other traditions, in Smith's view, one is actually claiming one's inheritance. The invitation includes engaging the world through the eyes of believers whose faith one may have previously considered as being alien or irrelevant. He can make such recommendations, he believes, because there is a common foundation to the experience that informs the traditions, in his words: "through participation in a religious tradition each of us participates in the life of God." And this, at bottom, is what authenticates and situates the possibility of an ideal religious community of global proportions.

Frank Whaling: Christian Theology in a Global Context

Something of both Ninian Smart and Wilfred Cantwell Smith can be seen in the proposals of Edinburgh scholar Frank Whaling (b.1934). Smart, as we have indicated, is known for astute comparative analyses of religious traditions on the basis of characteristic responses to common formal factors identified as "strands" or "dimensions." Whaling, following Smart, substitutes "observable elements" for strands and dimensions, but proceeds in much the same way, by examining the religions according to the categories of (1) community, (2) ritual, (3) social involvement, (4) ethics, (5) scripture and myth, (6) concepts (by which he means teachings), (7) aesthetics (music, painting, sculpture, architecture), and (8) spirituality. Smith, as we have observed, is primarily interested in the fundamental spirit of the various religions, to which spirit is attached the opportunity each one provides to fulfill primary human need. Whaling, following Smith, is intent on identifying that vital force, and discovers the fulfillment of human need to be linked to each tradition's understanding of transcendence and the mediation thereof.

Thus Whaling's work is both descriptive and hortatory. He believes that religions need to be understood, and that the focus on observable elements is the key to a broader understanding. He believes it highly useful that all citizens of the global society have this factual understanding of all of the major global religions. But he has also proposed that the distinctiveness of each tradition is based on the ways in which transcendence is conceived and is understood to relate to nontranscendence. Each of the traditions, that is to say, affirms a transcendent reality, but both construes that reality and understands how it becomes meaningful to "people on earth" in a distinct and characteristic way.

Whaling is insistent that devotees of any one of the religions "pass over" (through "the creative use of the imagination") into another religion so that all come to know, for example, "what it means for a Hindu to be a Hindu and a Muslim to be a Muslim." But this exercise should not be treated as a sampling of possibilities from which a potential adherent feels some obligation to make a specific choice. Rather, such "passing over" is designed to increase understanding of the dynamics of the global community, and, in a religious sense, to assist the devotee "to return to his or her own tradition" with increased understanding and renewed fervor.

> At this point, understanding world religions means not only having a mental grasp of what the other person's religious community, rituals, ethics, social and political involvement, scripture, concepts, aesthetics, and spirituality are all about, and how it might be possible for that person through those elements to be in contact with transcendent reality. It means passing-over into the world-view of another person in such a way that we have a joyful sense of what their world-view means to them emotionally, in addition to what it means to us intellectually. It gives us access, in some small but poignant way, to their faith and their experience. We are no longer on the outside; we are—in however minute a way—on the inside.

The benefits are not merely personal and individual, nor do they pertain only to increased religious understanding. Beyond this, Whaling is concerned about pressing problems of a global nature that challenge people of all religions.

The ecological threat to our global existence is obvious: the dying out of various species, the diminishing of the rain forests and woodlands, the pollution of our environment, the using up of non-renewable natural resources of minerals and energy, the contamination of the atmosphere and biosphere, the threat to the ozone shield, the cumulative effect of nuclear experiments. Human understanding of other humans is also obvious at a global level. . . . Moral and spiritual matters also have a global dimension . . . .

Whaling sees it as challenge. He also understands it as opportunity:

The natural, human, and spiritual riches of all cultures, religions and civilization are open to all the people on earth in a way that has never been true before.
   The global situation offers an unprecedented challenge and stimulus to Christian theology and world religions to forsake their parochial concerns and to seek the wellbeing of the planet as a whole over and above the vested interests of particular parties, or even of nation states.

Thus, Whaling is not proposing that there be some comprehensive global religious synthesis or that decisions be made about bases on which religious preferences might be adjudicated. Rather, he urges that advocates of the various religious traditions come increasingly to see themselves as belonging to a pluralistic global society within which they (and their traditions) face unprecedented challenges and opportunities. He believes he has provided a methodological basis on which the religions can be compared and contrasted, a spiritual basis on which the existence of each can be affirmed, and both intellectual and moral incentives for advocates of each to learn more about the others, in the midst of which he has also made a compelling request that Christian theology prepare itself for the global context.

John Hick: The Religions as Contributors to the Fullness of Religious Experience

We began this chapter with reference to John Hick's (b.1922) observation that autobiographical factors play a significant role in religious identification. We will continue this survey of proposals on the subject of comparative religion by allowing Hick to develop his perspective on this subject in more detail. We refer specifically to his article "The New Map of the Universe of Faith" that was published in his book *God and the Universe of Faiths* in 1973.

   In this sketch of the relationships between religious traditions, Hick begins by offering a definition of religion—"religion is an understanding of the universe, together with an appropriate way of living within it, which involves reference beyond the natural world to God or gods or to the Absolute or to a transcendent order or process"—that is inclusive enough, he believes, to encompass all religions. But his presentation does not begin to take off until he considers the universality of religious experience, confirmation of which he finds in Wilfred Cantwell Smith's observation that "in every human community on earth today, there exists something that we, as sophisticated observers, may term religion, or a religion." Smith continues: "And we are able to see it in each case as the latest development in a continuous tradition that goes back, we can now affirm, for at least one hundred thousand years." Acknowledging this, Hick looks carefully at the historical and cultural situations within which the great religions of the world were encouraged to find formation. He notes that the "two cradles of civilization"—Mesopotamia in the Near East and the Indus valley of northern India—were regions where "spirit worship" and "reverence for nature deities" were present long before there were identifiable religions. Thus, a kind of seed-bed had been cultivated in these two regions within which a subsequent "golden age of religious creativity" could come to fruition.

This latter, which Hick believes to have begun "sometime around 800 B.C.E.," is responsible for the origin and development of the world's religions. As he describes it:

> This consisted in a remarkable series of revelatory experiences occurring during the next five hundred years or so in different parts of the world, experiences which deepened and purified men's conceptions of the ultimate, and which religious faith can only attribute to the pressure of the divine Spirit upon the human spirit.

Included are the early Jewish prophets, Zoroaster in Persia, Lao-tse and Confucius in China, the Upanishads and the Buddha in India, Mahavira (the founder of Jain religion), then the writing of the Bhagavad Gita, and then Pythagoras in Greece, which eventuated in the golden age of Greek philosophy identified with Socrates and Plato. After "a gap of some three hundred years" came the origins of Christianity, and "after another gap" the beginnings of Islamic religion under the influence of Mohammed. Looking at the entire sequence Hick offers this proposal:

> The suggestion that we must consider is that these were all moments of divine revelation. But let us ask, in order to test this thought, whether we should not expect God to make his revelation in a single mighty act, rather than to produce a number of different, and therefore presumably partial, revelations at different times and places? I think that in seeing the answer to this question we receive an important clue to the place of the religions of the world in the divine purpose. For when we remember the facts of history and geography we realise that in the period we are speaking of, between two and three thousand years ago, it was not possible for God to reveal himself through any human mediation to all mankind. . . . If there was to be a revelation of the divine reality to mankind it had to be a pluriform revelation, a series of revealing experiences occurring independently within the different streams of human history.

This is the fundamental insight: that one and the same God has made something of God's nature and designs for the world known to peoples in all portions of the world, but in ways that were compatible with the patterns of social and cultural life that had already developed in these regions. The corollary is that "the great creative moments of revelation and illumination" were so formative that the religiocultural complexes they inspired remain the great civilizations of the world, and are recognized as such even in this last quarter of the twentieth century.

Hick recognizes that the evolution of religious consciousness has not always been smooth. On the contrary, because of the circumstances that brought them into being, the great religions of the world have frequently seen themselves as being rivals. And he is quick to acknowledge that the entire sequence of religious development can indeed be interpreted as "the history of man's most persistent illusion." But he prefers to view it, through "the standpoint of religious faith," as the consequence of divine revelation. For him, "the same divine reality has always been self-revealingly active towards mankind, and . . . the differences of human response are related to different human circumstances." In summary:

> These circumstances—ethnic, geographical, climatic, economic, sociological, historical—have produced the existing differentiations of human culture, and within each main cultural region the response to the divine has taken its own characteristic forms. In each case the post-primitive response has been initiated by some spiritually outstanding individual or succession of individuals, developing in the course of time into one of the great religio-cultural phenomena which we call the world religions.

It cannot be said any clearer than this:

> Thus Islam embodies the main response of the Arabic peoples to the divine reality; Hinduism, the main (though not the only) response of the peoples of India; Buddhism, the main response of the peoples of South-East Asia and parts of northern Asia; Christianity, the main response of the European peoples, both within Europe itself and in their emigrations to the Americas and Australasia . . . .
> [T]hese revelations took different forms related to the different mentalities of the peoples to whom they came, and developed within these different cultures into the vast and many-sided historical phenomena of the world religions.

After establishing this theoretical framework, Hick must face the crucial questions concerning the validity of this variety of forms of response. Here his attitude is twofold. On the one hand, he does not believe that "any and every conception of God or of the transcendent is valid, still less [are] all equally valid." But, on the other hand, he is willing to affirm that "every conception of the divine which has come out of a great revelatory religious experience and has been tested through a long tradition of worship" (in addition to having sustained individuals and cultures over long periods of history) is no doubt "likely to represent a genuine encounter with the divine reality." He can accommodate this insight by suggesting that these different accounts may be valid, though each is incomplete and imperfect, since none, by itself, is adequately capable of representing "the infinite nature of the ultimate reality." In short, at their experiential roots the various religious traditions of the world are all "in contact with the same ultimate reality." But "their differing experiences of that reality, interacting over the centuries with the different thought-forms of different cultures, have led to increasing differentiation and contrasting elaboration."

In the future, as the peoples of the world assume more and more the characteristics of a global community, Hick believes that the great religions will be less rivals and more contributors together in resisting "the universal wave of secularization" that seems so prevalent.

> Not that all religious men will think alike, or worship in the same way or experience the divine identically. On the contrary, so long as there is a rich variety of human cultures—and let us hope there will always be this—we should expect there to be correspondingly different forms of religious cult, ritual and organization, conceptualized in different theological doctrines. And so long as there is a wide spectrum of human psychological types—and again let us hope that there will always be this—we should expect there to be correspondingly different emphases . . . .

In the end, Hick envisions, the religions of the world will contribute toward assisting human beings to find a right relationship with that ultimate divine reality that is responsible for each one's occurrence. And "in the eternal life there is no longer any place for religions." For, "the pilgrim has no need of a way after he has finally arrived." Hick understands his interpretation of the situation to be a faithful reading of the Christian scriptures which affirm that in "the vision of the heavenly city . . . it is said that there is no temple—no christian church or chapel, no jewish synagogue, no hindu or buddhist temple, no muslim mosque, no sikh gurdwara . . . for all these exist in time, as ways through time to eternity."

Robert Cummings Neville: Systematic Comparative Theology

As previous examples within this chapter have illustrated, comparative studies in religion can be launched from numerous disciplinary standpoints, each of which seems to require the complementation of other disciplines, standpoints, and guiding intellectual interests. That is, theologians have ventured schemes to explain the relationship of one or more of the religions to the others, but, often in so doing, have ventured out beyond the range of their acknowledged competence. Similarly, historians have provided perspectives from which comparisons and contrasts can be drawn, but, often in so doing, find themselves involved in somewhat uncomfortable reflection of a metahistorical nature. The same tends to be true of philosophical approaches to the subject: conceptual analyses have proven themselves useful in this subject area, but primarily to the extent that they provide assurance of a tested cognizance of the data of the traditions that are being analyzed.

It goes without saying that the scholar who is best equipped to make an impressive foray into this subject is the one who is expertly trained in comparative critical thinking and who is also thoroughly familiar with the fundamental intentions of at least two of the major religious traditions of the world. This is precisely how one might approach the work of Robert Cummings Neville (b.1939), who is professor of theology, philosophy, and religion, and whose writings focus both on Christianity as well as on Chinese religions. From among his numerous publications, we have selected to trace the argument he has presented in his 1991 publication, *Behind the Masks of God: An Essay Toward Comparative Theology*, since it is fundamental to much of what appears in the other volumes.

Neville works under the conviction that comparative theology should be both intentional and systematic. He has no difficulty conforming to the first rule, but the second is daunting. To do comparative theology well, the scholar must possess a vast knowledge of the ins-and-outs of the traditions as well as have a thorough mastery of the intellectual tools by means of which such analyses are conducted. No one, Neville concedes, is properly up to the task. And yet it is a venture very much worth pursuing.

Neville approaches the comparative task by considering how philosophy of religion might produce a philosophy of world religions. This requires him to identify the categories by means of which at least two religions can be seen to exhibit some philosophical common ground. Neville recognizes that philosophy of religion, as it is practiced within most Western colleges and universities, is an invention of modern Western philosophy. Consequently, issues concerning theism, transcendence, the ontological grounding of religious affirmation, the understanding of relationships between causes and effects, and so on, are products of Western philosophical reflection, which are then drawn upon to lend philosophical interpretation to the religions of the non-Western philosophical world. Having made this concession, however, Neville does not search for Asian alternatives or contrasts to the Western mind. Rather he perceives Asian religions as phenomena that can be approached through similar kinds of principled differentia. That is, theism, transcendence, ontological grounding, and the like, are not restricted to Western conceptualization, and therefore are missing from the Asian examples, but are rather formulated in distinctive and sometimes strikingly dissimilar terms. Neville affirms that the insights of the several religious traditions can indeed be treated side by side. The religions themselves belong to an identifiable mode of philosophical discourse, within which framework they present identifiable varieties, contrasts, and similarities.

Christianity and Chinese religions, for example, cannot properly be compared on the basis of theistic intention, which the former exhibits but which the latter eschew. But they can be compared on grounds of ontological and cosmological principles. Indeed, Neville affirms that the category of ontological creativity is characteristic of each of these traditions, while there are significant differences as to whether such creativity is regarded as being transcendent or immanent, and whether relationships between determinative factors are understood as being symmetrical or asymmetrical. Further, within some ontological and cosmological schemes, the principle of noncontradiction applies, whereas in others apparent contradictions are sustained. Similarly, all religious traditions engage the question as to where and how fundamental harmonies are situated and grounded, and the interrelationships between such harmonies and prescribed virtues and values. Again, the details are complex, and the work of comparative analysis is a highly sophisticated investigative undertaking. Indeed, Neville's insights in this regard are stimulative of long-range projects in comparative philosophical analyses. But the findings to date indicate that there are comparative conceptual bases from which to suggest, for example, that Chinese thought is more adept at giving expression to creation *ex nihilo* as well as to Platonic cosmology than is Western thought. This suggests to Neville that creation *ex nihilo* is an intriguing and useful point of potential common ground from which both comparison and mutual understanding can progress. Neville's program places the work of comparative motif analysis within the framework of the comparative logics of the various traditions' ontological and cosmological orientations.

Critical Rejoinders

So far in this chapter, reference has been made to the efforts of a variety of theorists who have approached religion by comparing and contrasting selected religious traditions. In most of these instances, the theorists have been interested in providing more than a descriptive account. In addition, they have offered proposals regarding normative issues: Are all religions true? Are some of them more true than others? Is one or more of them more authentically religious than some of the others?

When comparative studies in religious traditions are extended to involve themselves in these normative issues, the theorists have proceeded in ways that are clearly traceable. No matter how the issue is approached and what procedural explanations are offered, theorists approaching questions about the extent to which religious traditions approximate sustainable truth must discover, select, or posit a *norm*. Then, having identified the norm, all relevant phenomena are judged in comparison with that norm. Sometimes the norm has been understood to have an actual historical manifestation, as, for example, when one of the religious traditions is reckoned to be an embodiment of the religious ideal. We have noted that some theorists have approached the Christian religion this way, then have judged the truth and falsity of other religions according to the extent to which they both match and deviate from that norm. More often, however, the norm is conceived in a projected manner, frequently as that toward which all of the religious traditions are tending, and which no one of them can claim, at least not yet, to embody. The projection of the ideal norm can be conceived in either hierarchical or linear fashion, and, at times, in both of these ways. Whether projected in linear or hierarchical fashion, or both, the ideal norm serves as the principle by which existing religions are judged, and perhaps updated and transformed. The projected norm enables the theorist to contend that none of the existing religious traditions—not even any of those that might be enjoying a privileged position—can be taken as a reliable and accurate representation of the norm. In these situations, the idealized norm can function as the principle of transformation. It can also be used to help specify the degree of deviation between present and ideal states of religion. Then, with reference to the deviation, the advocate of ideal religion—or some future idealized religious state or situation—can function as both analyst and visionary. The analyst is also visionary when the analyst portrays what might someday be when the norm is fully realized. In that day, so the vision might imply, peoples of various religious traditions will be at peace with one another. The barriers between them will have been lifted because the frustrations of religious differences will have been transcended. All hostility and competition can then cease, and persons of religious sensitivity everywhere can help usher in the time of global harmony and unity. We have observed in the preceding pages that comparative analyses of religious traditions have been employed as launching bases for such hopeful global anticipations.

It need not be pointed out, perhaps, that the comparative approaches to religious traditions that have been identified in this chapter have been viewed with suspicion, and not simply on grounds that their conclusions seem mistaken or unwarranted. Rather, the strongest objections have been raised about the propriety and legitimacy of the enterprise itself, particularly when this mode of inquiry carries the promise of being able to disclose the nature and substance of religion. Such objections have been raised on grounds that a comparative study of religion that intends to assist the religious traditions to form more extensive bases of cooperation involves agenda-setting that stretches far beyond the bounds of critical scholarship. The controlling interest seems to be motivated by theological interests, some critics have contended, or, perhaps, when engaged in such work scholars in religious studies have actually taken responsibility for the sponsorship of certain religious proposals. That is, they appear to be engaged in the very activity they purport to be examining. When so engaged, their own religious programs control the findings they claim to have uncovered. Thus religion, in Michael Pye's words, "casts its own deep shadow across the study of religion."

As early as 1959, Erwin R. Goodenough (1893–1965) addressed aspects of this problem in his now famous article "Religionswissenschaft," first published in the journal *Numen*. Goodenough made a plea for the strictly scientific character of the discipline, but he did so on grounds that were in keeping with his understanding of the nature of religion. Given all that he had written about the tendency to screen oneself off from the power of the *mysterium tremendum*—which screening is frequently attempted through the use of doctrinal or ideational formulations— Goodenough recommended that a new scientific approach to religion should inch its way into the unknown by tested empirical investigations. For Goodenough, there is a way to transcend the posture that approaches the unknown by surrendering to it or being absorbed into it, and this requires that one face the mystery openly, armed with the scientific method. The scientific method implies neutrality and objectivity and the requisite openness that is dictated by the powerful presence of the mystery. Goodenough believed in the abilities of the scientific method to approach that mystery appropriately, by respecting it for what it is. But in his desire to keep theological and religious inclinations from blocking the analyst's view, he muddied the waters again by speaking of the scientific approach as constituting a new religion.

Goodenough's article prompted Willard Oxtoby of the University of Toronto to offer a commentary. In his reexamination of Goodenough's proposal, Oxtoby contended that some of what was desired had come to pass: the history and phenomenology of religion had indeed become disentangled from Christian theological concerns and was gathering momentum as a respected field of teaching and research on its own terms. But Oxtoby saw the situation in a slightly different way. Instead of berating theologians for resisting the findings of *Religionswissenschaft* on grounds that such findings ran contrary to doctrinal or creedal affirmation, Oxtoby pointed to the still-fragile character of *Religionswissenschaft*. In fact, Oxtoby found scholars in divinity schools and seminaries to be remarkably open to the new theoretical and empirical possibilities made accessible within *Religionswissenschaft*. Had he desired to, Oxtoby might have added that much of the initial pioneering work of the academic study of religion was undertaken by scholars who had been trained in theology, or at least were conversant with its workings and intentions.

In the same year that Goodenough published his famous article, Zwi Werblowsky was raising similar questions in accusing Joachim Wach of confusing *Religionswissenschaft* with theology. Werblowsky made his critical points when reviewing Wach's book, *The Comparative Study of Religion*, which was published in 1958 in English translation under Joseph Kitagawa's editorship. Carrying his critical rejoinder into the 1960 congress of the International Association for the History of Religions in Marburg, Werblowsky was successful in having a plenary resolution passed that forbade the religious beliefs or convictions of any scholar from influencing "the color or character of the I.A.H.R."

Werblowsky's dramatic challenge was taken up a quarter of a century later by Donald Wiebe, a Canadian scholar, in a now well-known and frequently cited article, provocatively entitled "The Failure of Nerve in the Academic Study of Religion." With controlled but insistent vehemence, Wiebe chided too large a number of his colleagues for a rather dogged obedience to a work agenda that was both implicitly and explicitly theological. Wiebe attacked the methodological heresy from several sides. He believed, first, that it was an exercise in deception: so-called religious studies scholars are not actually engaged in the inquiries they purport to be pursuing. Second, the intrusion of the theological agenda sufficiently muddies the waters so that legitimate religious studies is not free to pursue valid research agendas on its own terms. Third, the theological enterprise itself is indefensible on strict philosophical grounds, being vulnerable to the same judgments that discredit metaphysics and other forms of fanciful philosophical speculation. In Wiebe's view, the perpetuation of theological reflection under religious studies' auspices simply robs the latter enterprise of the intellectual legitimacy to which, strictly on its own terms, it can rightly lay claim.

As a rejoinder to Wiebe, Eric Sharpe, to whom reference was made in chapter 3, observed that "practically the whole of the comparative religion establishment in the half century between about 1889 and 1939 was made up of scholars very much involved in the practice as well as the study of religion." In Sharpe's view, it was stimulation from the Protestant wing of Christianity that gave origin and impetus to the academic study of religion, specifically because of its "deeply felt desire to establish a principle of free inquiry on scientific principles within the churches." Instead of emancipation from any and all theological influences, Sharpe believed religious studies should continue to participate in the dialogue. His fear is that any progressive "secularization of the history of religions" will gradually remove such study from both "the world of religion and the world of the intellect." Moreover, as Sharpe viewed the matter, the methodological emancipation program is based on the assumptions of a "historical-empiricism" which, though highly regarded some time ago, have been widely challenged within the world of contemporary scholarship.

Some of Sharpe's concerns were enunciated further by Robert Wilken in his presidential address, provocatively entitled "Who Will Speak for the Traditions?" at the 1989 national meeting of the American Academy of Religion. Noting that the Enlightenment assumptions on which the scholarly study of religion is based encouraged a public forum free of external constraints but certainly accountable to the institutions within the society, Wilken charged that the deliberations of religious studies were tending to occur in the vacuum of professional peerage. Citing Kant's conviction that public reason functions "to make suggestions for the better organization of the religious body," Wilken called attention to missed or absent connections between contemporary scholarship and contemporary religious institutions.

> For too long we have assumed that engagement with the religious traditions is not the business of scholarship, as though the traditions will "care for" themselves. . . .

There are some in our company whose scholarly mission leads them along quite different paths. But that is hardly reason for all of us to approach "religion" as though it were the "creation of the scholar's study" or as if it existed only in the past.

Then, quoting an authority out of the past, Wilken continues: "As Ernst Troeltsch reminds us, it makes a difference for an interpreter whether one is simply engaged in decently interring a corpse or dealing with a reality that has a future as well as past." Wilken is thoroughly cognizant of the principles implicit in the separation of church and state, and he knows that the lectern is not the pulpit and the room is not a *yeshiva*. Yet he wishes to affirm that the scholarly study of religion does not consist solely of "dispassionate secondary discourse." To proceed this way is to "prune the list of things we [namely, professors and scholars in the field] talk about" and to "narrow the circle of people we will talk to, or better, of those who will talk to us." Moreover, Wilken believes that such a careful but sterile attitude consigns many of the vital ingredients of the subject-field to footnotes or into "historical sources invoked for the purpose of documenting an idea or illustrating a theory."

Sharpe's and Wilken's responses to the critical rejoinders of the strict emancipationists demonstrate that the controversy is occurring under the banner of comparative religion. Those affirming rapport have tried to show that while the two fields of endeavor are distinct from each other, they are not necessarily antithetical, conflictual, or even appositional to each other. In a number of schools, for example, programs in religious studies and programs in theological studies exist side by side, and in some of them the same scholar might serve as a member of both faculties, presumably functioning with a keen understanding of the differences in intentions, expectations, and modes of procedure that pertain between them. Yet, regardless of how successful these efforts at conducting parallel (or compatible without being competitive) undertakings have been, the suspicion remains that theological studies are not conducted with the same analytical rigor, or dispassionate scholarly attention, that is the prerequisite for analysis and interpretation in the field of religious studies. The comparative study of religion, particularly when it is approached in a comprehensive fashion, and when the relationship between religious traditions is placed within historical and global frameworks of interpretation, is understood to belong more to theology than to religious studies—thus, more to speculative theory than to rigorous analytical inquiry. All of this has given it something less than full stature as a vital contributor to the making of the intellectual discipline. Instead of being a full partner in this enterprise, it has been relegated to a somewhat fanciful adventure into imaginative speculation. There is hardly any way, so the critics charge, to contest the findings of such an enterprise, for no shared criteria exist on which such judgments can be based. Thus the speculative adventure tends to invite spiritual visionaries, or one-world ideologues, whose hope for the unity of the religious traditions is ordinarily linked to the desire for the realization of some conceived or imagined collective human aspiration.

Mark Juergensmeyer: Comparative Religion Applied

If the comprehensive comparisons of religious traditions draw intellectual criticism or suspicion, the more specific point-for-point comparisons and contrasts have no difficulty establishing academic respectability. These, one can be certain, will become the most prominent development within this framework in the near and even distant future. That is, less attention will be paid to ways in which the traditions themselves relate to one another, and attention will become more particularly focused on clear instances of joint or shared interest and intention.

Examples of specific comparative religion must include the collective scholarly work being undertaken as the Fundamentalist Project at the University of Chicago, under the combined direction of Martin E. Marty and Scott Appleby. In order to produce a multivolume study, supported by the American Academy of Arts and Sciences, Marty and Appleby have assembled scholars from throughout the world who have information about and insight into the so-called fundamentalist phenomenon. The joint inquiry is focused on the fact that religious and political fundamentalism seems to be on the rise throughout the world in the 1980s and 1990s. The Chicago group is dedicated to explaining why. Incorporated in this interest is the related question as to why the religions are giving prominence to their fundamentalist sides. Since all of the religions of the world are included in the range that is being examined, the project is producing some provocative and compelling specific comparisons.

Similarly motivated, Mark Juergensmeyer's book *The New Cold War? Religious Nationalism Confronts the Secular State* (1993) is a stimulating comparative study of the rise of contemporary religious nationalism. Focusing on the Middle East (particularly Israel and Egypt), the former Soviet republics of Eastern Europe, Central Asia, India, and Sri Lanka, and dealing with Muslims, Christians, Jews, Buddhists, and Hindus, Juergensmeyer (b.1940) examines the kinds of conflict that involve religion and politics together. He contends that "fundamentalism" is not the appropriate category of analysis and interpretation. Rather, what appears to be occurring is the resurgence of traditional religion as criticism of "secular nationalisms," and such occurrences do indeed constitute a worldwide phenomenon. For our purposes, Juergensmeyer's thesis is not as significant as the intellectual undertaking he has pioneered. A scholar could not competently engage in such comparative work without having a keen grasp of the religions and cultures in question. Here the overall intention is not to create face-offs between the religions themselves, but to examine them in their shared interest in responding effectively to secularizing forces. Along the way Juergensmeyer offers sophisticated comparative analyses of the religions, and yet such comparisons are not his driving intention. We call it applied comparative analysis in religious traditions, for the comparisons and contrasts are included in the analytical work that is required before theses can be proposed and interpretive considerations pursued. The fact that all of the religious traditions have a similar stake in a contemporary worldwide ideological problematic lends legitimation to the comparative work that is undertaken. But it is undertaken with specific purposes in mind, and thus falls outside the range of studies that are vulnerable to the charge of being fanciful or idealistic speculation.

Concluding Observations

Three considerations deserve to be mentioned in this context. The first derives from an observation that might seem to be altogether obvious from the outside, but appears not to carry heavy influence within the theoretical stances that prevail in comparative studies in religion. This observation is that the majority of the comprehensive comparativists approach the relationship between religions as being essentially friendly or benign. That is, most of the theories that have been surveyed in these pages treat the various religions as being components of some larger comprehensive unity, like-minded elements within some overarching design, participants in some ongoing cooperative process, or as candidates for fusion or eventual union. As illustration, Friedrich Heiler gave an address to the International Association for the History of Religions Congress in Tokyo in 1958 in which he argued that the study of religion would lead to the "unity of religions," a sentiment he underscored in an essay entitled "The History of Religion as a Preparation for the Cooperation of Religions" in 1959. More recently, Arvind Sharma has voiced like-minded irenicisms, when, after identifying the distinctive traits of the major world religions, he says, "there is something charming rather than alarming about religious plurality." Good wishes and high aspirations aside, the sober truth of the matter is, however, that these same religions have frequently understood themselves to stand in rival or competitive positions with respect to each other. Certainly at times, and in certain respects, the spirit of cooperation has existed between them. But prevalent too has been a non-irenic, overtly polemical, indeed hostile spirit even to the point of warring contentiousness. The majority of religious traditions that the comparative theorists would like to envision forming some beneficial and harmonious cooperative bond derive their own origins from clashes and conflicts with other traditions. One thinks of the rise of Christianity as belonging to Jewish self-criticism. One can cite the rise of Buddhism as belonging to a concerted attempt to find a viable alternative to the Hindu way. Islamic religion finds its roots in deviations from and opposition to both Christianity and

Judaism. Although most of the theorists have found the means to accommodate such differences within unitizing and expansive theoretical schematisms, the traditions themselves still remain great distances away from realizing the same like-mindedness in practical or explicit terms. But such disjunctures and discrepancies are hardly reflected in the scholarly literature on the subject.

The corollary is that efforts to establish effective rapprochement between religious traditions in nonabstract conceptual form are often fraught with stubborn difficulties. At one level of abstraction it may sound plausible to affirm that the variety among religious traditions might conceivably yield to a hypothetical unity. But in practical terms, such unities are elusive. Alfred Bloom, director of the Institute of Buddhist Studies in Berkeley, has been monitoring Buddhist-Christian dialogues from the time that they were first established with organizational seriousness. While believing in the resourcefulness of dialogue, for example, he thinks it is unrealistic to expect that "the problem of interfaith relations within society" can by solved "simply by dialoguing." Bloom reminds his readers that alongside dialogue are ignorance and prejudice, in all religious communities. Beyond this, some serious disagreements exist that no amount of good will and discussion can overcome.

Further, when one religion is compared with another, there are no guarantees that the instrument of comparison is an apt one. It does no good, Bloom suggests, to compare Christianity and Buddhism on belief in God, or on other points of apparently significant doctrine. The fundamental differences between the two religions lie in the realm of epistemology and regard the nature of consciousness. The problem is that one really needs to know both traditions rather thoroughly before one can do appropriate comparative work. This can only occur if one has been thoroughly immersed in the culture(s) with which the religion is most compatible, and through which it is also manifested. If one truly knew the religions this way, one would know better than to try to make variety subordinate to unity. In short, the variety of religions exists for good reasons.

The second consideration is prompted by the previous one. While comparative studies in religion can hardly match the reality of actual relationships between traditions, the approach does indeed constitute a useful theoretical framework by which important materials might be organized. In other words, speculative theory has a legitimate heuristic place within religious studies. Sometimes such theories prove themselves to be correct, or conversely are found wanting. But frequently they function as being catalytic or instigative, and can be looked to set important processes of creativity into motion, in spite of the fact that they stand more as the data studied by religious studies than the methods by which religious studies makes that data intellectually accessible.

Of course, there are huge risks involved in such imaginative and speculative theory-building. In this regard, Jonathan Z. Smith's sobering analysis stands as stern warning: Misleading uses of comparative analysis have produced grave distortions. In *Drudgery Divine* (1990), Smith traces the history of scholarship on differences and similarities between early Christianities and the religions of late antiquity, illustrating that the bulk of this scholarship was directed (or misdirected) by competing Protestant and Catholic claims regarding the nature of "true Christianity." It should surprise no one that Smith calls for a thorough examination of the workings and pretensions of prevailing comparative method. Allan Grapard sounds similar warnings in his book *The Protocol of the Gods: A Study of the Kasuga Cult in Japanese History* (1992), contending that studies of Japanese religion have been thoroughly skewed by the imposition of interpretive categories from Western scholarship for which the materials provide no justification. Instead of calling for a reassessment of comparative cultural methods, Grapard asks that the practice be halted so that appropriate interpretive approaches can be cultivated in their own terms, precisely to fit the subjects being investigated.

We are pleading here—and this is our third consideration—for some disciplined middle ground. We recognize that the questions are going to be asked, for the subject has roots in natural curiosity: Why should there be more than one religion? Are all religions true? Are some truer than others? Can religion aspire to function as a positive force in the world? Were UNESCO to approach the leaders of the religions of the world for assistance in helping to establish an international atmosphere of peace instead of violence, would there be any unifying guiding principles to which an appeal could be made? If the answer is yes, then the religions of the world do in fact have something fundamental and substantial to do with one another. And, if this is true, then the similarities between them—what they hold in common—ought to be just as discernible as the differences. And, if so, the intellectual work of comparison and contrast has sufficient grounds on which to proceed.

This does not provide license for extravagant, irresponsible flights of speculative fancy. Nor is the fact of commonality a substitute for the meticulous investigation and analysis that is the only reliable pathway toward enduring cross-cultural understanding. And certainly the pretense of knowing all about some other religions because one is devoted to one's own should be identified as the arrogance it most surely is. Nevertheless, religious studies has much to learn and much to contribute to this ongoing discussion.

CHAPTER • SEVEN

THE FUTURE OF RELIGIOUS STUDIES

Several conclusions become almost self-evident from the trajectories that have been traced and chronicled in this study. The first is that religious studies is a multiform subject-field within which a variety of disciplines are employed to treat a multiplicity of issues, interests, and topics. Religious studies has no single subject, nor does it sanction any one method of approach. Rather, the subject is multiple, and the methods of approach are numerous.

This implies, second, that religious studies has a deep and abiding relationship with a large number of academic fields and disciplines. It shares its content with other fields, for the topics and interests it addresses require the use of a multiplicity of disciplines. Religious studies has also borrowed and adapted many of its insights and discoveries from these fields and disciplines. Such facts become evident when one charts the contributions of sociologists, anthropologists, philosophers, historians, theologians, psychologists, art historians, mythologists, linguists, and others. All have contributed substance, materials, and means of access to religious studies.

Third, the dependence of religious studies on contributions originating from other academic fields and disciplines does not make religious studies parasitical. Rather, religious studies enjoys a rich life of its own. It has adapted these materials and methods to its own ends and purposes while maintaining a symbiotic relationship with the other fields and disciplines. Thus the larger conclusion must be that when religious studies was formed, it was primarily the sets of field and disciplinary associations and arrangements that were new. Many of the methods and materials had been available to scholarship before, but not the combination and manner by which they were joined. The arrangements, the interrelationships, the dynamics by which methods and substance were conjoined, and the specific intellectual foci and intention were new.

Yet this was not all that was new. Through the formation of religious studies, a wealth of new materials has been uncovered, and some innovative methodological approaches have been cultivated. None of this had been brought together in the same combinations before. When the associations were formed, certain intellectual legacies were tapped, and some new scholarly ventures were set in motion.

Because religious studies is a relatively new enterprise, we have attempted in this study to come to terms with some of its distinguishing formative characteristics. We have searched for these characteristics from among the several large constellations of intellectual interest on which deliberate and sustained scholarly attention has been focused. In wanting to come to terms with the sets of intellectual interest, we have found it useful to speak of models of inquiry. We have noted that these models of inquiry have enjoyed a certain prominence in religious studies' second-order tradition, that is, within the history of scholarship by which the subject-field has been formed. We have tried to illustrate that religious studies' second-order tradition is composed out of the interaction of these several conceptual models. For this reason, our analysis of religious studies has taken the form of a modified narrative account within which the historical and theoretical developments can be traced simultaneously.

Approaches to Religion: The Sequential Development

Methodologically speaking, religious studies takes its modern-day roots from René Descartes' interest in clear and distinct ideas. As refined and amended by Immanuel Kant, the same intellectual interest was translated into an attempt to isolate religion's essence.

The undertaking itself was motivated and undergirded by a simple *focal object* (namely, religion's clear and distinct single essence) and an isolative *interest of reason* ("What is that without which religion would not be what it is?"). The first chapter of this study was devoted to a review of some prominent examples of this point of departure within religious studies under the rubric of the quest for the essence or core element of religion. It was noted that a host of prominent scholars within the field sought to uncover religion's core element, or first datum, in both ontological and theological senses. They were motivated by a desire to establish intellectual coherence by means of a single organizational principle. This interest in singularity, in uncovering a distinct and clear idea that functions in a fundamentally formative manner, was also enunciated under the question: What is the origin of religion? This question was also pursued by a large company of scholars from within a variety of fields, beginning with the explorational inquiries of E. B. Tylor and stretching down into the current era. Indeed, many of the treatises that belong to the initial history of the subject-field are methodologically single-minded. Their desire is to uncover that without which religion would not be what it is or to identify its root cause, fundamental generative source, or the combination thereof.

In the course of the methodological development of the subject-field, the preoccupation with a single-datum question eventually gave place to a variety of attempts to describe religious phenomena in multiple terms. It was not that single-principle coherence had been effected with full satisfaction, nor was it a matter of recognizing that it had failed. Rather, the transition to intellectual interests of another kind seemed to occur quite naturally, as if the intention were simply to fill out the range of knowledge that could be known about the subject. Core elements, that is to say, are difficult to uncover, and if one should be successful one has accomplished little more than identifying a likely candidate and demonstrating its necessity and prominence. This leaves the multiplicity of data untended. Thus, in many scholarly quarters there was a relinquishment of the quest for a single principle in favor of descriptive accounts of multiple phenomena. Scholars affected by the transition soon learned that description can be approached in a variety of ways. So too can the contents of religion be brought together in numerous ways. The decision for description rather than explanation forced inquiry to cultivate distinctive grammars of description, and the shift from a single focus to plural foci required the postulation of a context within which multiple factors would become discernible.

Here some scholars have opted for defensible collections—sometimes almost random or arbitrary collections—of religious data. Others, desiring more integrational rigor, proposed tighter schemes for the classification of religious phenomena. Other approaches worked to identify "natural groupings." As it turned out, the most obvious pattern of "natural grouping" in religion is the religious tradition or the identifiable religion. Still other attempts to work with "natural groupings" have concentrated on patterns, structures, or themes that translate across the boundary lines distinguishing religious traditions.

Then, once the world of multiplicity was discovered, descriptive accounts could easily become functional accounts. That is, instead of portraying the ways in which religion is shaped and configured, the scholar can attempt to demonstrate and illustrate how it works in society, what it desires to achieve, what uses it has, what roles it plays, what services it performs, what societal and cultural places it

·occupies—that is, how religion functions. The same functional accounts have been drawn upon to lend definition to religion and even to provide compelling explanations of its origin. It goes without saying that radical multiplicity is difficult to name, and thus extremely difficult to classify or categorize. Thus, interpretation always looks for themes, structures, patterns, or other suitable nexes to encourage multiplicity to yield to identifiable order.

The preceding chapters have been dedicated to identifying these orientational points, these specific methodological stances, as they have facilitated understanding of the nature, substance, and function of religion. The cumulative evidence is that all of the distinctive approaches to the subject share the same intention, namely, to make religion intelligible. Intelligibility is the key motivational factor in the progressive development of the subject-field.

Several modes of inquiry, we have noted, belong to the process by which intelligibility has been pursued. All of these models can be conceived. All of them are methodologically possible. All of them make sense. All of them are workable. All of them can claim high academic respectability. All of them have adherents, representatives, devotees, spokespersons, and disciples. All of them can boast of historical and methodological traditions of significant durability and longevity as well as of measurable achievement. All possess impressive intellectual credentials. Thus, no one of them need feel incapable or inadequate alongside any of the others, nor should any feel obliged to defer or default to any of the others. Each has distinctive strengths. Each has stimulated remarkable insights. Many of these insights would have been inaccessible to all or most of the other approaches. Furthermore, the omission of any one of the models can lead to an impoverishment of the subject-field.

Against this background, it should not disturb the reader to consider that none of the models can be understood to be "right" or "correct" in any exclusive way. Instead, each approach is "correct" or "right" in that each discloses facts or truths that lie beyond the reach or the capacities of the others. Approaches are "right" and "correct" when they do what they are designed to do—that is, when they are resourceful, insightful, useful, polished, sophisticated, rigorous, strategic, timely, and appealing. And they can, of course, become impulsive, presumptuous, and imperialistic when their reach is larger than their capability, when they attempt methodological ventures for which they are not properly equipped, and when they regard their own qualifications as guaranteeing exclusive entitlement to access to the subject-field.

Approaches are like perspectives, and perspectives are like horizons and vantage points. They function to direct interests and to place certain subjects within reliable view. Apart from an approach, or a stated set of interests, there is no view. Understanding is formed through the workings of such models of inquiry. The interest the scholar brings to the subject gives shape to the subject. It stimulates accessibility. It directs one's perceptual abilities. Where one stands determines what one sees and what one can know. And much of what one sees and learns is about where one stands.

Furthermore, the same viewpoint is unavailable to any of the other standpoints. When the standpoint is shifted, the subject is altered. This implies a need for methodological self-consciousness from both sides. The investigator fashions a standpoint in order to make a subject accessible. In the process, the inquirer also learns something about the nature of the standpoint. After one has utilized a standpoint, one becomes aware of its relative strengths and deficiencies. One also learns that a shift in perspective allows one to reach out to other subjects. And one becomes aware that an inability to perceive a subject in the same way others do may be due to the fact that the inquirer is standing in a different place. Standpoints, insights, and discoveries go hand in hand. Without standpoints, there can be no discoveries. Discoveries depend on both insights and standpoints. And insights come to magnify and justify standpoints.

Each of the models of inquiry, regardless of what and where it is, must be regulated by a consistent pattern of conceptual arrangement. Thus, one model cannot comprehend another model within its own terms. For the same reason, the product of one disciplined viewpoint cannot easily be translated into the terms of another, nor are they easily blended or fused. Each model exhibits a specific logic of inquiry.

Overlappings between models occur, of course. The combined independence and interdependence of the several standpoints become very intriguing when, for example, a discovery within one of the frameworks is instrumental in changing the contours of one of the others. This happened, we noted, when the cultivation of developmental interests reached over to take enthusiasm and strength away from the effort to identify a *sine qua non*. As we also observed, one of the great stimulants toward uncovering the origin of religion was the difficulty scholars encountered when trying to specify religion's essence authoritatively. But it is also true that the interest in identifying the essence of religion did not stay submerged, even after it had been partially supplanted by the quest for origins. Rather, it has surfaced repeatedly since the beginnings of the nineteenth century, and can even boast of contemporary enthusiasts. The methodological situation becomes even more complicated when we note that the quest for origins, which, in some places, supplanted the attempt to identify a *sine qua non*, was itself supplanted when the transition from single to plural focus occurred. And yet, the search for origins was eventually reestablished, but on descriptive phenomenological grounds. Indeed, the search for origins was also reestablished on functional grounds. As indication of the variety of ways in which methods, interests, and foci are intermixed, the functional approach has even been employed as a basis for defining religion, that is, for isolating its *sine qua non*.

Standard methodologies never die, it seems, but simply assume new form, take on additional and sometimes borrowed and acquired characteristics, and, thus, are revived again. The pathway forward is forged by expanded awareness of what other schools of approach have set out to achieve. When an approach is stumped, when the obstacles it faces appear overwhelming, it frequently finds an open field only by going back to recover a ploy or an insight that had been discarded after having been used in another place. In the perpetual exchanges of methods, insights, perspectives, and scholarly intentions, and in the application of all of these to the content of the fields, lies the intellectual vitality of the academic study of religion.

There is an important corollary: namely, that the variety of subjects, methods, intentions, and insights that comprise religious studies requires the effective interaction between sub-fields and disciplines. Stated in bolder terms, religious studies is not the sociology of religion, or philosophy of religion, or history of religion, or anthropology of religion, and so on, but is comprised of the cooperation between all of these. A religious studies that has become history of religions, say, is no longer religious studies but is history of religions. Similarly, a religious studies that has become philosophy or sociology or psychology of religion is not religious studies either, but is philosophy of religion, sociology of religion, or psychology of religion. What distinguishes religious studies from any of its individual component parts is its composite nature: it consists of all of these methodological operations, and all of these selective foci of interest, working together.

A subcorollary can be attached to this important corollary: namely, that the various disciplines and subfields that belong to religious studies are not differentiable simply on the basis of the distinctive methodologies that belong to each. Psychology of religion, for example, does not employ some "psychological method" as distinct from sociology of religion, which uses, say, the "sociological method." On the contrary, within these various ranges of intellectual interest and inquiry, a variety of methods are employed. Sociologists of religion draw upon the resources of descriptive, analytical, and functional methodologies, as do psychologists, anthropologists, and historians. The method is selected on the basis of the nature of the investigative task to be performed. Consequently, representatives of the various fields and disciplines register as investigators and theorists who illustrate the workings of each of the points of methodological departure that have been chronicled in this book. Those who have sought to identify the origins of religion, for example, come from all walks of academic and disciplinary life. The same is true of those who have devoted their efforts toward making religion intelligible by working to identify its primary function(s). None of the fundamental approaches that have been identified in this chronicle belongs to any one of the fields or disciplines as its special preserve. Hence, no one of them lies under the control of any of the fields or disciplines. And, more importantly, the variety within religious studies, in the last analysis, is not due to the copresence of sociologists, psychologists, historians, and the like, somehow all working on the same materials but under the auspices or guidance of sociological, psychological, and historical interests and incentives. Rather, the variety stems from the fact that the work of religious studies is characterized by a variety of intellectual motivations, and, at least so far, all such motivations have been judged to pertain. Should any single motivation be allowed to dominate, religious studies would not be religious studies, but would be reduced to some limited version or aspect of the same. As it was phrased in a previous chapter: Religious studies is a subject-field before it is anything more discrete than this. And, as a subject-field, religious studies has many subjects, employs many disciplines, manifests many intentions, and gains insights from many sources. But, lest there be fear that a subject-field of such manifest variety would contain so much novelty that it resists comprehensive depiction, one must add that the subjects, disciplines, intentions, and insights can be distinguished on the basis of certain implicit logics. We have tried to distinguish such logics on the basis of fundamental questions that are asked about a subject. By cataloging and chronicling some of the more prominent and representative responses to these questions—certainly it was not our intention to identify all of them—we have tried to retrace some of the methodological steps involved in the making of an intellectual discipline.

Religious Studies: Still in the Making

The final pages of this volume must be about something other than the conceptualization of standpoints, viewpoints, and scholarly perspectives on the study of religion. For, as much as we are concerned about matters methodological, we are also intrigued by what the analysis that has been conducted is able to foretell concerning the future of religious studies. Preceding chapters have provided an illustrated chronicle of development of some prominent pathways from the past into the present. Now it is time to consider what courses of ongoing development might be expected and anticipated in the immediate and longer-range future of the discipline.

It is important to notice that religious studies made a large leap forward in the early to mid-1960s. Certainly a scholarly study of religion was conducted before this time, but this date marks the time of a significantly large flowering, particularly within educational institutions in the United States. This was the era in which new programs and departments were established in the colleges and universities. It was the time when the major professional societies in the field were either started or gained large increases in membership and influence. All this occurred against the background of the decision by the United States Supreme Court in the cases of *Engel* and *Schempp*, decisions that reinforced the separation of church and state while adding legitimacy to the academic study of religion. Later, the National Endowment for the Humanities included "comparative religion" and "ethics" as fields that may qualify for federal-grant assistance. This brought additional respectability to the subject, or, perhaps, was evidence or confirmation that the same respectability had been gained.

Looking back, the chronicler will note that religious studies attained academic stature during a time of considerable intellectual and collective spiritual ferment. Both the ferment and the prevailing *zeitgeist* of the time lent support to analyses of subjects that put the student or scholar in touch with cultures that had been unfamiliar territory just months or a few years before. It is arguable that there would have been no counterculture had the writings of Zen Buddhism, for example, not been available, and had they not stimulated literary, artistic, and philosophical responses within the first generation of Americans to claim them as being descriptive of their own experiences and aspirations. But *zeitgeist* alone cannot account for the development of religious studies. The subject-field is stronger now, after the *zeitgeist* has shifted, than at the time the *zeitgeist* was performing such catalytic and sustaining services. Religious studies' methods are clearer today than before. The materials at its disposal are much more extensive. The discipline's means of reaching them, and of knowing what to do with them once it has them in possession, are considerably more sophisticated than before. Thus, while the formation of the discipline received significant encouragement from the original *zeitgeist*, there was truly something that needed to be studied, which turned into an enterprise much larger than might have been envisioned at first.

When speculating about the future of religious studies, one encounters considerations whose long-term influence is difficult to calculate. The chapters in this study have focused on points of distinctive methodological departure in the study of religion and have provided illustrative examples of the ways in which such methodologies function in gaining access and lending definition to the subject of religion. It has been appropriate to trace intellectual developments within these methodological frameworks since, in many respects, they best explain the making of the discipline. But there are important serendipitous influences as well—unexpected insights or discoveries that come to play instrumental roles within the subject-field itself. In this respect, one thinks of the influence of structuralist insights, which occurred first in literary interpretation and then, as far as religious studies is concerned, came to influence philosophy, anthropology, and a host of other fields and disciplines. One thinks too of specific developments within one of the known subject areas of religious studies, for example, a breakthrough in the interpretation of a particular religious tradition. Louis Dumont offered a simple argument in his book *Homo Hierarchicus* in 1970, namely that the Hindu caste system is regulated by the principle of inequality, which is not the opposite of western culture's commitment to equality since the Hindu formulation builds from the idiom of purity while the West's viewpoint is about authority. It was a simple argument, but it powerfully affected understanding of differences and similarities between the religious traditions involved. Charles Long's views about the ways in which a prevailing colonial, social, political, and cultural structure also bestows privileges on selected religious perspectives and positions is another significant example in point. Similarly, if taken seriously, Luce Irigaray's analyses of differences between men's and women's discourse, together with her suggestions about seemingly impartial rules of gender and grammar being deeply rooted in phallocratic assumptions about the world, carry a thoroughly reformative (although still underrecognized and articulated) conceptual capacity. And the same powers lie inherent in Renato Rosaldo's plea that astute reflection on culture cannot be properly achieved by detached, "objective" observers who mistakenly believe it virtuous to avoid dealing with subjectivity. In these, and other instances, lie insights that have an ability to inform inquiry throughout religious studies, regardless of their distinctive internal methodological sponsorship. It goes without saying that, at this writing, the field is only partially cognizant of the authority of some of these intellectual events, but will be influenced accordingly as they become better known.

There is a very large issue on the horizon that will thoroughly transform the academic study of religion, namely, the growing recognition that religious traditions themselves are not static or monolithic phenomena, but find their constantly changing and shifting identity in contact and relationship with each other. Taken with utmost seriousness, this recognition means that no tradition can be defined in terms of its own singularity or self-created identity. In point of fact, there is nothing really new in this insight, for through the centuries the substance and form of each religion have been products of contact, fusion, and syncretistic activity with others. Judaism, Hinduism, Islam, Buddhism, Christianity, and the others have only achieved definition in relation to other religious and cultural perspectives with which they remain in contact, and in relation to which they are both similar, distinctive, and dissimiliar. Accurate depictions and portrayals of any one of them can only be rendered via an acknowledgment of the multiplex ways in which each tradition has been shaped in its contact with other social, cultural, religious, and political traditions and influences. One day soon this recognition will become thoroughly internalized within the discipline. And other insights, similar in force to this one, will offer infusions and permeations quite unpredictably. This, we recognize, is the way academic disciplines continue to develop, for the process of intellectual formation, fortunately, is ever-restive.

For example, for many years "comparative religion" was treated as a special subject or topic within the study of religion. Approached this way, it was regarded as belonging to religious studies, but not as being a fundamental or constitutive element. In fact, as we have noted, comparative religion made its entry into religious studies in close cooperation with institutionalized study programs in world missions. Gradually, however, comparative religion began to emerge from its world-missions base, to gain greater and greater independence. With increasing independence came heightened methodological circumspection, and a far more deliberate intellectual agenda. Thus, step-by-step, comparative religion moved from being an intriguing topic to sub-field status within religious studies. As it progresses to greater rigor, as Jonathan Smith urges, its utility will increase too.

There is an additional step to be taken, namely, from distinct subject to subfield to necessary component of an emerging methodological self-consciousness. Indeed, so compelling has comparative religion become that it tends now to pervade religious studies in all of its aspects. It belongs to the context, the framework, of religious studies. It helps define the field's direction and compelling intellectual interests. Indeed, from this time forward, no aspect of religious studies can be thought through systematically—no aspect of religious studies can even be approached—without explicit acknowledgment of its cross-cultural dimensionalities. Already it is impossible to conduct scholarly research in religious studies except within an intellectual framework that treats cross-cultural sensitivities as being regulative.

It is noteworthy, in this respect, that Jacob Neusner, the distinguished historian and interpreter of Judaism, has managed to accomplish all phases of this multifaceted expository work. In the first place, he has successfully approached Judaism as a subject that belongs inherently to the academic study of religion, from which resources he has drawn critical, analytical, and interpretive skills. That is, he has conceived the academic study of religion in a manner that is thoroughly congruent with his desire to make Judaism as intelligible as any other religion that would or could be considered under the same set of interpretive rubrics. And he has done a magnificent job of demonstrating that the academic study of religion, as he understands and practices it, belongs properly to the work of the humanities and social sciences within American higher education.

We have focused on the role of comparative religion to help trace the process by which a single, self-standing topic of intellectual interest is transformed into a component of a larger self-consciousness. Comparative religion stands as a prominent example of such methodological transposition, but does not stand alone in this respect. The same role has been assumed by psychoanalysis, which has moved from being a discrete subject to becoming a factor of methodological self-consciousness within a great variety of fields and disciplines within the humanities and social sciences. We propose that the same role will be assumed—one day soon—by second-order tradition. One day soon it will be impossible for any prospective development within religious studies to occur outside of an expressed methodological self-consciousness of the workings of the subject-field as a whole. An academic study of religion, fully cognizant of its history and objectives, represents the kind of disciplinary strength that is required if religious studies is to render uncontested vital and intellectual service.

Going Beyond the Paradigm

Another ponderable but incalculable factor needs to be taken into account when one assesses the future of religious studies. This factor can be approached through a recognition that the perspectives of religion that have been identified and surveyed in this study are ones that can be mapped, traced, and explained. The very fact that they can be mapped, traced, and explained is indicative of the fact that we are working with a known and discernible map. Thus, in working with approaches to the subject of religion, we have made use of mapwork that is equipped to plot the very points of methodological orientation that have been identified as components of religious studies' second-order tradition. Clearly the map and the approaches mesh. They can be articulated together because they engage two basic elements within the same conceptual framework. Mapwork is the analytical reflexive side, while the approaches are presentational and expository. Approaches deserve to be called expository and presentational because they expose various aspects or dimensions of religion in a coherent, self-consistent manner. The map is designed to help tease out the rudiments of the methodological strategies that are implicit in the approaches. Approaches register within the mapwork since the mapwork has been constructed to disclose the distinguishing contours and characteristics of the approaches.

But what about other approaches and other maps? What about approaches that are inaccessible to such mapwork? What about approaches that may fall outside the range of this present pattern of mapwork? What are they? Where are they? Can they be found? If found, can they be discerned? Can the analyst say anything about them? What influence might they have on the future of religious studies?

Here, too, we can only speculate. If a report instead of speculation were appropriate, the report would circumscribe the range of access that the present mapwork makes possible, and then would identify questions, problems, and possibilities that lie around the edges. The report could follow the lead of certain theorists in the field in identifying proto-extra-paradigmatic areas. For example, if C. J. Bleeker is correct, religious studies has been conducted so far via a focus on *components of stability*, that is, repeatable patterns. But Bleeker is quick to acknowledge that such stable factors represent "arrested pictures"—that is, patterns, essences, natures, structures, and the like. Such elements are methodologically accessible since the analyst encounters such factors again and again. But this is their nature: they are repeatable, recurrent, duplicable, and thus easily yield to analytical reproduction. In most instances, what qualifies as an element of stability is simply the name for the fundamental principle of determination or organization. Rudolf Otto, for example, identifies *"das heilige"* as the *sine qua non* of religion. Ninian Smart chooses "strands" or "dimensions" when identifying organizational or determinative factors that are present in a crossreligious context. When he proceeds to propose that the vitality of a religion depends on the interactive relationship between these several integral strands or dimensions, he is contending, in formal terms, for an integrated system of organic interaction wherein the relationship between plural determinants is regulated by functional reciprocation. Otto's, Smart's, and most of the others' methodological orientations are accessible because they employ formal principles to identify that which carries the status of being constant and invariable.

The alternative—or "other side"—would be subjects that are either incoherent, inconstant, and indeterminant, or those that fall outside the range of the determinant-indeterminant field to which the reigning methodological paradigm enjoys access. The contrast that is implicit here is somewhat analogous to differences between Apollonian and Dionysian modes—the former strict and circumspect, the latter contrapuntal and expressly free. Scholarship tends to concentrate on the Apollonian world, thus missing Dionysian realities and religious esotericisms, because the latter do not easily correlate with testable patterns of recurrence.

Consider, for example, what turmoil William Blake's insights would create for the methodological conceptualization of standard religious studies. How could any of them be fitted to any coherent scheme, or, if they were, would they remain what they were originally? Why is the mentality of the technician sanctioned in religious studies while the attitude of the artist is treated with suspicion? And consider how little of Native American religion is known to religious studies—except those portions of it that can be correlated and calibrated with standard history-of-religions analytical and interpretive procedures.

Similar comments can be made about any of the important subjects that are overlooked, underestimated, or deliberately shunned because they do not qualify for high-priority assessment given their place within the world from which intelligibility is being approached and by which it is also measured. Scholars are taken by surprise by hosts of topics that are not within the range and focus of that at which they have been trained to look. Certainly scholars do not boast about being able to train their attention on everything. And what they miss often lies outside the scope of what they understand to be intriguing or to carry the possibility of some intellectual payoff of calculable sums. Thus, scholars are often blind-sided by subjects and topics that force a recognition that had not been planned for.

This, certainly, has been the career of women's or feminist studies within religious studies. For generations religious studies scholars would talk about "man" when referring to human beings. The assumption was that the word "man" was being employed generically. No explicit thought was ever given to differentiations between men and women, or the impact of these distinctions, together with women's identity, on understanding religion. As consciousness of gender differences and distinctions was raised, the entire subject of religion would be looked at with fresh eyes. For example, interpretations of traditions would be advanced from the perspective of the cultural status and place of women. The contrast between patriarchy and matriarchy would be examined from within numerous historical and religious contexts. The evident correlations between male status in religion and male status in society and culture would be investigated. And religion's abilities both to give voice to women and to thwart that voice would be examined carefully. In short, the advent of women's or feminist studies carries the capacity significantly to alter the expectations by which intelligibility is discerned and constructed. And the ramifications with respect to the self-identity of the subject-field remain decidedly embryonic.

The same principle holds, though in varing degrees, with respect to the application of virtually any new interpretive standpoint that might enter the investigatory screen from whatever social or cultural source. In this regard, a considerable amount of intellectual activity within a subject-field is generated by the social, cultural, economic, and political challenges of the people on whose behalf the investigations are being conducted. Thus, whatever emerges as a powerful issue or challenge to the people is reflected in the direction and intensity given to the study of religion. As scholarship, it is not a matter of right or wrong, correct or incorrect, but of the operational circumstances in which inquiry is forged. There are places in the world today where academic study of religion is not allowed, or not encouraged, and for many it is a new and fragile undertaking. The seminal theorists considered matters that were rooted in the challenges faced by their own societies, communities, and traditions. It is just as true today, and the implications for the shape and direction of scholarly inquiry are just as compelling.

We return to C. J. Bleeker's comment about "arrested pictures." If "arrested pictures" can be likened to photographic slides, the alternative must be something resembling moving pictures. Thus, in considering an alternative to "arrested pictures," one must focus on the dynamics of time, change, and motion. Or, one might be thinking about that which happens only once—that is, a dynamic, spontaneous surprise element—or, perhaps, that which eludes photographic representation.

A parallel might be found in the treatment of catalytic and kinetic realities in art. Once upon a time, art was dominated by patterns of stability: Romanesque, Gothic, Baroque, Neo-Romanesque, Neo-Gothic, and the like. But gradually, then increasingly, an interest in kinesis developed—that is, in visual and structural sets regulated by the dynamism of perpetual motion. A similar transition would occur in religious studies if the object of analysis shifted away from such easily constructed elements as the Four Noble Truths, the Eightfold Path, the Ten Commandments—about which neat notations can be made in lecture notes—to, say, the experience of enlightenment, or personal conversion, and, as has been noted, to the manner in which religions are being continuously defined and redefined in contact with each other. Without recognition of these dynamic factors, the characteristic spirits of the various religious traditions remain only partially accessible. The corollary is that what is constitutive of religion may not be identical to that which would also function as effective organizing principles within paradigmatic-sanctioned schematic representations. Can the subject of religion be adequately fitted to the workings of the methodological framework? If, as Bleeker has observed, the prevailing methodologies only register "arrested pictures," are not those same methodologies giving partial or distorted impressions?

This leads to a larger observation. In entertaining the possibility of a kinetic mode in religious studies, we are considering a way to make the ingredients of the prevailing paradigm flexible. This is a significant change. Yet, with it, the paradigm remains as paradigm. The next advance would require an attempt to think, conceive, or project religious studies in extraparadigmatic terms. And this would involve placing it outside the sanctioned framework.

The first step in approaching this subject—or even in considering whether the subject can be approached—is to assess the power and range of the working paradigm. Its capacities must be carefully assessed. The analyst and interpreter must be confident about what the paradigm can and cannot be expected to accomplish. This reflexive analytical process can be set in motion through an evaluation of the implications of the truth that all of the approaches that have been identified in this study have been constructed through the workings of a single but fundamental paradigm, and all of the approaches have been sustained by that same paradigm. It is the paradigm, as has been illustrated, that was conceived and designed within Western intellectual history at a particular point in this history.

Therefore, one way of accounting for the plurality of methods that characterizes the subject-field is to consider that each one is necessary if the prevailing paradigm itself is to be articulated in its appropriate fullness. This consideration implies that none of the approaches, if taken separately, is sufficient to capture all of the nuances of "religion" to which the paradigm provides intellectual access. Our study has demonstrated, for example, that the attempt to capture an essence cannot expect to uncover an origin. The interest in reducing religion to its fundamental component parts cannot begin to do justice to religion's comprehensive wholeness. And the methodological procedures involved in underscoring wholeness are not mutually exclusive, though they can only be presented one at a time; there is always more to say about religion than can be said through the instrumentation of any one model or approach. We have selected the word *instrumentation* advisedly, for methodological approaches are not normative but instrumental. They perform a function—a logical, conceptual, and logistical function. They help put certain subjects into focus. They are responsible for constructing disclosive avenues of inquiry. They make analysis possible. They cultivate distinctive interests. They are absolutely necessary to the study of religion; indeed, they make such study possible. To seek descriptive or interpretive innovation by doing something other than (1) designing additional models, (2) probing existing models for additional insights and materials, (3) encouraging crossmodular borrowings and exchanges, or even (4) regulating all models by the insertion of a kinetic element is, in effect, to try to step outside the framework of the fundamental paradigms. Any of this, at least until now, has been impossible.

The very consideration of extraparadigmatic conceptual possibilities makes apparent how dependent religious studies is—and has been—on the comprehensive approach to human knowledge that was constructed and fashioned at the time of the Enlightenment. Indeed, at one time, the author considered including the word *parsing* in the title or subtitle of this book: methodological approaches designed under the influence of the scientific method have functioned to parse the subject, to break it down into its constituent elements. It has been noted repeatedly in this study that the overall intent was to make the subject of religion intelligible. Thus, it was (and is) the great achievement of religious studies that it has made the subject of religion intelligible by utilizing the analytical and interpretive methods that were sponsored and, thus, legitimated, by the Enlightenment. This was the objective from the beginning: to identify the core element, whether essence or origin, so as to be able to certify and then illustrate that religion has a necessary and proper place within the inventory of elements of which the scope of knowledge is composed. When the methodological range was expanded, the use of patterns and structures as organizing principles stands as testimony to the same expectation. That a subject-field called religious studies emerged as a result of this process simply confirms that material content and canons of analysis and interpretation were made coherent and congruent by the methods of inquiry that were applied. Academic respectability followed since it could be demonstrated convincingly that religious studies, like other fields and disciplines that have their roots in the Enlightenment, is the methodological translation of the subject of religion into workable and certifiable means and instruments of intelligibility.

Had the starting point been different, the consequences would have been different too. For example, had the compulsions of the Enlightenment not served as principal sponsorship, intelligibility might have been ventured from other grounds. We cannot specify with sufficient accuracy or depth what such grounds might be, but we are in position to affirm that the writers and scholars chiefly responsible for the making of the intellectual discipline called religious studies had no alternative to the methods they employed. Certainly they were free to make choices within the fundamental interpretive framework, but they would not have been able to conceive of alternative frameworks. So they worked with analytical tools that established congruence between a method and a subject. They made Enlightenment inquiry congruent with the subject of religion, and, as our analysis has demonstrated, they worked painstakingly to illustrate and prove that their findings and claims were congruent with the fundamental teachings of the dominant religious tradition. That is, they achieved congruence, or at least impressive compatibility, on all sides. Enlightenment philosophy was made congruent with religion's demonstrable intelligibility, and both of these were made congruent with a modified understanding of the teachings of Christianity (to which was sometimes appended Judaism, and, perhaps, the other religions of the world).

What if they had approached their subject from another vantage point? That is, what if they had fashioned methods of analysis and interpretation that were congruent or compatible with other religious traditions—say, the traditions of Asia? How, for example, would religious studies appear if it were approached through analytical and interpretive sensitivities formed out of Buddhist or Hindu experience? What would religious studies be if scholars within the Islamic world were to take the lead? And how would religious studies appear if the formative congruence were to comparative religion, say, instead of to the dominant religion within the culture within which the enterprise is undertaken?

This book has cited no examples of this kind, for we are aware of no systematic analytical approaches to the subject of religion with extra-Western sponsorship. But there is every reason to expect that such intellectual inquiry is possible and that it is probably occurring. A number of the approaches we have identified were designed to give the Christian religion top position. We Westerners may smile at this, or be disturbed by it, or try to diminish its force by identifying the circumstances out of which this tendency has come. But what if the tables were turned? What if religion as well as religious consciousness were approached not with an interest in identifying core features—as identified within the taxonomy of cause, source, root, and so on—but out of respect for the designs and intentions of traditions that are not intent on attaching intelligibility to substantiable formal factors? Do we know what such studies would look like? Have we any clear sense of their configuration? What we do know is that scholars in other parts of the world do indeed approach comparative religion from within religious interests that they intend to maintain and protect. That is, we know that interpreters outside the Western world do what Westerners typically do when engaged in comparative analysis of this kind: they establish their inquiry in such a manner that the congruence they hope for will be brought to accomplishment. But we do not have clear knowledge about distinctive study methods that are designed to explore the religious traditions from outside of Western scholarship that does not privilege any of the traditions themselves. This, without question, is an issue for the future. As the nations of the world learn more about each other, as international travel increases, and as the study of religion is ventured from distinctive vantage points, scholars in religious studies will learn more than content and data from their colleagues in other cultures. They will also discover analytical and interpretive methods that carry the promise of perpetually transforming the instruments and canons of intelligibility.

But this is work for the future. What about the consequences of our present analysis?

Here we must offer a qualification. The methods that have been chronicled in this study have indeed done their work. They have assisted in making the subject of religion intelligible. And yet, the paradox is that the very effort at intelligibility-making has disclosed that the subject yields only partially to the workings of the prevailing paradigm. That is, ever since Descartes' construction of the methodological apparatus—that knowledge derives from the decomposition of wholes into constituent elements, so that intellectual decomposition is dependent on the isolation of a single underlying principle—there has been protest, even by those who recognized the brilliance of the Enlightenment achievement. Blaise Pascal's famous "the heart has reasons which reason does not know" will find echoes in Kant's "I have denied reason to make room for faith." Moreover, the search for the locus of religion outside the sphere of rational intelligibility, the attempt to coin a language that applies exclusively to religion and to religious experience, a preoccupation with the world of *mythos* that is defined as being "prelogical," or an interpretive approach to the subject that focuses on symbols that do not conform to the rules of discursive reasoning, and even Ludwig Wittgenstein's well-known dictum in praise of silence stand as corroboration. The sequence is (1) that the methods of analysis and interpretation were devised in accordance with the prescribed Enlightenment mode and style of addressing problems and issues, (2) that the subject of religion was successfully approached and represented this way, and (3) that the translation of religion into these canons of analysis and interpretation leaves the analysts and interpreters manifestly dissatisfied, even after more than two centuries of investigative work. Thus the analysts and interpreters have concluded that religion does and does not yield to the canons of critical rationality.

Seen from the other side, religious studies itself stands as evidence (1) that the content of religious studies is not identical to the content of religion, and (2) that religious studies is not the only mode in which religion occurs or can be presented. All of this implies that there are aspects of the subject to which the established canons of critical rationality have no immediate access. In addition, there are senses in which religion resists the process of rationalization.

And yet, conclusions of this kind should not and need not be interpreted as a sign of failure. The fact is that the intellectual making of the discipline took place, and continues to occur, and that the analytical and interpretive achievements have been considerable. Indeed, even the fact that the subject does not translate fully into the analytical and interpretive apparatus is a discovery that the discipline made and continues to honor. In sum, religious studies recognizes that religion is not fully translatable into religious studies, and this is an analytical and interpretive truth.

Thus, the methodological procedures that have been identified in our study, and the intellectual orientations that have been chronicled, are disclosive of two simultaneous and virtually interchangeable processes. They illustrate how understanding functions in trying to come to intelligible terms with religion, and they explain just how much of religion can be made intelligible. No doubt both of these chronicles would be far less circumspect, but, alas, exceedingly more difficult to trace, had René Descartes, the methodological catalyst, been willing to settle for knowledge and not certitude. Had he done so, the story we have traced would have been a different one—a story that might also have been told. But it is not the story about the making of the intellectual discipline that eventually came to be known as religious studies. This latter, as we trust this volume has illustrated, is a story full of intellectual challenge and excitement, and provides so much to think about that it will keep scholars and inquirers energetically involved for generations to come.

BIBLIOGRAPHY

ALBANESE, Catherine L. *Nature Religion in America: From the Algonkian Indians to the New Age.* Chicago: University of Chicago Press, 1990.

ALTIZER, Thomas J. J. *Mircea Eliade and the Dialectic of the Sacred.* Philadelphia: Westminster Press, 1963.

AYER, A. J. *Language, Truth and Logic.* London: Penguin Books, 1936.

BACHELARD, Gaston. *The Poetics of Space.* Translated by Maria Jolas. Boston: Beacon Press, 1958.

BAIRD, Robert D. *Category Formation and the History of Religions.* The Hague: Mouton, 1971.

BANTON, Michael, ed. *Anthropological Approaches to the Study of Religion.* London: Tavistock, 1966.

BELLAH, Robert N. *Beyond Belief: Essays on Religion in a Post-Traditionalist World.* Berkeley: University of California Press, 1970.

BERGER, Peter. *The Sacred Canopy: Elements of a Sociological Theory of Religion.* Garden City, N. Y.: Doubleday & Co., 1969.

_____, and Thomas Luckman. *Social Construction of Reality: A Treatise in the Sociology of Knowledge.* Garden City, N. Y.: Doubleday & Co., 1966.

BLEEKER, C. J. *The Rainbow: A Collection of Studies in the Science of Religion*. Leiden: E. J. Brill, 1975.

BOAS, Franz. *The Mind of Primitive Man*. Reprint. New York: Greenwood, 1983.

_____. *Race, Language and Culture*. Chicago: University of Chicago Press, 1982.

BRANDON, S. G. F. *Religion in Ancient History: Studies in Ideas, Men and Events*. London: George Allen and Unwin, 1973.

CAHILL, P. Joseph. *Mended Speech: The Crisis of Religious Studies and Theology*. New York: Crossroad, 1982.

CAPPS, Walter H., ed. *Ways of Understanding Religion*. New York: Macmillan, 1972.

CARLYLE, Thomas. *On Heroes, Hero-Worship and the Heroic in History*. Lincoln: University of Nebraska Press, 1966.

CARMAN, John B. Majesty and Meekness: *A Comparative Study of Contrast and Harmony in the Concept of God*. Grand Rapids: Wm. B. Eerdmans, 1994.

_____, and Steven P. Hopkins, eds. *Tracing Common Themes: Comparative Courses in the Study of Religion*. Atlanta: Scholars Press, 1991.

CASSIRER, Ernst. *The Philosophy of Symbolic Forms*. 3 vols. New Haven: Yale University Press, 1953–57.

CHANG, K. C. *Early Chinese Civilization: Anthropological Perspectives*. Cambridge: Harvard University Press, 1976.

CHANTEPIE DE LA SAUSSAYE, Pierre Daniel. *Lehrbuch der Religionsgeschichte (Manual of the Science of Religion)*. Freiburg, 1897.

CHRISTIAN, William. *Meaning and Truth in Religion*. Princeton: Princeton University Press, 1964.

DANIELOU, Jean. "The History of Religions: And the History of Salvation." In Danielou, *The Lord of History: Reflections on the Inner Meaning of History*, pp. 107–21. London: Longmans, 1958.

DERRIDA, Jacques. *Dissemination*. Translated by Barbara Johnson. Chicago: University of Chicago Press, 1981.

_____. *Positions*. Translated by Alan Bass. Chicago: University of Chicago Press, 1981.

DESCARTES, René. *Discourse on Method*. London: Penguin, 1968.

_____. *Meditations on First Philosophy*. New York. Bobbs-Merrill, 1960.

DE VRIES, Jan. *The Study of Religion: A Historical Approach*. Translated by Kees W. Bolle. New York: Harcourt, Brace and World, 1967.

DEWEY, John. *Common Faith*. New Haven: Yale University Press, 1934.

DONIGER, Wendy. *Asceticism and Eroticism in the Mythology of Siva.* London: Oxford University Press, 1973.

_____. *Dreams, Illusion and Other Realities.* Chicago: University of Chicago Press, 1984.

_____. *Women, Androgynes, and Other Mythical Beasts.* Chicago: University of Chicago Press, 1980.

DOUGLAS, Mary. *Implicit Meanings: Essays in Anthropology.* New York: Metheun, 1978.

_____. *Natural Symbols: Explorations in Cosmology.* New York: Random House, 1972.

_____. *Purity and Danger: An Analysis of the Concepts of Pollution and Taboo.* New York: Metheun, 1984.

DUMÉZIL, Georges. *Camillus: A Study of Indo-European Religion as Roman History.* Berkeley: University of California Press, 1980.

DUMONT, Louis. *Homo Hierarchicus: The Caste System and Its Implications.* Chicago: University of Chicago Press, 1981.

DURKHEIM, Emile. *Elementary Forms of the Religious Life.* New York: Free Press, 1965.

_____. *The Rules of Sociological Method and Selected Texts on Sociology and Its Method.* Edited by Steven Lukes. New York: Free Press, 1982.

ELIADE, Mircea. *Cosmos and History: The Myth of the Eternal Return.* Edited by Robin Winks. New York: Garland Publishers, 1982.

_____. *Patterns in Comparative Religion.* New York: New American Library, 1984.

_____. *The Quest: History and Meaning in Religion.* Chicago: University of Chicago Press, 1984.

_____. *The Sacred and the Profane: The Nature of Religion.* Translated by Willard Trask. New York: Harcourt Brace Jovanovich, 1983.

ELLWOOD, Robert. *Many People, Many Faiths.* New York: Prentice-Hall, 1987.

ERIKSON, Erik H. *Gandhi's Truth: On the Origins of Militant Nonviolence.* New York: W. W. Norton, 1969.

_____. *Young Man Luther: A Study in Psychoanalysis and History.* New York: W. W. Norton, 1958.

EVANS-PRITCHARD, E. E. *Social Anthropology and Other Essays.* New York: Free Press, 1962.

_____. *Theories of Primitive Religion.* London: Oxford University Press, 1965.

FEUERBACH, Ludwig. *Essence of Christianity*. New York: Harper & Brothers, 1958.

FLEW, Antony. *God, Freedom and Immortality: A Critical Analysis*. New York: Prometheus Books, 1984.

FOUCAULT, Michel. *The Archaeology of Knowledge*. London: Tavistock, 1972.

_____. *The Order of Things*. London: Tavistock, 1970.

FRAZER, James. *Creation and Evolution in Primitive Cosmogonies and Other Pieces*. New York: Ayer, 1935.

_____. *The Fear of the Dead in Primitive Religion*. New York: Ayer, 1936.

_____. *The Golden Bough*. New York: Macmillan, 1985.

_____. *The Worship of Nature*. The Gifford Lectures. New York: AMS Press, 1926.

FREUD, Sigmund. *Civilization and Its Discontents*. New York: W. W. Norton, 1984.

_____. *The Future of an Illusion*. New York: W. W. Norton, 1975.

GADAMER, Hans-Georg. *Truth and Method*. New York: Crossroad, 1982.

GASTER, Theodore H. *The Dead Sea Scriptures*. New York: Doubleday & Co., 1976.

GEERTZ, Clifford. *Interpretations of Cultures*. New York: Basic Books, 1973.

_____. *Islam Observed: Religious Development in Morocco and Indonesia*. Chicago: University of Chicago Press, 1971.

_____. *Local Knowledge: Further Essays in Interpretive Anthropology*. New York: Basic Books, 1983.

GELLNER, Ernest. *Conditions of Liberty: Civil Society and Its Rivals*. New York: Viking Penguin, 1994.

GERHART, Mary. *Genre Choices, Gender Questions*. Norman: University of Oklahoma Press, 1992.

GIDDINGS, Franklin. *The Scientific Study of Human Society*. New York: Ayer, 1974.

GRAPARD, Allan G. *The Protocol of the Gods: A Study of the Kasuga Cult in Japanese History*. Berkeley: University of California Press, 1992.

GUNN, Giles. *The Culture of Criticism and the Criticism of Culture*. London: Oxford University Press, 1987.

HABERMAS, Jürgen. *Theory and Practice*. Boston: Beacon Press, 1973.

HAMMOND, Philip. *The Sacred in a Secular Age: Toward Revision in the Scientific Study of Religion*. Berkeley: University of California Press, 1985.

HARE, R. M. *Moral Thinking: Its Levels, Methods and Point*. London: Oxford University Press, 1981.

HEIDEGGER, Martin. *Being and Time*. New York: Harper & Row, 1962.

_____. *Existence and Being.* New York: Regnery Books, 1949.

HEILER, Friedrich. *Prayer: A Study in the History and Psychology of Religion.* London: Oxford University Press, 1932.

HICK, John. *God Has Many Names.* Philadelphia: Westminster Press, 1982.

_____. *Problems of Religious Pluralism.* New York: St. Martin's Press, 1985.

HUSSERL, Edmund. *Cartesian Meditations.* The Hague: Martinus Nijhoff, 1977.

_____. *Idea of Phenomenology.* The Hague: Martinus Nijhoff, 1964.

IRIGARAY, Luce. *je, tu, nous: Toward a Culture of Difference.* New York: Routledge, 1993.

JAMES, E. O. *The Beginnings of Religion.* London: Hutchinson University Library, 1948.

JAMES, William. *Varieties of Religious Experience.* New York: Penguin Books, 1982.

JASTROW, Morris. *The Study of Religion.* Edited by William A. Clebach. Atlanta: Scholars Press, 1981.

JEFFNER, Anders. *Filosofisk Religionsdebatt.* Stockholm: Skeab Verbum, 1967.

JUERGENSMEYER, Mark. *The New Cold War: Religious Nationalism Confronts the Secular State.* Berkeley: University of California Press, 1994.

KANT, Immanuel. *Prolegomena to Any Future Metaphysics.* New York: Liberal Arts Press, 1950.

_____. *Religion Within the Limits of Reason Alone.* New York: Harper & Brothers, 1934.

KATZ, Steven T., ed. *Mysticism and Philosophical Analysis.* New York: Oxford University Press, 1978.

_____. *Mysticism and Religious Traditions.* New York: Oxford University Press, 1983.

KITAGAWA, Joseph M. *The History of Religions: Retrospect and Prospect.* New York: Macmillan, 1985.

_____, and Charles H. Long, eds. *Myths and Symbols: Essays in Honor of Mircea Eliade.* Chicago: University of Chicago Press, 1982.

KRISTENSEN, W. Brede. *The Meaning of Religion: Lectures in the Phenomenology of Religion.* Translated by John B. Carman. The Hague: Martinus Nijhoff, 1968.

LACAN, Jacques. *Ecrits: A Selection.* New York: W. W. Norton, 1982.

LANG, Andrew. *Myth, Ritual and Religion.* 2 vols. London: Longmans, Green, 1899.

_____. *Magic and Religion.* London: Longmans, Green, 1901.

LANGER, Susanne K. *Philosophy in a New Key.* Cambridge: Harvard University Press, 1942.

LAWSON, E. Thomas, and Robert N. McCauley. *Rethinking Religion: Connecting Cognition and Culture.* Cambridge: Cambridge University Press, 1990.

LEACH, Edmund. *Social Anthropology.* London: Oxford University Press, 1982.

_____. *Dialect in Practical Religion.* Cambridge: Cambridge University Press, 1978.

_____, and Alan Aycock. *Structuralist Interpretations of Biblical Myth.* Cambridge: Cambridge University Press, 1983.

LENSKI, Gerhard. *The Religious Factor: A Sociological Study of Religion's Impact on Politics, Economics, and Family Life.* Reprint. New York: Greenwood, 1961.

LÉVI-STRAUSS, Claude. *Savage Mind.* Chicago: University of Chicago Press, 1966.

_____. *Structural Anthropology.* Chicago: University of Chicago Press, 1976.

LÉVY-BRUHL, Lucien. *Primitive Mentality.* Translated by Lilian A. Clare. New York: Macmillan, 1923.

LINCOLN, Bruce. *Discourse and the Construction of Society: Comparative Studies in Myth, Ritual and Classification.* New York: Oxford University Press, 1989.

_____. *Myth, Cosmos and Society: Indo-European Themes of Creation and Destruction.* Cambridge: Harvard University Press, 1986.

LONG, Charles H. *The Myths of Creation.* Atlanta: Scholars Press, 1963.

_____. *Significations: Signs, Symbols, and Images in the Interpretation of Religion.* Philadelphia: Fortress Press, 1986.

MACINTYRE, Alasdair. *After Virtue: A Study in Moral Theory.* South Bend, Ind.: University of Notre Dame Press, 1984.

MALINOWSKI, Bronislaw. *Magic, Science and Religion and Other Essays.* Garden City, N. Y.: Doubleday & Co., 1948.

MANNHEIM, Karl. *Ideology and Utopia: An Introduction to the Sociology of Knowledge.* New York: Harcourt, Brace & Co., 1955.

MARETT, Robert R. *The Threshold of Religion.* London: Methuen, 1914.

_____. *Tylor.* London: Chapman and Hall, 1936.

MAUSS, Marcel. *The Gift: Forms and Functions of Exchange in Archaic Societies.* New York: W. W. Norton, 1967.

MENSCHING, Gustav. *Structures and Patterns of Religion.* Livingston, N. J.: Oriental Book Distributors, 1976.

MERLEAU-PONTY, Maurice. *Primacy of Perception.* Translated by William Cobb. Evanston, Ill.: Northwestern University Press, 1964.

_____. *Themes from the Lectures at the College de France.* Translated by John O'Neill. Evanston, Ill.: Northwestern University Press, 1970.

MICHAELSEN, Robert. *The Study of Religion in American Universities.* New Haven: The Society for Religion in Higher Education, 1965.

MÜLLER, Friedrich Max. "Essays on the Science of Religion." Vol. 1 of *Chips from a German Workshop.* London, 1967.

_____. *Introduction to the Science of Religion.* London, 1880.

_____. *Sacred Books of the East.* Oxford: Clarendon Press, 1979.

NAKAMURA, Hajime. *A Comparative History of Ideas.* London: Metheun, 1986.

_____. *Ways of Thinking of Eastern Peoples.* Honolulu: East-West Center Press. 1964.

NEEDHAM, Rodney. *Structure and Sentiment: A Test Case in Social Anthropology.* Chicago: University of Chicago Press, 1962.

NEEDLEMAN, Jacob. *The Heart of Philosophy.* New York: Alfred A. Knopf, 1982.

_____. *Lost Christianity.* New York: Doubleday & Co., 1980.

_____. *The New Religions.* Garden City, N. Y.: Doubleday & Co., 1970.

_____. *A Sense of the Cosmos: The Encounter of Modern Science and Ancient Truth.* New York: Doubleday & Co., 1975.

_____, and Dennis Lewis, eds. *Sacred Tradition and Present Need.* New York: Viking Press, 1975.

NEUMANN, Erich. *Origins and History of Consciousness.* Translated by R. F. Hull. Princeton: Princeton University Press, 1954.

NEUSNER, Jacob. *The Academic Study of Judaism: Essays and Reflections.* Atlanta: Scholars Press, 1983.

_____. *Judaism in the American Humanities.* Atlanta: Scholars Press, 1981.

_____. *Judaism: The Classical Statement, the Evidence of the Bavli.* Chicago: University of Chicago Press, 1986.

_____. *New Humanities and Academic Disciplines.* Madison: University of Wisconsin Press, 1984.

_____. *Take Judaism, for Example: Studies Toward the Comparison of Religion.* Chicago: University of Chicago Press, 1983.

NEVILLE, Robert Cummings. *Behind the Masks of God: An Essay Toward Comparative Theology.* Albany: State University of New York Press, 1991.

NIELSEN, Kai. *An Introduction to the Philosophy of Religion.* New York: St. Martin's Press, 1983.

NYGREN, Anders. *Meaning and Method: Prolegomena to a Scientific Philosophy of Religion and a Scientific Theology.* Philadelphia: Fortress Press, 1972.

OBEYESEKERE, Gananath. *Medusa's Hair: An Essay on Personal Symbols and Religious Experiences.* Chicago: University of Chicago Press, 1981.

_____ . *The Work of Culture: Symbolic Transformation in Psychoanalysis and Anthropology.* Chicago: University of Chicago Press, 1990.

O'DEA, Thomas, and Janet Aviad. *The Sociology of Religion.* New York: Prentice-Hall, 1983.

OTTO, Rudolf. *The Idea of the Holy.* London: Oxford University Press, 1923.

_____ . *Mysticism East and West. A Comparative Analysis of the Nature of Mysticism.* New York: Macmillan, 1932.

OXTOBY, Willard G. *The Meaning of Other Faiths.* Philadelphia: Westminster Press, 1983.

PADEN, William E. *Interpreting the Sacred: Ways of Viewing Religion.* Boston: Beacon Press, 1992.

PAILIN, David A. *Attitudes to Other Religions: Comparative Religion in Seventeenth- and Eighteenth-Century Britain.* Manchester: Manchester University Press, 1984.

PANIKKAR, Raimon. *Intrareligious Dialogue.* New York: Paulist Press, 1978.

_____ . *Invisible Harmony: Essays on Contemplation and Responsibility.* Edited by Henry James Cargas. Minneapolis: Fortress Press, 1995.

_____ . *The Unknown Christ of Hinduism.* New York: Orbis Books, 1981.

PARSONS, Talcott. *Essays in Sociological Theory.* New York: Free Press, 1964.

PENNER, Hans H. *Impasse and Resolution: A Critique of the Study of Religion.* New York: Lang, 1989.

PETTAZZONI, Raffaele. *Essays on the History of Religions.* Leiden: E. J. Brill, 1967.

PETTERSSON, Olof, and Hans Akerberg. *Interpreting Religious Phenomena: Studies with Reference to the Phenomenology of Religion.* Stockholm: Almqvist and Wiksell, 1972.

PHILLIPS, D. Z. *Wittgenstein and Religion.* London: Macmillan, 1993.

PREUS, J. Samuel. *Explaining Religion: Criticism and Theory from Bodin to Freud.* New Haven: Yale University Press, 1987.

PROUDFOOT, Wayne. *Religious Experience.* Berkeley: University of California Press, 1985.

PYE, Michael, ed., with Robert Morgan. *The Cardinal Meaning: Essays in Comparative Hermeneutics.* The Hague: Mouton, 1973.

_____ , ed. *Marburg Revisited: Institutions and Strategies in the Study of Religion.* Marburg: Diagonal-Verlag, 1989.

_____ . *Zen and Modern Japanese Religion.* London: Ward Lock, 1973.

RADCLIFFE-BROWN, A. R. *Structure and Function in Primitive Society*. London: Cohen and West, 1952.

RADHAKRISHNAN, S. *Eastern Religions and Western Thought*. London: Oxford University Press, 1975.

RICOEUR, Paul. *Figuring the Sacred: Religion, Narrative, and Imagination*. Edited by Mark I. Wallace. Translated by David Pellauer. Minneapolis: Fortress Press, 1995.

_____. *Hermeneutics and the Human Sciences*. Cambridge: Cambridge University Press, 1981.

_____. *Symbolism of Evil*. Boston: Beacon Press, 1969.

RINGGREN, Helmer, and Ake V. Ström, *Religions of Mankind: Today and Yesterday*. London: Oliver and Boyd, 1967.

ROOF, Wade Clark. *A Generation of Seekers: The Spiritual Journeys of the Baby Boom Generation*. San Francisco: HarperSanFrancisco, 1993.

RORTY, Richard. *Consequences of Pragmatism: Essays: 1972–1980*. Minneapolis: University of Minnesota Press, 1982.

ROSALDO, Renato. *Culture and Truth: The Remaking of Social Analysis*. Boston: Beacon Press, 1993.

SCHLEIERMACHER, Friedrich. *On Religion: Speeches to Its Cultured Despisers*. New York: Harper & Brothers, 1958.

SCHUON, Frithjof. *The Transcendent Unity of Religions*. New York: Harper & Row, 1975.

SEZNEC, Jean. *The Survival of the Pagan Gods: The Mythological Tradition and Its Place in Renaissance Humanism and Art*. New York: Harper & Brothers, 1953.

SHARPE, Eric J. *Comparative Religion: A History*. London: Duckworth, 1986.

_____. *Understanding Religion*. New York: St. Martin's Press, 1984.

SMART, Ninian. *The Phenomenon of Religion*. London: Macmillan, 1973.

_____. *The Philosophy of Religion*. London: Oxford University Press, 1979.

_____. *Religion and the Western Mind*. Albany: State University of New York Press, 1987.

_____. *The Science of Religion and the Sociology of Knowledge: Some Methodological Questions*. Princeton: Princeton University Press, 1973.

_____. *Worldviews: Crosscultural Explorations of Human Beliefs*. New York: Charles Scribner's Sons, 1983.

SMITH, Huston. *Forgotten Truth: The Primordial Tradition*. New York: Harper & Row, 1976.

_____. *The World's Religions*. Revised and updated edition of *The Religions of Man*. San Francisco: HarperSanFrancisco, 1991.

SMITH, Jonathan Z. *Drudgery Divine: On the Comparison of Early Christianities and the Religions of Late Antiquity*. Chicago: University of Chicago Press, 1990.

_____. *Imagining Religion: From Babylon to Jonestown*. Chicago: University of Chicago Press, 1982.

_____. *Map Is Not Territory: Studies in the History of Religions*. Leiden: E. J. Brill, 1979.

_____. *To Take Place: Toward Theory in Ritual*. Chicago: University of Chicago Press, 1987.

SMITH, Wilfred Cantwell. *The Faith of Other Men*. New York: Harper & Row, 1972.

_____. *The Meaning and End of Religion*. Reprint. Minneapolis: Fortress Press, 1991.

_____. *Towards a World Theology: Faith and the Comparative Study of Religion*. Philadelphia: Westminster Press, 1981.

SMITH, William Robertson. *Lectures on the Religion of the Semites*. London: A. and C. Black, 1889.

SÖDERBLOM, Nathan. "The Place of the Christian Trinity and the Buddhist Triaratna amongst Holy Triads." in *Transaction of the 3rd International Congress for the History of Religions*. Vol. 2, pp. 391–410. London: Oxford University Press, 1908.

_____. "Holiness." In *Encyclopaedia of Religion and Ethics*. Vol. 6, pp. 731–41. Edinburgh, 1913.

_____. *The Living God: Basal Forms of Personal Religion*. London: Oxford University Press, 1933; reprint, Boston: Beacon Press, 1962.

SPENCER, Herbert. *The Study of Sociology*. Ann Arbor: University of Michigan Press, 1961.

_____, and Frederic Harrison. *The Nature and Reality of Religion: A Controversy between Frederic Harrison and Herbert Spencer*. New York: D. Appleton, 1885.

SPIRO, Melford E. *Buddhism and Society: A Great Tradition and Its Burmese Vicissitudes*. Berkeley: University of California Press, 1982.

STARK, Rodney, and William S. Bainbridge. *The Future of Religion: Secularization, Revival and Cult Formation*. Berkeley: University of California Press, 1985.

TAMBIAH, Stanley J. *Culture, Thought, and Social Action: An Anthropological Perspective*. Cambridge: Harvard University Press, 1985.

_____. *Magic, Science, Religion, and the Scope of Rationality*. Cambridge: Cambridge University Press, 1990.

TAYLOR, Mark C. *Erring: A Postmodern, A-Theology.* Chicago: University of Chicago Press, 1984.

_____, ed. *Deconstruction in Context: Literature and Philosophy.* Chicago: University of Chicago Press, 1986.

TIELE, Cornelis Petrus. *Elements of the Science of Religion.* 2 vols. New York: Charles Scribner's Sons, 1897–99.

_____. *Outlines of the History of Religion, to the Spread of the Universal Religions.* London: Trubner, 1877.

TILLICH, Paul. *The Future of Religions.* Edited by Jerald C. Brauer. New York: Greenwood, 1966.

_____. *Theology of Culture.* London: Oxford University Press, 1983.

TÖNNIES, Ferdinand. *Custom: An Essay on Social Codes.* New York: Regnery, 1971.

TURNER, Victor. *Dramas, Fields, and Metaphors: Symbolic Action in Human Society.* Ithaca, N. Y.: Cornell University Press, 1974.

_____. *The Ritual Process: Structure and Anti-Structure.* Ithaca, N. Y.: Cornell University Press, 1977.

TYLOR, Edward Burnett. *Primitive Culture: Researches into the Development of Mythology, Philosophy, Religion, Art, and Custom.* 2 vols. London: Murray, 1873, 1874.

_____. *Researches into the Early History of Mankind and the Development of Civilization.* London: Murray, 1870.

VAN GENNEP, Arnold. *The Rites of Passage.* Chicago: University of Chicago Press, 1960.

VAN DER LEEUW, Gerardus. *Religion in Essence and Manifestation: A Study in Phenomenology.* 2 vols. New York: Harper & Row, 1963.

WAARDENBURG, Jacques. *Classical Approaches to the Study of Religion.* 2 vols. The Hague: Mouton, 1974.

WACH, Joachim. *The Comparative Study of Religions.* New York: Columbia University Press, 1958.

_____. *Sociology of Religion.* Chicago: University of Chicago Press, 1947.

_____. *Types of Religious Experience: Christian and Non-Christian.* Chicago: University of Chicago Press, 1972.

WEBER, Max. *The Protestant Ethic and the Spirit of Capitalism.* Glencoe, N. Y.: Free Press, 1951.

_____. *The Sociology of Religion.* Boston: Beacon Press, 1956.

WERBLOWSKY, R. J. Zwi. *Beyond Tradition and Modernity: Changing Religions in a Changing World.* London: Athlone Press, 1976.

_____, E. E. Urbach, and Ch. Zirszubski, eds. *Studies in Mysticism and Religion, Presented to Gershom G. Scholem on his Seventieth Birthday*. Jerusalem: Magnes Press, Hebrew University, 1967.

WHALING, Frank, ed. *Contemporary Approaches to the Study of Religion*. 2 vols. The Hague: Mouton, 1984.

_____. *The World's Religious Traditions*. Philadelphia: Fortress Press, 1984.

WIDENGREN, Geo. "Evolutionism and the Problem of the Origin of Religion." In *Ethnos*. Vol. 10 (1945), Nos. 2–3.

_____. *Religionsphänomenologie*. Berlin: Walter de Gruyter, 1979. Translated from the original publication, *Religionens Värld*, Stockholm, 1953.

WIEBE, Paul. *The Architecture of Religion: A Theoretical Essay*. San Antonio: Trinity University Press, 1984.

WILSON, Bryan. *Religion in Sociological Perspective*. London: Oxford University Press, 1982.

WINCH, Peter. *The Idea of a Social Science and its Relation to Philosophy*. London: Routledge and Kegan Paul, 1971.

_____. *Moral Integrity: Inaugural Lecture in the Chair of Philosophy*. Oxford: Blackwell, 1968.

_____, ed. *Studies in the Philosophy of Wittgenstein*. New York: Humanities Press, 1969.

WUTHNOW, Robert. *The Religious Dimension: New Directions in Quantitative Research*. New York: Academic Press, 1979.

_____. *The Restructuring of American Religion*. Princeton: Princeton University Press, 1988.

YINGER, J. Milton. *The Scientific Study of Religion*. London: Macmillan, 1970.

ZAEHNER, Robert C. *Mysticism: Sacred and Profane*. London: Oxford University Press, 1957.

RELIGIOUS · STUDIES

INDEX —————————————————————————

CPSIA information can be obtained at www.ICGtesting.com
Printed in the USA
240496LV00001B/1/A

9 780800 625351